The Incarnate Text

The Incarnate Text

Imagining the Book in Reformation England

James Kearney

PENN

UNIVERSITY OF PENNSYLVANIA PRESS

PHILADELPHIA

Published by
University of Pennsylvania Press
Philadelphia, Pennsylvania 19104-4112

Printed in the United States of America on acid-free paper
10 9 8 7 6 5 4 3 2 1

Library of Congress Cataloging-in-Publication Data

Kearney, James
    The incarnate text : imagining the book in Reformation England / James Kearney.
        p.   cm.—(Material texts)
    Includes bibliographical references and index.
    ISBN 978-0-8122-4158-7 (alk. paper)
    1. English literature—Early modern, 1500–1700—History and criticism.   2. Books in literature.   3. Iconoclasm in literature.   4. Reformation—England.   I. Title.
    PR418.B66K43   2009
    820.9′357—dc22
                                                                                    2008050863

For my parents,
Kate Kearney and Jerry Kearney

CONTENTS

ILLUSTRATIONS

INTRODUCTION

THIS PROJECT BEGAN with a simple question: how were books imagined in early modern England? In the past thirty years we have learned a great deal about the history of the codex, the histories of manuscript and print production, the history of reading.[1] And so we have come to understand how daunting a question this might be. To conjure the early modern book would require a tremendous act of historical imagination. It would entail reconstructing the ways in which readers and nonreaders apprehended the physical object of the book: the smell of ink, the feel of parchment made from animal skin or paper made from rags, the way one might handle books of different sizes, books with different bindings, or books with no bindings at all. It would require understanding the ways in which books were embedded in a world of objects and a world of social relations: books as gifts, books as commodities, books as devotional objects, books as totems and trash. Given that this was a moment of technological change for the codex, such an inquiry would need to attend to print culture and manuscript culture, the changing ways books were produced and disseminated, as well as changing assumptions concerning the reliability and authority of different kinds of books. A study of this kind would need to consider the rich variety of things called books: from the stack of printed sheets one could purchase unbound from the bookseller to the elaborately wrought manuscript folio chained to a piece of furniture in a church or university library; from a book to be worn around the neck to a book on which one could play dice. To understand how books were imagined would entail positioning the early modern book in relation to other forms of written or printed artifact: the scroll, the pamphlet, the letter, the broadsheet. And it would be necessary to attend to writing outside the world of books and papers: writing on walls, on glass, on rings, on flesh. We would also need to consider the subjects imagining the book. Who could read in the early modern period, and what did it mean that they could read? What did the illiterate and semiliterate think of books and book culture? When and where did people encounter books, and when and where did they read? How did they read: alone or in groups, aloud or silently, passively or actively? Above all, perhaps, to imagine how the book might have been imagined, we would need to attend to what Ernst Curtius calls "the book as symbol" in his classic essay of the same name. Working a half century later, our methods and assumptions might differ from Curtius's, but the basic thrust of the inquiry would remain the same: in what way did this particular artifact become an emblem, an idea, a thing good to think with?

In this speculative exercise I have not yet scratched the surface of what it might mean to reconstruct how the book was imagined in early modern England. And yet even with the limited program I have outlined here, it is clear that a scholarly inquiry into this topic would require many books, many scholars.[2] My focus here is much narrower. In *The Incarnate Text*, I explore the ways in which the book was imagined during a crisis in representation and language, a crisis that was sparked by the Reformation. More specifically, I look at acts of the imagination—most what we would call literary, some not—that responded to a productive tension at the heart of the Reformation's conception of the book specifically and the graphic dimension of language more generally. I offer this book then as a contribution to a larger collective project of understanding the book in early modern England.[3] At the same time, I contend that the subject of this study—what we might call a crisis of the book, occasioned by the Reformation—is essential to any historical understanding of the place of the book in the early modern imaginary. When I initially asked the question with which this project began, all roads kept leading back to religion. When early modern writers reflected on language as artifact, they tended to so in religious terms. Insofar as the early modern period had a sense of the history of the book, that history was a Christian history. The key moments in that history were the Fall, the inscription of the Mosaic law, the incarnation, the writing of the gospels, the inspiration of biblical translators, the providential invention of the printing press. And the most recent turning point in that history for sixteenth- and seventeenth-century Christians, Protestant or Catholic, was the Reformation.

The Reformation was famously and self-consciously a return to the book within a religion of the book. With the rallying cry "*sola scriptura*," Protestants embraced a sacred text as the sine qua non of their religion. Many Reformers embraced written language as the medium and the book as the vehicle of godly authority and Christian truth. Many championed the vernacular Bible and Christian literacy as antidotes to ignorance, superstition, and idolatry. Indeed, for some the book became an emblem of the desire to transcend the merely material and irredeemably fallen world of objects, of things. At the same time, Reformers were suspicious of all human media, of the fallen material dimension of all representation. They distrusted the material dimension of text, of all that might be associated with the letter rather than the spirit, and so this return to the book, this embrace of text, was fraught with ambivalence. That Reformers distrusted the necessarily fallen aspect of representation is well known, and yet we lack a vocabulary for talking about this phenomenon. It is tempting to think of this distrust of representation as a form of iconoclasm, but it would be more accurate to think of iconoclasm as a form of this distrust. Iconoclasm narrowly defined, of course, concerns the destruction of images: statues, paintings, stained-glass windows, and so on. In this project I am interested only peripherally in either images or acts of violent destruction. Images are only one form of representation, and acts of violent destruction are simply the most spectacular of the possible responses to the problem of representation in Christian thought. Many fine studies have been devoted to the study of the destruction of images, and some have detailed the relationship of this iconoclasm to literature.[4] Insofar as I am concerned with language and letters, words and books, I am working the other side of the street. But I also want to insist that this opposition between word and image—an opposition that seems so natural to us—is itself, in part, a product of the history I am recounting. If Christians had consistently opposed books to images, words to icons, Reformation writers did so with a vengeance, and they did so precisely in response to the problem presented by the materiality of representation. Early modern scholars, at times, reproduce this distinction without analysis, and so merely repeat what the Reformation had to say about itself. But books are, among other things, *things*; they are images to be seen, objects to be held. Texts necessarily have a carnal dimension, and it is the carnal dimension of texts and the problems that that ineluctable dimension caused for those who wished to repudiate the flesh that I address here.

My exploration of the way that the book was imagined in Reformation England necessarily draws me into a larger conversation about the history of the object. Scholars have recently asked us to attend more closely to the things of the early modern world; we seem to have turned our attention in recent years from subjects to objects, from the realm of discourse to the world of material culture. Of course, the best of this work proceeds from the understanding that there is no such thing as an intelligible object world divorced from subjects; this work insists on the dialectic of subject and object, the interpenetration of self and world.[5] Although *The Incarnate Text* is indebted to and inspired by this larger movement, it maintains a slightly different emphasis than most recent studies of material culture. In the first instance, this project insists on attending to the ways in which writers in the period thought in materialist terms. To read Spenser or Marlowe, Nashe or Donne is to read writers deeply immersed in materialist ways of thinking about the natural world, human behavior, the soul. Moreover, writers in early modern England were actively engaged in what we might call theorizing about the culture's relationship to the realm of objects and things. This was an historical moment in which the human relation to the material world was being redefined. Natural philosophy's embrace of empiricism, the humanist reconceptualization of the texts and artifacts of history, the exploration and discovery of lands and things undreamt of in ancient philosophy, the transition to modern markets and global trade—all of these historical developments led to new ways of apprehending the physical stuff of the world. And none of these developments, I contend, was untouched by the religious crisis that I address in this study. The redefinition of the subject's relationship to objects and the material world cannot be understood without reference to early modern religious culture and the impact of the Reformation on this culture.

In *The Incarnate Text*, I seek to make a contribution to the history of the object by focusing on an object in crisis: the post-Reformation book.[6] More specifically, I attend to the ways in which some writers—especially literary writers—addressed the post-Reformation problem of language as artifact. The crisis I discuss in this project occasioned many attacks on artistic representation. Paintings, statues, entire buildings were destroyed, music was forbidden, theater and poetry were denounced—all in the name of eradicating superstition and idolatry. The Reformation, broadly speaking, was not friendly to the arts. At the same time, however, the crisis that sparked these attacks proved to be remarkably generative, producing a wide range of discursive and artistic works. Artists—sculptors, painters, musicians, dramatists, poets—are, of course, particularly attuned to the sensuous properties of representation, the textures of matter, the vibrations of sound, the rhythms of language. Since it was precisely the material, aesthetic, and imaginative dimensions of representation that were under attack, it is unsurprising to find artists responding to this crisis. Protestants and Catholics, more and less reformed, all had to negotiate the problems of artistic representation. Here, my concern is with literary artists and their response to the problem of language as artifact, language as aesthetic object. I have made no attempt to be comprehensive; while I draw on a wide range of writings, I analyze a handful of texts written by a handful of writers: Erasmus, Tyndale, More, Spenser, Marlowe, Shakespeare, Bacon. But if the story I tell is necessarily partial, I hope that it is also suggestive, drawing in a wide range of topics—from humanism and hermeneutics to secularization and enlightenment, from iconoclasm and anti-Semitism to barbarism and fetishism—that speak to the ways in which this crisis of representation both returned to some of the core concerns of Christian thought and anticipated the modern world.

Textual Asceticism and the Incarnate Text

In a "Sermon . . . preached vpon a good Friday" (ca. 1531–1534), John Fisher, Bishop of Rochester, ruminates upon the famous dream vision of Ezekiel in which the prophet "telleth that hée sawe a booke spread before him, the which was written both within and without." In his provocative exegesis of this passage, Fisher equates Ezekiel's "wonderfull booke" with the passion and crucifixion of Christ.[7] Fisher, however, does not merely suggest that his congregation should reflect on the crucifixion as a text containing the knowledge necessary for salvation; he insists on reading Christ crucified as a material book:

> But you maruell peraduenture why I call the crucifix a booke? I will
> now tell you the consideracion why. . . . A booke hath boardes,
> leaues, lynes, wrytinges, letters booth small and great. First I saye
> that a booke hath two boardes: the two boardes of this booke is the
> two partes of the crosse, for when the booke is opened & spread,
> the leaues be cowched vpon the boardes. And so the blessid body of
> Christ was spred vpon the crosse.
>
> The leaues of this booke be the armes, the handes, legges, and
> féete, with the other members of his most precious and blessed
> body. . . .
>
> You perceyue that this booke was full of lynes and small Letters,
> whyche were of dyuers coulers, (as I sayde) some black, some blewe,
> some reade, some blewyshe, that is to saye, full of stroakes, and

lasshes, where by the skynne was toarne, and rente in a thousande places. Besides these small letters, yet was there also greate Capytall Letters precyouslie illumyned with Roset colour: Roset is a reade colour lyke vnto the coulour of a Rose, which colour that most precyous bloude, whiche issued out of his hands and féete, doeth represent vnto vs, with this most precious blud was illumined the fyue great Capital letters in this wonderful booke. I mean by these capital letters the great wounds of his body, in his handes, and in hys féete, and in his side.[8]

I am interested in this sermon as an act of the imagination. Desiring his congregation to meditate on the crucified body of Christ on Good Friday, Fisher translates a scriptural text about an iconic book into a devotional image of Christ on the cross, an image he then "reads" as an illuminated manuscript. More simply, he asks his auditors to imagine a man being tortured to death and to imagine his suffering body as a book. In Fisher's inspired appropriation of Ezekiel's text, the congregation is invited to visualize an image in flux: Ezekiel's book transformed into the body of Christ, the body of Christ transformed into a fleshy book, bloody and beaten.

The ease with which Fisher moves from text to image and from body to book is striking to the modern reader. We live in an historical moment that tends to oppose texts and images, and tends not to think of the book as a thing of the flesh. Today, the book is only rarely seen as part of the world of bodies and things. Instead it is a vehicle for the transmission of text; it is an instrument and not an icon.[9] We might expect a sermon comparing Christ's body to a book to transport us from the suffering flesh to the redemptive message. For us, to *read* the body of the crucified Christ, to think of it as a text, would suggest an interpretive act in which the cross disappeared into meaning, body into figure. The particular situation of this body would become a window through which we could see what the suffering of that body means. The effect of Fisher's comparison, however, is precisely the reverse: the body comes into ever greater focus until it is all that one can see. Playing upon the figure of Christ as Word become flesh, Fisher makes the vision of an incarnate text come to life through a visceral conflation of body and book, through an insistence that books are flesh. To be sure, the effect of Fisher's sermon on his congregation depends on a certain shock value. How can one compare suffering flesh to a book? Fisher here offers an extended elaboration of a conceit that would make any metaphysical poet proud; the violent yoking together of the body and the book is reminiscent of a Donne or a Crashaw. And as so often with such conceits, Fisher asks us to attend to the very material ways in which these heterogeneous things are alike. The object Fisher describes in his conceit is a manuscript codex, made of parchment, written with ink. To understand the image he asks the congregation to see, we need to remember that parchment was made from animal skin, scraped and stretched and dried in the sun. Handling a parchment page even hundreds of years after it has been rendered into a writing surface, the reader is often well aware of its history as flesh: one can see hair follicles, tiny veins, discolorations where the living skin carried scars or blemishes.[10] In Fisher's sermon the crucified Christ is figured as a book *not* because it is to be read like a text but because the image of the book helps Fisher and his congregation imagine the suffering flesh in visceral ways.

Throughout *The Incarnate Text*, I look at acts of the imagination like Fisher's, acts that call on the book as both traditional emblem and familiar thing in the world. When I embarked on this project, I began with Fisher, with this sermon and this image. The sermon seemed like a way to mark an historical moment as it was passing; it seemed like a means of framing one end of the story I wanted to tell about new ways of imagining the book engendered by the Reformation. Written in the early 1530s, after a decade in which English authorities had battled the new Protestant faith with all the weapons at their disposal, but just as the marriage question was pushing Henry VIII to break with Rome, Fisher's sermon seemed like the last gasp of an era that was coming to a close. With its insistent conflation of body and book, Fisher's sermon seemed to me to belong to a medieval epistemology in which books were still part of the world of images and bodies. This was the Catholic backdrop against which I could present an image of a particularly Protestant book, or rather a particularly Protestant way of understanding and relating to the book. Fisher's fleshy book would be contrasted with a turn to text, a turn to spirit, a turn away from the letter and the body. If Fisher's sermon seemed somewhat alien to modern readers, all the better; it would help clarify that Fisher's material book was superseded by a modern conception of text as only having a contingent relationship to the book as object. This is in many ways a familiar narrative, applied here to a history of the book: the medieval and Catholic give way to the modern and Protestant; a culture of the image and the body, a culture of immanence, gives way to a culture of the text and the spirit, a culture of transcendence.

Nothing in my subsequent research, however, supported this familiar narrative. This is not to say that there was not a shift in the ways in which books were conceived; on the contrary, it will be the burden of this project to demonstrate that this shift was related to the religious crisis I discuss. Following Max Weber's famous formulation, one could map the disenchantment of the book onto the "disenchantment of the world." Just as a world of miracles and prodigies, analogies and resemblances, was transformed into a world of fact and method, analysis and representation, so the carnal and sacred book was transformed into the instrumental text. This is only, however, the end of the story. To view what happened in the sixteenth and seventeenth centuries through the lens of this narrative would be to read the end into the beginning; it would be to simplify and obscure a complex and contentious struggle over the ways in which images and books should be understood. And it would be to render inevitable what was neither inescapable nor foreseeable. Nothing had to happen the way it did. No one knew where this struggle over books and images would lead. Protestants and Catholics did not uniformly line up to take predetermined positions on either side of easily defined issues. In assuming a simple trajectory from immanence to transcendence, in assuming a Protestant book that simply replaces a Catholic one, this grand narrative fails to account for the variety and complexity of the responses to the crisis of the book. One of the aims of this book is to show the ways in which the history was much more contested and conflicted, much more interesting, than the familiar version of this narrative might suggest. To assume, for instance, that Fisher's way of imagining the book was simply a remnant of an earlier age, of a medieval era superseded by the modern, is to fail to see the complexity of the tradition that early modern writers like Fisher inherited. And it is to misunderstand the ways in which the crisis of the book occasioned by the Reformation was simply a particular historical manifestation of a problematic at the heart of Christian thought.

* * *

That Christianity is a religion of the book is axiomatic, but that it is a religion that has had a vexed relation to the book is a story less often told. One of the tenets of *The Incarnate Text* is that Christianity was a religion of the book that was always made uneasy by the materiality of text. This ambivalence toward the book is of a piece with, although not reducible to, Christianity's ambivalence toward icons. In his discussion of Christian iconoclasm in *The Reformation of the Image*, the art historian Joseph Leo Koerner contends that "the Christian image was iconoclastic from the start." In Koerner's account the Christian icon was "always already repudiated"; it was designed to be "crossed out." Even in those historical moments when the image seemed most powerful, when Christianity seemed to embrace the image, it was always bracketed off as image, always considered treacherous.[11] And if the Christian icon was always already iconoclastic, then the ambivalent relation to the image that we see in the Reformation—never more pronounced than in those images denouncing images—was simply a particularly consequential return to concerns that had always defined Christianity's relation to the world of icons. The ambivalence that Koerner finds at the heart of Christianity's relation to the image also informs Christianity's relation to the material object of the book. In *The Incarnate Text*, I contend that Christianity always enjoyed an ambivalent relationship to the book and that this ambivalence was exacerbated by the defining concerns of the Reformation. This analogy between a Christian understanding of the icon and a Christian understanding of the book can only take us so far, however; Christians did not *simply* treat the book as another icon, another aspect of the material world that needed to be repudiated. The issue is complicated, in the first instance, by the fact that books and images were so often opposed in Christian thought. Even Gregory the Great's famous—and in certain circles infamous—defense of images was an argument that both worked as a prophylactic against the threat that images represented and created a clear hierarchy of book and image. In a letter to Bishop Serenus of Marseilles in 599, Pope Gregory argues against the iconoclastic destruction of image

> Some time ago it reached us that your fraternity, seeing certain people adoring images, broke the images and threw them from the churches. And certainly we praise you for your zeal lest something manufactured be adored, but we judge that you should not have destroyed those images. For a picture is displayed in churches on this account, in order that those who do not know letters may at least read by seeing on the walls what they are unable to read in books. Therefore your fraternity should preserve those things and prohibit the people from adoring them, so that persons ignorant of letters may have something whereby they may gather knowledge of the story.[12]

The defense of images as books for the illiterate would become a recurrent refrain in medieval and early modern thought, repeated in a variety of contexts and finally institutionalized in the Council of Trent. It would lead to the notion of images as *biblia pauperum* (Bibles of the poor)—a phrase that Gregory did not use in his justification of images—and would help clarify the relation of image to text in Christian culture. It is important to note that this influential defense of images assumes a hierarchy of text and image, and it assumes that the proper way to understand images is to read them as one would read a book. Even when Christians defended images, they defended them as substitutes for, and supplements to, books; they defended them as "texts" that needed to be read. The image defended by Gregory is, as Koerner would suggest, an iconoclastic one. But if Gregory's influential conception of images as books works to clarify how Christians should apprehend the image, it muddies the waters when it comes to the material dimension of text, when it comes to all the ways in which the book is an icon.

* * *

From the beginning, it seems, Christianity enjoyed a peculiar relationship to the book. Not simply a religion of the book, Christianity is a religion of the codex. The codex replaced the roll or scroll as the dominant reading technology in Christian culture as early as the second century C.E. The historical evidence for the Christian preference for codices is unequivocal. Almost all non-Christian texts that survive from the first three hundred years of the Common Era are scrolls; almost all of the Christian texts that survive from the same time period are codices. By the fifth century, as the Christian religion rose in prominence and historical significance, the codex would overtake the scroll as the medium of choice for all kinds of texts in the Greek and Roman worlds. In *The Birth of the Codex*, C. H. Roberts and T. C. Skeat refer to this development—in which the book form familiar to us today replaced the traditional roll or scroll—as the "most momentous development in the history of the book . . . [before] the invention of printing."[13] Scholars have offered a variety of speculative arguments attempting to explain why Christians adopted the codex rather than the scroll: its greater portability and greater capacity to hold text made it more economical and convenient; the indexical technology of the codex lent itself to the interpretive strategies of Christians; an early influential text—Paul's letters perhaps—existed in this form and thus shaped expectations about what a Christian book should be; Christians wanted to distance themselves symbolically from paganism, and, especially, Judaism.[14] The lack of scholarly consensus seems instructive, suggesting the ways in which this shift, like all historical change, is overdetermined. Here, I prefer not to contribute to the speculation on the cause of this transition but to consider some of the possible effects of this development for Christianity's relation to the book. Whatever the reason for the "choice" of codex over scroll, the codex form became a material marker of the ways in which the Christian religion differentiated itself from competing traditions. As Guglielmo Cavallo notes, in the first centuries of the Common Era the codex was a form familiar to the lower classes of society. It was employed as a kind of notebook and was useful for business and other day-to-day transactions.[15] The scroll, on the other hand, was a form used by the more "literate" aristocratic elite; sacred texts, literary texts, and important historical and juridical documents were committed to the scroll form. The scroll was associated with permanence and reserved for that which was valued by society, while the notebook form of the codex was ephemeral and of little value, economically or culturally.[16] The emergence of the codex as the privileged textual form of this new religion, for whatever reason, meant that Christian culture was materially differentiated from pagan and Jewish cultures through the media form that it employed, a form that these competing traditions viewed as low, ephemeral, inconsequential.[17] As Christians came to be associated, and to associate themselves, with a form that was humble and debased, the codex seems to have become part of the repertoire of symbols whereby early Christians systematically overturned traditional notions of value: just as a criminal executed by the state was revealed as the godhead, so the humble codex was exalted over the prestigious scroll.

We know, of course, that the manuscript codex would soon cast off its humble origins to become the dominant medium for the preservation and dissemination of written text for the next thirteen hundred years or so. And we also know that in Christian culture the codex was often revered as both the material vessel of sacred text and one of the central symbols of a religion that defined itself by its relation to texts. In one of Jerome's most famous letters—his "Letter to Eustochium" (385 C.E.)—we find relatively early evidence both of Christians venerating the book and of Christians insisting on the humility of the embodied Christian text.[18] In the letter Jerome denounces the hypocrisy of wasting valuable resources on the creation of the Christian book as an aesthetic object while the Christian duty to care for the poor is neglected: "Parchment is stained with purple dye, gold is melted to form letters, books are studded with gems, and Christ dies in nakedness before their doors."[19] That the true image of Christ in the form of suffering human flesh is ignored while valuable resources are wasted on beautiful objects was a recurrent theme in Christian iconoclasm. Jerome's attack on gold and purple manuscripts is situated within an attack on Christian hypocrisy generally, an attack on aristocrats (especially aristocratic women) who are interested in various kinds of religious display rather than true virtue. In the preface to his translation of Job, Jerome makes a similar argument in which he associates the taste for such valuable books with the spiritually vulgar: "Let those who will keep the old books with their gold and silver letters on purple skins, or, to follow the ordinary phrase, in 'uncial characters' . . . if only they will leave for me and mine, our poor pages and copies which are less remarkable for beauty than for accuracy."[20] Written in "inch-high" (*uncial*) letters of gold or silver, these aestheticized objects are positioned in opposition to humbler forms of text, correct if not beautiful. A few manuscripts have survived from the fifth and sixth centuries that offer a sense of what Jerome was critiquing: scriptural texts, often the psalter or gospels, written in silver on purple parchment (Figure 1).[21] For Jerome, as for other influential figures, both rhetorical excess and lavish material ornamentation detract from the simple truth of Christian texts.[22] Jerome's attack on the heavily ornamented book is a product of what we might call a textual asceticism ("let me and mine have our wretched pamphlets") that dovetails with Christianity's ethos of denying the flesh and insisting on simplicity and humility in all things. This back and forth between the veneration of the book and the repudiation of such reverence would continue throughout the Middle Ages. The material evidence amply demonstrates that Jerome's critique would largely go unheeded, as the production of precious Christian manuscripts became a veritable industry. Famously, of course, some of the most impressive artistic objects that survive from the Middle Ages are elaborately illuminated manuscripts. Inscribed with precious metals or garnished with jewels, these books announced their spiritual value through their material worth. At the same time, a Hieronymian train of thought persisted that suggested that such books were dangerous. At best, they threatened to become icons that detracted from the properly spiritual meditation of text; at worst, they threatened to become idols that led away from proper veneration of the deity.[23]

Fisher and the Post-Reformation Book

Fisher's "Sermon . . . preached vpon a good Friday" reflects the ambivalence toward the book that he inherited from the Christian tradition. In Fisher's

Figure 1. "The Gospel of Matthew." *Codex Rossanensis* (sixth century), fol. 45r. Biblical uncial written with silver ink on purple dyed parchment. Biblioteca Arcivescovile, Rossano, Italy. Erich Lessing / Art Resource, NY.

sermon, however, this ambivalence is not simply a function of a textual asceticism but is a function of the fraught relationship of Christ as flesh to Christ as language. A strong strain of Christian thought asserted that the incarnation of the *logos* as flesh in the form of Christ transformed humanity's relation to the material and phenomenal world. If God takes on material form, the argument goes, then matter itself is transformed; if God takes on a body and becomes an image walking among us, then the prohibitions against images and icons expressed in the Old Testament can no longer pertain in the same way. Scholars have detailed how this tradition affects Christian notions of bodies and images, sacraments and relics.[24] My concern here is to address the ways in which this tradition affects Christian notions of language and text. Following the opening lines of John's Gospel (*In principio erat verbum*), Christian writers associated the second person of the godhead with language, with words. And Christ as *logos* not only had a powerful effect on Christian notions of language; it also had a profound effect on the ways Christians conceived scripture. Almost from the beginning, it seems, the incarnation of Christ as flesh was understood in relation to the incarnation of the word as scripture.[25] And this conceptual relation would result in elaborate metaphors of Christ as both text and book. As Beryl Smalley notes, Jerome himself "compares Scripture to the body of Christ in expressions which sound extravagant to modern readers."[26] The analogy between the body of Christ and the letter of scripture would become a Christian commonplace, leading to a long Christian tradition that attempted to apprehend the mystery of Christ as Word through visions of Christ as book.[27] In his fourteenth-century *Dictionarium seu reportorium morale* (ca. 1355), Pierre Bersuire offers a concise rendition of the conceit of Christ as book; he describes Christ as a "book written within the skin of the virgin. . . . That book was spoken in the disposition of the Father, written in the conception of the mother, exposited in the clarification of the nativity, corrected in the passion, erased in the flagellation, punctuated in the imprint of the wounds, adorned in the crucifixion above the pulpit, illuminated in the outpouring of blood, bound in the resurrection, and examined in the ascension."[28] The arc of Christ's incarnation and life, passion and death, resurrection and ascension is here comprised in the production of a book. The rich metaphorical tradition equating Christ's body with scripture generated a wide variety of cultural forms, ranging from the Charter of Christ, in which Christ's crucified flesh was equated with a written legal document, to children's alphabets in which a simple hornbook was figured as the body of Christ on the cross. The tradition that the Word is incarnate in scripture also led in various times and places to the veneration of the Bible and to the belief in its material efficacy in the world. The Bible was thought to ward off the devil and evil spirits, to cure disease, to protect crops. And the notion of Christ as book and scripture as the incarnate Word worked not only to sanctify the Bible in the minds of some but also to sanctify a variety of quasi-scriptural texts, ranging from the Agnus Dei to the Fifteen Oes.[29] This veneration accorded to scripture and quasi-scriptural texts could extend outward to encompass all writing as sacred. Ernst Curtius records an anecdote concerning Francis of Assisi in which "the saint picked up every written piece of parchment which he found on the ground, even if it were from a pagan book. Asked by a disciple why he did so, Francis answered: *Fili me, litterae sunt ex quibus componitur gloriosissimum Dei nomen.* [My son, these are the letters out of which the glorious name of God is formed]."[30] Here, the incarnation of the *logos* means that all language—fragments of text, scraps of parchment—has been glorified. Writing itself is sacred. Despite the authority of figures like Jerome who denounced the veneration of the book, it would be a mistake to assume that reverence toward the book was simply a falling away from Christian ideals, simply a function of the idolatrous impulses of the superstitious or ignorant. What we see in this seeming apotheosis of the book is that Christians used the codex as a way to think through some of the mysteries of the faith. It is not simply that the relation between ideal and material dimensions of language was central to the antitheses that structure Christianity: the letter and spirit, the word and Word. More specifically, it is that this relation provided a way for Christians to imagine the dialectic of immanence and transcendence at the heart of a religion with an ineffable, transcendent God who takes on human flesh.

Following in the long Christian tradition apprehending the incarnation through the image of the book, Fisher reads Ezekiel's observation that the book was "written within and without" as an invitation to reflect on the mysteries of Word made flesh:

> This booke was written with in and without. Fyrst within was wrytten but one word. . . . Of this worde Saint Iohn speaketh, saying, In principio erat verbum, the word was in the begynning before all creatures, thys worde is the second person in the godhead, the sonne of God which by the holie Ghost was written in the inward syde of thys parchment. For the Godheade of Christe was couered and

hidde vnder the lykenesse of man. The holy Ghost was the penne of almyghtie God the father, He set hys most mightie word vnto the body of Christ, within the wombe of the Vyrgine Marye, and so this booke was written within.

For as Sainct Paule sayeth . . . if they had knowne the sonne of God, which was and is the Lorde of euerlasting glorie, they woulde neuer haue crucified hym. They sawe his manhood which was in outwarde sight, but they sawe not hys Godheade whych was couered within the same. The Godhead was the inward syde, and the man-hoode was the outwarde syde.[31]

The one word written on the inside of Ezekiel's book is the "second person in the godhead, the sonne of God"; Christ's humanity, his "manhoode," is written on the outside of the book. Fisher gives us the codex as a metaphor for the hypostatic union. And Fisher's sermon here offers us a glimpse into the way the scroll is displaced by the codex in Christian thought. Ezekiel's book—like almost all books referenced in the Bible—is a scroll, a "roll of a book," as most English editions from the Geneva Bible to the King James Bible have it. In explicating Ezekiel's book, however, Fisher describes a manuscript codex in elaborate detail. Reading the codex back into the Old Testament as an embodiment of text that anticipates Christ, Fisher's sermon offers a palimpsest of forms: an image of a cross written over an image of a codex written over an image of a scroll. It is unclear whether this is a deliberate decision or a simple misreading. In any case, the substitution of codex for scroll alters the interpretive frame; the phrase "written within and without," for instance, means something very different when applied to the two sides of a scroll than when applied to the inside and outside of a codex. The codex form—a form that invites metaphors of container and contained, kernel and shell—shapes the ways in which Fisher imagines the relation of body to book.

While preaching his sermon, Fisher would have been surrounded by codices. One of the things that Protestants decried about the Catholic Mass was what they considered the unnecessary and confusing number of books that circulated on the altar during the service. It is likely that the liturgical books Fisher employed in the course of the Mass were not simply texts to be read but devotional objects, carefully considered icons designed to evoke pity and wonder in the congregation. As texts crucial to the performance of the central experience of Christian life, liturgical books—missals, ordinals, pontificals, psalters, antiphonals, processionals—were often treated as sacred objects. Displayed on the altar, these books often became ceremonial artifacts invested with the splendor and potency of the Mass. The covers and bindings of medieval and early modern books sometimes incorporated the fragmentary remains of saints, effectively transforming the book into a portable reliquary.[32] Yvonne Hackenbroch has called our attention to a golden prayer book binding that was converted into a pax, the tablet or plate kissed during the Mass.[33] Marking the presence of the sacred through the authority of the rare and precious, such religious books were key elements in a sacred economy of objects central to late medieval life. And yet we see little evidence of this economy in Fisher's evocation of book as body. Surrounded by books, Fisher asks his congregation to imagine a book, but the object that Fisher conjures does not resemble the aesthetic objects that Bibles and liturgical books had so often become; the object he conjures is not grand or even pretty. Certainly, Fisher exalts the book by equating it to the suffering flesh of Christ; just as Christ's body is glorified by the divinity it clothes, so Ezekiel's book is glorified by this comparison to Christ on the cross. But in Fisher's sermon this glorification does not lead to any kind of aesthetic magnificence; on the contrary, Fisher goes out of his way to depict the grotesque frailty of the flesh. Both body and book are, in Fisher's sermon, abject. This abjection, however, is as much a celebration of the incarnation as those books dressed in purple and gold that Jerome had denounced. The incarnation troubled any simple understanding of the world, of the flesh. If the presence of the divine in the fallen world and in human form worked to help transform that world and that form, it also worked to show how fallen and corrupt they truly were. For Christians, the incarnation was a supreme sign of God's love precisely because in assuming human flesh Christ chose to debase himself. In his sermon Fisher dwells on the physical horrors of the crucifixion, on the agonies that the embodied Christ must undergo. The image of the book helps to make these agonies more real, because it too is a sign of death and corruption. It is important to remember that the book—made from the skin of dead animals—was a traditional memento mori in the period. Like Christ's body, like all bodies after the incarnation, it was both glorified and corrupt. In Fisher's sermon we see ambivalence toward an object that pulls in two directions: it is a sign of letter *and* figure, flesh *and* spirit, of a fallen material realm that needs to be transcended *and* of the transcendence of that realm. And in the Reformation the almost structural ambivalence that shaped the Christian understanding of the book would be exacerbated as

Reformers simultaneously revered the text and rejected the flesh that embodied it.

To assume that Fisher's sermon was a remnant of an earlier age, that it was Catholic and therefore "medieval," is not only to misunderstand the complexity of the tradition he inherited; it is also to misunderstand the ways in which Fisher's conception of the book was profoundly shaped by Reformation concerns. Throughout *The Incarnate Text*, I use the term "Reformation" both to frame the historical moment I am addressing and to suggest the set of issues with which I am concerned, but I want to emphasize that this is not a book about Protestant, or for that matter Catholic, conceptions of the book. It is a book about the ways in which books were imagined after the historical break we know as the Reformation, how books were imagined during a crisis in Christian thought concerning representation. Everyone in sixteenth- and seventeenth-century England, and indeed Europe, lived in a post-Reformation world. To assume that Catholics of this time period were part of some kind of "residual" culture is simply anachronistic. This is not to say that Fisher's conception of the book was not decidedly Catholic or that he did not embrace a traditional Christian understanding of books. Fisher would be executed for his traditional beliefs not long after this sermon was written. And like all Reformation texts, Fisher's sermon embraced tradition, or an aspect of tradition, with a vengeance. Rather, it is to say that Fisher's sermon was a product of its place and time; it was not merely an imaginative act but a political act, part of an ongoing struggle for the hearts and minds of Christians. Fisher's striking conflation of cross and book was complicated by the significant role that Fisher played in this struggle, a role that involved him in the dramatic destruction of books.

The advent of the Reformation in England initiated an era of violence not only against the bodies of nonconformists but also against the books that embodied dissent.[34] And Fisher was intimately involved in these acts of violence. One of the first government- and church-sanctioned attacks on the nascent Reformation in England was Cardinal Wolsey's ritual burning of Lutheran books at Paul's Cross in 1521, an event that served to celebrate Luther's excommunication from the church. At the state-sanctioned book burning, Fisher preached a sermon "Agayn the Pernicyous Doctryn of Martin Luuther." In 1526 Fisher delivered a similar anti-Lutheran sermon at the recantation of Robert Barnes, an event at which Barnes and a group of merchants were forced to carry the wood that was used to burn the heretical texts found in their possession. In the interim between these two events, Fisher had been named an official censor of the book trade. In 1529 a priest named Thomas Hitton was seized in Kent for heretical preaching; under examination he confessed to smuggling a New Testament into England from the continent. Condemned by Archbishop Warham and the seemingly ubiquitous Fisher, he was the first Englishman to be burned alive in the cause of the Reformation.[35] Intimately involved in the administration's campaign against heretical and seditious texts, Fisher was a man with a particular interest in the ways in which the laity apprehended the material book of the Bible. Preached by a Catholic bishop at a time when Reformers were championing the authority of scripture over and against the traditions of the church, and when Catholic authorities were responding with censorship and violence, Fisher's sermon is more vexed than it would appear at first glance.

In the sermon, Fisher writes:

> Neuer anye Parchement skynne was more strayghtlye stratched by strength vpon the tentors then was this blessed body vpon the crosse. These lorells that crucifyed him, drewe by vyolence his moste precious armes, with ropes vnto either braunche of the crosse, that the sinowes burst in sonder, and so nayled his handes fast with spykinge nayles of yron, vnto the crosse. After they stretched his féete lykewyse vnto an other hole beneath in the crosse, and there nayled them with the third nayle thorough bothe his féete. And so they reared vp this body a loft against the sunne, euen as a parchment skinne is sette foorth before the heat of the Sun for to drye. It was set vp a loft to the entent that all the worlde might looke vpon this booke.[36]

And all the world should look upon this corpus in order to consume its redemptive message. One can imagine Fisher holding aloft a book to illustrate his dramatic conflation of Calvary and the production of parchment. But at this point in the sermon, a third image superimposes itself over the first two. The setting "vp a loft" of the "booke" that Fisher describes reflects the Catholic "prayer of oblation," that part of the Mass where the priest elevates the bread and wine as a reenactment of Christ's redemptive sacrifice; it is at this point in the Mass that transubstantiation is thought to occur. In the biblical passage Fisher is explicating, Ezekiel is instructed to eat the book. Given that we have a vision of the word being consumed, a traditional method of reading the passage was to equate Ezekiel's book with the eucharist. In an exegetical tour de force, Fisher manages to conflate three avatars of Christ—scripture, the cross, the eucharist—through the figure of Ezekiel's book. Or to look at it in another way, in Fisher's sermon the image of Ezekiel's book, the image of scripture, disappears into the two most potent images that the Catholic Church had to offer: the cross and the eucharist.

That this book—the book of the cross—was meant to be consumed, was meant to be transformed by and into the body, is brought home to the congregation by Fisher's discussion of how it is to be read. According to Fisher, the ideal reader for this book is Saint Francis:

> Sainct Fraunces coulde passe hys time with this booke, & was neuer wery thereof. . . . This holie Sainct Fraunces so profited in this lesson, that it caused in hys hearte such a feruent loue, such a deuotion, such an affection to Christ, that the capitall woundes which he behelde in the handes and féete, and syde of Christ, ware by myracle imprinted in hys owne handes and féete. . . . The meditation and imagination of this booke was so earnest, and so continuall, that the token of the fiue woundes of Christ, were imprinted and ingraued in thys holy Saynctes bodye.[37]

Francis's stigmata are emblematic of perfect reading, perfect meditation, perfect devotion.[38] Distinctions between subject and object collapse as the spectator becomes spectacle, as bearing witness to Christ's suffering in one's mind leads to bearing testimony on one's body. In the sermon Fisher keeps repeating the word "booke"—"Sainct Fraunces coulde passe hys time with this booke"; "the meditation and imagination of this booke"—but Ezekiel's book has long since disappeared into an image of the cross. The "reading" we see here is, of course, not reading at all but a devotional practice centering around the "earnest" and "continuall" "meditation and imagination" of the image of the cross. When examined in light of religious controversy, Fisher's sermon emerges not as a remnant of an earlier age but as an ideologically invested insistence on traditional devotional practices over and against the reading of scripture: we should read as Saint Francis did through continual meditation upon the cross. Lest there be any mistake as to his intention in transforming Ezekiel's book into an object of affective piety, Fisher suggests that devotional meditation upon the "book" of the crucifix is preferable to lay reading: "Thus who that list with a méeke harte, and a true fayth, to muse and to maruayle of this most wonderfull booke (I say of the Crucifixe) hée shall come to more fruitefull knowledge, then many other which dayly studie vpon their common bookes. This booke may suffice for the studie of a true christian man, all the dayes of his life. In this boke he may finde all things that be necessarie to the health of his soule."[39] In the sermon Fisher appears to be suggesting that "reading" the cross, "reading" the sacrament of the eucharist in the Mass is the only reading the laity need do.

In Fisher's sermon the book emerges as glorious and abject, as indispensable and superfluous, as an object that helps explain the fundamental mysteries of Christianity and as an instrument unnecessary to the dissemination of those mysteries. Fisher's sermon is a Reformation text because in the sermon he—like his Catholic cohort and his Protestant counterparts—responds to the crisis of the book with a vehement return to certain aspects of the Christian tradition.[40] In attempting to yoke that tradition to his purposes, Fisher attempts to shape the post-Reformation book, how it is read, how it is imagined.

Luther and the Fall into Writing

That Protestantism was a religion of the word was already a cliché in the early sixteenth century. To the extent that we repeat this commonplace without analysis, we simply reiterate one of Protestantism's most deeply held convictions and its most effective marketing campaign. That Christianity had always already been a religion of the book was one of the reasons this marketing campaign was so effective. Protestants had discovered—so it seemed to them—a contradiction at the heart of contemporary religious practices: the sacred text that should be at the center of this alleged religion of the book had been dislodged from its rightful place, replaced by nonscriptural traditions and acts of piety that had nothing to do with reading, hearing, or understanding text. Reformers like Luther promised a return to a true religion of the book and differentiated themselves from a Catholicism that they characterized as a religion of images and icons, bodies and things. With what seems in historical retrospect like a few swift strokes of the pen, those seemingly indelible categories—Catholic and Protestant—were written into being as diametrically opposed forces on a grand historical stage, as Christ and Antichrist. The simple antitheses at the heart of the dialectic I am describing here—word versus thing, writing versus image, text versus idol—have had, of course, wide-reaching repercussions for Western culture in the modern era. More locally, they necessarily shaped the experience of the book for Protestants and Catholics alike. Being a religion of the book in the way that Reformers proposed, however, is easier said than done; indeed, sustaining these fundamental antitheses in any kind of rigorous way is impossible. That this impossibility proved hugely productive, generating an unprecedented proliferation of written and printed text in the period—theological, polemical, confessional, literary—is one of the recurring concerns of this book. The problem for Reformation thought, of course, is that the things disavowed, the very things set in opposition to writing and text in these antitheses, are inescapably at the heart of language. Language cannot fail to have a material dimension; it cannot avoid being flesh or image. Catholics were not slow to call attention to the problem this posed for an iconoclastic religion of the book. In response to the Reformation's elevation of the book and denigration of the image, Thomas More asks a devastatingly simple question: if one can revere a book that tells us of "Crystes lyfe / and hys deth . . . expressed by wrytyng," why can one not revere an image depicting the same, since they are both forms of representation?[41] Likewise, he asks if "the name of Iesus is to be reuerenced and had in honoure," then "why and with what reason can they dyspyse a figure of hym carued or paynted" since the "name is but an ymage representynge his person to mannes mynde and ymagynacyon"?[42] This deconstruction of the difference between word and image works both ways, of course; later in the sixteenth century, more radical Protestants would reject the written word *as* an image. And many Protestants who did not adopt such an extreme position were acutely aware of the paradoxes at the heart of their fundamental beliefs. Luther himself would have to negotiate these paradoxes throughout his career. That his strategy was to embrace the paradoxes straightforwardly, and that he often did so brilliantly, should not obscure the fact that he and his interlocutors returned obsessively to the problem of language, the problem of the book.

When we think of Luther, we think of the great champion of scripture. We associate him with the translation and dissemination of the vernacular Bible, with the uncompromising doctrine of *sola scriptura*. He is the revolutionary who elevated scripture above the authority of the church and its traditions, and placed the Gospel at the center of Christian life and experience. And this is how he was defined in the period both by his supporters and, as in a photographic negative, by his opponents. To Catholics like More, Luther was engaged in bibliolatry; he was an idolater of the book who had reified the text of scripture and held it above and outside the histories and traditions that shaped and defined the texts in question. Those Reformers Luther derisively called the *Schwärmer* (fanatics or enthusiasts) accused him of exactly the same crime but for antithetical reasons. For radical Protestants who claimed to be more truly reformed than Luther, the letter of scripture was simply another mediating agent, an obstacle that could impede the movement of the spirit in the individual believer.[43] For the iconoclast Thomas Müntzer, for instance, the letter of scripture was useless without the internal movement of the spirit, what he called the "living witness": "The man who has not received the living witness of God . . . knows really nothing about God, though he may have swallowed 100,000 Bibles."[44] To insist on the text of scripture as the sine qua non of Christian experience—as Luther did—was to make a fetish of the word, just as Catholics made a fetish of their ceremonial forms. Embattled on all sides, Luther and his sacred book were wedded in the European imaginary.

Luther has become so associated with the book of the Bible and with a text-centered religion that it is easy to forget that he often and forcefully expressed his belief that writing—the graphic dimension of language—was an aspect of the fallen world. It is easy to forget that he associated the written word of scripture, in unequivocal terms, with sin and death. As Heiko Oberman observes, for Luther "the Bible is a necessary evil."[45] And it is a necessary evil because of the fallen nature of writing. In his *Lectures on Genesis*, Luther offers a reading of the Garden of Eden in which he suggests that the experience of the word of God was the defining feature of paradise. Luther reads the divine command to abstain from the fruit of the tree of knowledge of good and evil as the first preaching of the word. This injunction establishes the relationship between human and divine: "God gave Adam Word, worship, and religion in its barest, purest, and simplest form. . . . Only this He wants: that he praise God, that he thank Him, that he rejoice in the Lord, and that he obey Him by not eating from the forbidden tree."[46] This foundational prohibition then does not mark off the boundaries of Paradise but is itself the constitutive element of Paradise. And in this obedience to the word, the church is born: "here the Lord is preaching to Adam and setting the Word before him," and "in this passage the church is established."[47] In Luther's reading, both paradise and church are constituted by the ability before the Fall to hear the divine word directly and to understand and obey it perfectly. Disobeying this divine command, Adam and Eve are exiled from a perfect world of direct communication with, and knowledge of, the divine to a fallen world of material signs, the fallen world of the letter. The implication is that the absence of direct access to that word—an absence that necessitates writing and books—is the defining feature of the fallen world. Luther contends that "if Adam had remained in innocence, this preaching would have been like a Bible for him and for all of us; and we would have had no need for paper, ink, pens, and that endless multitude of books which we require today, although we do not attain a thousandth part of that wisdom which Adam had in Paradise."[48] Books, paper, ink—these are signs of the Fall, signs of the failure of human signification to be other than bodily, carnal.

When Luther was writing, the association of writing with the law and death already had a long history in Christian thought. Early modern writers inherited a tradition extending back to the church fathers who taught that writing had entered the world as a direct consequence of the Fall.[49] In one variant of this tradition, writing entered the world through the Mosaic law; thus, the letter and the law entered the world simultaneously, further establishing the link between the fallen letter and Christianity's Judaic inheritance. In Christian thought, however, writing and the law were not merely signs of the Fall but also signs of the possibility of redemption. Ambrose captures this facet of the tradition succinctly: "Because the authority of the natural law was corrupted and blotted out by disobedience, the written Law was determined necessary, that man who had lost all might regain at least a part."[50] Regaining at least a part of the divine word through the fallen material vessel of the written word, Christians are in the impossible position of attempting to overcome their fallen state by placing their faith in an aspect of the fallen world. For Luther and his theological descendants, this problem was exacerbated. They believed simultaneously that scripture alone could lead one to salvation and that the dead letter was not to be trusted. The solution to this dilemma is, of course, both simple and impossibly difficult: the spirit works through the word, bringing the letter to life. That this appeal to the spirit opened an interpretive Pandora's box is an aspect of Reformation history that has been well documented. My interest here is in the status of the letter. In its proximity to and distance from the word it can only ever represent imperfectly, the material letter of scripture is both the supplement that proves that humanity is fallen and the supplement that must help humanity transcend that fallen state. My point is not that Christians generally or Protestants specifically could not and did not negotiate these paradoxes. Many did so with seeming ease, never batting an eye over the problem of the material nature of representation, the problem of the letter. Nor is it my position that those who failed to attend to these paradoxes in a rigorous way were naïve in their understanding of language and representation. My contention is simply that these paradoxes, even for those far from the front lines of religious controversy, shaped this particular culture of the book in fundamental ways, shaped the ways in which the book was imagined in the period.

This Reformation ambivalence toward the letter is at the heart of the argument of *The Incarnate Text*. I begin, however, not with Luther's aversion to the written text of scripture but with Desiderius Erasmus's embrace of it. In the first chapter, "Relics of the Mind," I begin with Erasmus because one of the main threads I follow in this study—the movement from a piety focused upon the image to a piety focused upon the written text—is a fundamentally Erasmian one. Before Luther climbed onto the stage of Christian history, Erasmus was engaged in a campaign to make the reading of scripture the center of the Christian universe and to reform what he considered the ignorant and superstitious acts—veneration of relics, pilgrimages to holy sites, worship of images—that dominated contemporary devotional practices. That Erasmus laid the egg that Luther hatched was a commonplace of the period.[51] But my purpose here is not to pursue the idea of Erasmus as Reformer but to discuss Erasmus's influential understanding of the place of the text of scripture in Christian life. Although Erasmus was generally sympathetic to the Reformers' determination to return to scripture, he would have no patience for the radical implications of Luther's battle cry of *sola scriptura*. That scripture should be removed from history and tradition, that interpretation should be divorced from consensus, made no sense to the historically minded humanist. Nevertheless, Erasmus's double-barreled mission—the celebration of text, the denigration of image—would prove hugely influential to Protestants. Many of the major Protestant figures aside from Luther—Philipp Melancthon, Huldrych Zwingli, and Martin Bucer, among others—were persuaded by Erasmus's mission to reform contemporary piety before they made the leap with Luther to a new understanding of grace.[52] As I discuss in Chapter 1, Erasmus's desire to guide contemporary Christianity toward language and text, and away from icons and objects, led him to suggest that Christians should honor the writings of scripture in place of relics and images. In making his case for this reform of contemporary piety, Erasmus steps to the brink of what could be construed as an improper veneration of the word, especially the written word of scripture. This Erasmian veneration of the book, a reverence reproduced in the writings of many humanists and Reformers, led to tensions concerning the problem of scripture as material artifact. To explore the way some of these tensions were addressed in England, I turn in this initial chapter from Erasmus to the rancorous dispute between Thomas More and William Tyndale. Here, we see two brilliant writers grapple with the problem that the material dimension of language poses for Christianity.

"Bookworship" and Its Discontents

During this crisis of the book, Reformation writers returned again and again to the problem of the letter, to the troubling reality that the word of God was preserved and disseminated through the fallen medium of writing. The methods proposed to address the issue, however, inevitably introduced new complications, new challenges. Luther, for instance, attempted to resolve the problem by applying the fundamental Reformation division of word and image to writing itself. He did so through a radical division of language along experiential and sensory lines. Luther framed the matter simply: scripture experienced through the sense of sight is irredeemably fallen; the word experienced through the sense of hearing is not.[53] In his *Lectures on the Psalms* he insists that it is in the nature of God's word to be heard ("Natura enim verbi est audiri").[54] The crucial scriptural text here is Romans 10:17: "Faith commeth by hearing."[55] Since vision of the truth is not given man in this life, "the Word of God is perceived only by hearing."[56] At times, Luther seems to take this division quite seriously. And he reiterates this idea in characteristically striking and colloquial ways: "Do not look for Christ with your eyes, but put your eyes in your ears"; "The Kingdom of Christ is a hearing kingdom, not a seeing kingdom"; the church is a "mouth house" and not a "pen house."[57] At other times, this division of experience into vision and hearing seems simply to work as a metaphor for Luther's understanding of the proper way to apprehend scripture: through the spirit. After all, his account of his own conversion experience—the famous "tower experience" (*turmerlebnis*)—depicts him alone with the Bible, struggling to make sense of the "alien word."[58] Luther emphasized hearing the word preached because he wanted to insist that the word of God is present not on the page, not in the scriptural text, but through the working of the spirit, through the ghostly understanding. For Luther, the word is a speech-act, a promise made by God to his people, a promise that is renewed by faith when one hears the word preached: "When the preacher speaks, God speaks."[59] To be sure, preaching must rely on scripture, the spoken word on the written. Luther insisted, against those he dismissed as radicals and enthusiasts, that true preaching and any possible spiritual understanding of scripture are dependent upon a written word that is the sine qua non of the Christian experience. And yet, for Luther, that written word is an empty vessel in comparison to the word preached. The visual word is the dead letter; the aural word provides access to the living spirit.[60]

Although Luther mistrusted the visual dimension of human experience, it is important to remember that he was not an iconoclast in the narrow sense of the term. It is sometimes forgotten, for instance, that Luther's German Bible—that icon of the word's ascendance over the image—is full of woodcuts depicting scenes from scripture. In his polemic against the enthusiasts and iconoclasts, *Against the Heavenly Prophets in the Matter of Images and Sacraments* (1525), he writes that he wished these images would be "paint[ed] on walls for the sake of remembrance and better understanding. . . . Yes, would to God that I could persuade the rich and the mighty that they would permit the whole Bible to be painted on houses, on the inside and outside, so that all can see it. That would be a Christian work." Crucially for Luther, images "do no more harm on walls than in books."[61] Luther's distrust of the visual dimension of experience led him to treat, and to exhort others to treat, images with care; to reject icons outright, however, would be to evince a deference to the material dimension of representation that amounted to idolatry. For Luther, the radical iconoclasts were living contradictions: insofar as their actions and beliefs were determined by an obsessive relation to the material world, they embraced the very idolatry that they sought to eradicate. Luther's distrust of the graphic dimension of language, his embrace of the oral and aural, however, dovetailed with the iconoclasts' more vehement condemnation of visual experience. Although it was by no means the only way to address the problem of the materiality of the letter, this division of the graphic and aural dimensions of language proved extremely influential to Reformers generally and to the English Puritans of the late sixteenth and seventeenth centuries specifically.[62] Of course, this division produced its own problems. Sound is not immaterial; spoken language is not divorced from the flesh. More troublingly for the iconoclasts, sound and voice can be aestheticized, ritualized. Liturgical music, chant, repetitive prayer, iterations of holy formulae—all were denounced, at one time or another, by Protestant groups.

For some of the more radical Protestants, even experiencing the word of scripture aurally was not enough to ward off an idolatrous relation to fallen material forms. For these Protestants the distinction between graphic and aural became a distinction not only between hearing the word preached and reading the word on the page, but also between a minister preaching the word and a minister merely reading scripture or a sermon to his congregation. True hearing was aligned with the movement of the spirit in interpretation, while "bare reading" was aligned with the mechanical repetition of empty formulae that Protestants associated with the Catholic Mass.[63] In England the idea that preaching was necessary for salvation became so engrained in certain nonconformist circles that it was believed by some that the deaf were denied the means of salvation.[64] As early as the Admonition Controversy in the 1570s, the idea that the "bare word" of scripture was not enough for salvation was a central aspect of the debate between nonconformists and the Church of England. One of the problems facing the Church of England was the shortage of qualified ministers throughout the realm. There simply were not enough licensed "preaching ministers" available in the realm to provide one for every parish. To improve this situation, the English government sent out so-called reading ministers whose duty was simply to read the scripture and the prescribed sermons. To the nonconformists this rote preaching, this preaching by the letter, was anathema. The *Admonition to the Parliament* (1572) registers a strenuous objection to the Church of England's employment of reading ministers. John Field and Thomas Wilcox, the authors of the dissenting pamphlet, insist that administering "the worde of God" is properly "an offyce of preaching" but the Church of England makes it into "an offyce of reading":

> In the scriptures . . . [God's ministers] are enjoyned to fede Gods Lambes, and yet with these, suche are admitted and accepted, as onely are bare readers. . . . Reading is not feeding, but it is as euill as playing vpon a stage, and worse too. For players yet learne their partes wythout booke, and these, a manye of them can scarcely reade within booke. These are emptie feeders, darcke eyes, ill workemen . . . messengers that cannot call, Prophets that can not declare the will of the Lorde, vnsauery salte, blinde guides, sleepie watchmen, untrustie dispensers of Gods secretes, euill deuiders of the worde.[65]

Worse than playing upon a stage, the reading minister's performance of the text is mere theater, an empty recitation of words; the "bare reading" of scripture does not move past the letter to the spirit, does not move from text to interpretation, and so becomes a "mockerie" of Christ's scriptural injunction to "goe preache."[66] In this passage we see one of the recurring concerns of *The Incarnate Text*: the belief that any experience of text that is not properly edifying is idolatrous, a tarrying with the letter that does not engender a movement of the spirit.

If nonconformists claimed that scripture was a "sealed book" without the ministrations of a preacher, more mainstream Protestants rejected as "Puritan" the claim that that the "bare reading" of scripture was not enough for salvation. For them such a claim represented a return to Catholic idolatry and a betrayal of the doctrine of *sola scriptura*.[67] John Whitgift, the future Archbishop of Canterbury, railed against this "contempt of reading the scriptures," contending that the idea that reading the scripture is akin to "playing upon a stage . . . is an untolerable blasphemy."[68] For Whitgift, reading is a form of preaching:

> I say that St Paul, in that chapter to the Romans, by preaching doth generally understand all kinds of publishing the gospel by the external voice, which comprehendeth reading as well as it doth that which you call preaching; and it is greatly against the dignity and majesty of the scriptures, it also greatly confirmeth the error of the papists touching the obscurity of the scriptures and debarring the people from reading them, to say that faith cometh not by reading; for that is to make them dumb and unprofitable. . . . Surely I marvel what is meant by this your strange kind of doctrine, except you would have the people through ignorance of the scriptures brought again to this point, that they must only depend upon the mouth of the pastor.[69]

Whitgift's critique is twofold. By insisting that edification requires the intervention of a preacher, the nonconformists return to the hierarchical structure of the Catholic Church, where there must be some intermediary between the individual Christian and the text of scripture. By denying scripture the ability to move the spirit of one who reads or hears, the nonconformists deny the sacred text its efficacy. Scripture becomes a dumb thing, an idol. This is the heart of the issue, and on this, radical and orthodox agree. For the nonconformists it is idolatrous to reduce scripture to a stock or stone by merely reading it, by reducing it to a recitation, a performance; for the Church of England it is idolatrous to assume that scripture can be so reduced.

The polemical conflict between Henry Ainsworth and John Smyth helps clarify what is at stake in this debate. A radical separatist, Smyth offered an extreme version of the argument against "bare reading." In Smyth's argument the written word is a visual image, and the rote reading of the word was part of the ceremonial and ritual aspects of Judaism repudiated by Christ in the New Testament. For Smyth this meant that the material book could not be used as a "help" or "prop" during worship: "Here a question is to be discussed: wither a book be a lawful help to further vs in tyme of spiritual worship. . . . Bookes or writings are signes or pictures of things signified therby. . . . Hence it followeth that bookes or writinges are in the nature of pictures or Images & therefore in the nature of ceremonies: & so by consequent reading a booke is ceremoniall."[70] Books are a form of representation; therefore, they are "in the nature of" images and ceremonies. And books "are not to be given as helps before the eye in worship" because "reading wordes out of a book is the ministration of the letter . . . namely a part of the ministerie of the old Testament which is abolished." In Smyth's reading of the New Testament, Christ has shown decisively that "the ceremony of bookworship, or the ministerie of the lettere was now expired, and finished."[71] Smyth's rant against a Jewish "ministerie of the lettere" is standard-issue Christian anti-Semitism whereby the Christian differentiates himself from his Judaic inheritance by insisting that Jews were idolaters unable to move past forms and ceremonies, the law and the letter, to a proper religion of transcendence. Writing and the book, the law and the letter, all comprised in Smyth's "ceremony of bookworship," are the legacy of the Jew, whereas the Christian lives under the new dispensation of the spirit. Again, the debate circles around the dialectic of letter and spirit. True worship, "spiritual worship," cannot rely on reading, on the book; to do so is to abandon the spiritual word and embrace the Judaic letter.

In his response to Smyth, Ainsworth accuses the separatist of betraying the reformed cause by abandoning Reformation epistemology: "If M. Sm[yth] can prove *books & images* to be both of a nature, & both alike ceremonies: he may be a Proctour for the Pope, who hath brought *images* into the church, for *laie mens books*. And if the book be to him that readeth, of the nature that an image is to him that gazeth: who would not plead for them both alike, to be used or rejected?"[72] If books are things in the world *in the same way* that images are, if reading is simply a form of gazing, then how are Protestants different from Catholics? To accept that books are in some sense images, that written language is somehow part of a world of forms, of ritual and ceremony, is to embrace a Catholic epistemology and thereby give the game away to the Pope. Ainsworth refuses to accept this premise: "An image when it is looked vpon, affoardeth a man no edification (no not if it were an image sent from heaven, unlesse it had a *voice* withall) but a book when it is read, informeth the mind, and feedeth not the eye onely, as dooth a picture. An image & picture . . . speaks not; no spirit or breath of life is in them: but the book of God, is . . . inspired by *God*, his spirit & life is in it; it is not a dumb teacher."[73] Insisting that the difference between text and image lies in their relative ability to *speak* and thereby edify, Ainsworth metaphorically aligns books with the oral and aural rather than the visual. To speak, as a text does, is to edify, to offer itself up for interpretation, to "inform the mind." To be dumb, as images are, is to fail to enlighten, to resist or thwart interpretation, to merely "feed the eye." But Ainsworth's critique does not stop here; he accuses Smyth of throwing the scriptural baby out with the ritual bathwater. He asks what Smyth has "left unto vs" that is "not ceremoniall" and not therefore to be abolished; the answer it seems is "*the thing signified . . . by the book.*"[74] But Ainsworth asks, "where is this to be had? not in letters written with ynk, on paper, or parchment, for all these he sayth are ceremoniall and so abolished; but written in mens harts as in books, with the spirit as with inck. . . . If Satan can but perswade this point, he will bring out of mens harts, as out of the bottomlesse pit, a smoke of heresies."[75] Without the anchor of the letter, the material text of scripture, who is to stop the reader who would drift into confusion and heresy, who is to stop the preacher from substituting his own ideas, his own desires for God's? If Smyth accuses Ainsworth of replacing the true word with a mere thing, Ainsworth accuses Smyth of replacing the true word with the easily corrupted will of the reader.

This debate between conformists and nonconformists about preaching versus reading is just one of many such scenes from the early modern crisis of the book. I rehearse this particular debate not because the Admonition Controversy or, for that matter, the larger struggle between nonconformists and the Church of England, plays a huge part in the book that follows. They do not. Rather, I want to suggest that this debate is simply part of a larger conversation about representation and materiality, text and meaning. And I want to suggest that this larger conversation necessarily shapes conceptions of reading and the book. Here, the controversy arises because the different camps agree in principle that the word of God alone can bring one to salvation, but they cannot agree on where to *find* the word of God. As Ainsworth asks, "where is this to be had?" In "letters written with ynk, on paper, or parchment"? Written in "mens harts as in books"? Of course, this question—certainly one of the defining questions of the age—is not one that can be answered. And like many impossible questions it proves tremendously generative. In the second chapter of *The Incarnate Text*, "Rewriting the Letter," I address the inevitable complications that ensue when an iconoclastic religion accords iconic status to a material object, in this case the book. I do so through a reading of Book 1 of Edmund Spenser's *The Faerie Queene*, "The Legend of Holiness." A Reformation poet whose literary career can be read as an extended meditation on the problems and possibilities of language as artifact, Spenser attempts in various ways in *The Faerie Queene* to think through the problem of the materiality of language. Through a reading of "The Legend of Holiness," I examine the ways in which Spenser addresses both the veneration of sacred texts in Reformation England and the attendant anxieties concerning bibliolatry. Even as Spenser attacks the iconophilia of Catholic devotional practices, he grapples with the implications of the Reformation desire to treat the Bible specifically and the book generally as a sacred icon. More broadly, in his "Legend of Holiness," Spenser explores the paradoxes and contradictions generated by early modern Protestantism's desire to wrestle with the problem of the signifier, the problem of the materiality of language.

In post-Reformation England, the control of interpretation was crucial because reading was inherently dangerous. Reading was both the narrow road to salvation and the broad path to damnation. In Chapter 3, "The Reading of the Damned," I examine the dangers of reading through an analysis of Marlowe's staging of the book in *Doctor Faustus*. Books were frequently deployed as stage props in English Renaissance drama. Attending to the ways in which the book was staged helps us understand some of the ways in which the book was imagined in the period. In my reading of *Doctor Faustus*, the play dramatizes an intense ambivalence toward the book, drawing on the culture's fear of the book's capacity to generate error and to produce faction and apostasy. In Reformation thought, the experience of scripture was understood to be properly transformative; the individual encountering scripture, read or preached, must give him- or herself over to the word. And a transformative experience of scripture is at the heart of the multitude of conversion narratives in the period. These conversion narratives took a variety of forms, but one of the most widespread and influential versions of the narrative was what I am calling the readerly or textual conversion, a transformation resulting from the reading of scripture. In the debate discussed above, Whitgift, as representative of the orthodox in the Church of England, objects to the idea that reading the bare text of scripture lacks efficacy by noting that many Protestants were converted to "true religion" through acts of reading: "And, if you had been disposed to have called to remembrance that which you say you have so diligently read in M. Fox, you might have known that divers in the beginning came to the light of the gospel only by reading and hearing the new testament in English read."[76] Here, Whitgift points to the many conversion narratives recorded in Foxe's *Actes and Monuments* in which the bare text of scripture, read or heard, is the converting agent. And to examine conversion narratives in the period is to see what Whitgift means: in the period, textual conversion was epidemic. Of course, as the nonconformists might have responded, not all conversions are created equal. Christians of different confessional camps necessarily believed that many textual conversions were conversions to apostasy; in such transformations the convert turned away from truth and toward idolatry. The audience sees such a textual conversion in *Doctor Faustus*. By staging this conversion scene, Marlowe entertains his audience with the spectacle of a dangerous transformation through reading. In doing so, Marlowe foregrounds the inevitable aesthetic and affective dimensions of the life-altering reading experience. Wary of the aesthetic and material dimension of representation, Protestants nevertheless celebrated visceral responses to scripture. When English Reformers narrated their momentous experiences of scripture, they often described an affective response in explicitly sensory and somatic terms. In describing his conversion experience, Thomas Bilney speaks of beginning to "tast and sauour" scripture, which became "more pleasaunt vnto me than the hony or the hony combe."[77] In a sermon preached in 1552, Hugh Latimer credits Bilney as "the instrument whereby God called me to knowledge"; describing the aftermath of this conversion, Latimer contends that "from that time onward I began to smell the word of God."[78] Indeed, Reformers seemed to be especially fond of the conceit that one could smell or taste the gospel. As Peter Marshall observes, leading early Protestants like Bilney, Latimer, Tyndale, Cranmer, and Coverdale describe "vividly . . . the experience of 'tasting' God's holy word," and this "habitual substitution of 'tasting' for reading/ comprehending/ believing persisted" into succeeding generations of the English Reformation.[79] Reformers were fond of the conceit that one could smell or taste the gospel not because they wanted to locate authenticity in the body, but because they wanted to illustrate that their response somehow bypassed the intellect or will. This kind of affective response to scripture authenticates one's reading as the work of the spirit. Paradoxically, the movement of the spirit is depicted as visceral, the proper response to scripture framed as somatic. In *Doctor Faustus*, Marlowe thrills his audience with the spectacle of a man succumbing to the temptation of the book, dramatizing the dangers of an affective response to text, the dangers of transformation through reading.

Reading as Shibboleth

Narratives of textual conversion in the Reformation dramatize not only a transformation sparked by reading but also a transformation in how one reads. This transformation is almost always accompanied by a turn toward "truth" or "enlightenment" that is simultaneously a turning away from ignorance and idolatry, an idolatry frequently figured as a misunderstanding of the proper relation to the phenomenal world. In his conversion narrative, Latimer begins "to smell the word of God" when he is converted to "knowledge," a word he consistently uses to convey his enlightenment. For Latimer, a conversion to "knowledge" is a conversion to a properly reformed understanding that involves the forsaking of superstition, a forsaking of rites and rituals that bind one to the world and the flesh. In fact, Latimer's conversion narrative leads directly to a story in which he saves "an ignorant and simple woman" from superstition, from her credulous beliefs in the rites and rituals given "unto the Jews."[80] Throughout *The Incarnate Text*, I return to the idea that reading text and reading world were intimately related in Christian thought. To escape superstition and idolatry, to escape a misunderstanding of the proper relation to the phenomenal world, one must learn to read that world correctly, to read it not simply in accordance with scripture but to read it as scripture teaches one to read. In other words, the proper negotiation of the world of the flesh, the world of material things was intimately related to the proper negotiation of the letter. And both these kinds of reading were community defining, were essential to Christian notions of identity. Christianity consistently defined and redefined itself by invoking internal and external threats to the proper reading of scripture and world. We see this not only in Christianity's relation to other religions but also in the long and complex history of Christian heresy. On a smaller scale, we see it in the seemingly perpetual admonitions of Christian authorities against those who would pervert proper religion with their ignorant and superstitious ways.

The Reformation was, of course, a rather significant wrinkle in the long history of Christianity's often contentious struggle to understand book and world properly. Although this history was primarily a European one, it necessarily shaped, and was shaped by, Christian encounters with the wider world. And the Reformation coincided with an expansion of the globe that would have a significant impact on Christians' sense of the place and function of their hermeneutic community in that world. With the discovery of the Americas and the increase in global exploration and trade, exploitation and conquest, Europeans came into contact with a wide variety of cultures that needed to be accounted for in a Christian cosmology. Early modern ethnographers noted with interest whether cultures were lettered or unlettered, and what kinds of misapprehension governed a given society's relation to the world of objects and things. In these accounts, books and letters emerged both as crucial features of the technological superiority of the Europeans and as keys to spiritual liberty, to freedom from superstition.

* * *

From its inception, Christianity was not merely a religion of the book but a faith that needed to position itself against an older and more established religion of the book. Incorporating sacred texts of Judaism, Christianity differentiated itself from the more venerable religion through its different understanding of what these sacred texts meant. Central to this differentiation was an hermeneutic that worked as a shibboleth, as a marker of community. Following the relation of Christianity to its Judaic inheritance established in the New Testament generally and the Pauline epistles specifically, Christians believed the fundamental difference between Christian and Jew was reflected in their respective understanding of the relationship of the letter to the spirit; in other words, the fundamental difference was a function of their reading strategies. In *Living Letters of the Law*, Jeremy Cohen illustrates how crucial the figure of the Jew—as an embodiment of the wrong kinds of reading, as an embodiment of letter rather than spirit—was to Christian identity. Cohen documents the emergence of a useful construct for Christian self-definition: the "hermeneutical Jew." Augustine was the crucial figure in the development of an "hermeneutical Jew" who survived as a living witness to the truth of Christianity, one who was consigned to the pre-Christian historical era even as he survived as a living letter of the law. Here, Cohen offers a summary of Augustine's influential contention that the figure of the Jew is a "living letter": "Augustine explained, repeatedly and pointedly: The Jews preserve the literal sense, they represent it, and they actually embody it—as book bearers, librarians, living signposts, and desks, who validate a Christological interpretation of the Old Testament. Unlike the 'true bride of Christ,' the Jew knows not the difference between letter and spirit."[81] The Jew as the embodiment of the letter—a letter that must be preserved even as it is negated—was essential to the Christian understanding of the proper relation of letter and spirit, the proper method of reading scripture. And Jewish misreading extended beyond a misreading of the letter of scripture to a misreading of the flesh and the world.

* * *

Traditionally, Christianity has equated the material "letter" with both the sins of the flesh and the barren legalism and deadly literalism of the Old Testament, while it has equated the "spirit" with both the transcendence of the flesh and the transcendence of the law through Christ's New Testament of grace. However outside the mainstream his thought might be in general, John Smyth's notion of "bookish ceremony" captures perfectly the Christian sense that Judaic literalism is of a piece with Judaic idolatry: an idolatrous religion that confuses rites and rituals with true understanding is an extension of a literalism that makes an idol of text. Because the Jews fail to transcend the letter, they fail to transcend the flesh. The Pauline understanding of circumcision helped establish the relation of the flesh to the letter in Christian thought. In his epistles, Paul offered circumcision as one of the fundamental differences between Christian and Jew not because circumcision was a physical marker that separated the Jew from the Gentile, but precisely because indifference to such a mark established the new hermeneutic regime of the Christian religion. Rejecting a circumcision of the flesh was part of Paul's programmatic rejection of an alleged Jewish particularism in favor of a new Christian universalism; Christianity would not be a religion of the family or the tribe but a religion that transcended traditional borders of race and nation.[82] The classic formulation of this universalism is from the Epistle to the Galatians: "There is neither Iewe, nor Greeke, there is neither bond nor free, there is neither male nor female: for ye are all one in Christ Iesus."[83] Both conversion and reading—or, more accurately, conversion to a form of reading—were crucial to this desire to be a religion of Gentiles and Jews, a religion with global reach. Christian universalism was made possible because Christian conversion was figured as a conversion not of the flesh but of the spirit. And for Christians to understand the proper relation of flesh to spirit was to learn to read properly. It was not simply the repudiation of the materialist rites of Judaism and the acceptance of a spiritual understanding of religion; it was an hermeneutic that allowed one to transcend rites like circumcision while preserving the sacred texts that demand them. Circumcision was preserved as figure as it was rejected as letter; as Paul writes, "Circumcision is that of the heart, in the spirit, and not in the letter."[84] And it is this double move that established Christianity not only as a religion of the book but also as an hermeneutic community that embraced a certain reading of book and world.

Judaism was crucial to the formation of Christianity as a religion of the book that possessed a curious ambivalence toward the letter. And throughout Christian history, those who seemed to have an improper relation to the "letter"—a figure that comprises, among other things, both the literal sense and the material artifact of language—were denounced as "Judaizers," those who misunderstand the proper transcendence of the letter by the spirit. At the same time, however, Judaism represented for Christians only one of many possible paths to damnation. In Christian thought there were an infinite number of ways to misread the word and mistake the will of God, as there were an infinite number of ways to misread the world and commit idolatry. Other religions, of course, erred by definition. With the discovery of the New World and the expansion of the globe through conquest and trade, Christian nations found both more worlds to convert and conquer and further proof that Europe was both the source of global enlightenment and the center of God's work in the world. Even as Christian nations proselytized and attempted to convert, the hermeneutic community of Christians reestablished itself over and against the benighted cultures it found. In the early modern period, of course, the Christian community was not unified but splintered, and in the idolatrous rites and beliefs of non-Europeans, the different confessional camps found evidence both of the superiority of the Christian religion and of the benighted practices of their Christian adversaries.

In Chapter 4, "Book, Trinket, Fetish," I consider the significance of Reformation conceptions of reading and idolatry to European notions of barbarism. By investigating the new vocabulary that informed the Reformation's radical revision of the proper relation to the material world, this chapter examines the ways in which Reformation iconoclasm shaped European perceptions of the Christian self and the barbaric other. For seventeenth-century Protestant merchants traveling in the New World and Africa, to reveal a belief in the power of the material object was to engage in a fundamental category mistake that separated superstitious and credulous non-Christians from the rational European. And as William Pietz has observed, it was precisely when the Protestant Dutch supplanted the Catholic Portuguese as the primary trading power in West Africa that the modern discourse of the fetish emerged. An underlying premise of *The Incarnate Text* is that one can trace a history of the object by tracing a history of the object disavowed. In traditional Christianity the disavowed object par excellence was the idol, but by the end of the period in question, the fetish emerged as the paradigmatic misunderstanding of the material world in the European imaginary.[85] The early modern idol differs from the Enlightenment fetish in that the iconoclast imputes to the image or object in question extraordinary power; the idol is a threat to self as well as others. The fetish, in contrast, is always already demystified. Like the iconoclast, the modern observer of fetishism sees error and ignorance. He does not, however, see a threat; on the contrary, he sees a reminder of his own proper, enlightened perspective on the world. The fetish does not threaten him with the possibility of idolatry but comforts him with the knowledge that he is civilized. In this chapter I contend that the European discourse concerning "fetishism," a concept that developed in the cross-cultural space of Western Africa in the early seventeenth century, was articulated within the framework of a Reformation understanding of idolatry and materiality. By employing and critiquing Pietz's genealogy of the fetish, I argue that the early modern understanding of the fetish arose from the crisis I explore throughout *The Incarnate Text*. I then turn to William Shakespeare's *The Tempest*, which I read as an exploration of the function of Eurocentric notions of value and materiality in the power dynamic between European and non-European. I read *The Tempest* as a meditation on the place of the book in defining "civilized" and "savage" in early modern Europe. In the early modern imagination, the book is not only an icon of Reformation iconoclasm but also a privileged object in the emerging discourse of fetishism. Again and again in narratives of encounters between Europeans and non-Europeans, the savage is understood to be savage precisely because he or she cannot understand how to read the book as anything but a fetish. The canary in the Enlightenment coal mine, the book becomes a test case for the misapprehension of the material world.

One way to read the historical trajectory from idol to fetish is to read it through the lens of Weber's notion of the "disenchantment of the world." In "Science as a Vocation," Weber contends that the development of modern science and the concomitant and ongoing "process of intellectualization" have led to the "disenchantment of the world."[86] For Weber, the "increasing intellectualization and rationalization" of the West does not mean that the modern Western subject boasts a greater understanding of the conditions that shape his or her existence.[87] Rather, it means that the modern subject enjoys

> the knowledge or belief that if one but wished one *could* learn . . .
> [the "knowledge of the condition under which one lives"] at any
> time. Hence, it means that principally there are no mysterious incal-
> culable forces that come into play, but rather that one can, in princi-
> ple, master all things by calculation. This means that the world is
> disenchanted. One need no longer have recourse to magical means
> in order to master or implore the spirits, as did the savage, for whom
> such mysterious powers existed.[88]

Here, the divide between modernity and its premodern other is mapped onto different epistemologies, which are, at the same time, different faiths. Modern mastery (real or imagined) of "all things" is a function of a certain "knowledge or belief" in the intelligibility of the world in which one lives. Taken up by a wide range of writers, Weber's thesis has become one of the most influential of the many narratives describing the birth of modernity. Like most theories of modernity, Weber's "disenchantment of the world" is a narrative of a fall, a fall into technology, alienation, instrumental reason. As a narrative of a fall, it must, like all such narratives, posit a premodern world that is in some sense pre-fallen, and therefore outside history. One of the reasons that Weber's thesis is so influential is that it is a repetition in a different key of the fundamental narrative of modernity, a narrative invented by the early modern period itself.[89] And like all theories of modernity, Weber's thesis works better as a definition of the modern—or as a symptom of modernity's desire for definition—than it does as a description of the allegedly premodern. The notion of an enchanted world before modernity makes sense only from the perspective of the modern, "disenchanted" world; such an epoch is called into being by the very act of historicizing that would describe it.[90] And as is so often the case in such narratives, the Weberian divide between modernity and its premodern other is easily mapped onto the divide between civilized and savage. In the enlightened modern world, the enchanted world is conjured both as a relic of a misbegotten past and as the domain of the savage.

One reason a return to Weber's melancholy analysis of modernity is salutary is that he troubles this historical distinction between enchanted and disenchanted from the beginning. For Weber, the enchanted world persists as the shadow of enlightenment, not simply in uncivilized realms but on the periphery of the public sphere of modern society. Moreover, disenchantment has, it seems, almost always been with Western culture; the "process of disenchantment," he writes "has continued to exist in Occidental culture for millennia."[91] In *The Incarnate Text*, I contend that if the disavowal of the enchanted world we see in the discourse of fetishism is a recognizable aspect of modernity, this disavowal has nonetheless always been central to Christian thought. It is my contention that the modern epistemology that gave rise to the fetish was, in part, born of a particular historical manifestation of contradictions at the heart of Christian thought. As I suggested earlier, one can imagine the story I am telling as the "disenchantment of the book." The problem, of course, is that in the Judeo-Christian tradition there never was an enchanted book, or an enchanted world. Or, to be more precise, there never was a world or book not caught up in a dialectic of enchantment and disenchantment. Looking at the contemporary world, the anthropologist Michael Taussig suggests that "what exists now is perhaps best thought of as a new amalgam of enchantment and disenchantment."[92] In the modern world, Taussig finds enchantment in negation, defacement; today, he suggests, it is in desecration that the sacred emerges. When art is defaced, money destroyed, cultural or political icons vandalized, the category of the sacred object resurfaces. We see something similar and, at the same time, quite different in early modern acts of iconoclasm. On the one hand, the idol is called into being as idol by the conviction of the iconophobe or iconoclast; the idol is most powerfully an idol in the act of violence destroying it. On the other hand, the idol so conjured was not simply ritually destroyed but often aggressively demystified. In the stories that Reformers loved to repeat about their iconoclastic labors, they did not relish the toppling of the statue so much as the unmasking of the fraud. And these two impulses—to destroy an icon because it is dangerous, to belittle it because it is a sham—were often two aspects of a single act of iconoclastic destruction. The Reformation, I contend, was a particularly consequential moment in an ongoing dialectic of enchantment and disenchantment. It is one of the objectives of *The Incarnate Text* to trace some of the complexity of that dialectic before it emerged in its recognizable, modern form. At the end of the history I describe, many of the questions that I address in *The Incarnate Text*, questions concerning materiality and representation, were no longer urgent, no longer matters of life and death. As we move beyond the Reformation, as we move from idol to fetish, the threat of the fallen world of objects seems to dissipate. In this new era, the book is still a symbol of truth and enlightenment, but now its materiality seems to have disappeared into its function as a vehicle of text. If this can be described as a disenchantment of the book, it is a disenchantment that was always already an aspect of the Christian understanding of the book. If this is a demystification of the book, it cannot be understood without reference to the Reformation crisis of the book.

In the epilogue to *The Incarnate Text*, I briefly address the "enchantment" and "disenchantment" of the book through an analysis of the place of the sacred book in Francis Bacon's *New Atlantis*. Bacon is often considered an early modern prophet of modernity. His program for natural philosophy helped usher in modern science; his rationalist conceptions of language and the phenomenal world anticipated modern epistemology. In this epilogue I take seriously Bacon's own contention that his rationalist methods were the fruit of the Reformation's desire to eradicate superstition and ignorance. Bacon's battle against the idols of the mind was, in complex ways, an extension of the Reformation's struggle against idolatry. At the same time, I read his *New Atlantis* as a valediction to a religion of the book. *New Atlantis* describes a utopian community founded on Baconian principles, a utopian community that simultaneously espouses Christianity and brackets religion as a once and future concern. And the relation of the society of Bensalem to Christian revelation is established through a providential encounter with a miraculous book. In my reading of *New Atlantis*, Bacon employs this impossible book as a prophylactic against the influence of religion in his scientific utopia; he negates the impact of religion by fulfilling and preserving it. The book becomes an emblem of a religion that preserves revelation and awaits apocalypse. The place of the sacred book in *New Atlantis* becomes synonymous with the place of the unconverted Jew, Joabin; they are living letters that establish the relation to a past that is relevant precisely because it has been superseded. In the epilogue I suggest that Bacon evokes the disenchantment of the book through an impossibly enchanted book. In the new amalgam of enchantment and disenchantment that we see in Bacon's utopia, the sacred book is consigned to the miraculous past, the incarnate text deferred until the second coming.

CHAPTER ONE

"Relics of the Mind"

Erasmian Humanism and Textual Presence

From Caravaggio's *Matthew* to Erasmus's *Jerome*

IN THE EARLY YEARS of the seventeenth century, Caravaggio (Michelangelo Merisi, 1571–1610) was commissioned to paint three canvases for the Contarelli Chapel in the Church of San Luigi dei Francesi in Rome. The paintings were to depict crucial scenes from the life of Saint Matthew. Two of the canvases were narrative scenes intended for the walls adjacent to the altar: *The Calling of St. Matthew* on the left, and *The Martyrdom of St. Matthew* on the right. For the altarpiece, Caravaggio painted Matthew in the act of writing his gospel. His first rendition of this subject, *The Inspiration of St. Matthew* (Figure 2), was rejected.[1] According to Caravaggio's early biographer, Giovanni Pietro Bellori, the canons of San Luigi rejected the first *Inspiration* because they balked at the unconventional portrayal of the evangelist: "After he had finished the central picture of St. Matthew and installed it on the altar, the priests took it down, saying that the figure with its legs crossed and its feet rudely exposed to the public had neither decorum nor the appearance of a saint."[2] Following Bellori, most scholars have read the rejection of the painting as a reaction to the uncouth appearance of the evangelist.[3] With his bare feet and thick, stocky frame, Caravaggio's Matthew has the humble form of a peasant or common artisan. The pronounced physicality that the canons allegedly opposed in Caravaggio's Matthew is matched in the painting by the depiction of the act of writing. The androgynous angel who "inspires" the

Figure 2. Caravaggio, the first *Inspiration of Saint Matthew* (1602). Gemaeldegalerie, Staatliche Museen zu Berlin, Berlin, Germany. Bildarchiv Preussischer Kulturbesitz / Art Resource, NY.

writing of the text is not placed above and behind the evangelist in the classic position of the muse but is portrayed leaning into the evangelist in an intimate act of instruction. Caravaggio's angel reaches across the book to guide Matthew's hand, physically manipulating the gospel writer's awkward scrawl across the page. In Caravaggio's first version of *The Inspiration of Saint Mat-*

thew, it appears as if an otherworldly spirit is none-too-gently teaching an illiterate laborer how to write. After the first rendition of the subject was rejected, Caravaggio painted a second version of *The Inspiration* that the canons of San Luigi evidently found acceptable (Figure 3). This second painting still hangs in the Contarelli Chapel in Rome. The first *Inspiration* found its way to Berlin, where it was destroyed by fire in 1945.

Caravaggio's first *Inspiration* seems to draw on certain traditions surrounding the writing of St. Matthew's gospel. The Gospel of Matthew had a privileged place in the Christian canon: it was believed to be the earliest of the gospels and, therefore, was considered the first Christian text. A long-standing Christian tradition held both that Matthew wrote the gospel in his own hand and that he wrote it in Hebrew.[4] Jerome was the most authoritative source for the church's beliefs regarding the Gospel of Matthew, and in the preface to his *Commentary on Matthew* he writes, "The first evangelist is Matthew, the publican, who was surnamed Levi. He published his Gospel in Judea in the Hebrew language, chiefly for the sake of Jewish believers in Christ, who adhered in vain to the shadow of the law, although the substance of the gospel had come."[5] Matthew thus faces in two directions. He writes the first Christian text, but he does so in the language of the old dispensation for those attempting to escape "the shadow of the law." Famously opening with a genealogy of Christ that traces him back to David and Abraham, Matthew's gospel marks a transition, connecting Old to New, promise to fulfillment. In his first *Inspiration* Caravaggio shows the evangelist writing, with the vigorous encouragement of the angel, the first lines of the gospel that begin this genealogy. Viewed in a certain light, there is nothing particularly strange about Caravaggio's decision to portray the evangelist writing in Hebrew: the painting simply illustrates a traditional understanding of the writing of Matthew's gospel. Even as the painting follows the *textual* tradition authorized by Jerome, however, Caravaggio's depiction of a Hebrew gospel introduces a new element into a long *iconographic* tradition.[6] And I would suggest that this particular innovation in the iconography of the gospel writer addresses issues at the center of Reformation and Counter-Reformation debates. More specifically, I contend that Caravaggio's *Inspiration of Matthew* gestures toward an ongoing crisis concerning the authority of the Bible and the relation of scripture to history.

The issue of the legitimacy of various scriptural traditions, and the accuracy of Jerome's translation in particular, occasioned bitter polemic and horrific violence in the sixteenth and seventeenth centuries as various

Figure 3. Caravaggio, the second *Inspiration of Saint Matthew* (1602). S. Luigi dei Francesi, Rome, Italy. Erich Lessing / Art Resource, NY.

confessional camps clashed over the sacred writings of Christianity. This was not simply a battle over interpretation but a struggle over the *text* of scripture. Applying humanist innovations in the analysis of texts to the Christian archive, scholars like Lorenzo Valla and Desiderius Erasmus questioned the accuracy and validity of the Vulgate, a translation that had served as the textual cornerstone of the Catholic Church for a millennium. In doing so, they opened the philological floodgates: theology was soon engulfed by technical questions concerning everything from the nuances of Hebrew grammar to the provenance of manuscripts. Given this context, it is striking that Caravaggio was commissioned to have the Matthew altarpiece ready by Pentecost, the feast celebrating the descent of the Holy Spirit to the disciples of Christ.[7] The gift of tongues that marked the descent was read as a reversal of that second fall, the fall into languages occasioned by the Tower of Babel. Overcoming that fall and speaking to all people in all languages was understood to be an indication of Christianity's universalizing mission. In the sixteenth and seventeenth centuries, as humanist scholars returned *ad fontes* in an effort to recover a more perfect text, and as the Bible was translated into all the languages of Europe, it seemed to some as if Christendom was finally overcoming that second fall, finally fulfilling the promise of Pentecost. And as a cacophonous horde of variants and editions and translations descended on Europe, it seemed to others as if Babel had returned. I would like to suggest that Caravaggio's two depictions of *The Inspiration of Matthew* represent a response to a crisis of scriptural authority, a crisis of language and representation, a crisis that we tend to call the Reformation.

In the early sixteenth century, roughly eighty years before Caravaggio painted his 1602 *Inspiration*, humanist scholars challenged the long-standing tradition that the gospel of Matthew had been written in Hebrew. Conjecturing that Matthew had in all likelihood written in the same language as the other evangelists, scholars like Desiderius Erasmus cast centuries of Catholic tradition, and the testimony of Jerome himself, into doubt. Reformers seized on this allegedly erroneous tradition as a means of calling into question the customs and teachings of the Catholic Church. In the middle of this controversy, two Hebrew texts of Matthew's gospel were discovered and printed. In 1537 a Protestant Hebraist named Sebastian Muenster published an edition of the Gospel of Matthew in Hebrew based on an incomplete manuscript that Muenster maintained he had discovered in a Jewish community.[8] Jean Du Tillet, the Catholic Bishop of Brieu, claimed to have found a Hebrew manuscript of the Gospel of Matthew while traveling in Italy in 1553. Du

Tillet brought the manuscript back to Paris, commissioned the Hebrew scholar Jean Mercier to translate it into Latin, and published an edition of the text alongside Mercier's translation in Paris in 1555.[9] The Hebrew Matthew of the Protestant Muenster and the Hebrew Matthew of the Catholic Du Tillet are widely divergent texts. One might expect the Hebrew text depicted in Caravaggio's *Inspiration* to be drawn from one or the other. What is curious about Caravaggio's painting is that, as Irving Lavin has shown, it conforms to neither of these texts but is a perfect translation of the Latin of Jerome's Vulgate.[10] Either choosing to ignore or ignorant of this recently unearthed evidence, Caravaggio synchronizes the Hebrew text in his painting with the embattled Vulgate.

At a session held in April 1546, the Council of Trent had established the Vulgate as the official version of scripture for the Catholic Church:

> The same holy synod considering that no small advantage may ac-crue to the Church of God, if out of all the Latin translations of the sacred books in circulation it made known which is to be held as authoritative [*authentica*]: determines and declares that this ancient vulgate translation which is recommended by the long use of so many centuries in the church, be regarded as authoritative in public lectures, disputations, sermons, and expository discourses, and that no one may make bold or presume to reject it on any pretext.[11]

The Council of Trent's declaration is famously guarded. The Council does not suggest either that Jerome's translation is correct with respect to the original documents or that it is divinely inspired. In fact, Jerome himself is never mentioned. The underlying logic is that the Vulgate is authoritative precisely because it is the edition that was used by the universal church for the past thousand years. Since the divine hand guided the church and its traditions, the Vulgate must be a gift of the Holy Spirit and free of doctrinal error. The key word in the Council's declaration is *authentica*, which was understood to mean that the translation was more authoritative and authentic than any other text, including, it would seem, the original Greek and Hebrew manuscripts on which it was based. As the work of the Holy Spirit, Jerome's translation serves as the basis of all future translation and interpretation, and so replaces the originals in all respects.[12] Protestants were not slow to pick up on what they believed were the disturbing implications of the Council's declaration. Calvin was apoplectic. In his *Acta Synodi Tridentini cum Antidoto*

(Acts of the Council of Trent with the Antidote), he contends that the aim of the Council is to "make all revere a Scripture hidden in darkness like the mysteries of Ceres, and let none presume to aspire to the understanding of it."[13] Indeed, "they not only order us to be contented with a most defective translation," they also "insist on our worshipping it, just as if it had come down from heaven; and while the blemishes are conspicuous to all, they prohibit us from desiring any improvement. Behold the men on whose judgment the renovation of the Church depends!"[14] Calvin aligns what he considers a willful ignorance with paganism ("the mysteries of Ceres") and suggests that the Catholic Church wants its credulous flock to commit idolatry, to "revere" and "worship" this reified text "just as if it had come down from heaven." Here, Calvin's desire for a proper understanding of the historicity of language and the transmission of texts complements his critique of the idolatrous veneration of mere things. In this context, his humanist skepticism dovetails perfectly with his Protestant iconoclasm.

The Council of Trent had ruled that Jerome's translation was authentic and authoritative, but it also commissioned a revised, critical edition of the Vulgate, an edition that further clarified the status of the translation. When the Sistine and Clementine editions of the Vulgate were published (1589, 1592), they contained papal prefaces that, although worded carefully, came very close to suggesting that Jerome was divinely inspired to translate scripture.[15] Catholic artists seem to have taken up the claim that Jerome was divinely inspired. As Eugene Rice has shown, at the end of the sixteenth century there is a sudden glut of paintings in which Jerome's inspiration is embodied by a beautiful angel.[16] Rice suggests that this artistic development is a decidedly post-Trent phenomenon:

> Painters . . . instructed by ecclesiastical advisers anxious to reassure
> an audience more heterogeneous than learned and baffled in any
> case by the difficulty of representing pictorially so abstract a distinc-
> tion as that between the verbal and substantive inspiration of a text,
> supported without reservation or qualification the claim that God
> had guided the hand and pen of the translator of the Bible by show-
> ing Jerome taking dictation of the Vulgate from the Holy Spirit in
> the shape of an angel. . . . [Guido Reni,] Lodovico Carracci, Do-
> menichino, Albani, Rubens, van Dyck, Simon Vouet, and Johann
> Liss are some of the painters . . . who honored Jerome and the
> Vulgate in this way.[17]

Responding to the crisis of authority afflicting both the Vulgate and Jerome, these artists circle the proverbial wagons by transferring the iconography of inspiration from the writing of the gospel to its translation. And these representations of the inspiration of Jerome take their cue from the iconographic tradition surrounding the evangelists in general and Matthew in particular. The connection between Jerome and Matthew was a strong one as the two were often paired when the four doctors of the church were aligned with the four evangelists. And as Rice observes, "Representations of the inspiration of St. Matthew, of which Caravaggio's . . . Guercino's . . . and Rembrandt's . . . are late but celebrated examples, are the direct prototypes of the seventeenth-century inspirations of St. Jerome."[18] Rice reads the relationship in one direction, but there is no reason to assume that late versions of the inspiration of Matthew like Caravaggio's are not also influenced by recent developments in the iconography of Jerome. In this context, Caravaggio's two versions of *The Inspiration of Matthew* look like both the traditional depictions of Matthew writing the gospel and post-Trent paintings of Jerome translating the gospel. And, of course, in Caravaggio's first *Inspiration* the Vulgate is present—informing the Hebrew wording of a manuscript that does not exist—even if Jerome is not.

* * *

The origins of the scriptural crisis that, I suggest, informs Caravaggio's lost painting can be traced back to the publication of Erasmus's *Novum Instrumentum* in the early sixteenth century. The year 1516 was an *annus mirabilis* for Erasmus. Both his epoch-shattering edition and translation of the Greek New Testament (*Novum Instrumentum*) and his monumental, nine-volume edition of Jerome's works rolled off the presses of Johann Froben in Basel.[19] His edition of Jerome was hailed as a marvel of modern scholarship.[20] And *Novum Instrumentum*, the first translation of the New Testament to mount a successful challenge to Jerome's Vulgate, set Christendom on its ear. It was in *Novum Instrumentum* that Erasmus called into question the tradition that Matthew's gospel had been written in Hebrew.[21] But this was only one of the many ways that Erasmus's New Testament contested the traditions of the church. Although Erasmus himself would never break with Rome, it has been argued that the publication of the *Novum Instrumentum* was as crucial to the course of the Reformation as Martin Luther's nailing of his *Ninety-Five Theses Against Indulgences* on a church door in Wittenburg.[22]

The fact that Erasmus's two groundbreaking publications, his Jerome and his New Testament, arrived in the world in the same year is no mere coincidence. One could argue that Erasmus's edition of Jerome paved the way for his controversial translation of the New Testament.[23] In the *Life of Saint Jerome* (*Hieronymi Stridonensis vita*), published in the first volume of his edition of Jerome's works, Erasmus depicts the scholar rather than the saint, the man rather than the legend. He dispenses with the miraculous fictions that had sprouted up around the narrative of the translator's life and sticks to the works, the writings.[24] For Erasmus, "Nothing is better than to portray the saints just as they actually were, and if even a fault is discovered in their lives this very imperfection turns into an example of piety for us." In writing his *Life of Saint Jerome*, Erasmus insists, "I invented nothing, because to me the greatest miracle is the miracle of Jerome as he expresses himself to us in his many works of lasting and preeminent quality. And if extravagant tales of wondrous happenings are necessary for the reader's pleasure, let him take up Jerome's books, in which there are almost as many miracles as there are opinions."[25] Rescued from wonders and prodigies, Jerome emerges as an intrepid scholar whose miraculous work is the product of intense labor. As a variety of scholars have observed, the portrait of Jerome that Erasmus paints looks much like a self-portrait.[26] Erasmus's Jerome is, first and foremost, a scholar in his study, laboring to bring the word of God to his fellow Christians. Crucially, in his *Life of Jerome* Erasmus both celebrates the church father as a scholar and reduces the saint to a man. His Jerome is human and fallible, subject to doubt and error. For Erasmus, Jerome was "certainly a learned and pious man, but a man nevertheless."[27] This portrayal of the saint as an Erasmian scholar, of course, paves the way for a critique of Jerome's Vulgate. In his translation of the New Testament, Erasmus established the importance of such an endeavor by addressing directly the infelicities of the Vulgate, by showing that the venerable translation and its textual transmission were the work of fallible men. And whatever Erasmus's intentions might have been, this critique of the church's version of scripture opened a door for Reformers to challenge the authority and traditions of the church. If the translation of God's word the church had used for most of its history was so significantly flawed, how could the church's vision of Christianity be trusted?

In the contract drawn up for Caravaggio's first version of the *Inspiration of Matthew*, the canons of San Luigi dei Francesi specify that the angel is to be shown "dictating."[28] The traditional belief in the divine inspiration of the Bible was often expressed in the conceit that the Holy Spirit was the true author of scripture and that the human writers of scripture were merely the Spirit's amanuenses, and in Catholic doctrine this applied to both scripture and tradition. As Michael Mullett observes, one of the key concepts invoked at the Council of Trent was, in the words of the oft-repeated maxim, that "the traditions of the Church . . . were established with 'the Holy Ghost dictating' ('*Spiritu Sancto dictante*')."[29] Since the authority of Jerome's translation was one of the traditions the Catholic Church had confirmed at Trent, it follows that Jerome's translation, however cautiously the Church described its claims, was dictated by the Holy Ghost. In this conception of the history of the divine word, the translator is no less important in the transmission of scripture than the writer of the original text: Jerome takes his place next to Matthew as an author of the gospel. This conception of Jerome's authority helps shed light on Caravaggio's *Inspiration*. If Caravaggio's contract specifies that the angel is to be shown "dictating" to the gospel writer, the first *Inspiration* takes this conceit a step further, depicting a guiding spirit that foregoes dictation in order to write with or through Matthew.[30] The angel literally pushes Matthew's hand to sketch letters that seem to have no meaning for the astonished gospel writer. And the angel guides Matthew's hand to form words written by Jerome. Or, to be more precise, the angel manipulates Matthew's hand to write a passage in Hebrew in conformity with a Latin text that would be translated from the Greek more than three hundred years after the evangelist's death.

In Erasmus's Jerome and Caravaggio's Matthew, what is at stake is nothing less than the nature of scripture's relation to history. Erasmus had given the world a Jerome, and a Vulgate, divorced from miracles and prodigies, divorced from the intervening hand of God. He had given the world a Jerome who was human and flawed, but one with agency, one who was the prime mover in his translation. In contrast, one of the most striking features of Caravaggio's first *Inspiration of Matthew* is that the evangelist is portrayed as a man who seems to have no agency. It is not simply that Caravaggio represents Matthew as a humble man, but that the angel seems to use this humble Matthew as an instrument; the evangelist seems to be merely an extension of the quill that he grasps so awkwardly. And if Matthew disappears behind the angelic force that makes use of him in Caravaggio's *Inspiration*, Jerome disappears altogether. All that remains is the ghostly presence of the Vulgate, haunting Matthew's Hebrew text. Writing in a Hebrew perfectly aligned with the Catholic Church's preferred text, Caravaggio's Matthew seems to efface the human, historical labors of Jerome that Erasmus had brought to the world's attention. In responding to the crisis affecting both Jerome and the Vulgate, Caravaggio's inspiration is to remove the intermediary step, remove the problem of translation, remove Jerome. And in collapsing past and present, original and translation, Caravaggio seems to follow precisely the decision of the Council of Trent. If the Council of Trent had ruled that the Vulgate was authoritative, then Caravaggio's painting illustrates that the original text had always already corresponded to Jerome's translation. As the canons of San Luigi may have worried, however, the significance of this collapsing of past and present is not so clear. Depending on the perspective of the viewer, the painting might depict the hand of the divine shaping human history, guiding the *consensus fidelium* of the church, or it might reveal the hand of the church anxiously rewriting the past. By following through on the logic of the Council's decision, Caravaggio, whatever his intention, lays bare the way in which Jerome's translation now transcends its own textual history. In *The Inspiration of St. Matthew*, the word of God remains self-identical throughout history as some guiding hand, divine or otherwise, preserves the traditions of the Catholic Church.

The story of Caravaggio's Matthew and Erasmus's Jerome sounds very familiar to the student of early modern culture. In many ways, this is the story of Renaissance humanism. The intrepid scholar works to demystify an authoritative text by pointing to the vagaries of its history and transmission. The interrogation of the text works to destabilize orthodoxies, and the defenders of those orthodoxies respond to this threat by retrenching, by reestablishing the grounds of textual authority. But the role of humanist scholarship generally, and Erasmus specifically, in the demystification of scripture is not as clear-cut as this familiar narrative might suggest. We have come to expect the practices we associate with humanist philology—a critical understanding of the provenance of manuscripts, an attention to the materiality and historicity of written documents, an insistence on the social embeddedness of discourse—to lead to a certain desacralization of the text. But in what we might call the linguistic theology of humanist scholars like Erasmus we often find just the opposite.[31] Erasmus may humanize Jerome and challenge the Vulgate, but he does so as part of a mission to elevate the written text of scripture to the center of Christian experience. If Erasmus often plays the part of the scholarly iconoclast, especially in his gimlet-eyed scrutiny of the church's textual tradition, he also often looks like an idolater of the word. Indeed, many of his writings seem guilty of what Michael O'Connell calls logolatry, the identification of the Word of Christ with the merely material word of scripture.[32] From a twenty-first-century perspective, it seems as if Erasmus is able to hold two contradictory positions simultaneously. The humanist scholar understands that all texts are necessarily corrupt, that perfect translation is impossible, that words betray us. The linguistic theologian believes that this same fallen language, and the written word especially, is the medium of the sacred. Of course, this also is not a new story. Textual iconoclast and idolater of the word, Erasmus seems to embody the contradictions at the heart of Christianity's relationship to language. But these contradictions are exacerbated by the promise and threat of humanism's philological project and the conviction, shared by Erasmus and many early Reformers, that the written word should be the center of Christian life.

* * *

Much of *The Incarnate Text* is concerned with the ambivalence of poets to the materiality of the letter. In this chapter, however, I address the ways in which Erasmus flirts with logolatry, a veneration of the word that would help shape Reformation and Counter-Reformation thought. Although he was not an iconoclast in the traditional sense, Erasmus believed that one must attempt to transcend the fallen material world to apprehend the sacred. And in a fallen world, the best hope for this transcendence is language, particularly written language. Erasmus challenges the venerable translation of Jerome, but he does so because the text of scripture is the sine qua non of his theology. For Erasmus, divinity speaks most clearly through written text, and it does so precisely because writing, although necessarily material, is less embodied, less fraught with presence than the human voice. To avoid an improper attachment to the things of this world, to avoid the distracting presence of the human body, one needs the abstraction of writing. After discussing Erasmus's peculiar blend of iconoclasm and logolatry, I turn to England, where the contradictions at the heart of Erasmus's influential conception of the sacred text come undone in the heat of controversy. Erasmus's friend and collaborator Thomas More is often seen as representative of European humanism generally and the Erasmian project specifically in early sixteenth-century England. When it comes to the elevation of scripture to the center of the Christian experience, however, it is the Protestant William Tyndale who seems to inherit Erasmus's logocentric mission. In the controversy between Tyndale and More, we see two Erasmian humanists contending over the nature of scripture as written document. And in their bitterly polemical and frequently brilliant exchange, the two scholars grapple with the paradoxes at the heart of Christianity's fraught relationship to the notion of a sacred text. The problem faced by More and Tyndale, Erasmus and the Council of Trent, is a simple one: how to understand the relationship between the eternal Word of God, which is figured as unchanging, timeless, outside of history, and the word of scripture, which is time-bound and embodied, shaped by the forces of history, the pressures of language, and fallen human hands. If this is a question that has always vexed Christian thought, it is also a question that informs the crisis of the book in the sixteenth century. In this chapter, I explore the ways in which the humanist desire to attend to the historicity of text and the Reformation desire to exalt the text of scripture to the center of Christian experience strain the traditional ways in which scripture was conceived.

Erasmus, Iconoclasm, Textual Presence

In his 1516 edition of *Novum Instrumentum*, Erasmus publishes a dedicatory letter to Pope Leo X that offers the fruits of his scholarly labor both as a gift to the pontiff and as a means of redeeming contemporary Christendom:

> our chiefest hope for the restoration and rebuilding of the Christian
> religion . . . is that all those who profess the Christian philosophy the
> whole world over should above all absorb the principles laid down
> by their Founder from the writings of the evangelists and apostles, in
> which that heavenly Word [*verbum*]³³ which once came down to us
> from the Father still lives and breathes for us and acts and speaks
> with more immediate efficacy, in my opinion, than in any other way.
> Besides which I perceived that that teaching which is our salvation
> was to be had in a much purer and more lively form if sought at the
> fountain-head and drawn from the actual sources than from pools
> and runnels. And so I have revised the whole New Testament (as they
> call it) against the standard of the Greek original.³⁴

Erasmus here suggests that the reformation, or, as he writes, the "restoration and rebuilding," of the Christian religion (*restituendae sarciendaeque Christianae religionis*) will be a product of texts properly restored and properly read. For Erasmus the center of the Christian experience was, or should be, the text of scripture. To transform one's relationship to these texts, to transform one's reading, is to transform one's life. Offering both the first printed edition of the Greek text and a new Latin translation that he continually attempted to make more precise and powerful, Erasmus desired to reform all of Christendom through accurate philology and eloquent Latin.[35] In the "writings of the evangelists and apostles," made newly available to the world by Erasmus and Froben, the Word "still lives and breathes for us." And the status of these living and breathing writings *as writings* is crucially important to Erasmus.

Like almost everything else about Erasmus's daring publication, the title *Novum Instrumentum* occasioned some controversy. All subsequent editions were entitled, more traditionally, *Novum Testamentum*. In a letter of 1527 addressed to Robert Aldrich, Bishop of Carlisle, Erasmus clarified the title of his 1516 edition. In the letter Erasmus explains that the Latin word *testamentum* properly refers to a covenant or promise, whereas *instrumentum* is a written document that might describe such a covenant. Both the Old and New Testaments existed as covenants long before they were committed to writing, and by naming his edition *Novum Instrumentum* Erasmus implicitly asks the reader not to confuse the writings we read with the testaments they describe.[36] It would be a mistake, however, to assume either that Erasmus is merely making a pedantic distinction between act and record or that he is denigrating the written document in relation to the performative speech-act of the covenant. For Erasmus, as we shall see, the record is crucial to the comprehension of the act; the written document is more effective and valuable, in many ways, than the speech-act it records. First and foremost, Erasmus uses the term *instrumentum* precisely because it is novel in this context. He wants to announce for all to hear that he has returned to the sources and brought back the gospels in a "purer and more lively form," a form that he hopes will transfigure contemporary Christianity. And central to both the novelty and the transformative power of his endeavor is the status of the documents he presents as writings, writings in which the "heavenly Word . . . acts and speaks with more immediate efficacy . . . than in any other way." The radical nature of this statement is not often noted by modern scholars.[37] The implication is that the written record of the heavenly word speaks with more efficacy than the priest in the performance of the Mass, acts with more efficacy than the sacraments of the church. In making the *text* of Christ the center of his proposed transformation of Christian piety, Erasmus necessarily diminishes the relative stature of the institutions and functions of the church. And this would not go unnoticed by conservative defenders of the church or by reformers more radical than Erasmus.[38]

In the prefatory material to his *Novum Instrumentum*, Erasmus includes a summons to the reader, *Paraclesis*, which is his most stirring and influential exhortation to the reading of scripture. At the end of *Paraclesis*, Erasmus makes an astonishing claim for the power of the written word to represent, or *present*, Christ. Arguing against reverence for images rendered in wood or stone, Erasmus does not merely suggest that "the Gospel writings" express "the living image of . . . [Christ's] holy mind"; he contends that they offer us "Christ himself," Christ "speaking, healing, dying, rising."[39] We might expect Erasmus, the somewhat pedantic philologist who insisted on naming his testament *Novum Instrumentum*, to draw our attention to the potentially dangerous distance between the words Christ uttered and the rendering of that speech into writing. We might expect Erasmus the Christian exegete to discuss the fallen nature of language, the inadequacy of the written word to transmute the presence of Christ in the world into the experience of reading. Instead, the written text easily stands in the place of the historical Christ, speaking with his voice. Indeed, for Erasmus, the gospel—and by implication "these writings," Erasmus's *Novum Instrumentum*—"render . . . [Christ] so fully present" to the reader "that you would see less if you gazed upon him with your very eyes."[40] The Word made flesh is nothing compared with the flesh made word, the incarnate Christ nothing compared to the book that the reader of Erasmus's *Paraclesis* holds in hand. As O'Connell notes, this is "a theologically startling moment."[41] In fact, O'Connell finds the "devaluation of the actual incarnation in comparison with the textual record" so remarkable that he suggests that this "may not be a fully considered position of Erasmus. In context it seems rather an expression of the enthusiasm of presenting the first typographical edition of the Greek New Testament to Europe."[42] But this is not a new idea for Erasmus. That writing speaks to us more directly than speech, that the dead letter might inscribe more than absence, that it might, in fact, be the condition of a certain kind of "presence," is an idea that Erasmus elaborates again and again in his work.

In the Froben edition of Jerome's works, published in the same year as the *Novum Instrumentum*, Erasmus writes a dedicatory letter to William Warham, Archbishop of Canterbury, in which he suggests that the modern world should venerate the books of illustrious authors. According to Erasmus, "the most powerful and prosperous monarchs" of antiquity were so concerned that the memory of "great authors" not be effaced that they had their "maxims . . . inscribed everywhere in marble or bronze and set them up for all men to see; they bought their works at vast expense and had them faithfully and almost religiously copied, enclosed them in chests of cedar wood and rubbed them with cedar oil, then laid them up in their temples." These powerful monarchs treated the writings of human authors so carefully, so reverently because "something so sacred, so divine, should not be entrusted for safekeeping to any but the gods themselves . . . nor should works be allowed to die defenceless which confer immortality on all men."[43] Erasmus makes this argument in his dedicatory letter to Warham because he wants to claim that Jerome has been salvaged from the ravages of time, that the church father has been resurrected by Erasmus and Froben's press. But it is not merely writing's ability to overcome absence and death that Erasmus glorifies here. The language of divinity and sacrality, the striking image of "chests of cedar wood" anointed "with cedar oil" being laid up in temples, suggests a veneration for the book as object that transcends the desire to protect and preserve. Moreover, this veneration of the book that Erasmus extols seems inimical to Erasmus's own long-standing critique of the ceremonialism and superstition he saw everywhere in contemporary Christianity.

Whenever he touched on the state of contemporary religion in his writings, Erasmus indicted, often satirically, the tendency toward the veneration of "stocks and stones," the merely material things of this world. Pilgrimages, relics, statues, images: all were subject to his withering critique. Although, as I have said, it would be a mistake to call Erasmus an iconoclast, his scathing appraisal of the material manifestations of worship certainly anticipated and inspired the iconoclasm of Reformers.[44] One way in which Erasmus anticipated Reformation thought was in his disdain for the idea that the sacred might be localized in a specific place or object. In a discussion of the cult of relics in late antique and early medieval piety, Peter Brown contends that "*praesentia*, the physical presence of the holy, whether in the midst of a particular community or in the possession of particular individuals, was [in this period] the greatest blessing that a . . . Christian could enjoy." By the late Middle Ages the idea that the "holy was available in one place, and in each such place it was accessible . . . in a manner in which it could not be situated elsewhere" meant that significant numbers of people were mobilized at any given time in relation to holy places, sacred things.[45] And this notion of *praesentia* was at the heart of both a complex and extensive pilgrimage network and, more fundamentally, the church's conception of the relation of the earthly to the divine. It is precisely this idea of *praesentia* that first Erasmus and then sixteenth-century Reformers rejected as idolatrous. Although one can find an implicit critique of all kinds of devotional practices in Erasmus's writing, he reserved much of his venom for what he considered the irrational and superstitious acts of piety surrounding the pilgrimage and the relic. In the 1526 edition of his *Colloquies*, Erasmus added a new colloquy, *Peregrinatio religionis ergo* (A Pilgrimage for Religion's Sake), that offered a devastating critique of the abuses engendered by pilgrimages to reliquaries.[46] Since relics virtually embodied the notion of *praesentia* and inspired precisely the superstitious responses that he found offensive, it is not surprising that they were often the object of his critique. Moreover, for Erasmus the relic was more difficult to negotiate than the icon. The problem of the icon was a function of understanding representation improperly; images, icons, and all signs with a properly indexical function were *adiaphora*—things indifferent—as long as they were considered representations and not worshipped as physically embodying the holy. The relic, in contrast, is not something one can so easily "read through." The logic of the relic is metonymic rather than metaphoric; the holiness of the relic is a function of its contiguity with the world and the flesh, as well as the precise historical provenance of the material artifact. Its materiality is not incidental to its meaning, but essential to it. Relics even more than images have the potential to lead to a misunderstanding of the sacred.

The transformation of Christian piety championed by Erasmus necessitated the supplanting of relics and pilgrimages, images and icons, with text. Since Christians cannot hope for the presence of the divine in a fallen world, one must resist the desire for full presence and accept that one can only arrive at knowledge of God through the abstraction of the written word. The illusory "presence" of relics specifically and images generally distracts Christians from true religion: the metamorphosis of self through the absorption of the text of Christ.[47] Given his animus against relics and the relation to the material world they embody, it is all the more surprising then that Erasmus should use the metaphor of the relic to describe the proper way to venerate books. In the dedicatory "Letter to Warham" in his edition of Jerome, Erasmus explicitly pits the veneration of writing against the veneration of things. In his discussion of the monarchs of antiquity who seek at all costs to memorialize authors and preserve texts, Erasmus contends suggestively that these princes "perceived of course . . . that it was barbarous for the corpses of the dead to be so carefully embalmed sometimes with unguents and spices and woad to preserve them from decay, when their preservation served no purpose since they could no longer reproduce the features or figure of the deceased, which even a statue of stone can do, and to take no such care to preserve the relics of the mind."[48] Writings, texts, books are here "relics of the mind" (*animorum reliquiis*). The memorializing function of the relic is transferred to writing, as books are understood to speak across the ages as "corpses of the dead" never can. The proper vehicle of the spirit is not the flesh but the written corpus.[49] In case the reader misses the contemporary relevance of this figure, Erasmus spells it out:

> For my part, far as I am from despising the simple piety of common folk, I cannot but wonder at the absurd judgment of the multitude. The slippers of the saints and their drivel-stained napkins we put to our lips, and the books they wrote, the most sacred and most powerful relics of those holy men, we leave to lie neglected. A scrap of a saint's tunic or shirt we place in a gilded and bejewelled reliquary, and the books into which they put so much work, and in which we have the best part of them still living and breathing, we abandon to be gnawed at will by bug, worm, and cockroach.[50]

For Erasmus's more traditional contemporaries, relics were considered worthy of veneration because the body of which they were fragments was sanctified by the soul inhabiting it. Since the soul of the saint was informed by the divine, the relics were vessels of the Holy Spirit.[51] This understanding of relics is informed by an incarnational theology that embraces a notion of divine immanence. By taking on human form, Christ transforms the human relationship to the material world in such a way that it is proper to venerate (*dulia*), if not worship (*latria*), the fleshly and the material. But in Erasmus's *philosophia christi* the incarnation of the Word often seems less important than its manifestation as text.[52] In this passage, Erasmus insists that relics are merely fragments of the body, whereas writings bear the trace of the soul. The saints are properly remembered and venerated not through the fragments of flesh they leave behind but through the remains of the works on which they labored while alive. In their works, "the most sacred and most powerful relics of those holy men" (*sanctissimas et efficacissimas diuorum reliquias*), "we have the best part of them still living and breathing."[53] Through this devaluation of the relic and exaltation of text, Erasmus hopes to reform contemporary Christianity by denouncing a piety fixed upon spectacles of divine immanence and championing a piety that embraces transcendent acts of reading.

Throughout his career Erasmus makes it clear that a renunciation of flesh and attendant embrace of text is central to his hoped-for reformation of Christian piety. In the *Enchiridion militis christiani*, first published over ten years before the edition of Jerome and the *Novum Instrumentum,* Erasmus offers an entire treatise devoted, in various ways, to the eternal battle between the flesh and the spirit. In the "Fifth rule" of his *Enchiridion* Erasmus articulates a neo-Platonic ascent from the material to the spiritual realm: "Perfect piety is the attempt to progress always from visible things, which are usually imperfect or indifferent, to invisible."[54] In the course of describing a properly internal and spiritual piety, Erasmus condemns the material things and external rites that have come to dominate contemporary Christian worship. Throughout this discussion, his touchstone is the scriptural distinction between letter and spirit. Again and again in the *Enchiridion* Erasmus draws contrasts between the spiritual truths available through the written word and a superstitious devotion to the material world:

> With great veneration you revere the ashes of Paul. . . . If you venerate mute and dead ashes and ignore his living image still speaking and breathing, as it were, in his writings, is not your religion utterly absurd? You worship the bones of Paul preserved in a relic casket, but do not worship the mind of Paul hidden away in his writings? You make much of a piece of his body visible through a glass covering, and you do not marvel at the whole mind of Paul shining through his writings? You worship ashes . . . why do you not honor the written word more?[55]

Here, Erasmus appropriately uses a Pauline distinction between body and soul, letter and spirit, to suggest the proper way for the apostle to move through Christian history: as text. In his various efforts to champion text over flesh, however, Erasmus does not simply elevate the authorial presence he finds in writing in relation to the mystified presence the superstitious find in mere things; he elevates the dead letter of the text over authorial presence itself. In the letter to Warham, Erasmus suggests that writers "live on for the world at large even after death, and live on in such fashion that they speak to more people and more effectively dead than alive. . . . In fact, they then most truly come alive for us when they themselves have ceased to live." To illustrate his point that written text is more effective than spoken word, that the relics of the mind are more alive than the voice of the author, Erasmus turns to the classical world's most renowned orator: "For such is my opinion: if a man had lived in familiar converse with Cicero (to take him as an example) for several years, he will know less of Cicero than they do who by constant reading of what he wrote converse with his spirit every day."[56] For those who would converse with his spirit, the text is preferable to the man.

In his paradoxical contention that writers "most truly come alive for us when they themselves have ceased to live," Erasmus seems to echo a rich and strange passage in Augustine. In the last three books of the *Confessions*, Augustine turns from an explication of the self to an exegesis of scripture, specifically a commentary on the opening lines of Genesis. In the course of this exegesis, he imagines speaking with the figure traditionally considered the human "author" of the Pentateuch, Moses:

> May I hear and understand how in the beginning you made heaven
> and earth (Gen, I, I). Moses wrote this. He wrote this and went his
> way, passing out of this world. . . . He is not now before me, but if
> he were, I would clasp him and ask him and through you beg him
> to explain to me the creation. I would concentrate my bodily ears to
> hear the sounds breaking forth from his mouth. If he spoke Hebrew,
> he would in vain make an impact on my sense of hearing, for the
> sounds would not touch my mind at all. If he spoke Latin, I would
> know what he meant. Yet how would I know whether or not he was
> telling me the truth? If I did know this, I could not be sure of it
> from him. Within me, within the lodging of my thinking, there
> would speak a truth which is neither Hebrew nor Greek nor Latin
> nor any barbarian tongue and which uses neither mouth nor tongue
> as instruments and utters no audible syllables. It would say: "What
> he is saying is true." And I being forthwith assured would say with
> confidence to the man possessed by you: "What you say is true."[57]

As Augustine turns the thought of this imagined encounter over in his mind, the problem of different languages, and thus the problem of cultural and historical difference (as well as the problem of internal difference within the one text of scripture), recedes as the more fundamental problem of simple authenticity comes to the fore. Whatever language Moses speaks, whether I can understand him or not, how do I know that he speaks the truth? Thus, the epistemological problem of authenticity precedes the exegetical problem of meaning and understanding. And the authenticating voice is necessarily outside the body, outside language, outside history: the voice within speaks "a truth which is neither Hebrew nor Greek nor Latin nor any barbarian tongue and which uses neither mouth nor tongue as instruments and utters

no audible syllables."[58] The point of the imagined encounter with the patri-
arch is precisely that such an encounter is pointless: authenticity is a product
not of proximity, not of the presence of the author, but of the workings of
the spirit within the reader or auditor. The voice of Moses, the presence of
Moses, is not enough to guarantee the truth of his word. In Augustine's
account both the written word of scripture and the voice of the author are
dead letters. Augustine engages with the fantasy to illustrate that authorial
presence is a fiction. Only the movement of the spirit can authenticate and
explicate the truth.

Augustine seems to suggest through this vividly imagined encounter ("I
would clasp him . . . I would concentrate my bodily ears to hear the sounds
breaking forth from his mouth") that the bodily presence of the author offers
a false promise of an authenticating voice. For Erasmus, who helped edit
Augustine's works for Froben's press, this false promise of the flesh, of *praesentia*, is the crucial problem facing contemporary Christianity. If Augustine
reduces both authorial voice and writing to dead letters, Erasmus insists that
it is only in the absence of voice, the absence of the author, that the truth of
the text emerges. Indeed, in the *Enchiridion* Erasmus's denunciation of the
false promises of the flesh leads him to make the astonishing claim that
Christ's presence in the world was actually an obstacle to a proper understanding of his word. At the end of a characteristic discussion of the preference for relics of the mind over relics of the flesh, Erasmus writes

> You give homage to an image of Christ's countenance represented
> in stone or wood or depicted in color. With how much more reli-
> gious feeling should you render homage to the image of his mind,
> which has been reproduced in the Gospels through the artistry of
> the Holy Spirit. . . . And you do not gaze with wonder upon this
> image, do not worship it, scan it with reverent eyes, treasure it in
> your mind? With such holy and efficacious relics of the Lord at your
> disposal, do you disregard them and seek out much more extraneous
> ones? You gaze with awe at what is purported to be the tunic or
> shroud of Christ, and you read the oracles of Christ apathetically?
> You think it an immense privilege to have a tiny particle of the cross
> in your home. But that is nothing compared to carrying about in
> your heart the mystery of the cross. . . .
>
> As long as the apostles enjoyed the physical company of Christ,
> do you not read how weak they were and how crass was their under-

standing? Who could desire anything more to assure his complete salvation than this continuous familiarity between God and man? And yet after the performance of so many miracles, after they had been exposed for so many years to the teaching that proceeded from the mouth of God, after so many proofs of his resurrection, did he not upbraid them for their incredulity at the very last hour as he was about to be received into heaven? What reason can be adduced for this? It was the flesh of Christ that stood in the way, and that is what prompted him to say: "If I do not go away, the Paraclete [Holy Spirit] will not come. It is expedient for you that I go." If the physical presence of Christ is of no profit for salvation, shall we dare to place our hopes for the attainment of perfect piety in any material thing?[59]

The apostles are at a disadvantage when compared with sixteenth-century Christians. The apostles merely had Christ; Erasmus's contemporaries have his text. If Christ's human voice or material presence constituted true religion, "who could be more religious than the Jews" who saw him "with their own eyes, heard him with their own ears and touched him with their own hands"? Who could be "more fortunate than Judas, who pressed his lips upon the divine mouth?"[60] The apostles avoid the weakness and the crass understanding of materialists, cease to be Jews and become proper Christians, only in the *absence* of the human Christ. For Erasmus, authorial presence is an obstacle to understanding and an invitation to idolatry. The key then to Erasmus's textual piety is to avoid the false illusion of presence through an embrace of linguistic mediation. The abstraction of writing represents the best hope of a knowledge untainted by the false illusion of presence. Paradoxically, it is precisely through the abstract mediation of text that we can bring to life the voices of the dead, the presence of the divine. In a fallen world, absence is the precondition of presence, and a proper relation to the dead letter is the only prudent path to salvation.[61]

Philological Dreams, Sectarian Realities

Novum Instrumentum was rushed through the press because both Erasmus and the printer Johann Froben believed they were in a race against a rival printing of the Greek New Testament coming out of Spain. From the beginning of the sixteenth century, a team of scholars under the direction of Cardinal Jiménez de Cisneros at the University of Alcalá de Henares had been working on a monumental new edition of the Bible, which would come to be known as the Complutensian Polyglot. Although it rolled off the press of Guillén de Brocar in 1514–17, official publication of the Polyglot was delayed until the edition was authorized by Pope Leo X in 1521.[62] The massive scholarly undertaking resulted in a magisterial six-volume edition of scripture: the first four volumes contain the Old Testament in Hebrew, Greek, and Latin, printed in adjacent columns;[63] the fifth volume contains the New Testament in Greek and Latin, also printed in parallel columns; the final volume consists of various lexica and linguistic supplements (Figure 4). Even more than Erasmus's *Novum Instrumentum*, the Complutensian Polyglot is a testament to the possibilities opened up by the fruitful marriage of humanist scholarship and the new technology of print.[64]

In a prologue addressed to the reader in the prefatory material of the Polyglot, Cardinal Cisneros reads the physical page of the Old Testament as a visual metaphor of Calvary, in which the Latin Vulgate, positioned in the middle of the page between the Greek and Hebrew texts, is a figure for Christ on the cross between the two thieves. It is not surprising that Cisneros makes reference to thieves in this context: the idea that translation was a form of theft was a commonplace in the early modern period.[65] Here, however, the commonplace is inverted; the original texts on which the translation is based are figured as thieves, while the translation takes the place of Christ crucified. Seeming to anticipate the conflicts to come, Cisneros reads the translation as authentic and the Greek and Hebrew sources of the translation as, in some sense, false, counterfeit. Cisneros's preface seems to belie the principles of humanist scholarship that inform the Complutensian Polyglot. Why return *ad fontes* if the sources are thieves, infidels, and schismatics? But Cisneros's comparison does not end with this stunning image of Christ flanked by thieves; he also compares the polyglot page to the Roman Church flanked by the Synagogue and the Greek Church.[66] Desiring to protect the Vulgate against the incursion of Greek and Hebrew infidels, Cisneros reads the page as expressing the central position of the Vulgate in his vision of Christianity: it symbolizes the authority of the Roman Catholic Church and embodies the authentic Word of Christ. Through this extraordinary reading of the page, Cisneros does not simply conflate Christ crucified with scripture; he conflates Christ with a specific translation of scripture.

To a certain extent, Cisneros's extravagant reading seems to reflect Eras-

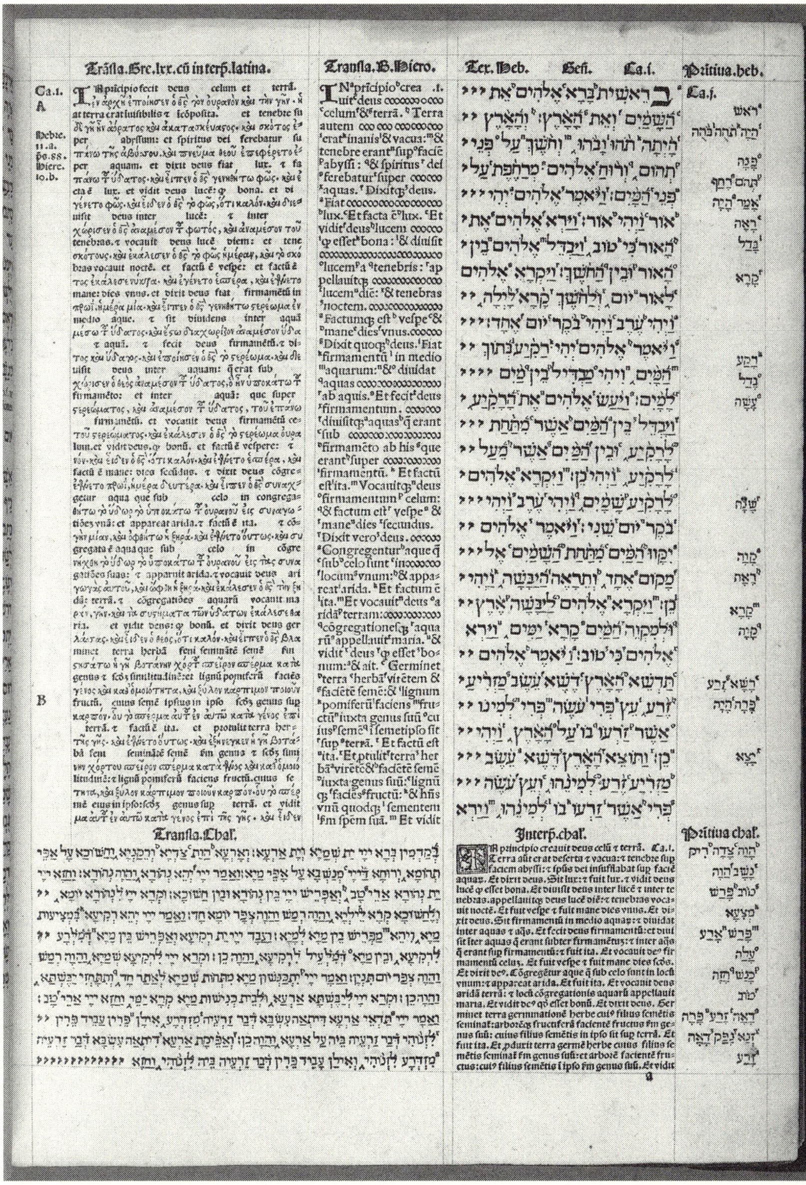

Figure 4. Page from *The Complutensian Polyglot* (1514–1517, 1521). This item is reproduced by permission of The Huntington Library, San Marino, California.

mus's desire to place the *text* of Christ at the center of Christian experience. But if Erasmus and Cisneros share a humanist enthusiasm that some of their contemporaries might construe as logolatry, as an idolatry of the word, they differ in their understanding of the relationship of God's word to history, to time. In Cisneros's dramatic reading of the page, the text of scripture is frozen in time; the authentic word of God persists unchanging through history. Here, Cisneros seems to anticipate both the Council of Trent and Caravaggio's first *Inspiration*, as he places the Vulgate outside of the purview of scholarship, outside of a merely human history. In this apotheosis of the Vulgate, we see the antithesis of Erasmus's desire to demystify both Jerome and his translation; we see the antithesis of Erasmus's desire to return man and book to a fallible human history. But if Erasmus's commitment to reading the text of scripture as part of human history would not allow him to place the translation above the original, it would also not allow him to imagine that the truth of the scripture resides only in the pure source, in the Greek. Unlike many of his humanist counterparts, Erasmus despised the kind of scholarship that would transform a text, a language, into a dead letter.[67] For Erasmus, the point was to make the text live. It is often thought that Erasmus's great achievement in the *Novum Instrumentum* is the printing of the Greek New Testament, but Erasmus himself understood his labor of love to be his translation.[68] For him it is the *Latin* New Testament that is his gift to Christian Europe. Erasmus's understanding of scripture lies in the *relation* between the two texts of scripture one finds in his *Novum Instrumentum*. He ultimately published the Greek and the Latin texts together so that one could be compared with the other, so that there could be a dialectical movement toward greater understanding. For Erasmus the unfolding of language, the unfolding of text through time is the movement of the spirit in the world. Erasmus's philology is essentially copious; humanist scholarship does not exist to pin down the word of scripture, once and for all, but to assist in the ongoing articulation of the text of God through time.

* * *

As discussed above, in the *Enchiridion* Erasmus argues that Christ's physical absence is essential to comprehension of his message. In the passage in which Erasmus makes this argument, he quotes John 16:7: "*Nisi ego abiero, Paracletus non veniet. Expedit vobis, ut ego vadam* [Nevertheless I tell you the truth, it is expedient for you that I go away. For if I go not away, that comforter will not come unto you. But if I depart, I will send him unto you]."[69] In this passage Christ prepares his disciples for his imminent ascension and promises to send the Holy Spirit. Erasmus's *Paracletus* is a translation of the Greek term used to describe the Holy Spirit in John's Gospel (14:16, 14:26, 15:26, 16:7).[70] Most early modern English versions, following Tyndale, translate the Greek as "comforter." Traditionally, the promise to send the Paraclete, or Holy Spirit, was understood to be dramatically fulfilled at Pentecost, when the gifts of the spirit manifest in the speaking of the one truth in various tongues. In the passage from *Enchiridion*, however, Erasmus reads the promise of the Paraclete in an unconventional way: "It was the flesh of Christ that stood in the way, and that is what prompted him to say: 'If I do not go away, the Paraclete will not come. It is expedient for you that I go.' If the physical presence of Christ is of no profit for salvation, shall we dare to place our hopes for the attainment of perfect piety in any material thing?"[71] Strikingly, Erasmus invokes the Paraclete not in a discussion of the movement of the spirit in the miraculous preaching of the word but in a discussion of the failings of voice, presence, charismatic preaching. Read in context, the implication of the passage seems to be that the promise of the Paraclete is fulfilled not in Pentecost but in the written text of scripture, "the image of his mind, which has been reproduced in the Gospels through the artistry of the Holy Spirit."[72] And as Erasmus suggests in his exhortation entitled *Paraclesis,* that image can be seen most clearly by the contemporary Christian in Erasmus's own *Novum Instrumentum.* The consonance between the Greek word used in John's Gospel to refer to the Holy Spirit and the title of Erasmus's manifesto on the reading of scripture (*Paraclesis*) is, of course, no accident. Erasmus wants to associate his *Novum Instrumentum,* the original Greek text of Christ that he resurrects for the modern reader through his humanist scholarship and Latin translation, with the ongoing presence of the Holy Spirit through Christian history. For Erasmus, the spirit is present through history in transcendent acts of reading, acts of reading that depend upon the letter of scripture.

That Erasmus associates the humanist revolution in biblical scholarship with the pentecostal gifts of the Paraclete can be seen in his colloquy *De incomparabili heroe Ioanne Reuchlino in divorum numerum relato* (The Apotheosis of That Incomparable Worthy, Johann Reuchlin). In this colloquy Erasmus recounts the dream of a pious man at the moment of the death of Johann Reuchlin, the renowned humanist scholar who helped revitalize the study of Hebrew in the Christian West. In the dream Reuchlin is welcomed into the next world as a "holy colleague" by Jerome, Christianity's most august linguist and philologist. The colloquy ends with a prayer: "O God thou lover of mankind, who through thy chosen servant Johann Reuchlin hast renewed to the world the gift of tongues by which thou didst once from heaven, through thy Holy Spirit, instruct the apostles for the preaching of the gospel, grant that all men everywhere may preach in every tongue the glory of thy Son Jesus."[73] Employed in the service of biblical exegesis, serving as the foundation of a *philosophia christi*, the humanist renaissance of letters will bring about a second Pentecost. This Pentecost, however, is brought about not by the Paraclete directly inspiring the charismatic preaching of the Bible in multiple tongues, but by the movement of the spirit through scholarship, through a rebirth of letters. Here, Erasmus offers a utopian vision of the radical dissemination of God's word that is emblematic of his relation to, and understanding of, language and writing. Of course, "The Apotheosis of . . . Reuchlin" was published in 1522, when it still seemed possible that philological method and literary zeal could restore Christian letters and thereby reform Christianity. In the ensuing decade, as divisiveness and violence won the day over amity and scholarship, Erasmus became much less sanguine about the prospects of reform.

The controversy concerning Erasmus's translation of the beginning of John's Gospel may have provided the first indication that the scholar's desire for a latter-day Pentecost was destined to go unfulfilled. The 1519 edition of Erasmus's Latin translation of the Greek New Testament was even more controversial than the 1516 edition. The significant changes that Erasmus made in the translation between the two editions moved his New Testament farther away from the Vulgate and orthodoxy. The most notorious of these changes was an alteration of Jerome's translation of the beginning of John's gospel. Where Jerome rendered the opening Greek phrase as "In principio erat *verbum*," Erasmus translated "In principio erat *sermo*." This change from what we might call "word" to what we might call "discourse" is indicative of the essentially time-bound and open-ended quality of Erasmus's linguistic theology. Terence Cave captures this aspect of Erasmus's thought beautifully:

> If Christ is *sermo*, he is not so much the once-and-for-all utterance
> of God (*verbum*) as a divinely present discourse, a living utterance
> which includes Christ's recorded (written) words yet is infinitely
> renewed in their re-utterance by readers of subsequent ages. Thus
> the translation of *logos* as *sermo* consecrates human discourse; but at

the same time it destroys the unity of the original utterance and initiates a movement beyond the scriptural circle into the fallen language of man.[74]

It is precisely this movement that is essential to Erasmus's linguistic theology. Paradoxically, it is through the abstract mediation of the dead letter that we can bring to life the voices of the dead, the presence of the divine. But in a fallen world this resurrection of the word can never be complete; it is part of the unfolding of the Christian text in history. The translation of this one word embroiled Erasmus in a dispute concerning the place of tradition in defining scripture and the place of scripture in defining tradition. In his desire to answer his critics and quell the turmoil, Erasmus published his *Apologia . . . In principio erat sermo* in February 1520. In a letter to Cardinal Wolsey addressing the impact of the controversy in England, we can hear Erasmus's concern about the potential consequences of the discord:

> In your country I hear tell of a man who protested noisily before a crowded congregation that I wished to correct the Gospel of John, because in my rendering I had used sermo instead of verbum—as though St. John had written in Latin, and as though the Son of God had not been called Sermo rather than Verbum before me by Cyprian, Hilary, Jerome, and countless others, or as though sermo were not a better equivalent than verbum for the Greek word logos. Before a learned audience could anything be more foolish? And before the unlettered multitude could anything be more inflammatory?

Erasmus then asks Wolsey to "defend the peace of sacred study" by urging the pope "to use his authority to suppress this passion for attacking other people." In his letter Erasmus seems to anticipate the troubles ahead:

> Some distempers of the body are the work of destiny, and I perceive that in the same way there are predestined epidemics of the mind, whatever their source; whether it be the stars, or the effect of different influences on our bodies or, as I tend to think, the Enemy of mankind, who rejoices in nothing more than in our discords. Who else could have infused such venom into our studies—even in theology, on which depends the sound health and honourable estate of the Christian religion? Such are the spite and bitterness with which

nowadays even the theologians everywhere dispute among themselves, so venomous the pamphlets in which they excoriate one another and the sermons before public audiences in which they tear
one another to shreds.[75]

Erasmus's sense as early as 1520 that this distemper would become epidemic
is remarkably prescient.

As sectarian conflict escalated in the mid-1520s, Erasmus, feeling besieged
on all sides,[76] returned to the Pentecostal theme of "The Apotheosis of . . .
Reuchlin" in *Lingua*, his treatise on the tongue as the all-too-human organ
that mediates between, but also divides, individuals and societies. But now
Pentecost is invoked not to celebrate but to lament the reforming times in
which Erasmus lives:

> when . . . [the apostles] had received the tongues of fire, what did
> they speak of? . . . They spoke the wondrous deeds of the Lord, and
> they began to speak with divers tongues, but with one accord, for
> they had one heart and one spirit, because one spirit had filled them
> all.
>
> But today we see the schools of the philosophers disputing with
> so many opinions, and all Christians battling to the death with so
> many conflicting dogmas. Are we not repeating the construction of
> the tower of Babel? What harmony can exist among those carried
> away by vanity, when no man yields to another? . . . What then is
> the cause of such a confusion of tongues and minds among us[?] . . .
> We are called into the community of the son of God, because we
> have been grafted by faith on to his body, that is, the church, but
> the name, *ecclesia*, church, means an assembly, not a separation of
> parts.[77]

Erasmus's dream of a Christendom reformed by the sacred letters of scripture
would be shattered by the shattering of his church. Erasmus would grow
disillusioned with an increasingly divisive reform movement and an increasingly reactionary Catholic Church. Erasmus's vision of a thoroughly text-
centered Christianity, however, would prove hugely influential to those less
interested in maintaining the *consensus ecclesiae* so dear to his heart. Although
Erasmus's reputation would suffer as both Protestants and Catholics rejected
him as part of the enemy camp, both the iconoclastic thrust of his thought

and his humanist embrace of the written word would have a lasting impact on Christian thought. In England, in particular, both an Erasmian logolatry and an Erasmian iconoclasm enjoyed a long afterlife.

It is notoriously difficult to estimate the effect of Erasmus's thought on the course of the English Reformation. Despite the fact that he visited England often in the early sixteenth century, despite the fact that he taught Greek and lectured on Jerome's letters at Cambridge from 1511 to 1514, that effect is almost certainly a product of Erasmus as text rather than a product of his charismatic presence in England.[78] As if to confirm his belief that writers "speak to more people and more effectively dead than alive," influential works like *Enchiridion* and *Paraclesis* converted more and more readers to an Erasmian faith in the written word's ability to transform the world well after their author's disillusionment and death.[79] Some of Erasmus's writings became part of the textual apparatus of the Church of England. Royal injunctions handed down by both Edward and Elizabeth stipulated that editions of Erasmus's *Paraphrases* on the New Testament were required in all the parish churches of the country.[80] For a full half century then, the *Paraphrases* of Erasmus, the reform-minded Catholic scholar, was the standard New Testament commentary in Protestant England. Furthermore, the enduring influence of Erasmus's *Paraclesis* can be found in one of the authorized homilies of the Elizabethan regime: "An Information for them which take offence at certayne places of the holy scripture."[81] Addressing those who might doubt the centrality of the text of scripture to the lives of Christians, the sermon contends that Christ's promise "to be present with his church, til the worldes end" is fulfilled not only "in that he is . . . with vs by his grace & tender pitie: but also in this, that he speaketh presently vnto vs in the holy scriptures."[82] Indeed, Christ is so fully present in scripture that it might be possible to see Christ more perfectly in text than if he were present among us: "The Scripture doth in suche sorte set foorth Christ, that wee may se him both God & man, we maye see hym (I saye) speakyng vnto vs, healyng our infirmities, dying for our sinnes, rysyng from death for our iustification. And to be short, we maye in the Scriptures so perfectly see whole Christe, with the eye of fayth, as we lackyng fayth, coulde not with these bodyly eyes see hym, though he stode nowe present here before vs."[83]

This is, of course, an unacknowledged paraphrase of the *Paraclesis*. The Elizabethan regime here offers its church a somewhat watered-down version of an argument that Erasmus had made so eloquently fifty years earlier: that Christ is present in language, in writing, in text. The sermon denounces those who would "pull with violence, the holy Bybles out of the peoples handes," those who "haue most spitefully destroyed, and consumed the same to ashes in the fyre."[84] That there would come a time in the near future when one Christian would pull the Bible out of another Christian's hands and that there would come a time when Bibles would be burned by those espousing the Christian faith would have horrified the Erasmus who wrote the *Paraclesis*. But the violence that would be directed at both texts and images, the schisms arising from conflicting ways of apprehending the presence of the divine in the world, are intimately related to the issues that he was exploring in 1516. The contradictions at the heart of the Erasmian project are emblematic of a fundamental problem facing both Protestant and Catholic in the sixteenth century: how can Christianity reconcile faith in a text that can only be apprehended in some material form with a profound distrust of all material forms? In England we see this question addressed in forceful and often startling ways in the controversy between two Erasmian scholars who would ultimately die for their beliefs: William Tyndale and Thomas More.

Tyndale's Persecuted Word

In *Actes and Monuments,* John Foxe records an encounter between William Tyndale and an unnamed "learned man." In the exchange Tyndale's interlocutor defends the papacy and the Roman Church against the scorn of the Reformers, contending, "We were better be without Gods lawe then the Popes." Tyndale's response has become part of his legend: "I defie the Pope and all his lawes, and . . . if God spare my lyfe ere many yeares, I wyl cause a boye that dryueth the plough, shall knowe more of the scripture then thou doest."[85] The words may be apocryphal, but they convey both the passionate conviction with which Tyndale embraced his mission to bring scripture to the English people and the prophetic persona created by Foxe that so shaped the translator's reputation for later generations. In his supremely confident claim that the plowman will know scripture, Tyndale echoes Erasmus, that other infamous translator of scripture. In one of the most well-known and controversial passages in *Paraclesis*, Erasmus expresses a desire that the gospel be available to all men and all women, accessible to all nations, translated into all tongues. In England, Erasmus's treatise was translated by William Roye, Tyndale's sometime amanuensis, as *An Exhortacyon to the Dylygent Study of Scripture*:

And truely I do greatly dyssent from those men, whiche wolde not
that the scrypture of Chryst shulde be translated into al tonges that
it myghte be redde dylygentlye of the pryuate and seculer men &
women. . . . I wolde desyre that all women shuld reade the gospel
and Paules epystles / & I wolde to god they were translated into the
tonges of all men / So that they myght not only be reade & knowen
of the skottes and Iryshemen / but also of the Turkes & sarazyns.
. . . I wolde to god the plowman wolde singe a texte of the scripture
at his plowbeme. And that the weuer at his lowme / with this wolde
dryve awaye the tedyousnes of tyme. I wolde the wayfarynge man
with this pastyme / Wolde expell the werynes of his iorney. And to
be shorte I wold that all the communycacyon of the christen shulde
be of the scrypture / for in a maner suche are we oure selves as our
dayly tales are. . . . Hym do I counte a true dyuyne, whiche not with
crafty & sotyll reasons. But that in herte, countenaunce, eyes, &
lyfe, dothe teache. . . . Yf any man beynge enspyred with the holy
ghost do preche and teache . . . he is a very and true deuyne /
thoughe he be a weuer / yee thoughe he dygge & delue.[86]

The proliferation of people and texts, media and arts is striking. Both Erasmus and Tyndale express a powerful faith in the ability of written text, and
writing in the vernacular in particular, to hold and transmit divine truth.[87]
But Erasmus's pentecostal vision is like and unlike Tyndale's prophetic excla-
mation.[88] Erasmus's vision is idyllic and inclusive: a world of readers as theologians, brought together by text, created by text. Tyndale's dramatic
proclamation, in contrast, is performative and political ("I defie the Pope"),
quickly sketching an adversarial and rebellious position. He aims his hypo-
thetically edified plowman at the church like a weapon.

For Tyndale the history of the Roman Church was not an apostolic
succession confirmed by consensus and tradition but a narrative of oppression
and violence. In his preface to the reader in *The Obedience of a Christian
Man*, Tyndale pits the authority of the word of God against the authority of
the church. Tyndale is arguing for the necessity of the Bible in English,
but he frames his argument with an overarching narrative describing the
persecution of the true church by the false. Like Luther, Tyndale believed
that word and church were indivisible.[89] And if the true church is to be
fostered in England, the English people need scripture in the vernacular.
Tyndale's ingenious rhetorical strategy is to offer consolation to the reader

who has been denied the Bible in English: "Lat it not make the[e] dispeare nether yet discorage the[e] O Reader / that . . . [an English Bible] is forbeden the[e] in payne of lyfe and goodes or that it is made breakinge of the kynges peace or treason vnto his hynes to reade the worde of thy soules health. But moch rather be bolde in the lorde & comforte thy soule."[90]

The reader should be bold and comforted because "soch persecucion" is definite evidence that the word they are denied "is the true worde of God." In an uncertain world, we know true scripture from false by the hatred and abuse it attracts. As the reader can see from the histories recounted in both the Old and New Testaments, the true word is known precisely because it is "euer hated of the worlde."[91] Sketching a quick history of the battle between the word and the world, a battle that "began at Abell and hath euer sens continued and shall / I doute not / untyll the last daye," Tyndale writes, "sens the beginnynge of the worlde . . . [God] euer sente his true prophetes and preachers of his worde / to warne the people. . . . [But they] hardened their hertes and persecuted the worde that was sente to saue them."[92] Those who fear to embrace the true word because they fear violent reprisal; those overcome by "the wekenes of the flesh" who "haue denied / as Peter did"; those who have surrendered their "boke or put it awaye secretlye" should be comforted by the history of persecution that the Bible records.[93] And this abuse is not simply an accident of history; it is a necessary consequence of the Fall. In a fallen world the word of God can be free of such conflict no more than "the sonne can be without his lyghte." This startling analogy suggests that persecution is fundamental to scripture, an essential aspect of its way of being in the world. As a marginal note succinctly suggests, "the nature of Gods word is to be persecuted."[94]

In Tyndale's agonistic conception of Christian history, the persecuted word engages in an eternal struggle with idolatry. For Tyndale, contemporary religion, under the influence of antichrist, is ruled by the idolatrous workings of human reason and imagination.[95] This dangerous reliance on human understanding is nowhere more pernicious than in the supplanting of God's word with the "wisdom" of philosophers and theologians. In the *Obedience* Tyndale responds to the claim that "the scripture is so harde" that one could never hope to understand it without the help of theologians by asserting that such claims turn the world upside down, put the gloss before the text, the imitation before the original: "then is the doctoure fyrst true & the trueth of the scripture dependeth of his trueth and so the trueth of God springeth of the trueth of man. Thus Antichriste turnith the rotes of the trees upp-warde."[96] This reliance on human wisdom deforms scripture and divides people: "Now there is no other division or heresy in the worlde saue mans wisdome and when mans folish wisdome interpreteth the scripture, Mans wisdome scatereth / diuideth and maketh sectes. . . . Mans wisdome is playne ydolatry / nether is there any other ydolatry then to imagen of God after mans wisdome. God is not mans imaginacion / but that only which he saith of hym selfe."[97]

For Tyndale, human opinion is monstrously various, while God's word is a single entity, indivisible and self-contained, a touchstone by which the truth of human beliefs is tested and proven.[98] The word is not merely self-contained but self-sufficient, in need of no elaboration or extension. The bare word of God's scripture is enough. To augment or supplement God's word with human "wisdom" is to engage in idolatry, displacing God with human, the word with the world.

Tyndale's insistence that God is "that only which he saith of hym selfe" is crucial to his conception of a moral universe in which scripture is at odds with all that is other than scripture. Tyndale insists, "God is no thinge but his law and his promyses / that is to saye / that which he biddeth the[e] doo and that which he biddeth the[e] beleue and hope."[99] That Tyndale believes that the revelation of God's law and promises can be found in scripture alone and not human traditions is unsurprising. This belief is Reformation boilerplate. But in his need to argue for the priority and self-sufficiency of scripture forcefully, Tyndale engages in rhetoric that seems to limit God to his scriptural revelation. Next to the supremely confident marginal note, "What God ys," he writes, "God is that only which he testifieth of hym selfe and to imagen any other thinge of God then that / is damnable ydolatry." And this well-nigh Manichean division of creation into word and world, scripture and idol, leads to Tyndale's radical reduction of God to text: "God is but his worde."[100] In asserting the primacy and authority of scripture, Tyndale is willing to circumscribe divinity in such a way that the godhead seems to begin and end with text. Here, Tyndale appears to make the error of which Luther accused Erasmus in *The Bondage of the Will*, where Luther takes Erasmus to task for "not making any distinction between God preached and God hidden, that is, between the Word of God and God himself."[101] Luther would agree with Tyndale that "God is but his worde" *for us*; that is, in a fallen world God is present to us only in scripture. But for Luther there is a hidden or naked God, ineffable and inscrutable, above and beyond his word.[102] To conflate God and his word is to deprive him of his freedom and make him an idol. Elsewhere, Tyndale seems to reproduce Luther's argument against Erasmus, contending that we should not delve too deeply into the secrets of God's inexplicable will.[103] Here, in the heat of controversy, he radically circumscribes that ineffable God to a text that is, in his argument, easily read, easily understood. And for Tyndale, this is, crucially, a written text.

It is often thought, with good cause, that Tyndale is Luther's counterpart in England. After all, Tyndale, like Luther, translated the Bible into the vernacular. Tyndale, like Luther, believed that scripture superseded all earthly authorities and that faith alone justified. Tyndale's polemical prefaces to various texts of scripture are not only Lutheran but, in many places, simply translations of Luther. But it would be a mistake to assume that Tyndale follows Luther in all matters. The two Reformers differ on several of the crucial theological and ecclesiastical issues of the day, and they certainly differ in their understanding of the transmission of the divine word.[104] As I observed in the introduction, for Luther the word of God is fundamentally oral and aural, spoken by God and heard by those with ears to hear. If, as Jaroslav Pelikan writes, Luther's God can be characterized as "the God who speaks," Tyndale's God is the God who writes.[105] Of course, the positions of Luther and Tyndale on this issue are not so different at the end of the day: they both believe that the word of scripture is the touchstone of Christian religion and that the word must be preached. But if Luther insists that the dead letter of scripture is dependent upon the voice of the preacher to bring it to life, Tyndale insists that the preaching voice is dependent upon a prior written text. For Tyndale, the word of scripture, and thus God, exist in the fallen world as written text. This insistence on the primacy of the written word emerges most forcefully in Tyndale's controversy with Thomas More.[106]

A year after Tyndale's *Obedience* described the oppression of scripture by Antichrist, the English government issued a proclamation, most likely written under the direction of the Lord Chancellor, Thomas More, that denounced and banned the "pestiferous, cursed, and seditious errors" of "certain heretical and blasphemous books lately made and privately sent into this realm."[107] The prohibited books included, of course, Tyndale's translations of scripture. In the same year, More published *A Dialogue Concerning Heresies*, in which he, as the full title suggests, takes on "the pestylent secte of Luther & Tyndale," begun by the one on the continent and by the other "laboryd to be brought in to England."[108] Written as a dialogue between Catholic and Protestant characters referred to only as "Author" and "Messenger," More's colloquy is, among other things, concerned with refuting the Reformation doctrine of *sola scriptura* and defining the proper relationship between the written word of God and the church. Central to More's conception of Christianity is the belief that scripture does not contend with the authoritative traditions of the church because it is a privileged example of those traditions. In his *Dialogue* More consistently refers to Augustine's declaration that he would not have believed scripture if it were not for the church: "For were it not for the spyryte of god kepynge the trouthe therof in his chyrche / who coulde be sure which were the very gospels?"[109] Indeed, More is quick to point out that "Luther hym selfe is dryuen of necessyte to graunte" that the church must decide what constitutes scripture.[110] Having established the canon of scripture, the church is necessarily more authoritative than sacred texts that depend upon it for their authority. For More, scripture is the yardstick against which all other traditions of the church are measured, and yet scripture logically cannot supersede those traditions.

Tyndale countered More's critique with *An Answere vnto Sir Thomas Mores Dialoge*. In his *Answere* Tyndale returns again and again to the relation between word and church. In response to More's claim that the church necessarily precedes and therefore has priority over scripture, Tyndale offers only scorn:

> whether the church or congregation be before the gospel, or the gospel before the church . . . is as hard to solve, as whether the father be elder than the son or the son elder than his father. For the whole scripture, and all believing hearts, testify that we are begotten through the word. . . . That is, Christ must first be preached, ere men can believe in him. And then it followeth, that the word of the preacher must be before the faith of the believer. And therefore inasmuch as the word is before the faith, and faith maketh the congregation, therefore is the word or gospel before the congregation.[111]

If the relation between church and word is for More a knotty dialectic, for Tyndale it is as complex as the relation between creator and created, father and son. In Tyndale's genealogic conception of Christian history, text begets faith and faith begets church. And since the reading of a text is for Tyndale the fundamental Christian act, it is crucial that we read that text properly. For Tyndale this means a return to the original languages of scripture; this means tracing etymologies, cracking idioms, inhabiting grammars, embracing and comprehending linguistic and cultural difference. Despite the mythologizing of the renegade translator and the celebration of his translation, Tyndale is not often appreciated as one of the great English humanist scholars.[112] As formidable a linguist and philologist as England produced at the time, Tyndale turned the new learning associated with Erasmus and More against the church they represented. If Tyndale's skepticism about the ability of human "wisdom" to comprehend scripture is Lutheran, his evident faith in the philological project to excavate and reclaim linguistic meaning is decidedly Erasmian.[113] And Tyndale does not ground his faith, his church, in some elaborate interpretive schema, or in the authenticity of his personal reading; he places his faith in the text itself. For Tyndale, as he writes in the preface to his translation of the Pentateuch, the word of God "hath but one symple litteral sense."[114] In asserting the primacy of the literal sense, Tyndale does not embrace what we might call literalism. His insistence on the "one symple litteral sense" is a critique of what he considers irresponsible, and therefore idolatrous, reading: reading that substitutes human "wisdom" for God's meaning.[115] He clarifies his position in the *Obedience*: "God is a sprite and all his wordes are spirituall. His litterall sence is spirituall, and all his wordes are spirituall. . . . Finally all gods wordes are spirituall / yf thou haue eyes of God to se the ryght meanynge of the texte and where vnto the scripture perteyneth and the finall ende and cause therof."[116] Letter and spirit are one, but this does not mean that they are collapsed or conflated. Rather, they are part of a single movement, a movement from divinely authored text to divinely authorized reader ("yf thou haue eyes of God to se"). For Tyndale, the letter is always pregnant with the spirit; God's word is always in motion from hermeneutic promise to fulfillment.

"Writing Hath Bene from the Beginning"

If Tyndale espouses an Erasmian faith in the ability of written language to transcend time and place, to transcend the material conditions of its own history, More insists, with his enemy Luther, that written language is a fallen medium. In his *Dialogue* More repeatedly asserts (through the voice of the "Author") that scripture constitutes an incomplete and imperfect representation of the word of God. Pointing to the historical and fallen nature of all writing, More insists that scripture is of necessity textually corrupt and incomplete. As he writes, "some partes" of scripture are "all redy lost / more peraduenture then we can tell of," and the books we do have are necessarily "in some parte corrupted with mysse wrytynge." He contrasts Christ's "godhed" or divinity "whiche is euer beynge and present" with "holy scripture," which "had begynnynge" and may not, he shockingly claims, "endure to the worldes ende."[117] More's assault on the materiality of the biblical text is devastating: scripture is embodied and time-bound and, therefore, fallen and flawed, subject to error and decay. For More, scripture is not merely a part of the fallen, historical world; it is a direct result of the Fall. While More acknowledges that in scripture God has given the world "an inestymable treasure," he laments that the world would not have needed such a gift "yf the woundes of our owne foly had not . . . requyred it."[118] In More's account of the Fall, once Adam and Eve had broken God's commandment in paradise, the earthly struggle between flesh and spirit began, and it became the "busynesse and occupacyon of man" to discipline the body so "that it were not suffered to mayster the soule." Since attempts to "rule & brydyll sensualyte," to render the flesh "subiecte & obedyent vnto reason," were failing, it became necessary for God to intervene.[119] In his "endless mercy," God inscribed the "lawe wrytten with his owne fynger . . . in the tables of stone" so that humankind would be "put in remembraunce" of "certayne conclusyons" that "reason (ouerwhelmed wyth sensualyte) hadde than forgotten."[120] Writing, therefore, entered the fallen world in the form of the Old Testament law, a disciplinary regime made necessary by sin. Following in a long tradition that read the Mosaic law as the establishment of writing,[121] More views writing as a necessary evil in the tragic arc of Christian history before Christ.

Having aligned writing with the dead and deadly letter of the Mosaic law, More then suggests that the new law of Christ supersedes that letter:

> Lo the dayes be commynge sayd our lorde / whan I shall ordre and dyspose to the house of Israell and the house of Iuda / a newe couenaunt or testament. I shall gyue my lawe in theyr myndes. And I shal wryte it in theyr harte . . . .
>   This is called the lawe of Crystes faythe / the lawe of hys holy gospell.[122]

The finger that had written in the tables of stone now writes in the tables of the heart. Employing the figure of "writing in the heart" that recurs throughout the Old and New Testaments, More asserts that this new covenant is a covenant not of the law but of the spirit.[123] And what is crucial here for More is precisely the move from literal to figurative writing, from letter to figure, a move that signals, for More, a disavowal of the necessity of the written form. As More insists, this New Testament of faith was "reueled" by Christ's "blessyd mouth" and "by the secrete inspiracyon of god / without eyther wrytynge or any outwarde worde."[124] Disseminated through oral preaching and secret inspiration, this new covenant comprises "not onely the wordes wrytten" in the books of the evangelists, but "*moche more specyally* the substaunce of our fayth it selfe / whiche oure lorde sayd he wolde wryte in mennes hartes."[125] Because modern scholars often reproduce uncritically certain strands of Reformation thought, we tend to associate Catholicism with a dependence on external forms and Protestantism with an uncritical embrace of some inner light. When the crux is the materiality of the word of scripture, however, such binaries often break down. Here, More insists on a "secrete inspiracyon" that does not depend on an external form of any kind: "without eyther wrytinge or any outwarde worde." And More's choice of the phrase "outwarde worde" is well considered given that Luther so often spoke of the need to hold onto the *eusserlich* (outward or external) word. For Luther the external word refers to God's promises revealed in scripture and sacrament. In *The Smalcald Articles*, Luther writes

> God gives no one his Spirit or his grace except through or with the outward [*eusserlich*] word which precedes it, and this is our defence against the enthusiasts, that is, the spirits which boast that they have the Spirit without and before the word, and judge, interpret and expound thereby the scripture . . . as it pleases them. . . . Thus, to sum up, enthusiasm lurks in Adam and his children from the beginning up to the end of the world, as a poison placed in them by the ancient serpent, and it is the source, power, and might of all heresy, including that of the papacy and Mahomet. Thus we must firmly maintain that God desires to do nothing with us men except through his outward [*eusserlich*] word and sacrament.[126]

For both Luther and Tyndale, faith is always faith in an *anterior* text, a text that must be external, outward, alien. Of course, Luther believes that the medium of this external word is properly speech, and Tyndale believes that it is necessarily writing. But in either case, to confuse this external word with some inner light is to replace the sacred with the merely human, to commit idolatry. For More, in contrast, it is precisely the move from outer to inner word, from literal to figurative inscription that Christ's New Testament makes possible.

In his *Answere* Tyndale responds to More's repudiation of the authority of scripture by attacking More's account of the history of the material word. Sounding like the figure in Freud's famous joke depicting "kettle logic," Tyndale insists that writing has existed from the beginning, that even if writing proper has not always existed, God's writing has always been evident in miracles, and, finally, that sacraments and sacrifices are a form of divine writing.[127] Critiquing More's claim that writing was a late invention or intervention, Tyndale first insists that writing was around well before Moses and even Noah: "Some man would ask, How did God continue his congregation from Adam to Noe, and from Noe to Abraham, and so to Moses, without writing, but with teaching from mouth to mouth? I answer, first, that there was no scripture all the while, they shall prove when our lady hath a new son."[128]

As "stories testify," there was "writing in the world long ere Abraham yea and ere Noe."[129] Tyndale then contends that *even if* "there had been no writing" before the Mosaic law, "the preachers were ever prophets, glorious in doing of miracles, wherewith they confirmed their preaching."[130] Given that Tyndale elsewhere suggests that true preaching is corroborated by either scripture or miracles, the argument here seems to be that scripture is not strictly necessary in an age in which miracles abound and preaching can be authenticated by divine intervention.[131] The corollary to this argument would be that in the absence of authenticating miracles, scripture is the epistemological ground of knowledge in a way that speech, for Tyndale, can never be. But Tyndale also seems to be suggesting that the authenticating gesture of the miracle is a *form* of divine writing. Tyndale expands the argument by expanding the concept of writing in intriguing ways:

And beyond that, God wrote his testament unto them alway, both what to do and to believe, even in sacraments. For the sacrifices which God gave Adam's sons were no dumb popetry or superstitious mahometry, but signs of the testament of God. And in them they read the word of God, as we do in books; and as we should do in our sacraments, if the wicked pope had not taken the significations away from us, as he hath robbed us of the true sense of all the scripture. The testament which God made with Noe, that he would no more drown the world with water, he wrote in the sacrament of the rain-

bow. And the appointment made between him and Abraham he
wrote in the sacrament of circumcision. And therefore . . . "He gave
them the testament of circumcision:"[132] not that the outward circumcision was the whole testament, but the sacrament or sign thereof.
For circumcision preached God's word unto them . . .[133]

This is an extraordinary passage. Appearing to have taken up More's side of
the argument, Tyndale insists that God writes his testament in sacraments,
signs and sacrifices in which the sons of Adam read the word of God as we
read books. Unlike More, however, Tyndale is not suggesting that scripture
and sacrament are traditions of equal importance, or that writing is unnecessary because we have ritual; he is suggesting that ritual is, properly understood, a form of writing. For Tyndale, sacraments, like the "sacrifices which
God gave Adam's sons," are not the instrumental cause of grace but God's
"law and his promises" written in human practice, instructing us "both what
to do and to believe." In this version of the history of God's word, sacraments
are a form of the "outward" or "external word," which Tyndale, crucially,
considers a subset of writing.

Given Tyndale's argument against the significance of the oral transmission of the word ("teaching from mouth to mouth"), it is curious that he
contends that "circumcision *preached* God's word." But this striking figure
helps us understand Tyndale's conception of the divine word. For Tyndale,
the material trace of the text must exist before any preaching of it. Because
the word is not to be confused with human imagination or wisdom, it must
precede understanding, and in a fallen world, this means that it must exist as
an anterior, material text. But that text must be pregnant with a word that
preaches. The rainbow and circumcision are then instances of divine writing
both because they are material traces of God's testament and because they
are texts that are pregnant with meaning, texts that *call for* reading. Or as
Tyndale frames the issue, the rainbow and circumcision are examples of divine writing because they are unlike "dumb popetry or superstitious mahometry." Throughout his *Answere* Tyndale contends that we can recognize
idolatry because it is not in scripture; here, we see that we can recognize
scripture because it is not idolatrous. Unlike the "dumb shows" of Catholic
ceremony or the "superstitious idols" of Islam, which are dead letters that
never arrive at a destination, the rainbow and circumcision are letters that
point beyond themselves, that invite a figurative reading. Here, we "read the
word of god, as we do in books," and as we should do "in our sacraments, if

the wicked pope had not taken the significations away from us." For Tyndale, sacraments are sacraments only if they signify properly: "all the ceremonies and sacraments that were from Adam to Christ had significations; and all that are made mention of in the new Testament." These proper sacraments are to be contrasted with "dumb ceremony," which "edifieth not, but hurteth altogether." For Tyndale, the referential movement of language is crucial; the text must speak and must speak to the reader: "for if it preach not unto me, then I cannot . . . put confidence therein."[134] In his embrace of the referential movement of language, Tyndale sounds a lot like More. For More, however, the referential movement of language leaves the written, the dead letter, behind. Tyndale, in contrast, expands the concept of writing to include any material trace that produces this referential movement, that asks to be read "as we do . . . books."

In the version of Tyndale's *Answere* found in the edition of his *Works* collected by John Foxe and printed by John Day, the marginal note to the passage outlining the history of the word makes the remarkable claim that "writing hath bene from the beginning." The following bit of marginalia asserts that "God from the beginning hath written his will in the hartes of his elect."[135] Here, Tyndale's editors defend the authority of the written word, and Tyndale's history of that word, with the very figure that More had employed to deny that authority and that history. I would contend that this represents an acute reading of Tyndale's *Answere* to More. If More employs the figure of writing in the heart to emphasize the fundamentally Christian movement from Old to New, from literal to figurative, from letter to spirit, Tyndale insists that the letter is the sine qua non of this dialectical movement. For Tyndale, writing in the heart does not supersede the letter, the *written*; it simply creates readers who can read God's word, readers who "haue eyes of God to se[e]." In Tyndale's conception of Christianity, the fundamental Christian act is the taking up of the word in an act of reading, an act of reading that connects God as text to believer as reader.

In the exchange between More and Tyndale, we see two humanist scholars employing all the resources of the new philology to undercut the other's conception of the relation of language to the divine. In his attempt to save the church from the book, More divorces the transcendent idea of the word from the fallen materiality and historicity of writing, buttressing his radical critique of writing with a traditional faith in the church and the guiding hand of the Holy Spirit. In his desire to place the word of God beyond the reach of the authority of the church, Tyndale appeals to a written text of scripture that transcends its own historicity and materiality when it is taken up in an act of reading. And the vexed dialectic of church and book articulated by More and Tyndale would be rehearsed ad infinitum in the course of the sixteenth century, with Catholics and Protestants adopting all positions along the possible spectrum. That the Lutheran Tyndale adopts an Erasmian optimism about the ability of writing to transmit God's word and will, while Erasmus's friend and colleague More adopts a Lutheran pessimism about the ability of written language to transcend its fallen condition, is not so much an irony of history as a symptom of the contradictions that structure Christian belief, contradictions brought to the fore by the age's need to wrestle with the paradoxes of the material letter.

CHAPTER TWO

Rewriting the Letter

Textual Icons and Linguistic Artifacts in Book 1 of
The Faerie Queene

IN A COPY of the 1611 edition of Spenser's *Works*, an early seventeenth-century reader records his or her response to the first book of *The Faerie Queene* in the margins of the folio pages. Stephen Orgel has drawn our attention to this valuable archival evidence; as he writes, it offers "a rare opportunity to watch an early reader responding to Spenser."[1] The reader has obvious Protestant sympathies, and as Orgel observes, the marginalia amount to "an early Puritan commentary on *The Faerie Queene*—a manuscript text in angry dialogue with the printed poem."[2] When the Redcrosse Knight is revealed as the patron saint of England, for instance, the marginal note condemns the figure of Saint George as a "popish saint, de-vised by idle Monks."[3] Decrying what is, to this reader, the obvious idolatry of *The Faerie Queene*, Orgel's Puritan uses the margins of the page to accuse Spenser of creating and disseminating "idle [f]iction[s]" and "idle fable[s]" that smack of Catholicism.[4] If this reading seems less than responsive to the nuances of Spenser's poem, its partisan blindness does provide insight. In this chapter I want to use Orgel's reader as a guide, however errant, to the complexities of the first book of *The Faerie Queene*, the "Legend of Holiness." These polemical marginalia are instructive not because they are consistently perceptive, but because the strange reading that they document reminds us how peculiar *The Faerie Queene* must have seemed to early readers. This reading, or misreading, reminds us that the poem's notorious difficulty is not just a product of our historical distance from it, but a consequence of Spenser's grand ambitions and conflicting objectives. Moreover, the comments in the margins respond to a feature of Spenser's "Legend of Holiness" that must have confused and concerned many of Spenser's early readers and yet has often been overlooked in the poem's subsequent reception. What this particular reader, it seems, cannot help but see is that the first book of *The Faerie Queene* is an unholy hybrid of the Catholic and the Protestant.[5] How is it that a poem so invested in Reformation thought figures England as a knight identified with an iconic red cross, let alone Saint George? Crucifixes were anathema to many in Reformation England, and the cross was a matter of considerable controversy.[6] When Spenser first introduces the errant knight, he describes the religious icon that becomes synonymous with his Protestant hero: "But on his brest a bloudie Crosse he bore, / The deare remembrance of his dying Lord, / For whose sweete sake that glorious badge he wore."[7] Orgel's reader responds to the knight's red cross with a predictable if understated note: "This is not the way to adore him."[8] But the ostentatious red cross is only the most obvious instance of a problem that pervades Spenser's poem: the forms and practices of Catholicism—pilgrimages and palmers, hermits and beadsmen, rosaries and penitence—are everywhere in *The Faerie Queene*. A Protestant poem whose hero is an apocryphal Catholic saint, an iconoclastic poem that consistently relies on elaborate Catholic imagery, a self-consciously "medieval" romance that decries the devotional forms of the Middle Ages, the "Legend of Holiness" is a work whose utter strangeness has not been fully appreciated by modern readers.

From the beginning, *The Faerie Queene* announces that it will boldly use forms and terms decried by some Protestants as idolatrous remnants of Catholicism. As readers have observed, Spenser's decision to name the books of his epic "legends" might have seemed peculiar to Protestant readers since "legend" was, in Reformation England, the term for the repudiated Catholic genre of the saint's life.[9] Attending to the term "legend," however, helps the reader grasp some of the strategies Spenser deploys in the poem more generally. In the first instance, Spenser wants the reader to cast off the word's medieval and Catholic associations and return to the Latin root of legend as "what is read," from *legendum*, "thing to be read," and *legere*, "to read."[10] In other words, the reader must *reform* "legend," stripping the term of the corruptions that accrued during the dark and idolatrous interim between the primitive church and the present. And to return to this pure source, to return to the Latin root, is to be reminded that *legere* can also indicate acts of

choosing or selecting.[11] This sense of the word helps evoke Spenser's understanding of reading as an act of discerning or judging, his conviction that
reading is an ethical act. As Leigh DeNeef writes, in Spenser's fictional world,
"a world in which we are saved or lost by the moral choices we make, we
must be reminded of the fact that every perception potentially dooms us to
such a choice. We do not simply 'see' another person or event; we 'read'
them. And unless we do read them, we are likely, literally, to misread them.
The analogy between reading and ethical action is here totally collapsed."[12]
Spenser's heroes and Spenser's readers must read and choose, read and judge.
And in the Christian allegory of *The Faerie Queene*, this conflation of reading
and ethical action is also a mapping of Protestant hermeneutics onto the
generic landscape of romance. Grappling with the phenomena of a romance
milieu (wizards and witches, dwarves and dragons), Spenser's knights engage
in concrete actions that render Spenser's ethics of reformed reading legible to
the reader. Ivan Illich reminds us that "legere" is a term that evokes not only
mental but also physical activity: "The Latin *legere* . . . connotes 'picking,'
'bundling,' 'harvesting' or 'collecting,'" connections stressed by both Virgil
and Cicero.[13] Reclaiming "legend" from its association with the Catholic
genre of the saint's life, Spenser asks the reader to return to a sense of legend
as a "thing that is read," where reading is an ethical activity that anchors a
way of being and acting in the world. Nowhere is this reclamation of "legend" as a term inflected by the imperative to read and to act more evident
than in Spenser's "Legend of Holiness."

The Puritan reader lurking in the margins of Orgel's copy of Spenser's
Works offers a reminder of the potential to misread, to misunderstand the
text. To give this reader credit, however, the potential for misreading is precisely his or her point. As Orgel's reader recognizes, Spenser's poetic enterprise is one that could easily lead the undiscerning or incautious to error and
heresy. When the Redcrosse Knight kills Sans Foy, for instance, the critic in
the margins worries about less sophisticated readers: "The good knight
should have saved him, & not killed. you will say heere is a mysticall meaning. I think so, but all know not that, & therefore it is not safe to teach
murther under such pretenses."[14] Readers cannot be trusted to interpret a
complex poetic fiction like *The Faerie Queene* correctly. Spenser, of course,
was well acquainted with this concern. It is the stated rationale for the "Letter
to Raleigh" appended to the 1590 edition; "knowing how doubtfully all Allegories may be construed," Spenser offers a supplemental text that attempts
to shape the reader's interpretation of the poem.[15] Moreover, as many critics

have noted in different ways, Spenser writes the difficulty of the interpretative act into the reader's experience of *The Faerie Queene*. In the "Legend of Holiness" he does so for the simplest of reasons: to insist on the necessity and danger of reading. The "Legend of Holiness" is, in a sense, Spenser's primer for the rest of the poem; in this initial legend, he provokes the reader to attend to the complexities of language and compels the reader to take responsibility for his or her interpretive choices, interpretive acts.

* * *

In the previous chapter I outlined the logocentric positions held by Erasmus and Tyndale that would prove hugely influential to the course of the Reformation in England. Indeed, Tyndale's position in this dispute is emblematic of the English Reformation's initial embrace of the written word of scripture. Many of the theological and hermeneutic nuances of the positions held by Tyndale and Erasmus, however, would be abandoned in a determined push to replace what Reformers considered the idolatry of Catholic images and practices with writing, with text. This campaign worked according to simple dichotomies: text versus image, spirit versus letter, reading versus idolatry. Within this campaign the written word emerged as the medium of the properly iconoclastic truth. Foxe's *Actes and Monuments* contains a woodcut that encapsulates the Protestant campaign to replace the idolatry of Catholicism with the word of God. In the woodcut Justice balances "the weight and substance of Gods most blessed word against the doctrines and vanities of mans traditions"; the scales are clearly tipped in favor of a single Bible over and against a mass of Catholic apparatus including crosses, rosaries, and papal decretals (Figure 5). The material conditions of reformed worship in the Church of England revealed again and again that the centrality of scripture was the salient difference between the reformed rite and its idolatrous counterpart. During the Edwardian and Elizabethan regimes, images on the walls of churches were whitewashed and written over with select texts from scripture, often the second commandment against the worshipping of false gods.[16] Not only did the Bible (or bare cross) replace the crucifix or host on the high altar in Edwardian and Elizabethan England, but church furniture was also rearranged so that the lectern, rather than the altar or table, became the point of focus for the congregation.[17] The title-page woodcut of Foxe's *Actes and Monuments* illustrates some of the ways in which these differences in worship might be imagined in Protestant thought (Figure 6). The woodcut, which

Figure 5. "Gods most blessed word against . . . mans traditions." John Foxe, *Actes and Monuments* (1596), 1949. By permission of the Rare Book and Manuscript Library, University of Pennsylvania.

depicts Foxe's version of the "Image of Both Churches," is organized into three panels, stacked vertically; each horizontal panel consists of a pair of juxtaposed images, the church of Antichrist depicted on the right, the True church on the left. The bottom panel of the woodcut draws a comparison between Catholic and Protestant forms of worship. On the right side of the woodcut, the side of Antichrist, the viewer sees the idolatrous devotional practices of the Catholics. The members of the congregation appear to be ignoring the words of the bishop as they attend to their beads and rosaries. The focus of the image is drawn away from the lectern and toward a procession of some kind, perhaps a Corpus Christi procession. On the left side of the panel, the viewer sees the godly preaching of the reformed. The lectern is the focal point of the image; as the minister preaches, the members of the congregation piously look to him while following along in the Bibles in their laps. Three members of the congregation appear to be experiencing the inspiration of the spirit, which is represented as a vision of an illuminating sun containing the letters of the tetragrammaton. The message of the bottom

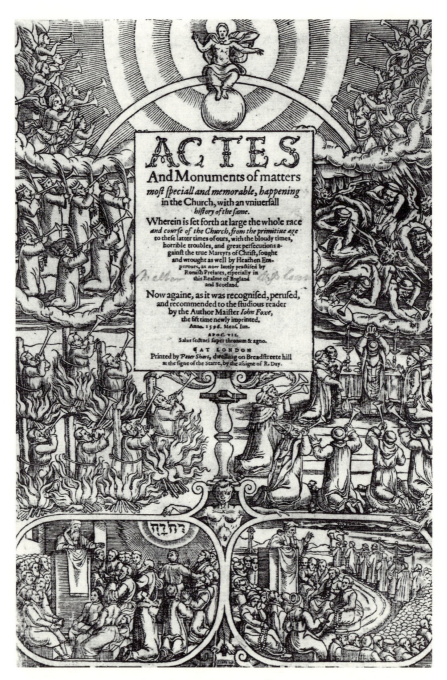

Figure 6. Title-page woodcut, John Foxe, *Actes and Monuments* (1596). By permission of the Rare Book and Manuscript Library, University of Pennsylvania.

panel is clear: the godly participate in the preaching of the gospel, which brings about spiritual edification and illumination. The papists, on the other hand, engage in ritualized processions and the recitation of empty formulae that work to obscure the gospel and maintain ignorance.

In opposing scripture and writing, books and language, to the idols and idolatry of the Catholic Church, Protestants were in danger of creating their own treacherous icon. The sacred text became the emblem of an iconoclasm that would do away with all icons, images, the stuff of Catholicism. But this sacred text—held up as the antidote to idolatry—was itself vulnerable to the charge that it had become an idol. Catholics, of course, wasted no time in denouncing the Reformers' bibliocentric dogma and devotional practices as a form of idolatry, an apotheosis of the book.[18] As I discussed in both the Introduction and Chapter 1, however, it was not merely Catholics but Protestants themselves who objected to the veneration or potential veneration of the book as object. For Reformers like Luther, writing was fallen, the physical artifact of the Bible a necessary evil. And all those supplemental and ancillary books that explained, and thus stood in the way of, the Bible were also suspect. In the preface to the 1539 edition of his German *Works*, Luther writes

> Herein I follow the example of St. Augustine, who was, among other things, the first and almost the only one who determined to be subject to the Holy Scriptures alone, and independent of the books of all the fathers and saints. On account of that he got into a fierce fight with St. Jerome, who reproached him by pointing to the books of his forefathers; but he did not turn to them. And if the example of St. Augustine had been followed, the pope would not have become Antichrist, and that countless mass of books, which is like a crawling swarm of vermin, would not have found its way into the church, and the Bible would have remained on the pulpit.[19]

In Luther's account, the Bible had been removed from its rightful place and replaced with other books, other voices, replaced with the words and arguments of men. The destruction or removal of this "countless mass of books, which is like a crawling swarm of vermin" would, in Luther's account, work to "liberate" the word of God from behind the barriers imposed by the Catholic Church. From the beginning of the Reformation, Protestants wanted to rid themselves of the plethora of ancillary books and texts that circulated in the Catholic devotional universe. Reformers maintained that in textually supplementing the word of God, the Catholic Church had displaced it. They, however, could not avoid doing the same. Luther, for instance, insists that if the church had followed Augustine's example and had been "determined to be subject to the Holy Scriptures alone," then it would not have wandered off the path of truth. The paradoxes of the familiar desire expressed here are instructive. On the one hand, Luther expresses a desire to remove from the church all those texts that surround and obscure scripture; on the other hand, he paradoxically chooses Augustine as his guide in determining that Christians be "subject to the Holy Scriptures alone." And, of course, anyone reading Luther's diatribe is reading something other than scripture; anyone assenting to Luther's argument is deferring to a nonscriptural authority.

In England, some of the more reformed Protestants, believing that the individual Christian did not need the mediating presence of the church in order to read scripture, demonized authorized, ancillary texts as a return to popery, as an idolatrous prosthetic that, in supplementing scripture, displaced it. In his *Shepheards Oracles*, Francis Quarles mockingly depicts a radical iconoclast who decries the book most emblematic of English Protestantism, the Book of Common Prayer, as

> That paper Idol; that inchaunting Spell;
> That printed Image, sent from Rome, from Hell;
> That broad-fac'd Owle, upon a carved Perch;
> That Bel and Dragon of the English Church.[20]

Quarles's radical turns the iconoclastic fervor of the Reformation toward the insufficiently reformed Church of England, and he does so by attacking the idolatry of that paper idol, the emblem of the Church of England, the Book of Common Prayer. Once an iconoclastic distrust of representation is unleashed, it can be turned on any form of representation, including language and text. For some, the Reformation desire to revere language and text as the antithesis of image, as the antidote to idolatry, only created another idol to be smashed. Spenser addresses this problem directly in his "Legend of Holiness," and he does so by littering his allegorical landscape with textual icons and linguistic artifacts, allegorical items that must be negotiated by both Spenser's hero and Spenser's reader. By examining some of the interpretive strategies Spenser embraces in the "Legend of Holiness," in this chapter I explore Spenser's quixotic attempt to write an epic poem for an iconoclastic religion of the book. Never lacking in ambition or audacity, Spenser, in his "Legend of Holiness," offers to teach Protestant England how to read.

Girdle Books and Gobbets Raw

Readers have long recognized that the problem facing the Redcrosse Knight is learning how to read. From the beginning of the "Legend of Holiness," Spenser establishes that the knight's negotiation of the allegorical landscape of faerie land is a function of his ability or inability to interpret signs—to read—and that this hermeneutic journey reflects and refracts the reader's experience of the poem.[21] At the outset of the "Legend," the knight wanders into danger having lost his way in a "shadie groue"; searching for a way out of the "labyrinth" by "tract," the Redcrosse Knight moves ever closer to Errour (1.1.11). In the first instance, "tract" here means "course, path, way, route," but it can also mean "a book or written work."[22] Reading "tract" as both track and treatise suggests that Spenser's "shadie groue" is, among other things, a specifically textual forest. A figure for both the fallen world of human experience and the fallen world of human language, the "shadie groue" in which the Redcrosse Knight loses himself is, as many commentators have noted, an offshoot of the *selva oscura* of Dante's *Inferno*. As Lawrence Warner has demonstrated, Dante's *selva oscura* can be read as part of the "topos of the Bible-as-forest, which enjoyed wide currency throughout the Middle Ages."[23] And it was not simply scripture that was a dark forest in which one could lose oneself but the textual universe that surrounded it. Tracing the sylvan metaphor from Augustine to Bonaventure, Warner argues that by the time that Dante was writing, the topos was as appropriate to the difficulty of making one's way through the daunting forest of biblical exegesis as it was to problems of contending with the obscurities of the Bible. In the *Breviloquium*, Bonaventure captures both senses of the metaphor: "These truths are so widely diffused throughout the works of saints and doctors that they could not all be read or heard by Scriptural students even in a long time. Beginners in the study of theology, in fact, often dread the Scripture itself, feeling it to be as confusing, orderless, and uncharted as some impenetrable forest."[24] Truth here is difficult to track; one could wander through the exegetes for a lifetime and not read or hear all the truths diffusely spread through their writings. Because the exegetes are themselves difficult to navigate, textual guidance is dubious, and the impenetrable forest of scripture becomes, for the beginning reader, something to dread. The darkness of Spenser's "sha-die groue" is, in part, a figure for the obscurity both of scripture and of the never-ending exegesis that envelops it.

Representing the divine truth that accompanies even fallen man, Una warns the knight of "the perill of this place" in which he finds himself; his wandering has led him toward Errour: "A monster vile, whom God and man does hate: / Therefore I read beware" (1.1.13). Reading the signs visible for those with eyes to see, Una "reads" or counsels "beware" because "this is the wandring wood, this *Errours den*" (1.1.13). Crucially, the "wandring wood" is not identical to the "shadie groue"; the Redcrosse Knight has found Errour's den by losing his way. As many readers have observed, Spenser's etymological mischievousness seems to shape the episode, as the errant knight's wandering (Latin *errare*) leads to his encounter with error; in the dream logic of Spenser's poem, the knight's errancy has created or engendered the "wandring wood."[25] If the "shadie groue" figures a dangerous thicket of text, the "wandring wood" suggests the generative capacity of misreading. When the knight persists in his resolution to move forward ("resoluing forward still to fare") despite Una's warnings that he should "stay the steppe" and "backe returne" (1.1.11, 13), he pushes onward into Errour's den and encounters a creature that is remarkably fecund:

> Of her there bred
> A thousand yong ones, which she dayly fed,
> Sucking vpon her poisonous dugs, each one
> Of sundry shapes, yet all ill fauored. (1.1.15)

Monstrous in its reproductive capacity, Errour engenders a thousand little misprisions. Misreading here is not sterile or static but dynamic and fundamentally generative; once off the path of truth, the fallen reader does not encounter an error that lies in wait but generates a capacity for error that is grotesquely limitless. The repellent image of "A thousand yong ones . . . Sucking vpon" Errour's "poisonous dugs" is reminiscent of Luther's diatribe against all those ancillary and supplemental books that surround and obscure scripture discussed above. In Luther's reading of the errors of Christian history, if the church had been "determined to be subject to the Holy Scriptures alone," then it would never have wandered off the path of truth, then "the pope would not have become Antichrist, and that countless mass of books, which is like a crawling swarm of vermin, would not have found its way into the church."[26] Earlier, I discussed the paradoxes that attend this desire to embrace scripture alone. Here, I want to note that in his metaphorical exuberance, Luther reifies Catholic error and any wandering away from the truth of the "Holy Scriptures alone" as "that countless mass of books," that "crawling swarm of vermin" that "found its way into the church." For Spenser—as for Luther in less polemical moments—such reification is itself an error. Avoiding error is not as easy as eradicating the textual vermin. In Spenser's "Legend of Holiness," the "shadie groue" is a textual wood that threatens the reader with the darkness of obscurity, but it would be a mistake to assume that the problem lies in books and texts, that error lies in wait for the unsuspecting reader and could be prevented by avoiding the dark places of the reading experience. "Errour's den" should not, of course, be sought out, but the "shadie groues" of reading cannot be circumvented. In Spenser's poem, there is no escape from text, there is no escape from the difficulties of reading; the *selva oscura* of text is simply the world in which the Redcrosse Knight and the Christian reader live and move.

When the Redcrosse Knight defeats the monstrous serpent-woman Error, she "spewd out of her filthy maw / A floud of poyson horrible and blacke" not only "Full of great lumpes of flesh and gobbets raw" but also "full of bookes and papers" (1.1.20). Editors and critics have read these "bookes and papers" as a figure for, among other things, the printing press, "Catholic propaganda directed against Elizabeth I and the established church," and the "theological books, tracts and pamphlets" of religious controversy.[27] All of these glosses reasonably point to "bookes and papers" that exist in the world and that might lead the Christian reader to error. These readings logically infer a Protestant animus against Catholic text, Catholic error. As readers of Spenser's poem, however, we are in danger of repeating the Redcrosse Knight's error if we assume that we can quickly grasp and easily constrain the allegorical significance of these "bookes and papers." Orgel's reformed reader is a surprisingly useful guide to the complexities of this passage. In the margins of this episode, Orgel's reader writes that a "part of this book"—in other words *The Faerie Queene* itself—is in the books and papers that Errour vomits.[28] If Spenser's figure for Errour gives rise to heretical writings, erroneous texts, then, according to this reader, Spenser's poem should take its place besides all the other treatises and tracts that lead readers astray. Although this reading in the margins consistently mangles the poem—or rather precisely because it consistently mangles the poem—it is not clear that Orgel's Puritan reader has the wrong idea about this passage.

As the hostile marginalia amply demonstrate, *The Faerie Queene* is always in danger of being read incorrectly, always in danger of becoming a source of error. If Spenser could write back to his reader, he would probably agree that the Puritan's rendering of the poem does belong in Errour's vomit. Whatever the Puritan reader intends, what this reading suggests is that Errour's vomit might be a figure not for erroneous texts to be avoided but for texts that have been misread.

Errour's book-ridden vomit is a parodic reversal of Revelation's strikingly material metaphor for receiving the word: the eating of the scroll that is sweet in the mouth and bitter in the stomach.[29] In his *Image of Both Churches*, John Bale glosses this passage in Revelation: "With good harte ought the scriptures to be receyued of all men, in faith deuoured, & in a pure loue digested. . . . Nothing but idlenesse worketh that man, which hath it not grafted within him, though he both fast & pray."[30] Errour's books and papers are not, to use Bale's terns, "in faith devoured" or in "pure love digested." Rather, like the other elements of Errour's vomit, they are "great lumpes" of undigested material, "gobbets raw" (1.1.20). The word "gobbet" was used in religious controversy of the early modern period to designate undigested scraps of text (usually from scripture or the church fathers) that were quoted out of context and thus misunderstood. This kind of reading was denounced both by Catholics and by Reformers as a reification of text that could lead to error and heresy. Bale himself uses the word in this way in his *Apology . . . agaynste a ranke Papyst* when he denounces his Catholic antagonist for employing "ragged gobbettes taken out of Ambroses glose" to shore up his argument; according to Bale, the "ranke Papyst" was always leaving the "best partes" of the church father "behynde."[31] Improperly citing scripture or other authoritative writings, improperly removing passages from context, and improperly arresting the movement of text are reifications viscerally captured in the term "gobbets." "Ragged gobbettes taken out of Ambroses glose" suggest undigested language, text unnaturally ripped from its proper place and swallowed whole. When addressing scripture or the texts that surround and supplement it, such reading necessarily leads to Christian error. Francis Bacon, in his essay "Of Studies" (1612), writes, "Some bookes are to bee tasted, others to bee swallowed, and some few to be chewed and digested. That is, some bookes are to be read only in parts; other to bee read, but not curiously; and some few to bee read wholly, and with diligence and attention."[32] For Spenser and most readers in Reformation England, scripture is a book to be "chewed and digested," to be "read wholly, and with diligence and attention." To fail to chew and digest properly, to fail, as Bale says, to have scripture "grafted within," is to reify text, to make it an object, a "gobbet" that can only be vomited up as error.

The danger for the reader of Spenser's poem is to fail to digest the complex significance of Errour. In a sense, to name or categorize the "bookes and papers" that are vomited up by Errour is to reiterate the erroneous reading strategies that produced them; it is to fix and reify error and to transform Spenser's poem into "gobbets raw."[33] To the consternation of censors and book-burners, error does not lie in wait for the reader within certain designated texts, texts that can be prohibited or destroyed to protect the reader from contamination. For Spenser, error is the inevitable result of textual wandering, and textual wandering is inevitable. The mistake is to assume that one can either avoid an error fixed in place or destroy an error reified as a thing, which is precisely the lesson that the Redcrosse Knight fails to learn in this early episode. The monster Errour that the knight encounters is, of course, a reification of error. That reification of this kind is one of the fundamental ways in which allegory works should not blind the reader to its dangers.[34] With the assistance of divine truth, with the assistance of faith ("Add faith vnto your force," 1.1.19), the Redcrosse Knight is able to overcome the monster, but how is the reader to understand this "defeat" of error? If we removed this episode from the context of the journey, if we read it as a ragged gobbet or gobbet raw, it would appear that the Redcrosse Knight, with the help of divine truth, had, once and for all, defeated error. To read further, however, is to chew on the fact that the knight will continue to err, that he will, in fact, be separated from divine truth in the very next episode. Having lost his way in the Wandering Wood, Redcrosse is always in proximity to "Errours den" and will remain so until he defeats error in its final incarnation as the infernal dragon of Canto 11, a monster that, like Errour, also has a mouthful of "gobbets raw" (1.11.13).

The allegorical reduction of error to "Errour" performs, I contend, important work in *The Faerie Queene*. At the beginning of his poem, Spenser presents his reader with the reification of error so that the reader is aware ("Therefore I read beware," 1.1.13) of the error of reification.[35] To transform abstractions into things is to falsify them, to misunderstand them, to misread. As Orgel's reader suggests, *The Faerie Queene* itself belongs in the "books and papers" vomited up by Errour—as does, crucially, scripture, as does any text improperly chewed and digested. At the same time, reification is not something that can be avoided; it is not simply a feature of allegory but a feature of human thought and language. When reading the episode of the "wandring wood," it is important to remember that "error" is already a reification before the reader ever gets to "Errour." The term "error" is simply an abstraction that affords the illusion of grasping a variety of human activities and experiences that are impossible to comprehend in all their permutations, impossible to grasp except by the reduction of naming and classifying. Spenser's monster "Errour" merely completes a process already begun by the naming of error as "error," already begun by language itself. If the poem alerts us to the dangers of such naming, it does not suggest that we can avoid these dangers. By staging the problem of reification, a problem endemic not only to allegory but to all reading, Spenser warns the reader of the danger of the book he or she holds in hand. The danger lies in the assumption that readerly error is easily found, easily avoided, easily overcome. The error lies in the assumption that error can be defeated in a fallen world.

* * *

In an elegant reading, Mark Rose suggests that the first canto of Spenser's "Legend of Holiness" forms a diptych. After the opening episode with Errour, the reader

> should notice that we are exactly midway in the first canto: the
> dragon episode has taken 27 stanzas; stanza 28, describing how the
> knight and lady found their way out of the forest and search for new
> adventure, forms a kind of pivot; and the canto's second episode,
> the adventures in Archimago's hermitage, occupies another 27 stan-
> zas. . . . The first canto may be thought of as a kind of diptych, with
> the two episodes balanced against each other like panels in a double
> painting placed side by side for comparison.[36]

In my reading of this opening canto, the two panels of the diptych present the reader with two errors relating to text and language, two errors that threaten acts of reading. The first panel confronts the reader with the error of reifying language, the error of treating texts like objects; the second portrays the error of fetishizing language, the error of treating the textual object like an idol. These encounters with erroneous reading would seem to be part of the reformation of both the Redcrosse Knight and Spenser's reader. Their adversary in this heuristic wandering is Archimago, the Spenserian embodiment of idolatrous misreading. Like Redcrosse's wayward course, however, Archimago's deception is potentially a salutary aspect of the journey for both hero and reader. Luther, when reflecting on his struggles in reading scripture, acknowledged both the importance of textual difficulty and the contribution of the devil: "my spiritual trials [*tentationes*] were of help to me . . . for one does not learn anything" without such struggles. According to Luther, these trials are what his rivals lack: "They don't have the right adversary, the devil. He would teach them well."[37] Archimago is the devil who would teach Spenser's knight how to survive in this strange land and teach Spenser's reader how to read this strange text.

The reader is fully made aware of Archimago's idolatrous nature through his engagement with text, specifically "His Magick bookes and artes of sundry kindes" (1.1.36). Consulting these "balefull bookes," Archimago

> . . . choosing out few wordes most horrible,
> (Let none them read) thereof did verses frame
> With which and other spelles like terrible,
> He bad awake blacke Plutoes grisly Dame,
> And cursed heaven, and spake reprochfull shame
> Of highest God, the Lord of Life and light. (1.2.2, 1.1.37)

On the one hand, Archimago's books seem to figure the perverted texts of the Roman Catholic Church. They seem to ally Spenser's "Legend of Holiness" with Reformation polemic that insisted that both the sacralized object and the verbal incantation were the playthings of Antichrist.[38] On the other hand, Spenser seems here to mock the notion of "baleful bookes," the idea of "wordes most horrible." The parenthetical aside—"Let none them read"—hints at the derision underlying the depiction of the wizard in his study. The aside stands in place of the words Spenser refuses to give to the reader; the narrator's hyperbolic interjection marks the spot where such words might have been, redundantly instructing the reader not to look. Skipping over these "wordes most horrible," the narrator rushes on to the evidently less horrible actions in which Archimago engages: conjuring figures from the netherworld, cursing heaven, speaking reproachfully of "highest God." These actions the narrator can, evidently, relate in good conscience, but he must intervene lest the reader see the "few wordes" that Archimago chooses. In the context of the sacrilegious actions described, the hilariously breathless aside works to deride the very notion of "wordes most horrible," works to scorn the idea that words can be "horrible" when divorced in some way from the actions that frame them. This movement back and forth between a desire to warn the reader of the dangers of idolatry and a desire to mock the absurd emptiness of idolatry seems characteristic of the "Legend of Holiness." In this episode Spenser's allegory concretizes and dramatizes the common Protestant rhetorical claim that Catholic priests were wizards and sorcerers by showing Archimago as a diviner of secret and bookish knowledge.[39] While some Protestants maintained that the Catholic Church had very real dealings with demonic forces, however, others accused Catholic priests of being charlatans preying upon the superstitious. What is curious about Spenser's allegory is that it attempts to have it both ways: Archimago seems to be both powerful conjurer and duplicitous fraud.

Although the invocation of his "Magick bookes" is the first explicit revelation of Archimago's diabolical practices in *The Faerie Queene*, Spenser throws suspicion on the "godly father" from his introduction to the poem (1.1.33). Early in the canto, two signs suggest heterodoxy: Archimago's apparent faith in the efficacy of mechanical devotional practice and his evident belief in the sanctity of material things.[40] I would contend that this faith in empty words and worthless things manifests itself in the very first clue to Archimago's idolatry: his girdle book. When the Redcrosse Knight and Una first "chaunst to meet" Archimago "vpon the way," they see

> An aged Sire, in long blacke weedes yclad,
> His feete all bare, his beard all hoarie gray.
> And by his belt his booke he hanging had. (1.1.29)

The book that "by his belt . . . he hanging had" is not a sign of Archimago's devotion to the Bible but the first clue to Archimago's affiliation with the various perversions of scripture found in Spenser's "Legend of Holiness." Usually a breviary or some other devotional aid, the early modern girdle book was used in Protestant iconography as a marker of Catholics' sanctimonious display of devotion to the gospel and of their misplaced trust in the props of piety (Figure 7). Identifying Archimago as either hypocritical fraud or superstitious idolater, the girdle book suggests that he is implicated in the errors of the Catholic Church.

Stephen Bateman's *Christall Glasse of Christian Reformation* contains a series of woodcuts depicting Catholic vices and reformed virtues in which the proper and improper use of books and scripture figure prominently. The

Figure 7. Girdle book of Boethius, *De Consolatione Philosophiae*. By permission of Beinecke Rare Book and Manuscript Library, Yale University.

proper relation to scripture is depicted in an image portraying Faith. In this woodcut a figure dressed in the Pauline "armor of a Christian man" stands astride the defeated devil and gazes up at a sun that blazes forth with the light of the tetragrammaton (Figure 8).[41] One of the more striking features of this woodcut is its use of the tetragrammaton as a kind of iconic inscription, an image invoking the properly textual inspiration of the spirit, an emblem of true reading.[42] The tetragrammaton enjoyed something of a vogue in the Reformation. Since representations of the deity were avoided as idolatrous within printed books and manuscripts of the period, the divine was often

Figure 8. "Of Faith." Stephen Bateman, *Christall Glasse of Christian Reformation* (1569), M4v. By permission of Beinecke Rare Book and Manuscript Library, Yale University.

figured in woodcuts by the untranslated tetragrammaton, God's name in the original Hebrew. Elizabeth Ingram and Ruth Luborsky's *Guide to English Illustrated Books, 1536–1603* reproduces a number of images in which the tetragrammaton is deployed in a Christian context. Some of these images seem to be simple representations of the deity presiding over creation. Other woodcuts mirror the image in Bateman's book insofar as the tetragrammaton depicts an experience of the divine as revelation. In many of these images, the tetragrammaton is placed within an image of a brightly shining sun so that the divine, or the human experience of the divine, is represented as an experience of language and light, or as enlightenment through text. In one—"The pope falling from an ass" (Figure 9)—the rays of the tetragrammaton-inscribed sun topple the pope from his mount. This scene seems to be an inversion of Saul's conversion to Paul on the road to Tarsus. In Christianity's

And then shal that wicked be vtte-
red, whom the lord shal consume with
the spirete of his mouth, and shal destroy with the apperaunce of his co-
mynge, euen him whose comming is
after the workinge of Sathan.

Figure 9. "The pope falling from an ass." Title-page woodcut, Walter Lynne, *The Beginning and Endynge of All Popery* (1548). This item is reproduced by permission of The Huntington Library, San Marino, California.

most famous conversion scene, Saul sees a light from heaven that forces him to the ground; a voice then speaks to him and he is converted to Christianity. Here, the pope falls from his mount not, presumably, because he is being converted to the true faith but because he is being defeated by it. The wood-cut is an anti-papal satire depicting the way that the light of the true gospel will illuminate what the pope and his Church would keep in darkness, thereby defeating darkness through light, ignorance through text. In the woodcut depicting Faith in Bateman's *Christall Glasse*, the iconic force of the untranslated tetragrammaton is used to signify the direct and unmediated communion between the gospel and the believer who has "put on Christ" (Romans 13:14); it functions as an icon of a properly linguistic faith. And here we can see that the tetragrammaton is useful to Reformers because it is an icon that is textual, abstract; the very abstractness of the tetragrammaton suggests that it does not represent but simply points to the deity. Paradoxi-cally, the linguistic icon of the tetragrammaton is employed to figure a certain iconoclastic directness and transcendent immediacy.

Other woodcuts from *Christall Glasse* illustrate the contrast between Faith's properly reformed relation to the Bible and that of the Catholic who turns scripture into an idol. Indeed, many of the woodcuts depicting the vices in Bateman's treatise portray Catholic figures with conspicuous girdle books (Figures 10–13). The depiction of Envy, for instance, portrays a bishop and friar attempting to drag a godly preacher bodily from the pulpit (Figure 10). According to the caption, "He which preacheth in the pulpit, signifieth godly zeale, & a furtherer of the gospel: and the two which are plucking him out of his place are the enemies of God's word, threatning by fire to consume the professors of the same."[43] The tonsured friar "plucking him out his place" is outfitted in robe and ostentatious girdle book.[44] The woodcuts depicting Wrath, Treason, and Lechery likewise portray idolatrous Catholics whose acccssory of choice is the girdle book. In the illustration of Lechery, a friar and nun are found in a carnal embrace flanked by two devils; not only does the lecherous friar wear a girdle book, but so does the more prominent of the two "deuill[s]" (Figure 13). Foxe's *Actes and Monuments* similarly employs the girdle book as an emblem of the hypocrisy of Catholicism. In a variety of woodcuts, the girdle book is employed to figure the posturing of idolaters who are, in fact, "enemies of God's word" (Figures 14–18). The woodcut depicting "Friers pulling Bilney out of the pulpit" depicts John Bilney, the Protestant preacher, literally plucked out of the pulpit while preaching the gospel; he is dragged away by a friar who wears a girdle book (Figure 14).[45]

Figure 10. "Of Enuie." Stephen Bateman, *Christall Glasse of Christian Reformation* (1569), G4v. By permission of Beinecke Rare Book and Manuscript Library, Yale University.

The woodcut suggests a clear contrast between scripture reading as meaningful action in the world and Christian text as ossified artifact.[46]

One way to make sense of the use of the girdle book in anti-Catholic iconography is to read it in relation to the anti-Semitic animus against Jewish phylacteries. In Deuteronomy, God enjoins Israel to remember and revere his word:

> Heare, o Israel, The Lord our God is Lorde onely, And thou shalt
> loue the Lord thy God with all thine heart, with all thy soule, and
> with all thy might. And these wordes which I commande thee this
> day, shalbe in thine heart. And thou shalt rehearse them continually
> vnto thy children, and shalt talke of them when thou tariest in thine
> house, and as thou walkest by the way, and when thou lyest downe,
> and when thou risest vp: And thou shalt binde them for a signe

Figure 11. "Of Wrath." Stephen Bateman, *Christall Glasse of Christian Reformation* (1569), C4r. By permission of Beinecke Rare Book and Manuscript Library, Yale University.

vpon thine hand, and they shalbe as frontelets betwene thine eyes. Also thou shalt write them vpon the postes of thyne house and vpon thy gates.[47]

In Judaism this injunction in Deuteronomy is honored by the wearing of *tefillin*, small boxes containing scriptural texts, on the head and arm, and the posting of the *mezuzah*, a box containing scriptural texts, to doorframes. This reading of the injunction in Deuteronomy was employed by Christian writers to invoke or describe the threat of literal reading, the danger of idolatrously embracing the letter rather than the spirit of scripture. Glossing this text in his *Sermons on Deuteronomy* (1583), Calvin writes that the "Iewes" method of reading this passage represents an occasion "to bewaile the corruption of mankinde" since "the Iewes which were Gods people" turned the text into

Figure 12. "Of Treason." Stephen Bateman, *Christall Glasse of Christian Reformation* (1569), D1r. By permission of Beinecke Rare Book and Manuscript Library, Yale University.

"a charme and sorcerie."[48] Following in a long anti-Semitic tradition, Calvin reads the *tefillin* and *mezuzot* of Judaism as idolatrous perversions of the passage in Deuteronomy; for Calvin the problem is a superstitious adherence to the letters of scripture: "the Iewes . . . haue abused euen the very letters" of the text. In Christian thought the "phylactery" became an emblem of this abuse. "Phylactery" is a transliteration of the Greek term employed in the New Testament to designate the *tefilla*, and in Reformation England, "phy-lactery" would become a byword for hypocritical displays of piety as well as abuses of the letter.[49] That the threat of this hypocrisy and this abuse is a pressing contemporary issue is clarified in Calvin's sermon when he compares the *tefillin* to the wearing of "the *Agnus Dei* in poperie, and to such other geugawes as the papists hang about their necks."[50] As I suggested in the Introduction, the Judaism imagined by Christianity was crucial to the articulation of a Christian ambivalence toward the letter. Those figures—like Ar-

Figure 13. "Of Lecherie." Stephen Bateman, *Christall Glasse of Christian Reformation* (1569), D4v. By permission of Beinecke Rare Book and Manuscript Library, Yale University.

chimago or Calvin's "papists" with their "geugawes" about their necks—who "abused euen the very lettres" of scripture were often denounced as "Judaizers," those who could not transcend the letter.[51]

If the passage in Deuteronomy was an occasion to "bewaile the corruption" of those who abused scripture, then it was also an occasion to celebrate proper Christian reading. According to Calvin, if this passage is interpreted correctly, the reader will understand that the fulfillment of the Deuteronomic injunctions "consisteth not in the doing of a sort of Ceremonies, nor in pretending faire countenances, by wearing texts of Gods law vpon our apparel." Rather, the passage enjoins the reader to keep God's word in sight and mind; for Calvin, the word of God must be "grauen in our heartes, as it may neuer be wiped out againe."[52] Read as an insistence that scripture remain always before the Christian reader, this passage in Deuteronomy became in

Figure 14. "Friers pulling [John] Bilney out of the pulpit." John Foxe, *Actes and Monuments* (1596), 912. By permission of the Rare Book and Manuscript Library, University of Pennsylvania.

the Reformation a touchstone for those who championed the vernacular Bible. In *The Obedience of a Christian Man*, William Tyndale uses this passage in his defense of an English Bible:

> Moyses [Moses] saith . . . Heare Israel let these wordes which I commaunde the this daye steke fast in thine herte / and whette them on thy childerne . . . & bynde them for a token to thine hande / & let them be a remembraunce betwene thine eyes / and write them on the postes & gates of thine house. This was commanuded generally vnto all men. How cometh it that Gods worde perteneth lesse vnto vs then vnto them? Yee how cometh it that oure Moyseses forbydde vs and commaund vs the contrary / & threate vs yf we doo / & will not that we once speake of Gods worde?[53]

For Tyndale it is unthinkable that Christians should be denied access to scripture when those born before the new dispensation of Christ were sur-

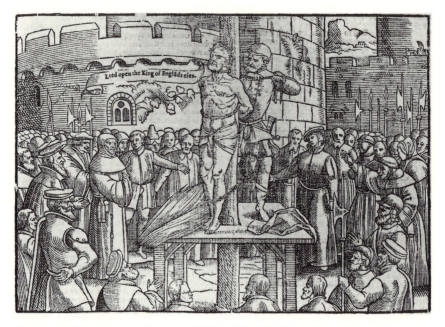

Figure 15. "The burning of maister William Tindall." John Foxe, *Actes and Monuments* (1596), 985. By permission of the Rare Book and Manuscript Library, University of Pennsylvania.

rounded by God's word: "What shulde be the cause that we which walke in the brode daye / shulde not se / as well as they that walked in the night / or that we shulde not se as well at none [noon] / as they dyd in the twylighte? Came Christe to make the worlde moare blynde?"[54] The "Moyseses" of the Roman Church would keep Christians from scripture, would keep Christians in darkness. In light of this Reformation reading of the passage, the animus against the girdle book one sees in Protestant iconography must be read carefully. Given Tyndale's reading of Deuteronomy, it would seem that any material form that allows one to keep the text of scripture close to hand would be beneficial to the Christian reader who desires to keep the word of God forever in sight and mind. And, in fact, in Foxe's *Actes and Monuments* there is at least one moment in which the girdle book is employed as an emblem of Protestant fidelity to scripture.

Depicting the degradation and execution of Hugh Latimer, Foxe lingers over a description of Latimer's clothing and accoutrements. Brought before the Bishop of Lincoln for examination, Latimer appeared "wearing an old three bare Bristow frise gown girded to his body with a peny leather girdle,

Figure 16. "The burning of . . . Thomas Cranmer." John Foxe, *Actes and Monuments* (1596), 1713. By permission of the Rare Book and Manuscript Library, University of Pennsylvania.

at the which hanged by a long string of leather his Testament, and his specta-cles without case, depending about his necke vpon his breast."[55] For Foxe, Latimer's threadbare apparel signifies that he has eschewed the trappings of this world and "put on Christ." The Testament that hangs from his girdle and the spectacles without case "depending about his neck" demonstrate that in wearing Christ he has properly divested himself of all idolatrous ornamen-tation and invested himself, body and soul, in the gospel. Always at the ready, the "Testament" as girdle book here serves as a sign of the kind of constant immersion in scripture that Reformers celebrated.[56] The fact that Foxe re-cords an example of a virtuous use of a girdle book in the text of *Actes and Monuments* while deploying the girdle book as a sign of Catholic hypocrisy in the images of his woodcuts helps explain the different ways in which the girdle book might signify. For Reformers like Foxe, books are meant to be read; in the medium of the woodcut, however, the girdle book—as long as it remains an ornament or accessory—tends to function as a static sign. To the extent that it is merely decorative, it is an idol. One of the woodcuts in Foxe's "Book of Martyrs" illustrates this distinction. In "The talke betwene M.

Figure 17. "Nicholas Burton . . . to the burning." John Foxe, *Actes and Monuments* (1596), 1865. By permission of the Rare Book and Manuscript Library, University of Pennsylvania.

Bradford and two Spanish fryers," the girdle book of one of the Spanish friars is juxtaposed with Bradford's Bible—a book of similar proportions, but a book that is held in the hand for use and not worn on the body for superstitious or ornamental purposes (Figure 18). This image dramatizes why the girdle book became such an ambivalent icon for Reformers. It is precisely because the proper veneration of scripture exemplified by Latimer's Testament or Bradford's Bible was so central to Protestants' sense of themselves that any Catholic perversion of that devotion must be denounced and ridiculed. It is, however, not always easy to read the difference between a book employed in godly edification and a book deployed for show. In Spenser's "Legend of Holiness," neither the Redcrosse Knight nor Spenser's reader can properly interpret Archimago's girdle book before they know more, before they know what kind of reader Archimago is. As is so often the case in the "Legend of Holiness," we read correctly only in retrospect. This is, in a sense, Spenser's point. That neither the Redcrosse Knight nor the reader can be expected to "read" the significance of Archimago's book at first glance is simply an aspect of the poem's solicitation of doubt and uncertainty, its invitation to salutary error.

Figure 18. "M. Bradford . . . and two Spanish Friers." John Foxe, *Actes and Monuments* (1596), 1469. By permission of the Rare Book and Manuscript Library, University of Pennsylvania.

The Labor Theory of Idolatry

In the "Legend of Holiness" Spenser not only depicts a range of idolatrous texts and books but also elaborates an iconoclastic hermeneutics that distinguishes between a properly transcendent reading and an idolatrous tarrying with letters and things. To make this interpretative program visible to the reader, he dramatizes the ways in which idolatry arises from spiritual and interpretive idleness. In Spenser's Palace of Pride, the first of Queen Lucifera's seven counselors, and thus the first of the seven deadly sins, is "sluggish *Idlenesse*," the "nourse of sin" (1.4.18). That Idleness leads the way in this pageant of sins suggests a diabolic inversion of the seventh as the day of rest. That he "all the rest did guyde" suggests both that he is the gateway to the other sins and that—as the resident authority on things indolent—he coordinates all repose (1.4.18). The curious prominence of Idleness in this procession is consistent with Spenser's conception of sin and idolatry throughout the "Legend of Holiness." The Redcrosse Knight repeatedly stops "in middest of the race," allowing his mission to languish as he engages in idle pursuits that inevitably result in idolatry (1.7.5).[57] In the Palace of Pride episode, the emblematic figure of Idleness is described as being arrayed like a "holy Monck"; in his hand he carries "his Portesse" that "much was worne, but therein little red" (1.4.18–19).[58] An unread "Portesse" or portable breviary suggests not only an idle reader but also an idle book. That Idlenesse's prayer book is "worne, but therein little red" suggests not only a calculated attempt to make the book look worn from use but also that the "portesse" is a bit of apparel, another girdle book. Unused, unread, the book presents a false image of godly edification. Derelict in the godly duty signified by his monk's garb, Lucifera's Idleness is a figure of the "idol shepherd." Drawn from Zechariah—"O idole shepherd that leueth the flocke"[59]—this figure was frequently employed in Reformation polemic to attack ignorant and negligent priests and ministers.[60] According to the *Oxford English Dictionary*, the term "idol" was used "sometimes with allusion to idolatry, sometimes with idol taken as 'counterfeit' or 'sham' . . . [and] sometimes associated with idle and so 'neglectful of duty.'"[61] In Reformation discourse, the proverbial figure of the "idol shepherd" articulated a strong cultural association between idleness as neglect and idolatry as bad faith. In Spenser's figure of Idleness, this idea is translated into the realm of reading as the unused or idle book becomes an emblem of indolence and idolatry.[62] The pun on "idol" and "idle" implicit in the notion of the "idol shepherd" was a common one in Reformation discourse, one that offered a kind of shorthand for the hermeneutic and spiritual negligence that led to idolatry. In *The Faerie Queene*, Spenser takes this pun seriously and employs it to articulate an iconoclastic hermeneutics, an ethics of reading the book and the world.

The Redcrosse Knight's epic quest is consistently threatened by romance digression. As Patricia Parker has brilliantly argued, the genre of romance is essentially digressive and dilatory, the characteristic deferrals and detours of romance holding off the quiescence and finality of narrative endings with endless story.[63] Epic, in contrast, is purpose driven, pushing forward toward some *telos*, the completion of epic labors.[64] As readers have long noticed, in Spenser's "Legend of Holiness," the traditional tension between epic and romance is mapped onto a Christian hermeneutics that insists that divine truth is the *telos* toward which all pilgrims must progress and all reading ought to advance. When the Redcrosse Knight is deterred from his path, from his mission, this signals interpretive danger as the knight is tarrying with false signs and barren idols. Harnessing the reader's generic expectations,

Spenser makes the sin of idleness crucial to Redcrosse's failures as both epic knight and Christian reader. Emerging wounded and weary from Lucifera's House of Pride, the Redcrosse Knight has survived but has not spiritually prevailed. Afflicted with lingering hubris, the knight decides to pause in an idyllic site to feed "vpon the cooling shade" and rest

> His sweatie forehead in the breathing wind,
> Which through the trembling leaues full gently playes
> Wherein the cherefull birds of sundry kind
> Do chaunt sweet musick, to delight his mind. (1.7.3)

Against the common sense dictated by both romance and allegory, Redcrosse then lays down his weapons; he subsequently finds himself not only "disarmed all of yron-coted Plate" but also "disgrast, and inwardly dismayed" (1.7.2,11). Guilty of the pride of complacency, he assumes he can do without the armor of a Christian man,[65] and with this assumption he not only proves himself foolish but renders himself faithless.[66] Dallying with the false Duessa, the weakened knight is "Pourd out in looseness on the grassy grownd, / Both careless of his health, and of his fame" (1.7.7). In a richly overdetermined allegorical moment, Spenser aligns romance digression and the sin of idleness with the infidelity that is idolatry. The Christian commonplace that idolatry was spiritual fornication arose from the recurrent Old Testament refrain that worshipping false idols was a form of whoring, a form of adultery that betrayed the jealous Christian God.[67] In a particularly Spenserian-sounding passage, the prophet Hosea warns that "the spirit of whoredoms hath caused them [the children of Israel] to err, and they have gone a whoring from under their God."[68] In his dalliance with Duessa, the Redcrosse Knight's idleness, his "spirit of whoredom," literally gives rise to the giant Orgoglio. The phallic giant has been read variously as a materialization of pride, lust, and the empty pomp of the Roman Catholic Church. He is, of course, all of these, as well as a manifestation of the Redcrosse Knight's idleness.

The relation between romance digression and the Christian sin of idleness is most fully developed in Book Two of *The Faerie Queene*, the "Legend of Temperance." Spenser elaborates this relation through his depiction of two romance idylls: Phaedria's isle at the center of the Lake of Idleness and Acrasia's enchanted bower. The latter episode in particular helps the reader understand the threat to chivalric and Christian identity that idleness and infidelity represent. At the heart of Acrasia's Bower of Bliss, Spenser unveils a *tableau vivant* of idleness in which another of his knights loses both self and purpose:

> There, whence that Musick seemed heard to bee,
> Was the faire Witch her selfe now solacing,
> With a new Louer, whom through sorceree
> And witchcraft, she from farre did thither bring:
> There she had him now layd a slombering,
> In secret shade, after long wanton ioyes. (2.12.72)

That Verdant, the wayward knight, has erred in wandering into Acrasia's "secret shade" is only too evident when the poem describes the tools of his trade:

> His warlike armes, the idle instruments
> Of sleeping praise, were hong vpon a tree
> And his braue shield, full of gold moniments,
> Was fowly ra'st, that none the signes might see. (2.12.80)

Having paused, like Redcrosse before him, to dally "in middest of the race," Verdant has abandoned his calling and had his identity as a warrior of Christ "fowly ra'st" (1.7.5; 2.12.80). The seemingly unmotivated apostrophe within "ra'st" indicates something missing at the heart of both word and knight. In describing the erasure of Verdant's shield, "ra'st" plays on the early modern understanding of "race" as "genealogy." Not only is Verdant emasculated and rendered purposeless through the neglect of his "warlike armes," but the foul erasure of his brave shield—"that none the signes might see"—also blinds him to his history and true identity. His idleness has made him both idolater, one who engages in spiritual fornication, and idol, a static sign that fails to signify.[69] In early modern England, the word "idle" referred not only to people "not engaged in work" and to objects "characterized by inaction" but to anything "void of any real worth, usefulness, or significance . . . hence, ineffective, worthless, of no value, vain, frivolous, trifling." The precise etymological development of the term is obscure, but the original sense was evidently "empty," "worthless," "useless," "vain."[70] The denizens of the Bower of Bliss are idle in all senses of the term: not working toward the truth of God, they are characterized by their inaction and become empty things without value. As Calvin suggests in his *Institutes*, the idolater will become like his idol: "Many are so delighted with marble, gold, & paintings, that they become as it were men made of marble, that they be as it were turned into metalles, & be like vnto painted images."[71]

For Spenser, this is the danger of a hermeneutic idleness: tarrying with the signs and things of this world will lead to an idolatry that hardens one's heart and renders one idle, a thing without worth or use. In *De Doctrina Christiana*, Augustine famously contends that *caritas* or love is "the motion of the soul toward the enjoyment of God for His own sake," while *cupiditas* or desire is "a motion of the soul toward the enjoyment of one's self, one's neighbor, or any corporal thing for the sake of something other than God."[72] For Augustine, Christian hermeneutics—a hermeneutics that teaches one how to read text and world—depends upon a fundamental distinction between use and enjoyment: "Some things are to be enjoyed, others to be used. . . . To enjoy something is to cling to it with love for its own sake. To use something, however, is to employ it in obtaining that which you love."[73] Use is a means to an end; enjoyment the end in itself. And, of course, God alone is to be enjoyed; to enjoy elsewhere is to commit infidelity, idolatry. Anticipating *The Faerie Queene*, Augustine translates this idea into a metaphor that speaks to the situation of Spenser's errant knights:

> Suppose we were wanderers who could not live in blessedness except
> at home, miserable in our wandering and desiring to end it and
> return to our native country. . . . But if the amenities of the journey
> . . . [themselves] delighted us, and we were led to enjoy those things
> which we should use, we should not wish to end our journey
> quickly, and, entangled in a perverse sweetness, we should be alien-
> ated from our country, whose sweetness would make us blessed.
> Thus in this mortal life, wandering from God, if we wish to return
> to our native country where we can be blessed we should use this
> world and not enjoy it . . . so that by means of corporal and temporal
> things we may comprehend the eternal and spiritual.[74]

In Augustinian hermeneutics as in Spenserian allegory, rest is only for the wicked. One must continue on the path of signification in the "endlesse worke" of reading toward the divine truth, the *telos* toward which all Christian labors must tend (*Faerie Queene* 4.12.1).[75] To stop in the "middest of the race," as Redcrosse and Verdant do, is to abandon the quest, to tarry with mere signs, to embrace idolatry. In the enervated and enervating idylls enjoyed by the two knights, Spenser dramatizes an Augustinian hermeneutic of transcendence in which any idle tarrying with the literal sign or the material world is spiritual fornication. Augustine associates this idle tarrying with a carnal understanding that will result in a kind of spiritual slavery: "There is a miserable servitude of the spirit in this habit of taking signs for things, so that one is not able to raise the eye of the mind above things that are corporeal and created to drink in eternal light."[76] Read through an Augustinian lens, the idylls of faerie land forestall the motion of the soul toward God and thereby transform the unwary into idle readers, idolaters enslaved to the signs of the world.

Separated from Truth (Una) and wandering through Errour, the Redcrosse Knight is an idle reader throughout much of the "Legend of Holiness." Blinded to his true identity and purpose by his spiritual idleness, Redcrosse, like Verdant, becomes an idol, a sign that fails to point beyond itself. It is not, however, that Redcrosse's "braue shield" has, like Verdant's, been "fowly ra'st"; rather, it is that his shield threatens to become a sign unmoored from its referent. When we first encounter that gentle knight pricking on the plain, he is clad in the "mightie armes and siluer shielde" of the Christian soldier "wherein old dints of deepe wounds did remaine" (1.1.1–2). Not only does he bear a "bloudie Crosse" on his armor for the "deare remembrance of his dying Lord" but "vpon his shield the like was also scor'd" (1.1.2). As Carol Kaske has established, the doubling of any image within *The Faerie Queene* is a marker of hermeneutic complexity and signals interpretive danger for both the Redcrosse Knight and the reader.[77] In this instance, the slippage from the "bloudie Crosse" on his armor—which the inexperienced knight properly wears for "remembrance"—to "the like" marks a slippage from a sign that points explicitly to its referent to a sign that refers ambiguously to another sign. And the word "like," of course, implies difference as well as similitude. In fact, the studied imprecision of "the like" that is "scor'd" on Redcrosse's shield seems to warn the reader that this sign—like all signs—harbors the potential to be misread.[78] Doubly removed from its referent and prefaced by the definite article, "the like" suggests the possibility of a slippage into reification and idolatry. Given the potential duplicity of "the like," it is important to note that "scor'd" in the early modern period could signify an object that is marked by writing or painting, or an object that is marked by cutting or incising. The distance between the Redcrosse Knight's breastplate and shield is itself a sign of the slippery slope from proper signification and holy contemplation of the divine to the graven image and idolatry. That the red cross has the potential to be misread can be seen in the Redcrosse Knight's battle with Sans Foy. In the course of the altercation, Sans Foy reads the knight's red cross as a magical talisman:

> Curse on that Crosse (quoth then the *Sarazin*)
> That keepes thy body from the bitter fit;
> Dead long ygoe I wote thou haddest bin,
> Had not that charme from thee forwarned it. (1.2.18)

As Orgel's reader helpfully notes, "The signe of the crosse can not preserve. It is an idole, if it bee so esteemed."[79] Understood properly as a "deare remembrance of his dying Lord," the cross is a proper sign of devotion. Reified and split apart from its referent, the red cross emerges as a potentially idolatrous icon.

Reading Gifts

The Redcrosse Knight's idolatrous tarrying with Duessa leads to the entrance of Arthur as the external agent who redeems the knight from spiritual bondage. Once the giant has been defeated, Duessa unmasked, and the knight liberated from Orgoglio's dungeon, Arthur's redemptive work is done. Before Arthur is allowed to exit the "Legend of Holiness," however, he and the Redcrosse Knight engage in a curious exchange of gifts:

> Prince *Arthur* gaue a boxe of Diamond sure,
>   Embowd with gold and gorgeous ornament,
>   Wherein were closd few drops of liquor pure,
>   Of wondrous worth, and vertue excellent,
>   That any wound could heale incontinent:
>   Which to requite, the *Redcrosse* knight him gaue
>   A booke, wherein his Saueours testament
>   Was writ with golden letters rich and braue;
> A worke of wondrous grace, and able soules to saue. (1.9.19)

In the romance narrative of *The Faerie Queene*—the story of knights and giants, dwarves and dragons—the reader seems to have been given a simple gift exchange, cementing social bonds between two men of the aristocracy.[80]

But the strangely unmotivated nature of the episode suggests that we are in the presence of allegory. The allegorical significance of the scene, however, has been notoriously hard to pin down. I take this elusiveness to be instructive as the episode is, in my reading, primarily an occasion for the Redcrosse Knight to misread.[81] There is a natural tendency to read this seemingly superfluous episode in traditional allegorical ways, and this means that the golden book and the healing liquor are often interpreted as emblems without regard to their status as objects in an exchange. Some of the issues at stake in this scene are clarified, however, if we simply attend both to the gifts as things exchanged and to the exchange itself.

At the level of the romance narrative, Spenser seems to dramatize the exchange of precious object ("boxe of Diamond sure") for precious object ("booke . . . writ with golden letters rich"). On a figurative level, however, the two objects perform very different work. Although the magically healing liquor is a traditional feature of the generic romance quest—or perhaps precisely because it is a traditional feature that the reader encounters in this strange poem—it seems to invite an allegorical reading. The fact that the diamond box that contains the liquor recalls one of the most symbolically resonant items in the poem, Arthur's diamond shield, also suggests that we are to read this romance object otherwise. Many scholars have offered readings of the "liquor pure," and although there is a general sense that it has something to do with God's grace, no consensus has emerged concerning a more precise referent. That the healing liquor seems to invite allegorical reading only to frustrate that reading is, I contend, significant. Of course, this kind of allegorical indeterminacy is characteristic of Spenser's poem. Often such imprecision means simply that the referents are multiple, that the allegorical element, like the Freudian symptom, is overdetermined by the various forces that bring it into being. On occasion, however, this indeterminacy is less a function of multiplicity than an invocation of the figurative qua figurative. To put it another way, what is signified by the wondrous liquor's teasing invitation to allegorize is not a specific referent or many possible referents but the possibility of reference. In the first instance then, the healing liquor seems to be a traditional romance object used here to invoke the prospect of allegory and the necessity of allegorical reading.

The "booke . . . writ with golden letters" is another story—indeed, seems to belong to another story. On a rudimentary level, the book is simply the other object in the exchange. Given that the gifts seem to call each other into being—neither appeared prior to this moment nor plays much of a part in the poem thereafter[82]—the reader might expect a certain reciprocity between the way the two objects signify in the poem. Curiously, however, the golden book, unlike the healing liquor, does not invite an allegorical reading. In part, this is simply a consequence of the fact that the book is named in the text: it is the "Saueours testament." And once it is named, it no longer asks the reader to look elsewhere for its meaning or significance. At the level of romance, at the simple level of story, the book is the New Testament; on a figurative or allegorical level, it remains the New Testament. In fact, no matter how the reader addresses it, the book that the Redcrosse Knight gives to Arthur is simply the New Testament. To paraphrase Gertrude Stein, in this scene a book is a book is a book is a book. The "Saueours testament" almost seems to become a three-dimensional object in a two-dimensional space, somehow heavier, denser, more fully realized or rendered than the things around it. The two objects in this exchange seem then to function in diametrically opposed ways: the magic liquor seems to invite allegorical reading in order to call attention to allegory, whereas the book neither invites nor allows allegorical reading. This is not to say that the book does not have a figurative function. On the contrary, the book is a remarkable addition to Spenser's collection of complexly resonant objects, one that works to perform the self-sufficiency of God's word. The "Legend of Holiness" is also, of course, a "Legend of Wholeness" with Una as the figure for the One Church, the One Word, and, more abstractly, the unity and indivisibility of truth. But if Una figures wholeness or oneness, she is at the same time a romance heroine and thus a figure that can only invoke or indicate these ideas. The "Saueours testament," in contrast, enacts the indivisibility she names. Its allegorical function is to refuse to function allegorically and thereby perform the perfect self-identity of God's word.

As I have suggested, the gift exchange is both unmotivated at the moment and amounts to naught in the long run. Nonetheless, there are spiritual repercussions for the Redcrosse Knight. In a brilliant reading, Maureen Quilligan contends that this exchange *generates* the knight's subsequent encounter with Despaire. The key to Quilligan's reading is Spenser's playful handling of the word "despair": "Despaire is not simply the personification of the lack of hope, which is what his name means etymologically (*de-spero*), he is one who 'dispairs' the natural wholeness of Christian teaching. By emphasizing the Old Testament virtue of justice to the exclusion of the New Testament virtue of love or mercy he 'dis-pairs' this true pair of testaments."[83] Elucidating the dream logic of Spenser's poem, Quilligan reads this "dis-pairing" of testaments as a consequence of the Redcrosse Knight having given the New Testament away. Given the consequences of the Redcrosse Knight's decision to exchange the book, it is tempting to look for some moral failing evident in this choice of gift. The poem, however, rarely works this way. The problem, rather, lies in the Redcrosse Knight's understanding of what has taken place, an understanding that the reader can infer only from his subsequent actions. In these actions the knight seems to reveal two fundamental errors in his understanding of the gift exchange: the first has to do with the nature of the book, the second with the nature of the gift. In the exchange with Arthur, the Redcrosse Knight has given away a book. In the dream logic of the poem, however, he subsequently acts as if he has given away a text. The problem, of course, is that one cannot—except in very special circumstances—give a text away.[84] This is especially true of a text like the New Testament, a text that any Christian reader ought to always "have" regardless of his or her proximity to any material manifestation of that text.

In a sermon on the first line of John's Gospel, "In the beginning was the Word," Augustine attempts to teach his congregation about the peculiar nature of language:

> Look, you are all listening to me; I'm making a word. If anyone goes out and is asked outside what's going on in here, he will answer, "The bishop's making a word." I'm making a word about the Word. But what sort of word about what sort of Word? A dying word about the undying Word; a changeable word about the unchangeable Word; a transitory word about the eternal Word. All the same, pay attention to my word. I mean, I did tell you, the Word of God is all of it everywhere. Here am I, making a word for you; what I am saying reaches all of you; in order for what I'm saying to reach all of you, have you divided up what I'm saying? If I was feeding you, and wanting to fill not your thoughts but your guts, and setting loaves of bread before you so that you could eat your fill, wouldn't you divide my loaves among you? Could all my loaves reach every single one of you? If they reached one, the rest of you would have nothing. Here I am, talking, and you all have it. It's not just that you all have it; you all have it all. It has all reached you all; it has all reached every one of you. Why, isn't my word marvelous! So what must the Word of God be?
>
> Here's something else. I have been speaking; what I have said

has gone out to you, and hasn't departed from me. It has reached you, and has not been separated from me. Before I spoke, I had it, and you did not have it; I have spoken, and you have begun to have it, and I have lost nothing. Why, isn't my word marvelous! So what must the Word of God be?[85]

The Redcrosse Knight's actions after the gift exchange suggest a misunderstanding of the marvelous nature of language, of text; he acts as if in giving the "Saueours testament," he has lost it, given it away. But a text can be uttered or inscribed an infinite number of times; Arthur's possession of the "Saueours testament" in no way precludes the Redcrosse Knight's possession of it. Furthermore, as I have been suggesting in different ways throughout *The Incarnate Text*, this simple distinction between book and text is, given the text in question, crucially important to Christian thought. Natalie Zemon Davis observes that when the translator Olivétan presented the French Protestant Bible of 1535, he offered it as "the most felicitous of gifts, made only to be given and yet never exhaustible."[86] The Redcrosse Knight, however, seems to believe that he has exhausted this wondrous gift. As Spenser so often does, he signals the Redcrosse Knight's potential confusion with syntactic ambiguity:

> . . . the *Redcrosse* knight him gaue
> A booke, wherein his Saueours testament
> Was writ with golden letters rich and braue;
> A worke of wondrous grace, and able soules to saue. (1.9.19)

An inexperienced reader of Spenser's poem like the Redcrosse Knight might interpret this passage to mean that the "booke" is a "worke of wondrous grace, and able soules to saue." The "worke of wondrous grace," however, is not the "booke" but the text, "his Saueours testament." In the dream logic of *The Faerie Queene*, the Redcrosse Knight's actions suggest that he has somehow given away "his Saueours testament" and in doing so has somehow decoupled or disarticulated the testaments of the Bible. It is this faulty logic that leads him to Despaire.

That the Redcrosse Knight has given himself over to an Old Testament logic of law and justice is evident from the moment he encounters Despaire. Seeing Despaire with one of his unfortunate victims, the knight with "firie zeale . . . burnt in courage bold / Him to auenge, before his bloud were cold." Addressing Despaire, he says, "Thou damned wight . . . / What iustice can but iudge against thee right, / With thine owne bloud to price his bloud, here shed in sight" (1.9.37). Despaire, of course, turns this logic on all sinners:

> Is not he iust, that all this doth behold
>> From highest heauen, and beares an equall eye?
>> Shall he thy sins vp in his knowledge fold,
>> And guiltie be of thine impietie?
>> Is not his law, Let euery sinner die:
>> Die shall all flesh?
>
> .   .   .   .
>
> The knight was much enmoued with his speach,
>> That as a swords point through his hart did perse,
>> And in his conscience made a secret breach,
>> Well knowing true all, that he did reherse,
>> And to his fresh remembrance did reuerse
>> The vgly vew of his deformed crimes,
>> That all his manly powres it did disperse,
>> As he were charmed with inchaunted rimes,
> That oftentimes he quakt, and fainted oftentimes. (1.9.47–48)

That the Redcrosse Knight's responds to these provocations as if "he were charmed with inchaunted rimes" alerts the reader to the artful way Despaire deploys text and language in the episode.[87] Despaire, of course, manipulates the message of scripture, emphasizing the law of the Old Testament and failing to convey the New Testament promise of mercy and grace.[88] Crucially, however, the New Testament has not disappeared from the text; Despaire employs New Testament passages readily and frequently.[89] This means that the Redcrosse Knight's error—his belief that he has given "his Saueours testament" away—is belied by the poem. Even in the midst of his despair, Redcrosse *has* the New Testament. The fact that the text of the New Testament is present in Despaire's Old Testament rhetoric is, I suggest, crucial to an understanding of the kind of error the Redcrosse Knight makes. To assume that one can give away one half of the Bible and thereby lose its redemptive message is not only to mistake a book for a text; it is also to mistake the nature of *this* text.

When narrating his conversion experience—the so-called tower experience (*turmerlebnis*)—Luther described his despair before his ultimate revelation. Famously, Luther despaired in the face of the law; he was a sinner who could never overcome his sinful nature to earn the love God offered. In his despair, Luther protested that God had added "pain to pain" since not only the decalogue and the Old Testament but also the *gospel* threatened the reader of the Bible with "righteousness and wrath."[90] One can see a version of the same idea in Spenser's "Legend of Holiness" when the Redcrosse Knight finally reaches the House of Holiness; taught by faith (Fidelia) to read the "sacred Booke, with bloud ywrit," the knight immediately despairs:

> Greeu'd with remembrance of his wicked wayes,
> And prickt with anguish of his sinnes so sore,
> That he desired, to end his wretched dayes:
> So much the dart of sinfull guilt the soule dismayes. (1.10.19, 1.10.21)

The knight despairs not despite his edification by faith but precisely because he now understands the redemptive message of the New Testament and thus the enormity of his sin. Moreover, that redemptive promise does not preclude the law or the prospect of damnation. The "heauenly documents" that Fidelia "preach[es]" address "iustice" as well as "grace"; if she can with her "goodly speech" raise "to life," the words she uses are also able "to kill" (1.10.19). Luther's perception that the New Testament threatened him with "righteousness and wrath" led to his despair, but it also subsequently became central to his understanding of scripture.[91] He came to see the significance of the fact that the threat of the law and the promise of grace were not consigned to the Old and New Testaments, respectively, but that the dialectic of law and grace was to be found everywhere in the Bible.[92] The part then is always read in relation to the whole, the scriptural text on a local level recapitulating the dialectical logic of the Bible as book. This means that in the act of reading scripture the reader continually confronts his or her inadequacy before the law and the specter of God's wrath, and the reader is consistently offered the promise of redemptive grace. Despaire can quote from the New Testament because, like the Old Testament, it contains both aspects of the Christian dialectic: justice and mercy, law and grace. When Una intervenes to save the Redcrosse Knight from his despair, she reasserts that dialectic.

As a figure for oneness or indivisibility, Una is, among other things, representative of the coherence and unity of the text of scripture.[93] It is Una who reminds the Redcrosse Knight of the whole message of scripture:

> In heauenly mercies hast thou not a part?
> Why shouldst thou then despeire, that chosen art?
> Where iustice growes, there grows eke greater grace,
> The which doth quench the brond of hellish smart,
> And that accurst hand-writing doth deface,
> Arise, Sir knight arise, and leaue this cursed place. (1.9.53)

Una stands in here not for the "Saueours testament" that the Redcrosse Knight had "lost" or "given away" but for the unity of scripture, the single movement from law to grace. Crucially, the "accurst hand-writing" is not expunged but defaced; the law is not erased but preserved, even as it is abrogated. The image is of a palimpsest, or an iconoclastic act that leaves the defaced icon as an emblem of the transformation from idolatry to transcendence. And the defaced "hand-writing" is not simply an image of a palimpsest; it is a reference to a textual palimpsest, the New Testament written over the Old. The "accurst hand-writing" alludes to Colossians 2:14: "Blotting out the handwriting of ordinances that was against vs, which was contrary to vs, and tooke it out of the way, nayling it to his Crosse."[94] Blotting out suggests a writing over or whitewashing, a supplemental marking that obscures but does not destroy the original.[95] The metaphor of the law as "handwriting" seems to read the threat of an Old Testament justice through the lens of the "handwriting on the wall" from Daniel 5, handwriting that announces judgment and imminent death. The palimpsest of the blotted-out handwriting suggests the movement of law and grace, Old Testament and New, a dialectical movement that the Redcrosse Knight is only now beginning to understand.

The Redcrosse Knight's despair in the face of an implacable Old Testament logic of righteousness and wrath is a function of his misapprehension of both the text of grace and the gift of grace. Luther's conversion experience, his reconceptualization of the relation of Old Testament to New, amounted to a radical reappraisal of the gift of grace, a radical reappraisal of the nature of the gift. In its fundamental reorientation toward grace, this conversion experience would be reiterated countless times in the sixteenth century. To return to the gift exchange after reading the ultimately redemptive message of the Despaire episode is to see that the Redcrosse Knight misunderstands Arthur's gift. As I suggested above, the "boxe of Diamond sure" with its "few drops of liquor pure" seems to resist precise allegorical reading. If no consensus has emerged about the precise allegorical referent, however, most scholars would likely agree with Thomas Roche's assessment that the liquor is "probably symbolic of grace" broadly construed, whatever more specific referent it might or might not have.[96] And if the liquor figures grace, however imprecisely, it transforms the nature of this exchange. In Reformation terms, if the gift given is the gift of grace, then there can have been no exchange. For Reformers, the gift of God's grace was, and must be, radically free. In articulating his theology of grace, Luther vehemently rejected the economic logic establishing the relationship between God and man in Catholic Christendom. In seeking to return to the purity of the true church, he rejected the economy of exchange in the Catholic doctrine of works and saw himself as recovering an essentially noneconomic relationship between man and the divine. And with a Reformation theology of grace in mind, the scene of the gift exchange is suddenly transformed. The gratuitous nature of Arthur's gentlemanly gesture—as well as the curiously gratuitous nature of this allegorical episode—is precisely the point. The gift of grace must be understood as pure gift; it is, therefore, superfluous, gratuitous, outside economies of exchange and narratives of heroic endeavor. From this perspective, the fact that the "liquor pure" simultaneously invites and resists allegorical reading makes sense; the significance of the liquor has nothing to with the object exchanged but with the nature of the exchange. The wondrous liquor resists any precise referent because its allegorical significance lies not in the object given but in its status as gift, "pure" gift.

That the Redcrosse Knight misunderstands both the gift he has been given specifically and the nature of the gift generally is revealed in the language of the exchange. Once Arthur gives the Redcrosse Knight the healing liquor, the Redcrosse Knight offers him an object in exchange to *requite* this gift: "Prince *Arthur* gaue a boxe of Diamond sure . . . / Which to requite, the *Redcrosse* knight him gaue / A booke" (1.9.19). The term "requite" suggests that the Redcrosse Knight reads the gift exchange as an economic exchange; he will "requite" or "repay" Arthur's largesse. "Requite," however, means "repay" both in the sense of "to make return for, reward (a kindness, service, etc.)" and in the sense of "to make retaliation or return for, to avenge (a wrong, injury, etc.)."[97] The ambivalence of the term "requite" suggests a Maussian exchange in which the Redcrosse Knight feels threatened by Arthur's gift, threatened with a debt or obligation that he cannot repay.[98] Of course, if we revisit the situation in which the gift exchange takes place, the "threat" of irredeemable obligation is very real. The Redcrosse Knight has just been saved from an horrific and self-imposed spiritual bondage; his debt to his savior is immeasurable. To add insult to injury, Arthur offers him this gift. That this gift is simply another avatar of the redemption he has been granted escapes the Redcrosse Knight, and so he avenges himself with a gift in response. The Redcrosse Knight falls victim to despair because he cannot accept his redemption freely, cannot accept the gift freely.

If the Redcrosse Knight's failure seems like a failure to understand rudimentary Reformation theology, it must be remembered that Luther insisted over and over again that it was almost impossible for the fallen human mind to grasp that God's gift of grace was free. For Luther the impossibility of thinking the free gift of grace is a measure of the distance between fallen man and the divine.[99] Fallen man simply cannot break out of the economic logic of exchange in order to grasp the free gift of grace; to do so "is farre aboue mans strength and capacity."[100] This is precisely why one cannot trust reason. The fallen faculty of reason naturally allies itself with the law and works righteousness and cannot fathom the doctrine of God's grace: "It is a kynde of doctrine neither proceedyng of free will, nor inuented by the reason or wisedome of man, but giuen from aboue."[101] The only way to understand the gift is through the gift of faith, and it is only through the gift of faith that one can learn to read the promise of grace in scripture. Only when Redcrosse is taught by Fidelia to "read aright" the "booke, that was both signd and seald with blood" does the knight learn the true meaning of the gift and the true meaning of the "Saueours testament."

Bidding Beads and Repurposing Language

The House of Holiness, the place in which the Redcrosse Knight learns to "read aright" and undergoes reformation, is a virtual funhouse of seemingly idolatrous Catholic figures (1.9.6). These figures are not denounced as idolatrous but embraced as the means of Redcrosse's reformation. I would like to focus here on two such figures—Caelia and the Bead-men—to ask why Spenser employs an obviously Catholic devotional form, the bidding of beads, in his House of Holiness. In his gloss of an earlier depiction of the bidding of beads, Orgel's Puritan reader asks the obvious question: "Is this a signe of holynesse, to pray on beades? A papist would lyk this well."[102]

In Bateman's *Christall Glasse of Christian Reformation*, the woodcut illustrating the sin of Sloth (idleness by another name) depicts a friar not with a girdle book but with rosary or paternoster beads. According to the caption,

Figure 19. "Of Sloth." Stephen Bateman, *Christall Glasse of Christian Reformation* (1569), G2v. By permission of Beinecke Rare Book and Manuscript Library, Yale University.

"the Fryers weede and Beades signifieth hypocrisie and lothsomnes of the truth" (Figure 19).[103] Frequently depicted along with girdle books in representations of hypocritical and credulous Catholics, these "superstitious" beads are just the kind of idle trumpery condemned by Reformers (see Figure 13). In the "Homily of Good Works," published in the authorized Elizabethan *Book of Homilies*, Thomas Cranmer "rehearse[s]" a catalogue of "papistical superstitions and abuses" in which he writes "of Beades, of Lady psalters, and Rosaries, of xv. Oos, of S. Barnardes vearses, of S. Agathes letters, of Purgatorye, of Masses satisfactory, of Stacions, & Iubilies, of fayned Reliques, or halowed Beades, Belles, Bread, Water, Palmes, Candels, Fire, & such other."[104]

The rosary is here placed among an abundance of idolatrously venerated objects (relics, beads, bells, breads), and a catalogue of superstitious texts.[105] Both the presumed efficacy of the reiterated prayer and the holiness of the beads as objects made the Catholic rosary an object of the Reformers' wrath. As Cranmer's list demonstrates, beads and the rosary were not synonymous: devotional beads were used for prayers other than the rosary (most famously the paternoster), and the rosary could be prayed without the assistance of beads. At the same time, as Anne Winston-Allen has pointed out, "From its inception onward, the rosary devotion was intimately tied to the string of beads that came to represent it."[106] Lending "the devotion an added aesthetic dimension and a certain concreteness," the conflation of beads and prayer meant that the rosary was both text and image, a prayer intimately tied to the body and an object that one "bids" as an act of devotion and supplication.[107] It was precisely this confusion of word and thing, this tarrying with the material sign, that so infuriated Protestants. That the rosary is read as a kind of perversion of scripture and is seen as displacing the Bible and proper devotional guides can be seen in the title-page woodcut of Foxe's *Actes and Monuments* (see Figure 6). As I discussed at the beginning of this chapter, the woodcut depicts Foxe's version of the "Image of Both Churches." The viewer sees three different representations of the church of true believers engaged in different kinds of godly activity extending down the length of the left-hand side of the image; extending down the right-hand side is a corresponding set of images depicting the church of Antichrist. For my purposes, the important parallel is drawn in the bottom two panels that depict, on the one side, the godly preaching of the reformed in which the members of the congregation can be seen piously reading their Bibles and, on the other side, the benighted devotional practices of the Catholics in which the members of the congregation ignorantly bid their beads.

In *The Faerie Queene* Spenser addresses the problem presented by the rosary and the bidding of beads in the third canto of the "Legend of Holiness." In this canto, Una, separated from the Redcrosse Knight and wandering in "wildernesse and wastfull deserts," comes upon the unholy pair Abessa and Corceca. When she first sees Una, Abessa, who cannot "heare, nor speake, nor vnderstand," flees from Divine Truth and back to the dark dwelling where her blind mother, Corceca, "Sate in eternall night" (1.3.11–12). Once Una reaches the benighted residence, she finds both mother and daughter "in darkesome corner pent." The same corner

> Where that old woman day and night did pray
> Vpon her beades deuoutly penitent;
> Nine hundred Pater nosters euery day,
> And thrise nine hundred Aues she was wont to say.

And to augment her painefull pennance more,
Thrise euery weeke in ashes she did sit,
And next her wrinkled skin rough sackcloth wore,
And thrise three times did fast from any bit:
But now for feare her beads she did forget. (1.3.13–14)

Defined by fear and ignorance, Corceca combines her obsessive ritual acts with compulsive iterations of "holy" formulae repeated in numerically super-stitious sets of three and nine. Associated with the false devotional practices of the monastic tradition through her daughter Abessa, Corceca, or "blind heart" (Latin *cor caecum*), is clearly emblematic of the unenlightened Catholic who mortifies the flesh and revisits the dead letter not out of faith and devo-tion but out of ignorance and "needlesse dread" (1.3.14).

What is peculiar about Spenser's "Legend of Holiness," however, is not that he portrays the idolatry inherent in the bidding of beads and the reifica-tion of texts but that he also depicts a virtuous instance of bead bidding. At the beginning of Canto 10, as the Redcrosse Knight is entering the House of Holiness, he comes across Corceca's reformed counterpart, Dame Caelia,

Whose onely ioy was to relieue the needes
Of wretched soules, and helpe the helpelesse pore:
All night she spent in bidding of her bedes,
And all the day in doing good and godly deedes. (1.10.3)

Certainly, the "heavenly" mother of Fidelia, Speranza, and Charissa is unlike Corceca in her altruistic attention to the problems of the fallen world, but what is Spenser's reader to make of the "bidding of . . . bedes"? Orgel's Puritan reader asks the obvious question: "Why beades, & not prayer?"[108] Later in the same canto, the Redcrosse Knight, still progressing through the House of Holiness and having just met the "auncient matrone" Mercie, comes upon "an holy Hospitall"

In which seuen Bead-men that had vowed all
Their life to seruice of high heauens king
Did spend their dayes in doing godly thing:
Their gates to all were open euermore,
That by the wearie way were traueiling,

And one sate wayting euer them before,
To call in-commers by, that needy were and pore. (1.10.36)

Traditionally, "beadsmen" were poor Christians paid to pray for benefactors or for the souls of the dead. Epitomizing everything that Protestants despised in the Catholic theology of works—the mechanical efficacy of prayer, the purchasing of redemption, and the performance of good works by proxy—it seems incomprehensible that Spenser would locate beadsmen in his reformed House of Holiness.

Spenser's Bead-men, however, are beadsmen of a different stripe. Given that traditional beadsmen were associated with what Reformers thought of as a bankrupt Catholic theology of works, it is of some significance that Spenser's Bead-men are revealed as allegorical figures for the seven corporal works of mercy. Prominent figures in a Protestant allegory, Spenser's Bead-men embody a doctrine that might sound suspiciously Catholic to the reformed reader. They do so because Spenser is attempting to redeem "beadsmen" for Protestantism by emptying out the term of its Catholic content and reclaiming it for a different kind of "good work": one that acknowledges that only through faith in the gospel and by the grace of God can one attain salvation. In a "Sermon upon the Epistle to Timothy," Calvin (via Lawrence Tomson's translation) refers to deacons as "Beade maisters": "Knowe we, that the Deacons, that is to say, the Beade maisters, and such as see to the pore, haue not onely an earthly office, but a spiritual charge, which serueth the Church of God, and therefore that they must bee nigh the Ministers of the word of God."[109] Here, the traditional understanding of beadsmen is turned inside out. They are not poor Christians paid to turn words into good works but those who work to care for the poor, and whose earthly office is seen as close in spirit to the preaching of scripture. Like Calvin, Spenser rewrites this Catholic term as a Protestant one, condemning an idolatrous Catholic practice only to repurpose the traditional sign of that practice for Protestant use. At the same time, he manages to redeem a vocabulary, if not a theology, of "good works" by distancing the term from the kind of "works" Catholic beadsmen traditionally did.

One might assume that the linguistic correlation of beads with prayers came about because beads as objects were so often used in the act of praying—that the innocuous material accessories to prayer accrued, over time, a certain amount of sacred resonance by association—eventually becoming as important, if not more important, than the prayer itself. In fact, the history is just the reverse; the word "bead" meant "prayer" before it ever referred to the "small ball-shaped object" with which we associate it now. As the *Oxford English Dictionary* tracks the history, "the name was transferred from 'prayer' to the small globular bodies used for 'telling beads,' i.e. counting prayers said, from which the other senses naturally followed."[110] Spenser seems to have been well aware of the connection between the bidding of beads and prayers. In the annotations to the September eclogue of *The Shepheardes Calender*, the bidding of beads is glossed in the following way: "For to bidde, is to praye, whereof commeth beades for prayers, and so they say, To bidde his beades. s. to saye his prayers."[111] When Caelia bids her beads, she can be read as merely praying. Always playing on the etymological senses of words, Spenser's poem attempts to salvage the bidding of beads for a Protestant poetics not by disassociating the term "bead" from prayer but by reclaiming "bead" as prayer. In just this fashion, Spenser attempts to redeem all the Catholic elements—beads, penance, works, Saint George—of the House of Holiness.

In *The Allegory of Love* C. S. Lewis accounts for the seeming Catholicism of Spenser's House of Holiness by suggesting that "all allegories whatever are likely to seem Catholic to the general reader":

> In part, no doubt, [this phenomenon] . . . is to be explained by the fact that visible and tangible aspects of Catholicism are medieval, and, therefore, steeped in literary suggestion. But is this all? Do Protestant allegorists continue as in a dream to use imagery so likely to mislead their readers without noticing the danger or without better motive than laziness for incurring it? By no means. The truth is not that allegory is Catholic, but that Catholicism is allegorical. Allegory consists in giving an imagined body to the immaterial; but if, in each case, Catholicism claims already to have given it a material body, then the allegorist's symbol will naturally resemble that material body. The whip of Penaunce is an excellent example. No Christian ever doubted that repentance involved "penaunce" and "whips" on the spiritual plane: it is when you come to material whips . . . that the controversy begins. It is the same with the House of Holiness. . . . When Spenser writes about Protestant sanctity he gives us something like a convent: when he is really talking about the conventual life he gives us Abessa and Corceca.[112]

Of course, Lewis overstates his case.[113] One would neither want to suggest that Catholicism *is* allegorical nor apply his thesis to all Protestant allegories as he does. Still, when applied to Spenser, his argument has a certain logic. Catholicism does seem to be allegorical in Lewis's sense within the "Legend of Holiness"; Spenser does employ the material forms of Catholicism to embody allegorically the spiritual truths of Protestantism. To suggest, however, that "the allegorist's symbol will naturally resemble" the material forms of Catholicism is to miss the point. It is not, as Lewis would have it, that there are a finite number of words and images to materialize spiritual things and the Catholics have taken them all; it is rather that the words and images of Catholicism are the very stuff of English history and English literature. Spenser does not rely on Catholic imagery because it is "natural" for him to do so; he appropriates it in order to reclaim it for a reformed history. Spenser's almost obsessive incorporation of older forms—words, styles, genres—creates an epic poem that is also a museum, a poetic anteroom that reclaims the very language of English history that had been consigned to the dustbin of history by the Reformation. And it is not that Spenser continues "as in a dream to use imagery so likely to mislead . . . [his] readers without noticing the danger"; on the contrary, Spenser employs the Catholic associations of these old forms precisely in order to mislead his readers. As I have been suggesting throughout this chapter, the "Legend of Holiness" is a text designed to compel the reader to face and experience the danger of reading.

The "Legend of Holiness" seems to entertain two ambitions that are not precisely compatible. In this poem Spenser seems to want to attempt to reclaim the stuff of English language and English history, to purify it of its Catholic associations and repurpose it for a reformed present. At the same time, the poem seems designed to employ those same Catholic associations to create an iconoclastic hermeneutics. If this iconoclastic hermeneutics works to cancel those idolatrous forms and images, it also works to preserve them, and it preserves them as idols. We tend to think of Protestant iconoclasm as the destruction of images, the purification of religious space and devotional practice through the eradication of offending objects, and, for the most part, the destruction of the medium is the message of iconoclastic acts. Nevertheless, it is curious how often Reformation iconoclasts left the defaced image in place, or left the marks of iconoclastic violence as a trace of the history of their encounter with the image or object.[114] This desire to preserve the act of iconoclasm is, I contend, something that is written into the "Legend of Holiness." It is a desire to sustain the iconoclastic *movement* from idolatry to transcendence, and it is a recognition that the iconoclastic imagination requires the idol for its redemptive work. The result of this desire to preserve the transcendent movement of iconoclasm is a kind of iconoclastic icon. In the "Legend of Holiness," Spenser trains his reader to read dialectically, tarrying with the letter in order to transcend it. Of course, as Spenser understands, the letter is never transcended, never overcome. Spenser knows that reformation is not a sudden and fully realized transformation that leaves the past of an individual or society behind but a habitual act, a devotional practice, the "endlesse worke" of reading (*Faerie Queene* 4.12.1).

Coda: Epic Reading, Heroic Madness

In *The Laboryouse Journey & serche of Johan Leylande, for Englandes Antiquitees* (1549), John Bale presents the reader with an account of John Leland's unfinished work, a search, as the title suggests, for the textual antiquities of England. This search was occasioned by the monumental transfer of land, goods, and authority known as the dissolution of the monasteries. Humanist scholar and early antiquarian, Leland was a servant of the king, commissioned, as Bale records, by "the noble Prynce, Kyng Henry the viii" to "serche and peruse the Libraries of hys realme in monasteries, co[n]uentes, and colleges, before their vtter destruccyon."[115] In 1546 Leland offered his king and patron, Henry VIII, a small book, a "New Year's Gift." This "Gift" is both a memorandum describing his progress in his state-sanctioned mission to preserve and catalogue books, and a promise of the various works of historical scholarship that will emerge from this project. In 1549 Bale reworked this gift and presented an augmented version of it to a new king, Edward VI, as *The Laboryouse Journey*. Only three years after all of Leland's documented progress and glorious promises, Henry was dead and Leland was incapacitated. Bale records the words of a "wytnesse" who wrote to him "lamentynge" Leland's "soden fall": "Surely my frynde, I can not therfore but lament this hys estate, boldelye affirminge that . . . Englande had yet neuer a greater losse. But what shall we saye? It hath pleased god that he shuld . . . be depryued of hys wyttes."[116] In the course of his laborious journey, Leland had, evidently, lost his way.

In his repackaging and repurposing of Leland's gift, Bale insists on reading Leland's efforts and the momentous historical change of which they are a part as an aspect of a millennial Reformation history, a history in which

England was emerging from a thousand years of darkness into the light. At the same time, Bale is more than sympathetic to Leland's desire to preserve the antiquities of that past, even if those antiquities are often a product of that dark and dismal interim. His dedicatory epistle to Edward is a lament that England has been so "negligent" toward its "hystoryes," a negligence that reached sinful proportions in the recent "ouerthrow" of the "Abbeyes & Fryeryes" when "the most worthy monumentes of this realme, so myserably peryshed in the spoyle."[117] Bale, of course, does not disapprove of the dissolution of the monasteries, a destruction "whyche God" himself had "appoynted for their wyckednesses sake";[118] rather, he bemoans the fact that in this just suppression of the monasteries no steps had been taken to preserve the antiquities they contained:

> thys is hyghly to be lamented, of all them that hath a naturall loue to their contrey, eyther yet to lerned Antiquyte, whyche is a moste syngular bewty to the same. That in turnynge ouer of the superstycyouse monasteryes, so lytle respecte was had to theyr lybraryes for the sauegarde of those noble & precyouse monumentes. I do not denye . . . [that the monasteries were] most iustly suppressed. Yet this would I haue wyshed (and I scarsely vtter it wythout teares) that the profytable corne had not so vnaduysedly and vngodly peryshed wyth the vnprofytable chaffe, nor the wholsome herbes with the vnwholsome wedes.[119]

Bale's lament here is not that many of the monuments of England have been destroyed, but that many of the "noble & precyouse" monuments have. It is the indiscriminate nature of the actions taken that brings him almost to tears. For Bale, some of the antiquities were quite rightly destroyed, just as some that survived still require destruction. He laments that these decisions were not in the hands of those suited to the task: "Oh, that men of learnyng & of perfyght loue to their nacyon, were not then appoynted to the serche of theyr lybraryes, for the conseruacion of those most noble Antiquitees."[120] Bale's desire for some discerning intelligence to sort the profitable corn from the unprofitable chaff reflected Leland's mandate. As James Simpson has reminded us in a brilliantly evocative essay, Leland, as an agent of the king, was engaged in acts of preservation that were part of the larger project of destruction. In his mission to salvage a textual tradition, Leland was himself, as Simpson points out, "an agent of the destruction of the very past" he sought to recuperate.[121] After Leland's "soden fall," having been "depryued of his wyttes," it would be left to Bale to continue these labors.[122] Bale frames this mission to recover and catalogue the books lost or threatened by the dissolution of the monasteries as a heroic quest to salvage an English textual heritage from imminent destruction. In Bale's vision of it, Leland's "laboriouse journey" seems to become emblematic of the Reformation itself: an act of iconoclastic destruction that will result in the preservation and salvation of the chosen. For Bale, this preserving and destroying, this selecting and judging is the work of Reformation edification and should be undertaken by the learned and morally upright, readers who can discriminate and stand in judgment.

In the more reflective moments of Bale's edition of Leland's incomplete *Journey*, the reader bears witness to the pathos of both the dissolution itself and Leland's strange quest.[123] Simpson follows the seventeenth-century antiquarian Anthony Wood in suggesting that Leland's madness is the consequence of his impossible mission.[124] However we read that madness, that "soden fall," there is something melancholy about the image of these men wandering the countryside preserving certain books and effectively marking others for destruction. There is also something quite literally quixotic in their attempt to preserve and destroy the textual traces of the past, in their attempt to rewrite history. As in Cervantes' *Don Quixote*, Bale and Leland work in the service of an idyllic past that never existed and work to recreate the present in that past's image. As with Cervantes' errant knight, there is something heroic and tragic and mad about their attempt to transform the world through the texts they champion, through reading. In *Don Quixote*, Cervantes presents the reader with that unforgettable scene of reading, the inquisition of books. In the novel, Don Quixote's niece and housekeeper escort the curate and the barber to the library, to "the onely authors of his harme." In the library, where "they found more then a hundred great volumes," the curate

commanded the Barber to fetch him downe the bookes from their shelues, one by one, that he might peruse their arguments; for it might happen some to be found, which in no sort deserued to be chastised with fire. No, replyed the Niese, no, you ought not to pardon any of them, seeing they haue all beene offendors; it is better you throw them all into the base court, and there make a pile of them, and then set them a fire; if not, they may be carried into the

yard, and there make a bon-fire of them, and the smoake will offend
no body. The olde woman said as much, both of them thirsted so
much for the death of these innocents, but the Curate would not
condiscend thereto, vntill he had first read the titles at the least of
euerie booke.

The first that Master *Nicholas* put into his hands, was that of
Amadis of *Gaule*; which the Curate perusing a while . . . [said] this
is the first booke of Knighthood that euer was printed in *Spaine*,
and all the others haue had their beginning and originall from this;
and therefore me thinkes that we must condemne him to the fire,
without all remission, as the *Dogmatizer* and head of so badde a sect.
Not so . . . quoth the Barber, for I haue heard that it is the very best
contriued booke of all those of that kinde, and therefore he is to be
pardoned as the onely complete one of his profession. That is true,
replied the Curate, and for that reason we doe giue him his life for
this time. Let vs see that other which lies next vnto him.[125]

The ensuing inquisition of books is fundamentally about selective reading,
about literary taste, about judgment and discernment. The niece and the
housekeeper would gladly burn all the books (they "thirsted so much for the
death of these innocents") that led to Don Quixote's madness. But the barber
and the curate must linger over the books, discussing their merits, invoking,
it seems, an entire textual tradition in order to sort the corn from the chaff.
As the barber and the curate squabble hilariously over which books will be
committed to the flame and which saved from destruction, a certain pathos
emerges from the absurdity of the situation, a pathos that speaks to the nostalgic desire evoked in complex and conflicting ways by Cervantes' novel, a
desire for preservation, for things not to be lost.

Spenser's "Legend of Holiness" is, I would suggest, another quixotic text
avant la lettre. Like Leland or Bale or Don Quixote, the Redcrosse Knight
wanders the countryside, encountering error and championing truth. Traveling in the strange allegorical landscape of faerie land, encountering textual
icons and linguistic artifacts, he is challenged to read and to choose, to read
and to judge. For men like Leland and Bale and Spenser, reading and ethics,
reading and heroic action in the world, are conflated. Viewed from a certain
angle, the "Legend of Holiness" presents the reader with a romance quest
that allegorizes the iconoclastic destruction and memorial preservation that
one finds in works like *The Laboriouse Journey*. For Spenser, however, the

point is not to preserve some antiquities and destroy others but to reclaim antiquities tainted by an errant history and to redeem an English literary language. The manifestly Catholic forms that the reader and the Redcrosse Knight encounter in the poem are not destroyed but salvaged for Spenser's nationalist epic and co-opted for the poet's iconoclastic purposes. The point, for Spenser, is not to eradicate certain books, not to change the textual landscape in which the reader wanders, but to transform the reader. In the "Legend of Holiness," the laborious journeys of Spenser's knight and Spenser's reader are quests in which both hero and reader are, in Spenser's vision, remade. Readers, however, are notoriously resistant to a text's designs on them. As Spenser knew all too well, readers are not so easily bent to an author's purposes. They read as they wish, the world be damned. The errant marginal notes in Orgel's book remind us of the melancholy reality of readers reading past or beyond or against a text. The blindness of this strange marginal reading, however, allows us to see with new eyes the sheer audacity of Spenser's poetic enterprise. Tilting at windmills, Spenser attempts nothing less than to reform English literature by reforming the English reader.

CHAPTER THREE

The Reading of the Damned

Doctor Faustus and Textual Conversion

CHRISTOPHER MARLOWE'S *Doctor Faustus* famously begins with the scholar in his study. Marlowe's Faustus addresses himself to a series of disciplines—philosophy, medicine, law, theology—each of which he ultimately rejects. In early modern performances of the play these arts or disciplines were almost certainly represented on stage by a book or succession of books. Dessen and Thomson's *Dictionary of Stage Directions* records roughly 130 examples of directions that call for a book or tablebook in plays performed between 1580 and 1642.[1] This number is in addition to the stage directions that call for such objects as parchments, scrolls, or paper and, of course, does not include all those moments when a play implicitly rather than explicitly calls for a book as prop. Easily procured and theatrically useful, the codex seems to have been a fairly common stage property in early modern drama.[2] Nevertheless, Marlowe's insistence on keeping the book on center stage in the opening acts of *Doctor Faustus* is extraordinary. Faustus, from his first moment on the stage until he leaves Wittenberg for the wider world, never appears in a scene in which he does not read some text, never appears in a scene in which he does not hold some book.[3] In Marlowe's play, Faustus's legendary dance with death begins as an elaborately choreographed dance with books.

Reading on stage, particularly reading a manuscript or printed book on stage, produces the illusion of the mind at work. As Dessen and Thomson suggest, "A book frequently conveys a state of contemplation, prayer, or melancholy in the figure who enters with it."[4] The reading subject is the thinking subject. In the opening scene of *Doctor Faustus*, however, it is precisely the scholar's rejection of the texts he reads that seems, in the first instance, to produce the illusion of a self-sufficient intelligence at work in the world. The opening scene of *Faustus* contains a dizzying mixture of languages, arts, idioms, all embodied in the texts Faustus rapidly invests himself in, and just as quickly divests himself of. Performing this sequence of reading acts, performing this series of selves, Faustus comes into being as an independent entity, as he emerges as the questing agent behind the various performances. The effect, however, does not produce precisely a sense of an inner self nor even what we might call inwardness; rather, it produces a kind of intentionality, a directedness toward the world. As many readers of the play have noted, Faustus is all hunger and revulsion, desire and disdain. It is characteristic of Marlowe that our sense of his characters as subjects is the product of a dramatic searching that is directed *outward*. Moreover, these subjectivities are often produced by addressing a succession of objects, a succession of props. In a discussion of the performance of the Marlovian subject, Michael Goldman suggests that this deployment of props is typical of Marlowe's tragedies:

> Initially, Marlowe's heroes present themselves to us as ravished by
> referring to an object, a prop. . . . We are urged to perceive the prop
> in its particularity—this book, this heap of money—and to enjoy its
> particular, practical power in a world whose physics and politics are
> well understood and briskly evoked. At the same time, however, the
> hero further defines himself by in some sense rejecting the prop. The
> prop is a source of bliss, but it is also—in some part or aspect—
> trash. Out of this double-valued attack on the prop emerges the
> audience's sense of character as definite, and definite in a way we
> usually think of as Marlovian—intensely appetitive, restlessly in mo-
> tion.[5]

On the one hand, Marlowe's use of props is theatrical shorthand; he uses the cultural resonance of the given prop to sketch in his characters. On the other hand, the audience sees from the beginning that these tragic figures are, in some sense, compromised by a perverse relationship to an object that defines them. In the opening scene of *Doctor Faustus*, the privileged object—the book—is, to the scholar in his study, a source of hope and despair.

Scholars have long recognized that this intense ambivalence toward the book—as that which renders Faustus both more than human and less than godly—is crucial to an understanding of the play. It is often read as both celebration and indictment of a peculiarly Renaissance and humanist aspiration. But this ambivalence must have also tapped into anxieties stemming from Reformation concerns with reading and representation. In Marlowe's deployment of the book as icon in this opening scene, he invokes both the Reformation's celebration of the book as the instrument of salvation and an iconoclasm that mistrusts all venerated objects.[6] Discussing Faustus's rejection of the Bible in favor of the necromantic books that ravish him, Anthony Dawson contends:

> The play's ambivalent preoccupation with books links the scene
> with the persistent strain of iconoclasm in sixteenth-century English
> culture. Although within Protestantism the book was seen as an
> antidote to idolatry, here we have the book that is venerated by
> Protestant, "iconophobic" England as the foundation of their reli-
> gion held up as an authoritative visual, as well as verbal, symbol, and
> then rejected because of a certain individualistic spin given to the
> interpretation of the sacred words. The Bible is dismissed as a kind
> of idol and then magical books are enshrined as idols in its place.
> The production of faction and apostasy is dramatized in a move that
> depends on both theatrical display of the book as icon and cultural
> wariness about its capacity to generate error.[7]

Dawson's insight concerning the book's capacity to generate error and produce faction and apostasy is central to my reading of *Doctor Faustus*. That *Faustus* dramatizes the dangers of reading goes without saying. I maintain, however, that we have not fully explored the ambivalence toward reading and the book that Marlowe exploits dramatically in *Faustus*. In post-Reformation England, reading is the way to both salvation and damnation. Both conversion and apostasy are time and again the consequence of an encounter with a text. In this chapter I contend that Faustus's apostasy is an example of an influential form of the conversion narrative: the readerly or textual conversion. By staging apostasy as textual conversion, Marlowe points not only to the seductive charms of the text and to the dangers of reading but also to the disturbing implications of the conventional Christian notion that texts penetrate and transform readers.

Textual Apostasy

It is not often noted that the opening scenes of Marlowe's *Doctor Faustus* dramatize a conversion experience. At the outset of the play the audience sees a man of learning grappling with his books, a man almost desperately searching for some kind of revelation. An encounter with a venerated text captivates or, as he says, ravishes him. Immersing himself in the world of this text, he finds a community of the like-minded and prepares for formal instruction. Finally, after an encounter with an otherworldy spirit, he commits himself body and soul to this new faith. The arc of this narrative would be recognizable to an audience living in an age in which conversion was epidemic. Of course, depending on one's perspective, depending on one's confessional camp, a given conversion narrative might also be a confession of apostasy.[8] As we see in the opening scene of *Doctor Faustus*, conversion is always a turning toward that is also a turning away, and Protestant and Catholic, radical and more traditional Reformer, might view a given conversion as a turn toward sin and damnation. Karl Morrison describes the double-edged nature of conversion: "Turning toward (conversion) and turning away from (aversion) were two aspects of the same act. One person turned to another by turning aside from some earlier object of attention." Given the two-sided character of conversion, "there could be bad conversions, as when the human heart fell into idolatry, turning from the Creator to worship the creature."[9] In an age of religious division and widespread conversion, the world was necessarily full of souls turning toward damnation.

That Faustus's spiritual change begins with books and reading is striking but not surprising. In the early modern period an increasing number of conversion narratives featured texts as agents of change. The prototype of what I am calling the readerly or textual conversion is the influential conversion scene in Book Eight of Augustine's *Confessions*.[10] If Saul's transformation into Paul on the road to Damascus established the generic conventions for conversion as unmediated divine revelation, Augustine's agonized conversion in the garden set the standard for the readerly conversion.[11] In the Reformation this kind of textual conversion would become ubiquitous as Reformers turned to scripture as the principal instrument of Christian revelation. Throughout the sixteenth and seventeenth centuries, scenes of reading served as the dramatic focal point of countless conversion narratives. Leading European Reformers like Luther and Zwingli famously attributed their conversion to an encounter with the letter of scripture.[12] Foxe's *Actes and Monuments* is

full of depictions of English men and women of the sixteenth century coming
to their beliefs through dramatic conversion experiences in which written
texts, often the Bible newly translated into English, played the crucial role.[13]
Foxe records the narrative of Thomas Bilney's conversion, which is both
idiosyncratic and broadly representative of many such conversion experiences:

> But at the last I harde [heard] speake of Iesus, verely when the new
> testament was first set fourth by Erasmus, which when I understode
> to be eloquently done by him, being allured rather for the latten
> [Latin] then for the word of god (which at that time I knew not
> what it mente), I bought it, euen by the prouidence of God, as I
> doo now well understand and perceiue. . . . [And that] first reding
> as I remember . . . did so exhilerate my hart, beyng before wounded
> with the gilte of my sinnes, and beyng almooste in dispayre, that
> euen immediately I semed vnto my selfe inwardly, to feele such a
> comfort and quietnes . . . that my brused bones lepte for ioye.[14]

The allusion at the end of this passage is to Psalm 51: "Make me to heare
ioye and gladnes, *that* the bones, *which* thou hast broken, maie reioyce." The
speaker of the psalm asks to be purged and cleansed, asks to be transformed
by God.[15] Lured to the New Testament by the siren song of Erasmus's elegant
Latin, Bilney is called to his spiritual redemption through the appeal of the
letter, and that glittering letter leads him to an experience that is terrifically
visceral. The act of reading so exhilarates his heart that he immediately feels
"such a comfort and quietnes . . . that my brused bones lepte for ioye."

Textual conversions were, of course, not merely the province of Protestants. Both Protestants and Catholics, more and less reformed, experienced
religious transformation through acts of reading. Textual conversions were
also not limited to encounters with scripture. Martyrologies like Foxe's *Actes
and Monuments* and John Gibbons's *Struggle of the Catholic Church in England* were written with an eye toward the conversion of the curious reader.
As Brad Gregory observes, "One of the martyrologists' clearest purposes was
propaganda in the etymological sense: they publicized the martyrs to prosely-
tize for Protestant [or, as Gregory argues later, Catholic] Christianity. . . .
[The texts] might make open supporters of the sympathetic or the curious,
just as martyrs' dying behavior sometimes converted spectators. . . . The
martyrs' witness would stun scoffers into silence and turn skeptics into believ-

ers."[16] In *The Lattre Examinacyon of Anne Askewe*, John Bale writes, "Full manye a Christen hart haue rysen and wyll ryse from the pope to Christ through the occasyon of . . . [the martyrs] consumynge in the fyre. As the saynge is, of their ashes wyll more of the same opynyon aryse."[17] And the ashes were made visible to Christian hearts through publications like Bale's. Texts of various kinds—polemical tracts, confessions of faith, conversion narratives—were cited by converts as catalysts for religious change. The serial convert William Alabaster attributed one of his conversion experiences (to Catholicism in this instance) to a text written by one William Rainolds in defense of the Douai-Rheims New Testament. In fact, Alabaster compares his textual conversion to the sequence of textual conversions that Augustine records in Book Eight of the *Confessions*.[18] Like Augustine, Alabaster hopes that the textual record of his conversion will help to turn his reader.

In all of these textual conversions, acts of reading bring about a certain transformation of the self. Tracking the ancient etymology of the term, Morrison notes, "In the languages of philosophy and theology, 'conversion' was a metaphor taken over from arts and crafts, especially from those employed in transforming raw materials into works of art or achieving some such alteration of metals as occurs in the production of bronze." Something of this early usage of the term "survives when the word *conversion* is used to describe, for example, chemical or metallurgic change."[19] We can see both senses of conversion in the arresting, if theologically conventional, final lines of John Donne's "Goodfriday, 1613. Riding Westward":

> I turne my backe to thee, but to receive
> Corrections, till thy mercies bid thee leave.
> O thinke mee worth thine anger, punish mee,
> Burne off my rusts, and my deformity,
> Restore thine Image, so much, by thy grace,
> That thou may'st know mee, and I'll turne my face.[20]

Here, the conversion experience, the turn toward the divine, is made possible by the transformation of the self. Always figured as the work of God's grace, this metamorphosis of the self was also often seen as the function of a transformative reading experience. Indeed, it was conventionally thought that the reading of scripture should properly be transformative. The meditative and devotional reading practices of the medieval and early modern periods insisted upon the transformation of the self through reading.[21] The first of the sermons appointed to be read in the Elizabethan Book of Homilies—"A frutefull exhortacion to the reading and knowledge of holy Scripture"—urges that readers of scripture not merely turn toward scripture but transform into it: "in reading of Gods word, he most profyteth not al wayes, that is most ready in turnyng of the boke . . . but he that is moste turned into it . . . moste in hys heart & life altred and changed into that thing, which he readeth."[22] But, of course, wherever an individual Christian fell on the confessional spectrum in the early modern period, he or she believed that many calling themselves Christians either failed to be transformed by their reading or were transformed improperly. In this chapter I want to suggest that Faustus's apostasy is not merely the wrong kind of transformative reading experience, not merely a turn away from salvation and toward damnation, but a parody of readerly conversion. Marlowe gives us conversion as burlesque, reading as travesty. He captivates the audience with the voyeuristic thrill of watching a virtuoso reader surrender to the seductions of the text. Putting the audience in the position of scorning the absurdity of Faustus's conversion, the absurdity of placing one's faith in such bookish ravishment, he calls into question what many considered the central act of Christian experience: the transformation of the self through text.

Two hugely influential conversion narratives, one ancient and one modern, set the stage for Faustus's readerly metamorphosis. The ancient narrative is Augustine's dramatic conversion in the garden. The modern is Luther's: the conversion heard round the world. All three scholars—Augustine, Luther, Faustus—experience a religious epiphany through an encounter with a text. In fact, one could argue that their spiritual change is a product of their encounter with the same text: Paul's Epistle to the Romans.[23] And for all three scholars, spiritual transformation is accompanied, and perhaps dependent upon, their transformation as readers.

Augustine's Finger

In Book Eight of the *Confessions*, Augustine depicts himself in crisis, urgently desiring to make a spiritual change but unable to do so. He explicitly frames his crisis as a *psychomachia* in which the old man and the new, the carnal and the spiritual, do battle: "A harsh bondage held me under restraint. The new will, which was beginning to be within me a will to serve you freely . . . was not yet strong enough to conquer my older will, which had the strength of old habit. So my two wills, one old, the other new, one carnal, the other spiritual, were in conflict with one another."[24] Desperate to reform his life, he wanders off in a garden in Milan and throws himself down "under a certain figtree":

> As I was . . . weeping in the bitter agony of my heart, suddenly I heard a voice from the nearby house chanting as if it might be a boy or a girl (I do not know which), saying and repeating over and over again 'Pick up and read, pick up and read.' At once my countenance changed, and I began to think intently whether there might be some sort of children's game in which such a chant is used. But I could not remember having heard of one. . . . I interpreted it solely as a divine command to me to open the book and read the first chapter I might find. . . . So I hurried back to the place where . . . I had put down the book of the apostle when I got up. I seized it, opened it and in silence read the first passage on which my eyes lit: [Romans 13:13–14]. . . . At once . . . it was as if a light of relief from all anxiety flooded into my heart. All the shadows of doubt were dispelled.
>   Then I inserted my finger or some other mark in the book and closed it.[25]

I include this seemingly incongruous final finger or other mark in my excerpt of this famous scene because I want to stress how crucial the materiality of language is to the narrative. In fact, the scene almost seems to exist as an instructive example of the dramatic and surprising ways in which the letter might serve as a vehicle for the spirit, might serve as an instrument of spiritual transformation.

However disembodied the genderless child's voice might seem, the "tolle lege" imperative escapes its immediate context and penetrates Augustine's garden only because it is vocalized, given physical form. Its material existence as utterance also underpins what we might call its iterability, its potential to be repeated and redeployed in different contexts, its potential to be read by Augustine as an imperative intended *for him*.[26] In his decision to appropriate the child's chant, Augustine commits himself to reading spiritually, allegorically.[27] And once he decides to read in this way, the entire episode is transformed. The garden setting, the fig tree, the genderless voice of the child—all of these now carry symbolic weight and suggest that a divine hand has set the stage for Augustine's famous turn. And, of course, the crucial prop in the scene is the codex that contains Paul's epistles.

By the time Augustine was writing, the codex had replaced the roll or scroll as the reading technology of choice in Christian culture. This development, in which the book form familiar to us today replaced the traditional roll or scroll, has been called the "most momentous development in the history of the book . . . [before] the invention of printing."[28] If Christians adopted the codex almost from the beginning, however, this technology did not simply replace older technologies like the scroll or wax tablet but existed alongside them. The codex, like all new media technologies, was defined within and against other, older forms with which it coexisted. Throughout the *Confessions* Augustine describes a variety of books and writing surfaces. In fact, as Eric Jager observes, the scroll and the wax tablet are referred to more frequently than the codex, and the codex does not appear in the text until "the series of readerly conversions leading up to Augustine's own conversion in the Milanese garden." In the *Confessions* then, the "codex as object and symbol" not only "stands out against" a "background of tablets and scrolls" but is also unmistakably associated with Christian conversion.[29] And in Augustine's drama the crucial prop of the codex again emphasizes the ways in which the materiality of the letter might serve as an instrument of spiritual revelation, as Augustine's manner of taking up the book seems to emphasize its physical properties as object. Augustine here plays a Christian version of *sortes Vergilianae*, or Virgilian Lots, a form of divination by chance selection of a passage in a text.[30] By doing so, Augustine emphasizes the indexical nature of the codex, the way it lends itself to random access and discontinuous reading, fragmented reading.[31] Unlike the scroll, the codex allows the easy movement from one portion of the text to another, allows one to mark or point to a passage and move or return to it instantly.[32] The finger that Augustine sticks in the codex at the end of the scene almost seems to literalize this indexical function.[33]

Paradoxically, it is precisely the contingency of the two events—the child's cry and the chance discovery of the relevant passage—that points to the working of some divine hand. In both cases the seemingly errant letter miraculously arrives at its destination. In my reading of this scene, the materiality of the letter is emphasized at every turn so that the reader can see the letter being transcended. Augustine is reborn as a Christian who will put off the flesh and put on Christ, but he is also, crucially, reborn as a reader, transformed into one who can transcend the letter in the service of the spirit.[34] That Augustine reads silently is, of course, essential to the scene: his silent reading of scripture, anticipated in the narrative by his famous rumination on the silent reading of Ambrose, marks the internalization and thus the spiritualization of the letter.[35] By staging the movement from letter to spirit, Augustine dramatizes a reading strategy that is at the same time a template for Christian conversion, turning away from the merely material things of the world and turning toward the divine.

Luther and the Alien Word

In 1545, a year before his death, Martin Luther wrote a preface to the Latin edition of his works that contained a brief account of his theological breakthrough and spiritual transformation. If Luther's conversion scene had not yet become what Brian Cummings calls an "historiographical fetish" in the latter half of the sixteenth century, it was already a crucial component of his legend.[36] At the outset of his narrative, Luther reminds his readers that he was "once a monk and a most enthusiastic papist"; or, as he puts it, a Saul. His breakthrough, however, is described not as a sudden revelation on the road to Damascus but as a product of intense, solitary labor, the labor of reading and writing. As he says, "I was all alone and one of those who, as Augustine says of himself, have become proficient by writing and teaching." Like Augustine's conversion, Luther's breakthrough is a product of his reading in Paul's Epistle to the Romans:

> I had . . . been captivated with an extraordinary ardor for under-standing Paul in the Epistle to the Romans. . . . But a single phrase in Chapter 1 . . . had stood in my way ['In the Gospel the righteous-ness of God is revealed']. For I hated that term 'righteousness of God.' . . . Though I lived as a monk without reproach, I felt that I was a sinner before God. . . . I did not love, yes, I hated the righteous God who punishes sinners, and secretly . . . I was angry with God, and said, 'As if, indeed, it is not enough that miserable sinners, eternally lost through original sin, are crushed . . . by the law of the decalogue, without having God add pain to pain . . . by the gospel threatening us with his righteousness and wrath!' Thus I raged with a fierce and troubled conscience. Nevertheless, I beat unrelentingly

upon Paul at that place, most ardently desiring to know what St. Paul wanted.

> At last, by the mercy of God, meditating day and night, I gave heed to the context of the words . . . I began to understand that the righteousness of God is . . . a gift of God . . . the passive righteousness with which merciful God justifies us by faith. . . . Here I felt that I was altogether born again and had entered paradise itself through open gates. There a totally other face of the entire Scripture showed itself to me.[37]

Luther's transformation, like Augustine's, begins with a desire for transformation. Crucially for Luther, that desire is not an expression of human will; instead it is a sign that he has already been ravished, or as he says captivated, by a desire that seems to arise outside the self. This desire is explicitly a desire for a revelatory reading experience: "I had . . . been captivated with an extraordinary ardor for understanding Paul in the Epistle of the Romans." Like Augustine, he isolates a passage and reads his sinful life through the lens of that passage. Also like Augustine, he is reborn into a different mode of reading: "Here I felt that I was altogether born again and had entered paradise. There a totally other face of the entire Scripture showed itself to me."

Unlike Augustine, however, Luther is not reborn into reading as transcendence, not reborn into allegory. For Luther, the resistance of the letter to interpretation is as important as his breakthrough; indeed, it is the cause of his breakthrough. In a letter to Nicholas Housemann from 1527, Luther writes, "The Prince of Demons himself has taken up combat against me; so powerfully and adeptly does he handle the Scriptures that my scriptural knowledge does not suffice if I do not rely on the alien Word [*alieno verbo*]."[38] In a brilliant reading, Heiko Oberman suggests that the concept of the alien word is fundamental to Luther's relationship to scripture. Ventriloquizing Luther, Oberman writes, "The 'alien Word' is the Gospel, which is not 'my own,' but which I must hear spoken 'to me.'"[39] Since the word of God must never be confused with the work of man's reason, the work of man's imagination, it remains alien, external, resistant to the will. In Luther's conversion scene this means that the resistance of the passage from Romans is a sign of God's grace, a sign of his hand in authoring this scene. For Augustine, since the letter kills and the spirit gives life, we must transcend the letter in a reading that is spiritual. But in his writings Luther wants to emphasize that the letter kills *so that* the spirit can give life. Death is necessary for rebirth, despair necessary for conversion—and conversion is never complete for Luther. He returns again and again to the alien word, insisting on its resistance to him and his alienation from it, so that again and again he can be reborn and shown the other face of scripture.

Luther here seems to follow in a long Christian tradition of meditative reading practices that work toward the transformation of the self, a tradition dominated by the reception of Augustine.[40] More specifically, he seems to be engaged in a version of *lectio divina*, a form of monastic asceticism focused on the reading and contemplation of the biblical text. *Lectio divina* incorporated reading (*lectio*), meditation (*meditatio*), and prayer (*oratio*), and it was a crucial component of the monastic reformation of the self.[41] Characteristically, Luther does not merely inherit but transforms this tradition. In the preface to the 1539 edition of his German works, the erstwhile Augustinian monk writes: "I want to point out to you a correct way of studying theology. . . . This is the way taught by holy King David (and doubtlessly used by all the patriarchs and prophets) in the one hundred nineteenth Psalm. There you will find three rules, amply presented throughout the whole Psalm. They are *Oratio, Meditatio, Tentatio*."[42] For Luther, the sequence was crucial. *Pace* meditative traditions like the *lectio divina*, prayer (*oratio*) must come first since one cannot rely on "reason and understanding" but can only hope to read scripture with the help of the Holy Spirit.[43] After prayer comes meditation (*meditatio*), which for Luther is a form of meditative reading practice ("reading and rereading . . . with diligent attention and reflection") that insists on returning again and again to the alien or external (*eusserlich*) word.[44] Finally, one's reading and meditation bring about a kind of spiritual affliction (*tentatio*), an affliction that is a sign of God's grace: "Thirdly, there is *tentatio, Anfechtung*. This is the touchstone which teaches you not only to know and understand, but also to experience how right, how true, how sweet, how lovely, how mighty, how comforting God's Word is, wisdom beyond all wisdom. . . . For as soon as God's Word takes root and grows in you, the devil will harry you, and will make a real doctor of you, and by his assaults will teach you to seek and love God's Word."[45]

In his own conversion narrative the *tentationes* or *anfechtungen* that he experiences as he beats upon Paul are the necessary precondition for his transformation. Only through suffering and despair can man be humbled enough to turn toward God and receive his grace. This is the alien work (*opus alienum*) of God that ultimately allows one to grasp the alien letter.[46] For Luther all conversion is a turning to the text of scripture, and scripture cannot be read without a transformation of the reading subject. As he writes in his *Lectures on the Psalms*, "No one can worthily speak or hear any Scripture, unless he is touched in conformity with it, so that he feels inwardly what he hears and says outwardly and says, 'Ah, this is true!'" But the Christian reader cannot be touched by scripture in this way unless God "humbles and afflicts him and brings him to remorse." In the *Lectures*, Luther explains this *tentatio* by making reference to Augustine's trauma in the garden in Milan. In "the conversion of Saint Augustine in Book 8 of his *Confessions*," we see the "remorse and meditation" without which one cannot begin to understand scripture.[47] Only in affliction can one begin to understand, and be transformed by, God's word.

Faustus Shrugs

In his opening speech, Faustus enjoins himself to

> Settle thy studies, Faustus, and begin
> To sound the depth of that thou wilt profess.
> Having commenced, be a divine in show,
> Yet level at the end of every art,
> And live and die in Aristotle's works.
> Sweet *Analytics*, 'tis thou hast ravished me![48]

From the beginning of the play, Faustus seems to desire a transformative reading experience. Having been ravished by the text of Aristotle in the past, he turns to it again. The nature of his absurdly quick tour through the disciplines of philosophy, medicine, law, and divinity suggests that he is restlessly searching for some kind of revelation. Faustus seems to stage a scene in which he will be converted by some text. But none of the texts he addresses seem to address him, and so the audience bears witness to a series of stillborn seductions as Faustus's books again and again fail to ravish him.

The opening scene also reads as if it is an extension of Augustine's game of Virgilian Lots with Faustus haphazardly opening his books, hoping to light upon a text that will speak to him. But the indexical character of the codex, which leads Augustine to the passage that will save him, leads Faustus to the fragmenting reading strategies that work to damn him. As the audience sees almost immediately, Faustus's desire to "settle [his] studies" and "sound the depths" is fatally compromised by his desire to "level at the end of every art." Restlessly in motion, Faustus is unable to meditate upon and "sound the depths" of the texts he reads. His initial turn to philosophy comes to an abrupt end when Faustus encounters the Ramist commonplace that disputing well is logic's greatest end:

> Affords this art no greater miracle?
> Then read no more; thou hast attained the end. (1.1.9–10)

His foray into medicine yields a similar response. If "the end of physic is our body's health," then Faustus, having "attained that end" and more, bids "Physic, farewell!" (1.1.17, 18, 27). And so it goes. As David Bevington and Eric Rasmussen note, the "end" in Faustus's desire to level at the end of every art can mean either "purpose" or "utmost limit."[49] But in every instance Faustus seems to read the purpose of the discipline as its limit or fulfillment; he reads the objective as an object that can be obtained or consumed and, once consumed, discarded like the book he holds in his hand.[50]

In this opening scene of *Doctor Faustus*, the scholar in his study continually misreads by equating the part with the whole, by reading an entire discipline through the lens of a textual fragment. As I mentioned in Chapter 2, this kind of reading in which undigested gobbets of text were removed from context and read as if whole, as if complete, was condemned by all sides as a splintering of the text that could lead to error and idolatry.[51] In his *Lectures on Genesis*, Luther rehearses a conventional line about the dangers of the "truncated Scripture text":

> It is the part of a good dialectician to take note of the tricks and devices of the devil which his slaves, the abominable sophists, also use as their own. Indeed, they support themselves with Scripture, because they would look laughable if they tried to force only their own dreams on men; but they do not quote Scripture in its entirety. They always snatch up what appears to favor them; but what is against them they either cleverly conceal or corrupt with their cunning glosses. . . . For the unwary are deceived when cunning men, according to their habit, switch from the parts to the whole, make uses of the fallacy of composition and division, or fail to cite passages in their entirety. . . . [A common trick is that] the text is not quoted in its entirety but is truncated in an utterly dishonest manner. . . .

Is it not a monstrous crime to jumble passages this way when so much is at issue?[52]

Of course, the most famous scene of reading in *Faustus* is the reading of just such a "truncated Scripture text." Like Augustine and Luther, Faustus famously latches on to a passage from Paul's Epistle to the Romans.[53]

Holding Jerome's Bible before him, Faustus first reads a passage from Romans suggesting that "the reward of sin is death" without, as every editor of the play points out, completing the passage by making reference to the gift of eternal life in the second half of the verse. He then reads a passage from John, and again Faustus truncates and thereby misreads the verse. Relying on fragments, Faustus fixes and reifies the text.[54] Faustus concludes with what Luther calls the "devil's syllogism," proving by logic the damnation of all of fallen humanity:

> Jerome's Bible, Faustus; view it well.
> [*He reads*]*Stipendium peccati mors est*. Ha!
> *Stipendium*, etc.
> The reward of sin is death. That's hard.
> [*He reads*] *Si pecasse negamus, fallimur*
> *Et nulla est in nobis veritas.*
> If we say that we have no sin,
> We deceive ourselves, and there's no truth in us.
> Why then belike we must sin,
> And so consequently die.
> Ay, we must die an everlasting death.
> What doctrine call you this, *Che serà, serà,*
> What will be, shall be? Divinity, adieu! (1.1.38–50)[55]

We tend to take Faustus's misreading of scripture both too seriously and not seriously enough. Faustus's truncation of scripture is often read as a sign of either despair or reprobation, and thus the scene is read as tragic. But if the scene is tragic when read in relation to Faustus's ultimate fate, it is, like so much in the play, comic in the moment. When searching out the theological implications of this moment of misreading, we sometimes miss its absurdity. As we are told again and again, the passages from Romans and John would be well known to any self-respecting Christian. In arguing for Faustus as a learned fool, Judith Weil asks an important question: how should we respond to "a 'divine in show' who . . . seems to be reading St. Paul for the first time?"[56] The answer, in the first instance, is a simple one: we laugh. And the laughter is not simply a product of the folly of Faustus's reading of the passage, it is also a product of his sublimely offhand dismissal of Christianity and all its grand paradoxes. The absurdity of Faustus's reading of scripture becomes even more pronounced if we line it up with the scene of reading in Luther's conversion narrative, a narrative that was available to the literate in Marlowe's England.

Between 1575 and 1578 a Protestant printer working under the auspices of John Foxe published several texts of Luther, newly translated into English.[57] This "little library of Luther," as Patrick Collinson calls it, would represent most of the Lutheran texts available in English for the next three hundred years.[58] Luther's *Commentary on Galatians* was the most theologically significant of these translations. The prefatory material introducing the *Commentary on Galatians* includes a brief biography of Luther, probably written by Foxe himself. The commentary and the biography would be printed in 1575, 1577, and 1588. In the English version of the biography the reader finds a slightly bastardized version of Luther's conversion narrative. In one of the more striking differences from Luther's autobiographical account, the English narrative suggests that Luther's battle with the text of Romans forces him to his bed without food, drink, or sleep, for three days and nights. He is "like a dead man . . . labouring in soule and spirite vppon a certaine place of S. Paule."[59] Here, the English version rewrites Luther's spiritual transformation so that it lines up more closely with Paul's conversion, whose experience on the road to Damascus similarly led to three days' suffering without food or drink.[60] Furthermore, the conversions of both Paul and Luther necessarily bring to mind the three days of Christ's death and resurrection. Although the English version takes liberties with the conversion narrative, in this respect it captures the spirit of Luther's despair and conversion. For Luther, conversion necessarily comprises death and rebirth. In the *Commentary on Galatians*, Luther discusses the depths of his despair as a monk who could not overcome the flesh to follow the spirit. His conclusion is that the despair that forces sinners to throw themselves on the mercy of God is "not onely a true, but also a godly and an holy desperation."[61] This despair is a function of reading. In the act of reading one continually confronts the law, the letter, the alien word, and in this existential confrontation with the letter that kills, the reader must die. Again and again in his writings, Luther insists that his readers must be converted, dying to their old selves and turning toward the spirit that gives life.[62]

In Lutheran terms then the problem with Faustus is not that he despairs, but that he does not despair enough. Faustus experiences no *tentatio*, no *anfechtung*. The letter of God's word, the letter of God's law, the specter of God's righteousness, do not, in Faustus's case, kill. And without that spiritual death, there can be no hope of redemption, rebirth. Much has been made of Marlowe's decision to place his Faustus in Luther's Wittenberg. The decision is, I think, overdetermined, but in this scene, Luther becomes the straight man in one of Marlowe's somewhat serious jokes. Rehearsing the most momentous conversion scene of the age, we get the scholar in his study wrestling *briefly* with Romans, wrestling *briefly* with God's justice, and his response is the wonderfully cavalier "Divinity, adieu." Faustus's apostasy is, crucially, not simply an errant conversion but a parody of conversion. Faced with the prospect of eternal damnation, Faustus shrugs. And when he does, the audience laughs at both the absurdity of Faustus's misreading and his magnificent insouciance in the face of eternal damnation. But the audience's laughter, I would contend, is also anxious. In this scene of textual impropriety, any Christian should read the possibility of his or her own damnation.

If taking Faustus's bungling of scripture too seriously prevents us from seeing its absurdity, not taking the episode seriously enough prevents us from seeing its universal relevance. Because the specific misreading is so egregious, it is often read simply as a sign of a flaw in Faustus's character. But Faustus's misprision, however erroneous, is a symptom of a much larger problem for the Christian reader: no reading strategy can avoid the problem that Marlowe dramatizes here. Reformers, of course, championed the Bible as a single book, as a coherent text that stands apart and alone from all other texts. They decried medieval works like the *Gloss Ordinaria* and Peter Lombard's *Sentences* that atomized scripture, works that seemed to encourage Christians to read scripture as a series of discrete texts.[63] Faustus's patently unorthodox reading seems to reflect the Protestant animus against the atomization of the text. Indeed, if Faustus errs in his reading of Romans, he errs in the same way that Luther did before his breakthrough. Luther too fixated upon a textual fragment and read it as a sign of his own damnation. Luther too despaired of his own salvation. Crucially, Luther's breakthrough in reading Romans came about when, as he writes, "at last, by the mercy of God . . . I gave heed to the context of the words."[64] Thus, Luther's dramatic revelation is the consequence of observing one of the simplest of hermeneutic principles.

He simply changes the frame and so transforms the textual fragment that so tormented him. But there's the rub. Before we follow the early modern polemicists who insist that the kind of truncation of scripture we see in Faustus is transparent folly, we might remember that the history of Christianity is the history of fragmented reading. More broadly, we might remember that there is no reading that can circumvent the essential friability of text. While the Reformers' conception of the Bible certainly changed the ways in which people read scripture, the texts of the Bible stubbornly remain, for Reformers as for everyone else, multiple and various. Bringing the texts into some kind of alignment requires interpretive choices about the relation and relative significance of different parts of scripture. Even for a "good dialectician," the fragmentation of scripture is inevitable. The converted Luther, like all readers, could not avoid some kind of splintering of the text. Because it did not fit with his *sola fide* convictions, and was so often used by his enemies to confound him, Luther famously dismissed the Epistle of James as an epistle of straw.[65] As Catholic polemicists were quick to point out, Reformers too "snatch[ed] up what appear[ed] to favor them"; they too failed "to cite passages in their entirety." They, like all readers, selected passages that spoke to them and discarded others.

* * *

If Luther frames his conversion as a consequence of his returning a fragmentary text to its proper place in the Christian dialectic, Faustus's conversion is a consequence of his following the logic of reification and fragmentation through to the end. In Christian thought, this is the logic of idolatry. In early modern England idolatry is often conceived of as a violation of the properly teleological thrust of interpretation.[66] This is an essentially Augustinian hermeneutic in which the chain of signifiers, the play of signification, must not stop until it reaches its ultimate endpoint in the divine.[67] All things are potentially signs, and all signs must ultimately refer to God. Thus, the Augustinian reader can never rest at the level of the sign. To interrupt the reading process, to halt the play of signification before arriving at the divine, is to be in thrall to the signifier. Faustus's dynamic reading performance in the scene in the study apes the restless movement of Augustinian hermeneutics, but his inclination to interrupt the progress of signification, to read at the level of the fragment, and ultimately to tarry with the signifier is the mirror image of Augustinian hermeneutics. The audience sees the endpoint of Faustus's reading strategies when Faustus locates divinity, locates transcendence, in the letter, when he reads "these necromantic books . . . [as] heavenly":

> Lines, circles, signs, letters, and characters—
> Ay, these are those that Faustus most desires. (1.1.52–54)

Here, we see a willingness to arrest the progress of signification, to embrace the letter that kills. The wonderfully telling "these are those" performs for us the short circuit in Faustus's hermeneutic, the way in which Faustus empties the sign of referent and so creates a sign that doubles back on itself, that fails to point to anything but itself. His reading transformed, Faustus is reborn as an idolater.

That Faustus's transformation is a conversion to idolatry is wonderfully clear. This clarity, however, should not obscure the fact that Faustus's transformation is not so different from the transformations of Augustine and Luther, or indeed the transformation of any Christian converted by an encounter with a text. To the iconoclast, Faustus's conversion is suspect because he grounds his new faith in his affective response to the text: "these are those that Faustus most desires." But this seems true of all textual converts. To be converted by a text is to give yourself over to the affective experience of reading. As Augustine describes it, his conversion is a product of a sudden emotional response to a text, an abrupt conviction that the text in question spoke directly to him: "it was as if a light . . . flooded into my heart. All the shadows of doubt were dispelled." In Augustine's drama in the garden, the encounter with a very material text becomes a certain sign of the spiritual dimension of his life, an indication that the hand of providence was at work shaping events. Luther's conversion is, in some sense, more intellectual: his encounter with a text forces him to change his conception of the relation of man to the divine. But that scholarly conversion is authenticated by an emotional transformation. Indeed, for Luther abjection before the letter of God's law is the necessary precondition for a transformation that is both emotional and conceptual, a transformation that is never complete. In *Doctor Faustus*, we see Marlowe's theologian frustrated, bored, and ultimately seduced by text. If his conversion is transparently heresy, it is also the mirror image of the readerly conversions so prevalent in the age. As always, Marlowe seduces his audience with the specter of its own fears and desires. In his conversion to idolatry, Faustus foregrounds the hopes and anxieties of a religious culture that grounds its faith in a transformative encounter with a text.

Bloody Deeds

In a play that attempts to shock through blasphemy, that asks us to imagine Bibles being burned, the lukewarm blood of newborn babes offered as sacrifice, perhaps the most blasphemous moment is Faustus's declaration of a simple, well-known, Latin tag: *Consummatum est*. With this line, the apostasy of Marlowe's Faustus would seem to be complete. Having abjured his faith, committed himself body and soul to the devil's party, he seals the pact—the so-called deed of gift—by appropriating Christ's dying words, mocking Christ on the cross:

> *Consummatum est.* This bill is ended,
> And Faustus hath bequeathed his soul to Lucifer. (2.1.74–75)

Faustus bequeaths his soul in the form of a "deed of gift," a contract written in Faustus's blood. This deed is reminiscent of the Charter of Christ, a popular late-medieval lyric in which Christ's crucified flesh is figured as a textual document. A staple of Middle English religious poetry, the "Charter of Christ," in its various incarnations, used the metaphor of a legal document to establish the crucifixion as a contract exchanging Christ's sacrificed body for Man's deliverance.[68] As Andrew Galloway notes, Faustus's " '*Consummatum est*: this bill is ended' . . . precisely echoes the words Christ uses in most English versions of the Charter to seal his bill: '*Consummatum est* this chartre es done.' "[69] Faustus's deed of gift is then an inverted form of the Charter of Christ; Faustus sells what Christ has purchased.

   In the conceit of the Charter, Christian redemption is figured as the inheritance of property or land.[70] And that inheritance is conditional: man must merit the inheritance through good works and proper penitence. Likewise, Faustus's "deed of gift" is anything but a gift. Having been reassured of the powers he will have once the devil has his soul, Faustus deduces:

> Then there's enough for a thousand souls.
> Here, Mephistopheles, receive this scroll,
> A deed of gift of body and of soul—
> But yet conditionally that thou perform
> All articles prescribed between us both. (2.1.88–92)

The word "gift" that Mephistopheles repeats throughout the exchange is a clumsy screen for what is transparently not a gift but an exchange of goods for services, legally documented. The term "deed of gift," invoked three times in this scene, seems to be Marlowe's addition to the Faust legend. It is not a term used in the *English Faust Book*, which refers to the document alternately as a covenant, promise, or obligation.[71] As Lowell Gallagher notes, a "deed of gift" is properly understood as "the unilateral transfer of property," whereas the kind of "bilateral concessions" Faustus describes in this passage "would be more typical of a contract."[72] By using the language of the gift to describe what is clearly understood to be a quid pro quo contract, Marlowe muddies the theological waters. As discussed in the previous chapter, the Reformation brought about a revolution in the conception of the gift.[73] As Luther insisted, comprehending the free gift of grace was impossible for the fallen faculty of reason; it could be grasped only through faith. Trusting reason, Faustus falls into a legal and economic logic that does not allow him to understand the nature of the gift, the nature of grace.

In the contract scene the "deed of gift" comes to embody both the exchange of Faustus's soul and his desire to convert his soul into an object of exchange. "Deed" is a word that encodes the way speech acts can be committed to text, the way documents reify actions. The rare triple rhyme—souls/ scroll/soul—draws our attention to the way in which the document here stands in for Faustus's soul, materially embodying both the performance of Faustus's deed and the alienable property Faustus sees fit to exchange. Of course, the corporeal nature of the document is viscerally underscored by the blood with which Faustus writes the text. And the emblem of Faustus's desire to treat his soul as property, as marketable object, is a scroll. As I noted earlier, Dessen and Thomson's *Dictionary of Stage Directions* records roughly 130 examples of directions that call for a book or tablebook between 1580 and 1642; by contrast, they record only five examples of stage directions that call for a roll or scroll.[74] Of course, stage directions only tell us so much, and we know that there are many more than five instances in which scrolls were used as props on the early modern English stage. Nevertheless, a twenty-five-to-one ratio seems to indicate that the scroll was a much less common stage prop than the codex. Given the number of codices that have been on display in the opening acts of *Doctor Faustus*, the scroll would stand out as a text of a different kind, one that works to clarify the ongoing transformation of Faustus.

As props on the early modern stage, scrolls often seem to signal the workings of what we might call, following Emily Steiner, documentary culture.[75] Onstage, scrolls often signify decrees, records, bonds: texts that act instrumentally within political, legal, and economic institutions. Even more than the codex, they are seen as an extension of bureaucracy, the textual glue of a society based upon the written word. Given the contractual contexts in which the scroll so often appears, the prop would seem to reinforce the audience's sense of the "deed of gift" as a legal and economic exchange. One thinks of the test of the suitors in *The Merchant of Venice*, a scene in which the scrolls in the caskets represent the legal and economic will of the father, a dead letter that extends beyond the grave to control the living. By alluding to the culture of legal, political, and economic institutions, the scroll figures Faustus's spiritual degradation. That degradation, however, is not merely a product of confusing spiritual and economic registers. The scroll is emblematic not merely of law but of the Law. Faustus embraces not merely the logic of documentary culture but the logic of the Old Testament. Scholars have shown the ways in which Christians and Jews adopted codex and scroll precisely to differentiate the two communities.[76] In certain early modern contexts, the scroll becomes a form associated with law rather than grace, old rather than new, letter rather than spirit. Perhaps as we watch Faustus move from codex to scroll, from Jerome's Bible to his bloody deed, we can chart the "form of Faustus' fortunes" through the forms of the texts he reads and writes (Prologue, line 8).

Both on the early modern stage and within the fiction of the play, the scroll is a piece of stage business. Like Augustine's codex, the scroll is the central prop in a scene that has been staged to *convert* Faustus, to turn or twist him toward his new faith. It is telling that it is Mephistopheles who insists again and again on both the writing of the "deed of gift" and the legalistic rituals that attend it:

> But, Faustus, thou must bequeath it solemnly
> And write a deed of gift with thine own blood,
> For that security craves great Lucifer.
>
> .   .   .   .
>
> Then stab thine arm courageously,
> And bind thy soul that at some certain day
> Great Lucifer may claim it as his own
>
> .   .   .   .

> But Faustus, thou must write it in manner of a deed of gift.
>
> . . . .
>
> Speak, Faustus. Do you deliver this as your deed? (2.1.34–36, 49–51,
>   59–60, 114–15)

As Luke Wilson notes, the very idea of a contract with the devil is preposter-
ous: "Faustus, and perhaps even Mephistopheles himself, accept the strange
premise that it makes sense to enter into a contract with the devil, that such
a contract has some sort of validity. But what sort? What could such a contract actually mean?"[77] Of course, there is no reason to believe that *Mephistopheles* accepts this "strange premise"; it seems clear from evidence within this
scene and from elsewhere in the play that the audience is supposed to understand that Mephistopheles engages in a ritual centered around texts because
he is putting on a show for the credulous Faustus.

Earlier in the play Mephistopheles had dismissed the notion that "magical" language was either efficacious or binding. After he performs his ritual
incantation and successfully conjures a devil, Faustus believes that there is
"virtue in my heavenly words" and exults over the "force of magic and my
spells" (1.3.28, 32). Mephistopheles suggests, however, that he came of his
"own accord," that the incantation was the cause of his arrival, but only "*per
accidens*":

> For when we hear one rack the name of God,
> Abjure the Scriptures and his Saviour Christ,
> We fly in hope to get his glorious soul,
> Nor will we come unless he use such means
> Whereby he is in danger to be damned. (1.3.47–52)

In other words, the performance of the words is not efficacious but only
indicative of Faustus's desire to turn toward sin and damnation.[78] The "lines,
circles, signs, letters, and characters" that Faustus ritually deploys are irrele-
vant; what matters is what Faustus desires. This notion that ritual language
is empty theater gets reproduced later in the play when the curses of the pope
and his minions ("*Maledicat Dominus!* . . . *Maledicat Dominus!* . . . *Maledicat
Dominus!*" etc.) prove both inconsequential and, in the face of the mockery
of Faustus and Mephistopheles, absurd (3.1.91–99). And like the other examples of ritualized or performative language, the efficacy of the contract is
undermined as the play proceeds. After a moment of backsliding in which

Faustus looks to heaven for mercy, he offers to write the "deed of gift" a
second time to receive the pardon of Lucifer:

> Sweet Mephistopheles, entreat thy lord
> To pardon my unjust presumption,
> And with my blood again I will confirm
> My former vow . . . (5.1.70–73)

Here, we have none of the ceremony of the "former vow," however, as
Mephistopheles commands Faustus to "do it . . . quickly" lest he fall into
"greater danger" (5.1.74–75). Of course, that Faustus writes the "deed of gift"
a second time only serves to render the contract suspect in the eyes of the
audience. And yet Faustus continues to believe.

Capitalizing on Faustus's belief in the power of text to bind, Mephistopheles seeks to ensnare the scholar with the hoariest of morality play contriv-
ances, the devil's contract. To the end of the play and his allotted days,
Faustus continues to see the "deed of gift," wherein he sells his soul for his
cunning, as the unforgivable sin. At the end of the *English Faust Book* it is
the contract that keeps Faustus from believing in the possibility of redemption. When Faustus confesses to his students that he has sold his soul to the
devil and that his payment is due, they implore him to turn to God: "This
they repeated unto him, yet it could take no hold, but even as Cain he also
said his sins were greater than God was able to forgive; for all his thought
was on his writing; he meant he had made it too filthy in writing it with his
own blood" (179). At the end of Marlowe's play, when the scholars remind
Faustus that God's mercies are infinite, he replies, "Faustus' offence can ne'r
be pardoned. The serpent that tempted Eve may be saved, but not Faustus."
His list of offenses ends with a fatalistic reference to the "deed of gift": "I
writ them a bill with mine own blood. The date is expired, the time will
come, and he will fetch me" (5.2.41–43). But, as every reader of the play
knows, the problem is not that the contract is binding, and it is not that
Faustus has made it too filthy by writing it with his own blood. What is
crucial is that in writing it, in signing it, he comes to believe. Faustus is
undone by his faith in text.

Reading God's Handwriting

A funny thing happens on the way to Faustus's damnation: the sorcerer's
retrograde progress toward the dead letter of the law is interrupted by techni-

cal difficulties—difficulties, as it happens, in reading and writing. Encouraging the scholar to "stab . . . [his] arm courageously," Mephistopheles instructs Faustus to "bind [his] soul" by writing the contract with his own blood. Faustus agrees to do so, but in the act of writing, his blood famously congeals and he "can write no more" (2.1.49–50, 62). When Mephistopheles leaves to "fetch . . . fire to dissolve it straight," Faustus is left alone on stage to ponder the significance of his recalcitrant blood:

> What might the staying of my blood portend?
> Is it unwilling I should write this bill?
> Why streams it not, that I may write afresh?
> "Faustus gives to thee his soul"—ah, there it stayed!
> Why shouldst thou not? Is not thy soul thine own?
> Then write again: "Faustus gives to thee his soul." (2.1.63–69)

Faustus immediately reads the staying of his blood as a sign, but it is a sign that he has trouble deciphering. Scholars often interpret Faustus's failure to read what the staying of his blood portends as akin to his inability to read scripture. They read this failure—as well as his misapprehension about the ownership of his soul—as an indictment of his spiritual acumen. Luke Wilson asserts, for instance, that "the theological point is fairly simple, and Faustus is as usual a poor theologian."[79] As the scene progresses, Faustus's evident interpretative deficiencies only become more pronounced.

When Mephistopheles returns with fire to dissolve his blood, Faustus attempts to make an end of the business, declaring his allegiance: "*Consummatum est.* This bill is ended, /And Faustus hath bequeathed his soul to Lucifer" (2.1.74–75). The progress of the transaction is arrested again, however, this time by an "inscription" on Faustus's flesh:

> But what is this inscription on mine arm?
> *"Homo, fuge!"* Whither should I fly?
> If unto God, he'll throw thee down to hell.—
> My senses are deceived; here's nothing writ.—
> I see it plain. Here in this place is writ,
> *"Homo fuge!"* Yet shall not Faustus fly. (2.1.76–81)

Faustus's inability to read properly what is right in front of him is wonderfully absurd. Reading the injunction to fly as a threat rather than an invitation, Faustus cannot see the significance of the prodigy: quite simply that he is being called—for a second time—to turn away from the demonic and toward the divine. But the farcical nature of this second moment of reading cuts two ways. It is not simply a function of Faustus's mulish obduracy but a function of the gross literalization of the previous scene of reading. And if the peculiar repetition and literalization of the invitation to read seems to call Faustus's theological literacy into question, it also works to undermine the entire hermeneutic enterprise. By staging this scene of reading twice, the first time as interpretative tragedy and the second time as farce, Marlowe draws the audience's attention to the difficulty of attempting to read the workings of divine providence in the world, a difficulty exacerbated by the epistemological crisis in Christian thought occasioned by the Reformation.

Writing on the flesh has a long history in the stories Christians tell about themselves. Among the many wonders to be found in *The Golden Legend*, one can read an account of the legible body of Ignatius of Antioch:

> It is read that S. Ignatius in all his torments and all the pains of martyrdom that he suffered, that his tongue never ceased to name the name of Jesus, and when they that tormented him demanded him wherefore he named this name so oft, he answered: Know ye for certain that I have in my heart this name written. . . . And because hereof, when he was dead, they that heard these words opened his body and drew out his heart and cut it open, and they found within the name of Jesus written with fair letters of gold, for which miracle many received the faith of Jesu Christ.[80]

Here, the metaphor of writing on the heart—a metaphor often deployed to demonstrate the transcendence of the letter—is marvelously literalized.[81] The miraculous transformation of Ignatius's figurative expression to embodied text is then the cause of future conversions. Inscriptions on the body like that of Ignatius often point in two directions: they are signs of exceptional faith and signs that engender faith. The most famous inscriptions on the body were the stigmata of Saint Francis. *The Golden Legend* informs its readers that "the wounds of the crucifying" appeared "in his hands, his feet, and in his side." During his life, he "did hide these tokens as much as he might, that no man should see them," his humility further evidence of the scrupulous imitation of Christ that the miraculous wounds disclose. Nevertheless, the wounds were made public and therefore could do the work of engendering faith since "some saw them in his life, and at his death they were seen of many." And lest there be any doubt concerning this miraculous writing on the flesh, the fact that these truly were the stigmata was made manifest "by many miracles."[82] Here, the epistemological regime of the miracle leads to an infinite regression as the truth of the miraculous is confirmed by further evidence of the miraculous. Accounts of the miraculous textualization of the flesh were not simply part of the Catholic archive; they were alive and well in sixteenth-century Europe. In 1585 it was claimed that Maria Maddalena di Pazzi's flesh became word during an act of reading. According to her biographer, while she read the Gospel of John, her heart was inscribed by none other than Augustine: "St. *Augustine* at two different times engraved upon her heart these four words, *Verbum caro factum est, the word was made flesh*: the first time in letters of bloud . . . the second time in letters of gold."[83] The miraculous legibility of the flesh is here a product of the transformative power of reading. The import of the miracle is fairly straightforward: through transformative reading the word metaphorically becomes flesh, and therefore, we understand one of the fundamental truths of Christianity, that the Word was indeed made flesh. But the recursive character of the miracle is remarkable: not only is the word literally made flesh but the word that is made flesh is precisely the phrase *Verbum caro factum est*. Increasingly in post-Reformation Europe the miracle has to work to shore up the epistemology that subtends it as the miraculous becomes evidence of the miraculous, evidence that we live in a world of divine immanence.

In a post-Reformation world, evidence of a given confessional camp's privileged relationship to the deity was imperative. Faced with a bewilderingly chaotic religious landscape, many Catholic writers explicitly grounded their faith in the miraculous. Leading figures like Robert Bellarmine, Justus Lipsius, and Robert Chambers contended that the miracles consistently associated with reliquaries and pilgrimage sites demonstrated both that Catholicism was divinely favored and that the devotional practices associated with these places, decried by Reformers, were legitimate in the eyes of God.[84] They asked what miracles Protestants could offer to confirm that Reformation teachings were divinely sanctioned. For their part, Protestants ridiculed what they considered the Catholic reliance on miracles. Reformers insisted again and again that the age of miracles was over and that anything that appeared miraculous in the present day was either fraudulent or demonic.[85] In his *Institutes* Calvin argues that miracles have "vanished away." They were a temporary gift no longer necessary for those who have true scripture; in this latter age miracles give way to the marvel that is "the new preaching of the gospel."[86] Reformers embraced a text-based faith and rejected ways of knowing grounded in the body, the flesh, the world.[87] For Reformers, to refuse to believe unless one could see or touch was to commit the error of doubting Thomas, which became an important scriptural reference in the period. As Glenn Most has shown, the story of doubting Thomas was read in "a new and quite different" way in the Reformation, and this new interpretation reflected a disavowal of faith grounded in the evidence of the senses.[88] In Protestant terms, the error of doubting Thomas is twofold. He is wrong to doubt without seeing, and he is also wrong to believe *because* he has seen. In his *Commentarie vpon the Euangelist S. Iohn*, Calvin contends that the "dulnes of Thomas is wonderful & monstrous" since "he wold also haue his hands to be witnesses of his resurrection." Thomas's evident "need to be drawn vnto the faith violently by the experiences of his senses" is to be scorned since it "is quite contrary to the nature of faith," which does not arise from "the bare experiments of things" but "from the word of god."[89] Of course, even as Reformers rejected Catholic miracles and the empirical mindset they betrayed, Reformation thought encouraged the reading of the hand of divine providence in the world. The Calvinist deity, in particular, was decidedly interventionist. As scholars have shown, belief in a vigorous providentialism was widespread in early modern England.[90] In the providentialist conception of the relation of man and the divine embraced by most English Protestants, the age of miracles was over, and yet God's hand could be discerned everywhere in the world.

A version of the "writing on the flesh" scene in *Doctor Faustus* can be found in Marlowe's source, the *English Faust Book*: Faustus "tooke a small penknife, and prickt a vaine in his left hand, & for certaintie therevpon, were seene on his hand these words written, as if they had been written with blood, *o homo fuge*; whereat the Spirit vanished, but Faustus continued in his damnable minde."[91] The scene is described with remarkable conviction. The *Faust Book* insists that it is a "certaintie" that these words—"O HOMO FUGE"—"were seene on his hand." As with many accounts of the miraculous and the providential in the period, the confidence of the assertion here seems strangely defensive. How could we know with any certainty that the historical Faustus saw these words? Even if some kind of first-person account existed, Faustus could hardly be described as a reliable narrator. And, if not Faustus, then who witnesses the inscription? The use of the passive voice whitewashes the problem of subjective perception: it is a certainty that the words "were

seen." In the play, of course, Marlowe foregrounds the problem of perception: "My senses are deceived; here's nothing writ: / I see it plain. Here in
this place is writ." Not content to believe what he sees in front of him,
Faustus doubts his senses. And in his doubt Faustus is perfectly orthodox,
according to both Catholic and Protestant doctrine. In *De Doctrina Christiana*, Augustine warns that the fallen signs of this world can be shaped by the
demonic: "For it is brought about as if by a certain secret judgment of God
that men who desire evil things are subjected to illusion and deception . . .
by those lying angels to whom . . . the lowest part of this world is subject."
Good Christians then should denounce and avoid "imaginary signs."[92] Luther's *Table Talk* records a conversation in which Luther speaks of "sorcerers
and the art of magic and of how Satan blinds men." In the course of the
conversation, Luther makes reference to Faustus: "Much has been said of
Faustus, who called the devil his brother-in-law. . . . If I, Martin Luther, had
done no more than extend my hand to him, he would have destroyed me."
After a brief discussion of seemingly supernatural encounters that have been
reported in the German countryside, Luther suggests why figures like Faustus
are so threatening: "You see, such is the power of Satan to delude men's
outward senses. What must he do to their souls?"[93] That Marlowe's Faustus
doubts his senses when he sees the writing on his flesh ("My senses are deceived; here's nothing writ") is not further evidence of a lack of faith but a
proper questioning of the signs of the fallen world. Without that doubt, the
miraculous writing would produce a credulous and passive "reader" who
need only respond with wonder to a visible sign and obey the injunction.
Both Protestants and Catholics accused those in the other camp of just such
a blind credulity, of believing not wisely but too well in the things of this
world. In doubting what he sees, Faustus, initially at least, reads properly.

The "writing on the flesh" scene is part of the documentary record, but
the "staying of blood" is not. This earlier incident seems to be another addition by Marlowe to the Faustus legend, an addition that forces the audience
to read the two dramatic moments in relation to each other and in relation
to the larger cultural conversation about the nature of divine intervention.
The "staying of blood" invites a providential reading of the hand of the
divine at work in the world, but it is not an example of the miraculous. There
is nothing unnatural about congealing blood; rather, it is the uncanny way
in which the mundane occurrence seems to address the situation at hand that
suggests the possibility of some other agency at work. The "staying of blood"
here is reminiscent of the seemingly contingent events in Augustine's conver-

sion narrative. As in Augustine's narrative, in this scene it is a serendipitous timeliness that suggests that a divine voice is speaking to those with ears to hear. The inscription on the flesh, in contrast, is a disruption of nature and, therefore, must be read as either miracle or demonic illusion. If the inscription is real, then it is a subversion of the natural order, and Christians of various confessional camps agreed that only God could overturn the natural order. If the inscription is a product of Faustus's deluded senses, then it must be of demonic origin, since signs and wonders that work to deceive man's fallen senses are the province of the devil.

The difference between a Protestant insistence on the workings of providence and a Catholic insistence on the workings of the miraculous was crucial to polemicists on both sides of the confessional divide. At the same time, as Alexandra Walsham has argued, the distinction was often difficult to maintain:

> It is important to remember that all of these categorical assertions were made in the heat of controversy, by commentators braced for combat in the confessional boxing ring. . . . When the clergy discussed the question in other discursive contexts their answers were not so cut and dried. . . . Theologians . . . preserved room in Reformed cosmology for events that occurred "beside the order so appointed" at creation: they simply subsumed them under the category of "special" or "extraordinary providences." "By a metonymy of the effect," conceded William Ames, an occurrence of this kind could be "called a Miracle." But the concept was hedged about with a number of significant qualifications. . . . Most examples of providential interference were *miranda* not *miracula*, preternatural wonders brought about by divine manipulation of secondary causes and elemental forces. Calvinist theoreticians insisted that these two types of occurrences were generically distinct, but in practice, application, and above all collective perception, the line of demarcation between miracles, providences, and prodigious but entirely natural vents was very hazy indeed. . . . As contemporaries recognized, there was plenty of potential for confusion.[94]

Given this potential for confusion, it is striking that Marlowe alters his source material to offer the audience two distinct signs. Playing with his audience's preconceptions, Marlowe dramatizes in rapid succession what look like a

Protestant and providential reading of the divine hand in the world and an "idolatrous" and Catholic reliance on signs and wonders. By adding the staying of the blood to the scene he finds in his source, Marlowe allows the audience to see the different kind of reading that each entails. He emphasizes the difference by making the latter a vulgar repetition of the former. Marlowe seems to be asking his presumably largely Protestant audience to laugh at, or react in dismay to, the vulgarity of Catholic miracles. He seems to be inviting reformed members of his audience to "read" the hyper-legibility of the writing on the flesh as cause for doubt, if not laughter. The point here is not that the audience is responding to fine theological distinctions but that Marlowe makes these distinctions visible as *aesthetic* differences. But this is one of Marlowe's traps, because, of course, despite the difference in the way the signs address themselves to Faustus, the play ultimately makes no distinction between them. In the morality play logic of *Faustus*, anything that works to dissuade the scholar from his path toward damnation would seem to represent the workings of providence. In context, both the congealed blood and the inscribed flesh seem to be examples of divine intervention, and both interventions are equally ineffective in persuading Faustus to turn away from the contract.

Faustus's relationship to these two wondrous signs is clarified by a third intervention. When Mephistopheles sees Faustus attempting to determine the meaning of the inscription on his flesh he decides to "fetch him somewhat to delight his mind" and exits the stage (2.1.82). He returns with devils who give "crowns and rich apparel" to Faustus, "dance," and "then depart." When Faustus demands that Mephistopheles speak, that he tell Faustus, "What means this show?," Mephistopheles responds, "Nothing, Faustus, but to delight thy mind withal" (2.1.83–84). That Mephistopheles cannot be bothered to hide the emptiness of the spectacle he presents is wonderfully telling. Through Mephistopheles, Marlowe repeats what the audience already knows, that this is a dumb show, a spectacular sign that fails to signify. Marlowe offers the audience three spectacles: the first invites an allegorical reading, the second invites a literal reading, and the third forecloses reading in favor of the pleasures of the senses. Given the Reformation's rejection of ways of knowing grounded in the flesh, it is tempting to suggest that we can trace Faustus's spiritual decline in this descent from abstraction to sensuality. But Marlowe consistently collapses the distinctions his audience might make between "carnal" and "spiritual" signs. Just as Marlowe shows us that books and words can be icons, so he shows us that "dumb shows" can be signs that signify "properly." Here, the audience is expected to read Mephistopheles' dumb show correctly, to understand that it is a demonic intervention into events, which attempts to distract Faustus from the divine signs that would save him. For the audiences, if not for Faustus, it is not merely a spectacle but a sign that signifies properly. In the world of *Doctor Faustus*—as in the world inhabited by Marlowe's audience—there is no aspect of the material world that cannot be given a spiritual reading by a discerning "reader." Likewise, there are no signs that are not carnal.

Marlowe's play reflects the problem at the heart of a providentialism that would do away with all flesh: if one is to see the hand of God in the world, one must necessarily place one's trust in the senses that apprehend that world; if God's writing is to be found in the world, then it is inescapably material. Moreover, one's experience of that world is shaped by one's aesthetic responses to the world, by one's response to form, beauty. By staging these three interventions in the way that he does, Marlowe asks the audience to consider the role of the aesthetic in interpretation. This is not to suggest that Marlowe champions one confessional camp over another, or even that he is fundamentally concerned with the difference in confessional camps. Rather, it is to suggest that Marlowe stages for us the impossibility of escaping the aesthetic dimension of experience. In Marlowe's play, the theatricality of Mephistopheles' spectacle allows us to see retroactively the theatricality of—the aesthetic dimension of—the two divine interventions. One cannot escape the aesthetic just as one cannot escape the affective experience of reading. Indeed, to live in a providential world is to embrace the world as artfully crafted, shaped by a discerning intelligence.

Transformative Desire and the Incarnate Text

As the play progresses and we move from the scholar's study in Wittenberg to the wider world, Faustus seems to leave his bibliophilia behind as his magic and existence are increasingly devoted to spectacle. One of the final books that Faustus contends with before he leaves Wittenberg is a miraculously encyclopedic book that Mephistopheles offers him. Here, we see Faustus turn away from the scholarly desires that seemed to animate him. In this scene Faustus makes a series of requests for further knowledge. In response to each request Mephistopheles refers him to this magically comprehensive book:

> *Mephistopheles.(Presenting a book)* Hold, take this book. Peruse it
>   thoroughly. . . .
> *Faustus.* Thanks, Mephistopheles. Yet fain would I have a book
>   wherein . . .
>
> *Mephistopheles.* Here they are in this book. *There turn to them.*
> *Faustus.* Now would I have a book where I might see . . .
>
> *Mephistopheles.* Here they are too. *Turn to them.*
> *Faustus.* Nay, let me have one book more . . .
>
> *Mephistopheles.* Here they be. *Turn to them.*
> *Faustus.* O, thou art deceived.
> *Mephistopheles.* Tut, I warrant thee. (2.2.162, 169–70, 172–73, 176–77,
>   180–82)

Seemingly frustrated by the encyclopedic book that would satisfy his every intellectual want, Faustus abruptly turns away from the world of books to the world of experience, specifically to those experiences he can no longer have:

> When I behold the heavens, then I repent
> And curse thee, wicked Mephistopheles,
> Because thou hast deprived me of those joys. (2.3.1–3)[95]

Faustus fancies himself a connoisseur of both knowledge and books, but this book threatens him with a bland functionality, a limitless capacity to answer all questions. It threatens to exhaust his inexhaustible thirst for knowledge with a banal plenitude of answers. So he intuitively finds its limit, the limit of all earth-bound books: "the face of God" (1.3.79). This, of course, is precisely what neither Mephistopheles nor the book can offer. A mirror image of the opening sequence in the study, this scene shows us the horrors of the deal Faustus has struck. Looking to transcend his human limits, he strikes a deal that will offer everything but transcendence. In a Christian hermeneutic, without the possibility of transcendence, without the possibility of referring to the divine, turning to the face of God, all signs become mere spectacles. Curiously, this scene is reprised in miniature with Lucifer himself playing the role of Mephistopheles. Lucifer even repeats his lieutenant's words, as he enjoins Faustus to "take this book. Peruse it throughly" (2.3.171–72). Here, however, the book offered to Faustus promises the ability to change his human form: "Take this book. Peruse it throughly, and thou shalt turn thyself into what shape thou wilt" (2.3.171–73). Now, Faustus will literally be transformed by his reading. But, of course, the transformation will be merely literal. A pale substitute for true transformation, this playing with forms must ultimately taste bitter to the hugely ambitious soul who rejected books and knowledge that left him "still but Faustus, and a man" (1.1.23).

Denied transcendence, denied the face of God, Faustus will choose the next best thing: beauty, the face of Helen. And when he conjures the figure of Helen of Troy, we see Faustus's inclination to reify texts, to transform words into images, reach a kind of demonic apotheosis. It is important to remember that when Faustus first conjures Helen, he does so for the entertainment of his fellow scholars. She is here clearly figured as a piece of theater, a spectacle for the literate, an aesthetic object. After the Homeric dumb show is over and the scholars leave praising Helen's beauty and Faustus's "glorious" art, the Old Man appears and pleads with Faustus to turn toward God. The appearance of the Old Man is the catalyst for an episode in which Faustus again faces his damnation and despairs. Abject, he turns to Mephistopheles and begs him to conjure Helen once again to "glut the longing of my heart's desire" (5.1.86). This is not only the second time that Faustus has conjured Helen but also the second time that he has conjured a Homeric figure out of a desire for solace in a moment of despair. Earlier in the play, of course, the audience learned that Faustus had conjured Homer himself. In this earlier scene, a despairing Faustus claims that he would have slain himself long since if not for the pleasures that his art affords:

> My heart's so hardened I cannot repent.
> Scarce can I name salvation, faith, or heaven
> But fearful echoes thunder in mine ears:
> "Faustus, thou art damned!"
>
> . . . .
>
> And long ere this I should have slain myself
> Had not sweet pleasure conquered deep despair.
> Have not I made blind Homer sing to me
> Of Alexander's love, and Oenone's death? (2.3.18–27)

Alexander is, of course, another name for Paris, and Oenone the wife he had forsaken for Helen. In most versions of the story, Oenone kills herself after

Paris's death. If we simply look at the content of the tale told, the choice of text seems peculiar. Faustus stays his hand, turns away from self-slaughter, because he has heard a song of despair and suicide. But Marlowe chooses this seemingly strange text precisely so that we can see that it is the formal pleasures of Homer's art that console Faustus. Transformed by the poetry of Homer's song, Alexander's love and Oenone's death, do not, for Faustus, signify loss and despair but beauty, form. Or more precisely, Homer's art creates beauty and form out of death and despair.

Late in the play, when Faustus once again finds himself in despair, he begs Mephistopheles to conjure "That heavenly Helen" to be his paramour (5.1.88). From Homer's song to Helen herself: Faustus seems to be progressing or regressing from a desire for the mediation of the poet to a desire for some kind of direct apprehension of the aesthetic object. And, as always, Faustus is moving backward from the end of the story to the beginning, ignoring tragic consequence to arrive at desire:

> Was this the face that launched a thousand ships
> And burnt the topless towers of Ilium?
> Sweet Helen, make me immortal with a kiss. (*They kiss.*)
> Her lips sucks forth my soul. See where it flies!
> Come, Helen, come, give me my soul again. (*They kiss again.*)
> Here will I dwell, for heaven be in these lips,
> And all is dross that is not Helena. (5.1.94–100)

Here the audience sees the word made flesh, the literary text incarnate. The language of Homer's poem has become an image to be seen and touched. Choosing to dwell in the heaven of these lips, Faustus is converted again, turning toward Helena and Hell, beauty and damnation. Despite the sensual nature of the turn, however, Faustus's conversion is not simply an embrace of the bodily. In this scene the theatrical image of Helen fails to obscure completely the underlying text that gives that image weight and shape. Despite the immediacy of the scene, despite the sense of intimacy evoked by Faustus's lines, it almost seems that it is the *provenance* of the image, its place in history and literature, that seduces:

> Was this the face that launched a thousand ships
> And burnt the topless towers of Ilium?

The figure of Helen is not yet an idol to be worshipped but an indexical sign that points elsewhere. One could argue that Faustus is seduced not by beauty but by a proper name. It is important to remember that Marlowe's most famous line of poetry comes in the form of a question. That question holds signifier and signified, present image and historical text, separate even if only for a moment. *Was this* the face? Faustus's epistemological doubt is the doubt of every convert before he or she sees the light. The kiss dramatically— emphatically—rejects that doubt in a leap of faith that fuses text and image. And in that leap of faith Faustus is converted once again.

From the beginning, Faustus's textual conversion was an aesthetic conversion:

> Lines, circles, signs, letters, and characters—
> Ay, these are those that Faustus most desires. (1.1.53–54)

It is often said that Faustus here fetishizes the material letter, but it is important to note that Faustus does not indicate any particular lines, circles, letters, characters. These are not the material traces of signification but signs that point to the idea of the materiality of signs. Unlike the traditional idolater who makes an idol of a statue, or an image, or a cross, Faustus seems to make an idol of form itself. Marlowe seems to want his audience to understand that Faustus's conversion is shaped by an aesthetic response, and he seems to be asking his audience if such aesthetic responses do not shape all such conversions.

At the beginning of this chapter I discussed the narrative of Thomas Bilney's conversion in Foxe's *Actes and Monuments*. Bilney is lured to the "truth" of the Gospel, lured to his conversion experience through the appeal of the beautiful Latin of Erasmus's *Novum Testamentum*. How is this different than Faustus being tempted by the fruit of "letters and characters"? Having been lured by Erasmus's Latin, Bilney's reading "did so exhilerate my hart . . . that euen immediately I semed vnto my selfe inwardly, to feele such a comfort and quietnes . . . that my brused bones lepte for ioye."[96] Bilney's response is visceral, bodily. Bilney's conversion narrative dramatizes the ways in which the reader's experience of a given text is inevitably related to both an aesthetic and an affective experience of the text. As I discussed in the introduction to the book, when English Reformers described their experience of scripture, they often described an affective response in explicitly sensory terms. In describing his conversion experience, Bilney speaks of beginning to "tast and sauour" scripture, which became "more pleasaunt vnto me than the hony or the hony combe."[97] His conversion is so profound that he can *taste* scripture. There is something visceral in such a response that transcends reason and will, that paradoxically transcends the flesh. In conversion narratives, such responses work to authenticate conversion. In their conversion narratives both Luther and Augustine record an affective response ("it was as if a light . . . flooded into my heart"; "I felt that I was altogether born again") that marks their experiences as authentic. Moreover, both offer up their narratives as aesthetic objects, as stories that partake in and develop a recognizable genre, and as stories designed to convert the reader. They are stories designed, in other words, to seduce, to lead the eye and turn the soul.

* * *

At the end of the play, as the stars move, time runs, and the clock threatens to strike midnight, as God stretches "out his arm and bends his ireful brows," as Faustus faces damnation with no end, he seeks a more *elemental* conversion:

> Ah, Pythagoras' *metempsychosis*, were that true,
> This soul should fly from me and I be changed
> Unto some brutish beast.
> All beasts are happy, for, when they die,
> Their souls are soon dissolved in elements. (5.2.107–11)

When the clock strikes twelve, Faustus wills his body to "turn to air" (5.2.116), his soul to be "changed into little waterdrops, / And fall into the ocean, ne'er be found" (5.2.119–20). In an effort to escape the eternal pains of hell, Faustus desires to undo himself. But in his final moment of desperation he offers to undo not himself but his books:

> My God, my God, look not so fierce on me!
> *Enter* [Lucifer, Mephistopheles, and other] *Devils.*
> Adders and serpents, let me breathe a while!
> Ugly hell, gape not. Come not, Lucifer!
> I'll burn my books. Ah, Mephistopheles! (5.2.120–23)

In the early modern period the ritual destruction of books was the conventional means whereby the sorcerer turned away from necromancy and toward a more godly life. The scriptural precedent for the burning of necromantic books can be found in the Acts of the Apostles where Paul's miraculous deeds in Ephesus inspire conjurors, or "them which vsed curious artes" to bring "their bokes" and burn them "before all men."[98] But Faustus's desperate cry seems less like a deathbed conversion than a sacrificial offering. Having sold his soul, Faustus would pawn it back by offering up his books. This desperate effort to redeem himself through his books serves only to highlight his dependence upon them. Like all iconoclasts Faustus here confers on the offending object a perverse respect, confirming the power of the book in the very act of violence intended to destroy it.

In the ritual destruction of books one sees the theatrical potential of the book that Marlowe attempts to harness in *Doctor Faustus*. Committing books to the flame forcefully clarifies their status as objects and icons. The burning of books is the final testament to their transformative power, their ability to seduce, to ravish. Given that the difference between conversion and apostasy is simply a matter of perspective, it is unsurprising that the epidemic of book burning in early modern England seems to mirror the epidemic of textual conversion. Protestants and Catholics, radical and more conservative Reformers, all insisted, as Faustus says, that there is danger in words. Ravished by the necromantic books he finds so heavenly, Faustus is transformed as a reader, converted to a faith in the letter that will damn him. But that conversion and that faith are not so different from those of Augustine and Luther. All Christians must wrestle with the paradoxes of the spirit and the letter, must attempt to transcend the letter without actually losing sight of it. In the final scene of the play Faustus wishes that he had "never seen Wittenberg, never read book!" (5.2.20–21). But as the morality play structure of Marlowe's *Faustus* suggests, if every soul is saved or damned by his or her reading, by the ways in which that reading is or is not transformative, then no one can be secure in the knowledge of salvation. Harnessing the anxieties surrounding the act of reading in his culture, Marlowe thrills his audience with the specter of damnation at the hands of a book.

CHAPTER FOUR

Book, Trinket, Fetish

Letters and Mastery in *The Tempest*

PROSPERO'S STORY BEGINS and ends with books. The narrative of loss and restoration, exile and return recounted in Shakespeare's *The Tempest* begins with a turn toward a world of letters and ends with a turn away from the power and authority conferred by the magic of books. The event that sets the revenge plot in motion is, of course, Antonio's overthrow and expulsion of his brother Prospero, the Duke of Milan, an incident that predates the action of the play. In Prospero's unfolding of the history that led to his exile, Antonio's insurrection was both provoked and facilitated by Prospero's turn away from the fallen world of men and toward the rapture offered by what he calls "the liberal arts" (1.2.73).[1] That Prospero was cast out to sea equipped with little more than his books seems a cruel literalization of his claim that he had been "transported" by his "secret studies" (1.2.76–77). Ultimately, Prospero will engineer his return from exile with the help of his books, and yet these powerful artifacts will not return with him to Milan. At the end of the drama, as the plot swerves from revenge to redemption, Prospero decides that "the rarer action is / In virtue than in vengeance" and elects to show mercy to his enemies (5.1.27–28). Curiously, this decision is concurrent with, and seemingly directly related to, a decision to destroy his book: "And deeper than did ever plummet sound / I'll drown my book" (5.1.56–57). The book or books that save Prospero and allow him to return to his former state must, it seems, be renounced before he can fully realize his restoration.

In the critical tradition, Prospero's books have become invitations to allegory. They have been read as an embodiment of the unbounded ambition of Baconian science and as a remnant of the culture of medieval magic, as an idealization of a superior European technology and as a materialization of European letters and literacy, as the enchanted "book" of the theater and as the corporeal incarnation of the sorcery of Shakespearean language. Perhaps the tradition's need or desire to allegorize Prospero's books is symptomatic of the fact that the books never materialize within the pages of Shakespeare's play. That is, in all the descriptions of this ostentatiously material object—which is, at various points in the drama, to be stolen, drowned, and burned—the enchanted tome fails, by some secret sorcery or other, to materialize within the printed text of *The Tempest*. The books (or is it a single book?) are mentioned four times within the text of the play, and each time they seem to be positioned off stage (1.2.166–68, 3.1.94, 3.2.87–93, 5.1.57). Prospero says that he will go to his book, that he will drown his book, but it is never clear that he has his book or books or that the audience is expected to have seen these books. This is particularly curious since, as I observed in the previous chapter, the codex seems to have been a fairly common prop on the early modern stage. In *Doctor Faustus*, books and other textual artifacts consistently occupy the stage as Marlowe invites the audience to join Faustus in fetishizing the written word. In *The Tempest*, in contrast, Shakespeare writes a play about the power of books that refuses to make a spectacle of the book.[2] Certainly, theatrical productions can and have staged Prospero's book or books,[3] but the printed text suggests that *The Tempest* consists of plots and characters that revolve around an archive that is always elsewhere, always off stage. The significance of this shaping absence is, I would suggest, related to *The Tempest*'s exploration of the book as an icon of European enlightenment and Christian transcendence.

In *The Tempest*, Shakespeare yokes together two conventional narratives concerning the book and its discontents: the sorcerer who must renounce his books in order to regain his humanity, and the disaffected subject or subjects who desire the destruction of books that they see as instruments of oppression. We could even attach these storylines to recognizable names from the early modern stage: Doctor Faustus and Jack Cade. Playing these traditional narratives off of each other allows Shakespeare to stage some of the complexity of his culture's profound ambivalence toward writing and books. His crucial dramatic decision, however, is to stage these familiar plots in an exotic and powerfully evocative setting, an island somewhere between "civilized" Europe and "barbarous" Africa.[4] This productively imprecise space calls to mind all those enchanted Mediterranean isles from the literary tradition, even as the play's allusions to the Americas point toward the discovery of the New World as the historical event that gives those literary isles new weight and significance.[5] By resituating these traditional narratives concerning the book in this resonant setting, *The Tempest* invokes a Christian ambivalence about writing and books that informs European notions of cultures without letters. This ambivalence was particularly pronounced in discourse concerning the New World. The alleged illiteracy of the societies encountered in the Americas helped create an image of the New World as either an Edenic land of pre-fallen innocence or a land of savagery and barbarism. Throughout *The Incarnate Text*, I examine various articulations of the idea that reading text and reading world were intimately related in Christian thought. In this chapter I explore the fact that Christians generally, and Protestants more forcefully, posited a negative correlation between reading and idolatry, a negative correlation that helped shape European notions of barbarism. To avoid savagery and idolatry one must not only learn to read the world correctly but also learn to negotiate books and texts, learn to grapple with and transcend the letter. In early modern Europe, the immense cultural capital of the book was, in part, a function of the conviction that literacy offered freedom from idolatry and superstition, that reading granted the ability to negotiate and transcend the fallen material world. This sense of freedom from superstition and idolatry was, of course, essential to Christian and European notions of community and identity. In the logic of early modern encounter narratives, the book seems to have been the counterpart of the fetish, the former evidence of enlightened reason and God's favor, the latter evidence of damnation, of intellectual and moral darkness. In *The Tempest*, Shakespeare plays with the fact that books had become a sign in the early modern period of one man's mastery of another, one culture's mastery of another. I read *The Tempest* as a meditation on the function of the book as both instrument and justification of European dominion.

A Prehistory of the Fetish

> *Infant reason cannot reach above a material God.*
> —John Atkins, *A Voyage to Guinea, Brazil, and the West-Indies*
> (1737)[6]

In *The Philosophy of History* Hegel famously removes Africa from human history altogether.[7] He describes the African continent as a "land of childhood, which lying beyond the day of self-conscious history, is enveloped in the dark mantle of Night" (91). For Hegel, the fundamental characteristic of Africans, or as he writes, "Negroes" (*die Neger*), lies in their inability to attain "the consciousness that there is something higher than man" (93). Without this "consciousness of a Higher Being" and the concomitant consciousness of "Universality," Africans, in Hegel's view, have no understanding of human freedom. This purported misunderstanding of freedom finds its historical realization in the institution of slavery: "Another characteristic fact in reference to the Negroes is Slavery. Negroes are enslaved by Europeans and sold to America. Bad as this may be, their lot in their own land is even worse, since there a slavery quite as absolute exists; for it is the essential principle of slavery, that man has not yet attained a consciousness of his freedom, and consequently sinks down to a mere Thing, an object of no value" (96).[8] This conceptual slavery that is far worse than human manumission is a product of Africans' inability to raise their eyes above the merely material things of this world. They become objects of no value, mere things, because they do not understand the proper relation to the natural world. African religion, a religion of magic and fetishism, is, for Hegel, evidence of this conceptual bondage: "Even Herodotus called the Negroes sorcerers:—now in *Sorcery* we have not the idea of God, of a moral faith; it exhibits man as the highest power, regarding him as alone occupying a position of command over the power of Nature. . . . It is they who command the elements, and this they call 'magic'" (93–94). This belief that man controls the natural world leads the Africans to give

> an outward form to this supernatural power—projecting their hidden might into the world of phenomena by means of images. What they conceive of as the power in question, is therefore nothing really objective, having a substantial being and different from themselves, but the first thing that comes in their way. This, taken quite indiscriminately, they exalt to the dignity of a "Genius"; it may be an animal, a tree, a stone, or a wooden figure. This is their *Fetich*—a word to which the Portuguese first gave currency, and which is derived from *feitizo*, magic. Here, in the Fetich, a kind of objective independence as contrasted with the arbitrary fancy of the individual seems to manifest itself; but as the objectivity is nothing other than the fancy of the individual projecting itself into space, the human individuality remains master of the image it has adopted. (94)

For Hegel, the people of the "the land of childhood" are excluded from human history because they are already slaves to the merely material world, slaves to their barbarous fetishism.

For Enlightenment thinkers and their nineteenth-century successors, the fetish was the marker of the barbarous par excellence. To evince a belief in the power of the object was to engage in a fundamental category mistake that separated superstitious and credulous others (nonwhites, non-Christians, Catholics, the lower classes, women) from the rational European man. In a series of important essays, William Pietz has traced the emergence of the Enlightenment concept of the fetish back to "the cross-cultural spaces of the coast of West Africa during the sixteenth and seventeenth centuries."[9] The word "fetish" is a derivative of the Latin *facere* (to make) via the Portuguese *feitico*, a term that refers to magical or diabolical practices. As Pietz argues, medieval Christianity conceived an elaborate theology of the falsely "made" or manufactured object in its attempt to develop a coherent theory of witch-craft (*feiticaria* in Iberian languages). The Portuguese who encountered African religious practices tended to understand them either as harmless superstition or as black magic proper; in either case, an inverse equivalence was established between the true sacramental objects of medieval Catholicism and the idolatrous *feiticos*. Indeed, Pietz suggests that the Portuguese employed this potential equivalence in their attempts to convert the Africans they encountered: "Crosses for idols, and crucifixes and images of saints for *feiticos*, was the proposal of the crusading Portuguese."[10]

The crucial juncture in Pietz's genealogy of the fetish is the historical moment when the Protestant Dutch ousted the Catholic Portuguese from the Gold and Slave coasts. In the seventeenth-century voyage accounts that followed this transfer of power, the Portuguese *feitico* became the pidgin *fetisso*, a related but fundamentally different concept that tended to be set within the "theoretical frame . . . of Protestant Christianity's iconoclastic repudiation of any material, earthly agency" (39). The potential equivalence between the false sacramental object and the true that the Catholic Portuguese tried to exploit for proselytizing purposes became, for the Protestant Dutch, simply another way to establish the barbarity of both Catholics and Africans through their shared dependence on external forms and material objects. The Protestant merchants themselves were quick to draw connections between African fetishism and a Catholic veneration of objects. As the Dutch merchant Willem Bosman would write in the eighteenth century, "If it was possible to convert the Negroes to the Christian Religion, the Roman-

Catholics would succeed better than we should, because they already agree in several particulars."[11]

Despite the kinds of evidence he cites from the merchants' narratives, Pietz downplays the importance of religion in his account. He argues persuasively that the merchants' denigration of all barbarous attachments to objects reflects their belief that the "truth of material objects" should be "viewed in terms of technological and commodifiable use-value" and not in religious terms (36). For Pietz this belief is itself fundamentally secular. Pietz's groundbreaking study here reverts to a familiar history: the early modern encounter with different value systems, both religious and economic, led to the secularization of the economic realm that has come to be associated with the Enlightenment. I would argue to the contrary that the impulse to secularize the economic was a fundamentally religious impulse. Dismissing the religious from his analysis of the emergence of the fetish too quickly, Pietz does not analyze the division between economic and religious spheres and the concomitant secularization of objects as historical developments in their own right. It was certainly part of the program of the Reformation to remove both economics and materiality, broadly construed, from the religious realm. Protestant diatribes against indulgences or purgatory illustrate that one of the fundamental purposes of the Reformation was to purge Christianity of the language and logic of economics encoded in the Catholic doctrine of works.[12] For Reformers, a doctrine of works and a belief in the efficacy of objects distorted the essentially noneconomic and immaterial relation between God and man.

As I have been arguing throughout *The Incarnate Text*, Protestant divines—entrenched in controversies surrounding icons and idols, vestments and sacraments—had been engaged in a century-long meditation on materiality and representation prior to the emergence of the notion of the fetish in the early seventeenth century. In the course of this meditation, Reformation thinkers had begun to develop a polemical vocabulary to describe the improper veneration of objects. In Africa, Protestant merchants encountered a society that they perceived to be based on a false belief in the efficacy and power of the material object. As these encounter narratives were disseminated throughout Europe, Protestants used this image of African societies to confirm their understanding of Catholicism as barbarism, and barbarism as essentially idolatrous. In early modern England the term *fetisso* was disseminated within a new vocabulary that was giving shape to the Reformation's revolutionary intervention in Christianity's relation to, and understanding of, the material world. The idea of the fetish thus emerges within the conceptual frame of Reformation iconoclasm.

* * *

The concept of the fetisso was disseminated in northern Europe through the various translations of the Dutch explorer Pieter de Marees's 1602 tract *Bechryvinghe ende Historische Verhael van het Gout Koninckrijck van Gunea*. In England, a partial translation of Marees's treatise found its way into Samuel Purchas's 1613 edition of *Purchas his Pilgrimage* as "A description and historicall declaration of the golden Kingdome of Guinea." Marees's "description and historicall relation" purports to describe the "belief, opinions, traffiquing, bartering, and manner of speech" of "the golden Kingdome of Guinea."[13] Marees's description is dominated by his elaboration of the fetisso, a concept that he clearly theorizes as the fundamental principle governing the social order in Guinea. In the translation found in Purchas, Marees argues that the Guineans "are altogether wild, rough, and unciuill, hauing neither Scripture nor Bookes nor any notable Lawes that might be set downe, or declared to shew the manner of their policie and liuing" (941). All they have are disparate customs structured by the fetisso. Guinean society relies, Marees claims, on the power of the fetisso to bless newborn children (930); to protect children against vomiting, falling, bleeding, wild beasts, and diseases (931, 942); to prove or disprove charges of adultery (929); to protect and assist warriors in battle (947); to catch fish (942); to conduct trade (942); to bring rain (944); and to help carry the dead to the "othe[r] world" (942–43).

From Marees's account, it is unclear whether the fetisso is simply the Guinean god that manifests itself through the use of the "man made objects" that are also called fetissos, or if these "amulets" are themselves worshipped as gods (943). What is clear is that Marees believes the Guineans live in a confused and confusing world of immanence where their god or gods are deeply imbricated with, and implicated in, the fallen, material world. It is precisely this confusion that brings out the Protestant wrath of Marees, who refers to the Guineans' practices as "witchcrafts," "Idolatry," and "superstition" (930, 933, 943). The last of these epithets most accurately reflects Marees's understanding of Guinean religion; his disdain for the idea that any power might be attributed to the fetisso is evident throughout the tract. Marees assumes that the Guineans themselves are ashamed of their "superstitious" practices: "when the *Netherlanders* saw them vse such vaine toyes, which were so foolish, and laught and iested at them, they were ashamed, and durst make no more *Fetissos* in our presence, but were ashamed of their owne apishnesse" (943). Marees's attacks on the "Idolatrous gods" of the Guineans are often couched in the terms of Protestant censure of Catholic superstition (940). Marees refers to their *Fetisseros*, or holy men, as *Priests*, and compares the fetissos to "golden crosses," "Saints," "Paternosters," and "trinkets" (931, 935, 943). This last term might not seem particularly Catholic or superstitious, but words like "trinket" and "trifle" emerged in early modern England as specifically Protestant markers of Catholic superstition.

Anecdotes describing non-Europeans overvaluing "trinkets" and "trifles" are scattered throughout early modern travel narratives. Pietz argues that the "key notion that was elaborated to explain perceived African confusion regarding the religious and economic value of material objects was that of the trifle." Trading trifles "of little or no value" not only "thematized the issue of differential value systems among different cultures" but also "evoked a contempt for a people who valued 'trifles' and 'trash'" (41). Of course, neither the successful trading of "trifles" nor the attendant disdain for "savages" who valued "trinkets" was confined to European contact with Africa. Jeffrey Knapp has argued that for the English in the New World, "the most salient fact about savages is that they always hold the wrong thing in 'precious estimation'—not gold, for instance, but trifles."[14]

In his *Briefe and True Report of the New Found Land of Virginia* (1588), Thomas Harriot observes that the natives of Virginia "doe esteeme our trifles before thinges of greater value," and he notes that the first contact between the natives and the English voyagers on his excursion was negotiated through "trifles":

> as soone as they saw vs . . . [the natives] began to make a great an horrible crye, as people which neuer befoer had seene men apparelled like vs, and camme a way makinge out crys like wild beasts or men out of their wyts. But beenge gentlye called backe, wee offred them of our wares, as glasses, kniues, babies, and other trifles, which wee thougt they deligted in. Soe they stood still, and perceuinge our Good will and courtesie came fawninge vppon vs, and bade us welcome.[15]

Similarly, in his *True Report, Of the Late Discoveries . . . of the Newfound Landes* (1583), Sir George Peckham tells his readers, "It is not to be forgotten what very trifles they be that the Sauages require in exchange" for "legiti-mate" commodities. Trifles such as "looking Glasses, Bells, Beads, Bracelets, Chains, or Collars of Bugle, Crystal, Amber, Jet, or Glass etc.," can be traded for "Pearle, Gold, Siluer, and precious stones."[16] In fact, Peckham sees an entire mini-economy for England in the trading of trifles to the "savages," an economy that might cure some of England's social ills: "it will prooue a generall benefite vnto our Country, that . . . not onely a great number of men which doo nowe liue ydlely at home, and are burdenous, chargeable, & vnprofitable to this Realme, shall heereby be sette on worke, but also children of 12. or 14. Yeeres of age or vnder, may be kept from ydlenes, in making of a thousand kindes of trifleing thinges, which will be good Marchandize for that Country."[17] The discourse promoting the trade of trifles in the New World became so prevalent in England that Francis Bacon felt the need to repudiate the practice in his essay "Of Plantations" (1625): "If you *Plant*, where savages are, do not only entertain them with Trifles, and Gingles; But use them justly, and graciously."[18]

For Pietz, both the discourse of the fetisso and the concomitant con-tempt for the misvalued trifle are "expressions of a new historical problematic outside the horizon of Christian thought" (36). I contend to the contrary that these developments are a central feature of Protestantism. Pietz's claim rests on the assertion that the discourse organized around idolatry and icono-clasm is not adequate to describe the fetisso. He writes, "The understanding of Europeans . . . was that Fetissos were not false gods in the traditional sense, but rather . . . quasi-personal divine powers associated with the materiality of the sacramental object" (38). Pietz's argument is that fetissos are fundamen-tally different from idols in the traditional Christian sense precisely because the fetisso is neither a false god nor a *representation* of a false god (45). The fetish has a certain semiotic opacity, a certain nonrepresentativeness that is "utterly alien to the Christian theory of idolatry" (45).[19] In making this argu-ment, Pietz turns to Augustine's *On Christian Doctrine*, which outlines "two distinct forms of idolatrous worship": "the worship of what is created . . . as God," and "consultations and arrangements . . . with devils" (29). For Pietz, neither of these, nor their many elaborations in medieval Christianity, are adequate to explain the peculiarly nonrepresentative fetish. But in returning to Augustine and medieval Christianity, he loses sight of his important obser-vation that the emergence of the fetisso can be traced to the historical mo-ment when the Protestant Dutch supplanted the Catholic Portuguese on the coast of Africa. By considering the impact that the Reformation had on "traditional" Christian iconoclasm, I hope to suggest a different prehistory of the fetish.

Trinkets, Trifles, Trumpery

In *The Winter's Tale*, Autolycus, Shakespeare's roguish peddler, gloats over his ability to pass off his shabby merchandise, his trinkets and trumpery, to an undiscriminating public: "Ha, ha, what a fool Honesty is! and Trust, his sworn brother, a very simple gentleman! I have sold all my trompery; not a counterfeit stone, not a ribbon, glass, pomander, brooch, table-book, ballad, knife, tape, glove, shoe-tie, bracelet, horn ring, to keep my pack from fasting. They throng who should buy first, as if my trinkets had been hallow'd, and brought a benediction to the buyer."[20]

In this passage Autolycus associates the fervor of his naive consumers with those who throng after all things hallowed, those who believe in the power of the sacred object to bring a benediction to the godly buyer. That is, he associates his credulous patrons with Catholics. This association not only is suggested by his explicit reference to hallowed objects and bought benedictions but is implicitly present in the words "trinket" and "trumpery." As David Kaula argues, "The terminology Autolycus applies to his wares belongs to the verbal arsenal of anti-Catholic polemical writing in reformation England. Again and again such words as 'trumpery' and 'trinkets' appear in the Protestant diatribes against what were considered the mercenary and idolatrous practices of selling indulgences, crucifixes, rosaries, medals, candles and other devotional objects."[21] The word "trinket" is of particular interest here. The term seems to enter the English language in the 1530s when, according to the *Oxford English Dictionary*, three different meanings of the term were theoretically operative: "a tool, implement, or tackle of an occupation"; "a small ornament or fancy article"; and "decorations of worship" or "religious rites, ceremonies, beliefs, etc. which the speaker thinks vain or trivial."[22] In practice, the *OED*'s third definition relating to "vain or trivial decorations of worship" tends to color other uses of the word. Indeed, many of the early uses of the term denigrate women, rustics, and Catholics as people who not only misunderstand the value of objects but might also have powerful and unnatural relations to them.

The significance of the fact that "trinket" seems to have entered the

The Ship of the
Romiſh Church.

Burning of
Images.

Ship ouer your
trinckets &be pac
king you papiſts.

The Temple
well purged.

The Papiſtes packing away
their Paltry.

Figure 20. Detail, "The Papistes packing away their Paltry." John Foxe, *Actes and Monuments* (1610), 1178. By permission of the Rare Book and Manuscript Library, University of Pennsylvania.

language—or, at least, become prevalent enough to register in the historical archive—during the decade of the Henrician Reformation is strikingly apparent when we turn to the *OED*'s first entry under the "vain or trivial decorations of worship" rubric. In a 1538 letter to Richard Rich, Dr. John London recounts some of his iconoclastic efforts in the Henrician dissolution of the monasteries: "I have pullyd down the image of your lady at Caversham, with all trynkettes abowt the same, as schrowdes, candels, images of wexe, crowches, and brochys, and have thorowly defacyd that chapell."[23] Hugh Hilarie provides a similar list of papist objects in his 1554 anti-Catholic poem *The Resurrection of the Masse: The Masse Speaketh* when he denounces "Aultare clothes, corporasses and cruettes / Copes, vestementes, albes, boke, bell and chalice / Candelstickes, paxe, and suche other trynckettes."[24] The word "trinket" recasts both London's odd inventory and Hilarie's motley collection as catalogues of Catholic folly. Unlike more traditional forms of iconoclastic discourse such as the Elizabethan Church's authorized "Homilie against perill of idolatrie," which granted enormous power to the treacherous material object, the reformed language of "trinkets" worked to demystify the material dimension of religion by rendering it trivial.[25]

No English reformed work did more to denigrate the "idolatrous" materialism of the papists than John Foxe's *Actes and Monuments*. At the beginning of the ninth book, "containing the Actes and thinges done in the Reigne of King Edward the sixt," Foxe includes a woodcut that portrays "The Papistes packing away their Paltry" (Figure 20). Depicting the removal of statues, crosses, mitres, elaborate folios, and, of course, Catholics from England, this woodcut represents a graphic version of the iconoclastic lists of London and Hilarie. The woodcut portrays the Catholics loading themselves and their "paltry" onto a ship of fools and trifling baubles ("The Ship of the Romish church") headed for foreign shores, with the decree—"Ship ouer your trinkets & be packing you papists."[26] The text that the woodcut purports to illustrate, however, does not discuss Catholic trinkets and papist paltry. Rather, it celebrates the ascension of Edward VI, declaring him the second coming of the biblical boy-king and revered iconoclast Josiah. The implication is that just as Josiah clashed with Old Testament idolaters so his antitype Edward would contend with the superstitious and idolatrous papists. The term "trinket" could also be extended outward from lists and images of pernicious material objects to include any manifestation of religious materialism. In one of his *Sixe Sermons*, Henry Smith associates "trinket" with all the "inventions" of Catholic doctrine and ritual: "then they inuented Purgatory, Masses, Prayers for the dead, and . . . all their trinkets."[27] Similarly, Foxe associates trinkets with the idolatrous innovations of the Catholic Mass itself. In a section of *Actes and Monuments* mocking the elaborate ceremony of the Mass, the running header is "The popes trinkets with the Canon of the Masse described."[28] Having reproduced and ridiculed the Catholic Salisbury Use, and recounted a reformed history of "how and by whom this popish or rather apish masse became so clamperde and patched togither," Foxe turns his attention to "such trinkettes as were to the foresaide Masse appertaining or circumstant, first, the linnen albes and Corporasses."[29] Foxe then mockingly provides an index of frivolous objects and absurd innovations. As Foxe's example makes clear, terms like "trinket" helped the Reformers cast their indictment of religious materialism as satire. If the established discourse of iconoclasm described the satanic work of the idolatrous object, the language of "trinkets" dismissed the material dimension of Catholicism as farce. Iconoclasm struggled with the fundamental problems of representation and materiality that have shadowed Christianity throughout its history, but the "common sense" language of trinkets suggested that the ridiculous innovations of Catholicism were both easily perceived and easily sent "packing." By enabling Reformers to rethink iconoclasm as a demystifying and trivializing discourse, "trinket" and related terms anticipated the fetisso and laid the groundwork for the modern discourse of fetishism.

* * *

Iconoclastic discourse and the discourse decrying fetishism are distinguished by the relative power each imputes to the material object. Traditional iconoclasm grants the idolatrous object an extraordinary power. As Ann Kibbey argues, "What historians and critics have misconstrued as an opposition to images was actually a devoted, if negative, act of reverence, and a very self-conscious one at that. Although iconoclasm appears to have been a rejection of all images, in their own way the iconoclasts believed very deeply in the power of icons."[30] In the writing of Elizabethan separatist Henry Barrow one can find evidence of the kind of "negative reverence" that Kibbey argues is constitutive of iconoclasm. Barrow was an iconoclast for whom, as Keith Thomas argues, "the arrangement of the very stones of church buildings was so inherently superstitious that there was nothing for it but to level the whole lot to the ground and begin again."[31] Barrow writes, "The idolatrous shape so cleaveth to every stone, as it by no means can be severed from them whiles there is a stone left standing upon a stone."[32] Understanding the objects of "superstitious" worship as spiritual materializations of the demonic, iconoclasts like Barrow treat the material dimension of religion with a perverse respect.

If a vehement iconoclasm is always a kind of idolatry insofar as it grants the offending object immense power, the discourse of antifetishism is an exercise in demystification. The modern conception of the fetish implies distance, implies an anthropological gaze that suggests that the barbarous or perverse other is guilty of some fundamental error in his or her relationship to objects. Protestant polemic of the sixteenth century tacked back and forth (sometimes in the same treatise, sometimes in the same sentence) between a negative iconoclastic reverence for the bewitching and beguiling object and a series of belittling gestures that reduced the material dimension of Catholic worship to the superstitious and unenlightened veneration of trash, trumpery, and trinkets. The allegation that a society was unable to read material values correctly, especially the allegation that a society was unable to think in nonmaterialist terms, was a fundamental means of defining the "other" in the early modern period, prefiguring the Enlightenment discourse of fetishism. The copious anecdotes describing "idolatrous" non-Europeans overvaluing trinkets and trifles are surpassed only by the abundant diatribes against the trumpery and trinkets of the "barbarous" Catholics. By placing these travelers' tales concerning the improper veneration of the object within the larger frame of reference of Reformation discourse concerning value and materiality, one can begin to discern the ways in which the mutually reinforcing discourses of iconoclasm and barbarism worked to define the non-European other as a slave to the physical world.

"The Booke Materially & of Itself"

In *The Tempest* the inability to read the proper value of things is not simply an aspect of the play's exploration of notions of barbarism but crucial to the unfolding of the plot. The various narrative components of the play—the love plot, the clowns' rebellion, Prospero's revenge, Prospero's redemption—lurch toward resolution in the wake of Prospero's masque. The theatrical centerpiece of the play, the masque is the fullest articulation of Prospero's bookish magic and his civilizing vision. The failure to bring the masque to a successful close is also the first glaring sign of human weakness in the magus, and it is designed to startle the audience, onstage and off, out of their complacent reception of Prospero's easy command of the play. After the interruption of the most spectacular demonstration of his magic, Prospero regains control of the island and the plot not with a grand display of his power, not with an authoritative demonstration of his knowledge, but with a simple trick that relies on the naive credulity of the would-be insurgents. Knowing that he can count on the ignoble trio of Caliban, Stephano, and the aptly named Trinculo to fail to read the true value of things, Prospero lures them away from the completion of their "foul conspiracy" with the promise of glittering trinkets and trifles.[33] His humanist "pageant" disrupted by the uncivilized rebellion of the clowns, Prospero orders Ariel to bring the "trumpery in my house . . . / For stale to catch these thieves" (4.1.186–87). The rebellion is thus derailed by the conspirators' inability to resist the temptation of mere "trash" (4.1.223). Given the focus of his anger—"A devil, a born devil" (4.1.188)—Prospero's belief that the clowns will fall for the ruse seems to arise from an easy contempt for the non-European Caliban. But if Shakespeare seems to employ this plot device to summon the widespread cultural conception of misguided savages who do not know the true value of things, he does so in order to tweak his audience's assumptions.

Strikingly, it is only the European characters who are transfixed with the "frippery" (4.1.224). The "beast Caliban" is, against type, the one character not distracted by the trumpery (4.1.140). In fact, it is Caliban who calls his confederates fools for doting on such "luggage"; it is Caliban who knows that they must ignore this "trash" in order to get to Prospero's book (4.1.231,

223). Playing with the European propensity to decry the fetishism of the barbarous other, Shakespeare here stages the overvaluation of the "enchanted trifle" as a European error (5.1.112). Given the status of the characters in question, we might assume that the inclination to such error is here marked as a trait not of exotic savages but of the all-too-familiar lower classes. Trinculo and Stephano, however, are not depicted as innocent simpletons who do not understand value; rather, they are the characters in the play who talk most about potential European markets for the island's commodities. When Trinculo first comes across Caliban, he pronounces him "a strange fish" and remarks, "Were I in England now, as once I was, and had but this fish painted, not a holiday-fool there but would give a piece of silver. There would this monster make a man—any strange beast there makes a man. When they will not give a doit to relieve a lame beggar, they will lay out ten to see a dead Indian" (2.2.27–32). Upon seeing Trinculo's dead Indian, Stephano thinks, "If I can recover him, and keep him tame, and get to Naples with him, he's a present for any emperor that ever trod on neat's leather" (2.2.66–68). The clowns' attempts to divine the value of the exotic native on the European marketplace is played for laughs, but the humor is a function of the critique of holiday-fools and idle aristocrats, the low and the high alike portrayed as having a taste for the exotic, portrayed as rubes taken in by monsters and strange beasts. Insofar as Stephano and Trinculo are thinking about profiting from the credulous, they are, in fact, thinking in the very terms used by the seventeenth-century merchants who would demonize the "fetish" as irrational. Here, however, the easy-to-fleece are Europeans who are mesmerized by commodified wonder. The depiction of Trinculo and Stephano suggests that the savvy would-be exploiters of the naive of Act Two are the holiday fools of Act Four. This is less an inconsistency of character than a fundamental principle of the play: the anthropological gaze that imputes an improper relation to objects or a misunderstanding of value can be trained on anyone. By easily avoiding the "stale" or bait of the "glistering apparel" Caliban seems to emerge as more "enlightened" than his European allies (4.1.187, 4.1.193.1). Of course, this ostensible enlightenment seems to be undermined by the fact that his grand strategy is to destroy the power of his enemy by burning his books.

The desire of the non-European savage to burn books would have conjured a powerful set of cultural assumptions in an early modern audience. In European travel narratives of this period, writing was consistently figured as a crucial technological difference distinguishing rational Europeans from the barbarous cultures they encountered. As Walter Mignolo notes, in the early modern period, "human societies were ranked in the chain of being according to their lack of possession of alphabetic writing. . . . The ability to create a system of writing, and the access to the power and knowledge that such a system conferred, was the ultimate token of the superiority of the 'civil man' over the 'barbarian,' who lived always as a slave to those with greater wisdom than himself." [34] In an English context, Samuel Purchas offers the classic formulation of writing as a sign of technological and moral superiority. In *Purchas his Pilgrims*, Purchas maintains that writing is "the litteral advantage" that raises one man, one culture over another: "amongst Men, some are accounted Civill, and more both Sociable and Religious, by the Use of letters and Writing, which others wanting are esteemed Brutish, Savage, Barbarous." [35] Stephen Greenblatt contends that "Purchas' use of the term 'barbarous' signals an important shift from the Greek distinction between self and other, a distinction based on the difference between those who speak Greek and those who did not. In Purchas the linguistic community is assumed to have a legitimate multiplicity; the crucial difference is a technological one—the achievement of literacy." [36] This technological difference is, I would add, crucially tied to religious difference. Lack of literacy is consistently figured in these early travel narratives as a sign either of God's disfavor or of a fundamental inability to achieve true religion. It is telling that in his catalogue of the differences between those who have and do not have letters, Purchas creates an opposition not simply between the "Brutish" and the "Civil," or the "Savage" and the "Sociable," but between the "Barbarous" and the "Religious." For Purchas, the Protestant minister, the technological difference of literacy is, I contend, not a new wrinkle in the distinction between civilized and barbarous but an old distinction between civilized Christians who read the book and the world properly and barbarous cultures condemned to savagery and damnation. As I discussed in the Introduction to *The Incarnate Text*, in early modern culture, proper reading—a reading that transcended the letter on the page and the things of the world—functioned as a shibboleth, a performative act that established those on the inside (and outside) of Christian community. If we can, following Greenblatt, characterize the multiplicity of the linguistic community as in some sense "legitimate," it is no less fallen. If linguistic difference is not a definite sign of barbarism, linguistic multiplicity is a reminder to men like Purchas that barbarism is the direction in which the human animal tends without divine assistance. For Purchas, the "legitimate multiplicity" of the "linguistic community" is a function of man's second fall at the Tower of Babel. As Purchas describes it, the "diuision and confusion of Tongues" that resulted from that fall was a perversion of those faculties whereby God distinguished men from other creatures.[37] If there is a remedy for the pernicious effects of this fall, if there is a way to overcome the barbarism that attends the "diuision and confusion of Tongues," it is through the salutary effects of proper reading; it is through the "literall advantage," which is a gift of God. The grace of Christian literacy, however, has not been given to all, and it is on this basis that Purchas distinguishes among human societies.

The logic subtending Purchas's "literall advantage" can be found throughout the archive of early modern encounter narratives. In this logic the brutishness of the non-European manifested itself not only as an inability to read but as an inability to understand the book as anything but a fetish, as anything but enchanted. Indeed, accounts of native misconceptions concerning the "magic of books" were a staple of early modern travel narratives and ethnographic accounts. A recurrent feature of these narratives was the anecdote of the "speaking page" or "talking book." Purchas himself references such stories in his discussion of the "literall advantage" of writing: "Want of letters hath made some [savages] so seely as to thinke the Letter it selfe could speak, so much did the Americans herein admire the Spaniards, seeming in comparison of the other as speaking Apes."[38] From the sixteenth century forward, the anecdote of the "speaking paper" or "talking book" seems to have become one of the tales almost reflexively told about the "illiterate primitives" of the New World. In his *History of a Voyage to the Land of Brazil* (1578), Jean de Léry recounts an incident in which the Tupinamba of Brazil marveled at the ability of paper to translate for the French pastor; according to Léry, writing was to them "some kind of witchcraft."[39] To provide a frame of reference for this episode, Léry mentions a similar story in the *General History of the West Indies* (1552) written by the Spanish historian Francisco Lopez de Gómara.[40] Léry's repetition of similar anecdotes indicating comparable errors in Brazil and the West Indies establishes the generic quality of such accounts and thus the uniformity of New World savagery. That "generic" quality helps Léry divide the world into those with and without the "marvelous" technology of writing:

> Here is a fine subject for anyone who would like to enlarge upon it: both to praise and to exalt the art of writing, and to show how the nations that inhabit these three parts of the world—Europe, Asia,

and Africa—have reason to praise God more than do the savages of that fourth part, called "America." . . . This invention of writing, which we possess and of which they are just as utterly deprived, must be ranked among the singular gifts which men over here have received from God.[41]

The technology of writing is a gift of God that establishes with elegant clarity which societies live in a state of barbarous idolatry, which societies must do without the grace of God.

In his *Generall Historie of Virginia, New-England, and the Summer Isles* (1624), John Smith records an incident in which writing is both a way to dupe the illiterate savage and an invitation to barbarous wonder. As Smith tells the story, he was imprisoned by the native Virginians as they were planning an attack on Jamestown. After entering into negotiations with the "Salvages," he sent some of them to the fort at Jamestown with written instructions. His purpose was both to request goods as a part of these negotiations and to send a warning to the English. In Smith's words, "he writ his minde to them at the Fort" in "part of a Table booke," which he sent with the "Salvages." When it became clear to the messengers that Smith had successfully communicated with the English at the fort, they returned with the requested goods and a marvelous tale to tell "to the wonder of them all that heard it, that he could either divine, or the paper could speake."[42] Narratives like Léry's and Smith's not only establish the illiteracy of the New World "salvage" but also suggest a fundamental inability to navigate successfully within either the realm of material artifacts or the world of human representation. Often such narratives suggested that the wonders of writing demonstrated to the savages that the Europeans either were gods or enjoyed a privileged relationship with the gods. This "mistake" was sometimes used in ethnographic accounts to mark the natives as naive and superstitious, childlike beings at a further remove from divine understanding than the properly literate, properly Christian Europeans. Writing roughly one hundred years after the publication of Smith's *General Historie*, Daniel Defoe returned to this by now famous anecdote in his *Essay On the Original of Literature* (1726). In Defoe's version of this "Story, which happen'd at our first planting of *Virginia*," the native messenger was so amazed at the ability to communicate across time and space that he insisted that "Capt. *Smith* was a Deity and to be Worshipp'd, for that he had Power to make *the Paper speak*."[43] Technological wonder here produces both savage idolatry and European divinity.[44] If the savages are misguided in their idolatry, that idolatry ironically proves that their inclination to venerate the European is based on a correct valuation of European superiority. The Europeans are closer to the divine precisely because they are not guilty of the idolatry that would so exalt them. In Defoe's account, this spontaneous idolatry is only natural since the divine gift of writing works to banish false gods: "Since the use of Letters, since Writing came into the World, and since History has preserv'd the true Account of the Actions of Men, we have had no new Gods set up; no Statues have been nick-nam'd, nor infamous Men exalted after their Death to the Rank of Deities."[45] Writing is for Defoe a divine invention that drives out certain kinds of idolatry and allows truth to emerge in human history. Without writing, human society—past or present—is condemned to error and superstition.[46]

The anecdote of the "talking book" became ethnographic shorthand to explain the ways in which the primitive and illiterate misunderstood the all-important technology of reading. These narratives did not need to elaborate on the significance of the "talking book" incident as its meanings and morals were, for those with ears to hear, largely self-evident. But the "talking book" anecdote was simply a minor variation on the much larger theme concerning the relation of the savage to these marvelous objects called books. One of the earliest and most searching discussions of New World wonder at the technology of the book can be found in Thomas Harriot's *Briefe and True Report of the New Found Land of Virginia* (1588). Often considered one of the first European ethnographies, the *Briefe and True Report* would have been available to Shakespeare as he wrote *The Tempest*. In the *Report*, Harriot discusses the ways in which the Algonquian society of Virginia responded to the technological "marvels" of the English:

> Most thinges they sawe with vs, as Mathematicall instruments, sea
> compasses, the vertue of the loadstone in drawing yron, a perspec-
> tiue glasse whereby was shewed manie strange sightes, burning
> glasses, wildefire woorkes, gunnes, bookes, writing and reading,
> spring clocks that seeme to goe of themselues, and manie other
> thinges that wee had, were so straunge vnto them, and so farre ex-
> ceeded their capacities to comprehend the reason and meanes how
> they should be made and done, that they thought they were rather
> the works of gods then of men, or at the leastwise they had bin
> giuen and taught vs of the gods.[47]

In Harriot's analysis, various European technologies are so alien and wondrous that the native Virginians must view them through a theological or mystical lens. That accounts of such savage wonder reflected back the Europeans' own desire for technological superiority and their own reverence for their creations goes without saying. Here, the alleged wonder of the Algonquians results in the crucial "mistake" of thinking that these extraordinary technologies indicated that the Europeans enjoyed a special relationship with the gods. Of course, the fact that the Europeans themselves believed that they enjoyed such a relationship does not prevent them from being amused at the idolatry of the savages. In response to this "mistake," Harriot endeavors to teach the natives true religion and to acquaint them with the technology that provides his people privileged access to this true religion.

When Harriot describes his attempts to teach the Algonquians about Christianity, however, their misunderstanding of the book of the Bible reinforces both technological and religious difference:

> Manie times and in euery towne where I came, according as I was
> able, I made declaration of the contentes of the Bible; that therein
> was set foorth the true and onelie GOD, and his mightie woorkes,
> that therein was contayned the true doctrine of saluation through
> Christ, which manie particularities of Miracles and chiefe poyntes
> of religion, as I was able then to vtter, and thought fitte for the time.
> And although I told them the booke materially & of itself was not
> of anie such vertue, as I thought they did conceiue, but onely the
> doctrine therein contained; yet would many be glad to touch it, to
> embrace it, to kisse it, to hold it to their brests and heades, and
> stroke ouer all their bodie with it; to shew their hungrie desire of
> that knowledge which was spoken of.[48]

According to his narrative, Harriot's attempt to tell the natives that "the booke materially & of itself was not of anie such vertue" meets with resistance or misunderstanding and with the desire to treat the book as totemic, as a fetish. On the one hand, in his capacity as scientifically accredited pitchman for "plantation" in the New World, Harriot takes pains to construct a tractable native population amenable to religious instruction: by showing "their hungrie desire of that knowledge which was spoken of," the Algonquians demonstrate their desire to emulate the godlike Europeans and embrace Christianity as their religion. On the other hand, insofar as Harriot's description creates a barbarous people whose conceptual difficulty lies in both their want of writing and their inability to think in nonmaterialist terms, it produces an alien society that seems inassimilable to a Protestant and European understanding of proper religion. Their naive enthusiasm—"yet would many be glad to touch it, to embrace it, to kisse it, to hold it to their brests and heades, and stroke ouer all their bodie with it"—suggests both the possibility and impossibility of evangelistic efforts. For Harriot's readers, to learn to read this book correctly is to learn to read the world correctly. Whether the inhabitants of the New World had the wherewithal to do so is an open question for Harriot and his readers.[49]

The alleged conceptual confusion of the Algonquians is a function of Harriot's, and English Protestantism's, own fraught relation to the materiality of representation. As I have argued throughout *The Incarnate Text*, in early modern England the codex was often deployed as an emblem of correct and incorrect ways of conceiving one's relation to the material world. That the book should be so deployed in a New World context seems almost inevitable. Like many of his contemporaries encountering native "fetishism," Harriot seems to read Algonquian beliefs and practices through the lens of Protestantism's repudiation of Catholic "idolatry." That the Bible is the object on which he focuses so much attention is striking, however, given that the transformation of the Bible into an idol was not only a charge Catholics leveled against Protestants but also an anxiety acutely felt, at times, by Protestants. Whatever Harriot's understanding of this particular cultural crux might be, the repetitive language he uses in this passage—a language of inside and outside, container and contained—is revealing. Many times and in every town, Harriot makes declaration of that which the Bible *contains* (the "contentes of the Bible"); he proselytizes that the "true and onelie GOD" is set forth "*therein*." His insistence that "the booke materially & of itself was not of anie such virtue" is bracketed by repetitive statements that the book is a material vessel within which one might find the secrets of this Christian God: "therein was contayned the true doctrine . . . but onely the doctrine therein contained." The "conceptual confusion" of the natives seems unavoidable given the metaphors that Harriot employs. Of course, the metaphors themselves are inevitable. However enlightened the Christian religion is supposed to appear in relation to a people who would embrace "the booke materially & of itself," Harriot's language reveals that the materiality of representation is inescapable and that the Christian religion is dependent upon an ineluctably material text. In attempting to differentiate European from Algonquian through the technology of the book, in attempting to articulate the illiteracy and fetishism of the savage, Harriot manages to rehearse a central problem of his culture: the materiality of representation as it pertains to divine revelation. Given the nature of this problem, it seems revealing that in Harriot's account of native wonder at European technology, he lists *both* "writing and reading" *and* "books." Of course, one can read and write in things other than books, and books can be used for things other than reading or writing; nevertheless, this curious juxtaposition suggests that the book, for Harriot, is a marvel not simply insofar as it is an instance of writing or occasion for reading, but as an object in its own right. As singular as Harriot's *Briefe and True Report* is in so many ways, it is typical in this respect: the alleged confusion the Englishman finds in the savages' understanding of the book is a reflection of Christian Europe's own fraught relationship to the book.

Turning from Harriot's ethnographic account to Shakespeare's play, one is struck by Caliban's apparent confusion about the significance of the material object that is Prospero's book. When plotting the overthrow of Prospero with Stephano and Trinculo, Caliban insists repeatedly that any attempt on Prospero's life must be preceded by the seizure and destruction of his books:

> Why, as I told thee, 'tis a custom with him,
> I' th' afternoon to sleep. There thou mayst brain him,
> Having first seized his books; or with a log
> Batter his skull, or paunch him with a stake,
> Or cut his weasand with thy knife. Remember
> First to possess his books; for without them
> He's but a sot, as I am, nor hath not
> One spirit to command—they all do hate him
> As rootedly as I. Burn but his books. (3.2.85–93)

Critics have argued that Caliban's violent insistence on the importance of the book *as object* not only fetishizes the book but materializes Prospero's power as something distinct from both Prospero and his knowledge. Like Harriot's natives, Caliban, it would seem, fails to understand that "the booke materially & of itself was not of anie such vertue, but onely the doctrine therein contained." Mark Taylor, for instance, argues that if the rebels had succeeded in their rebellion, if they had

> succeeded in burning the books, Caliban might have received another lesson in how partial is his understanding of the ways of Euro-

peans, in how little he has ever shared in their community, even
their community of rhetoric. . . . He might have learned that a
"book" is not mainly a physical object but rather a convenient way
of representing that which can reside in such an object and also in a
human head, but only the head of a man taught the reading lessons
that were never offered to Caliban.[50]

Taylor reads Caliban in the way that Harriot reads the Algonquians: Caliban
grasps that writing and books are associated with power but does not understand how the technology works. In this argument the ignorant savages fail
to comprehend that the key to unlocking the power of writing lies in tran-
scending the material object through an act of reading. Caliban, however,
seems to be correct not only in his understanding of the book's value to
Prospero but also in his intuition about how this particular technology works.
The physicality of the object does seem to matter in this instance. After
all, Caliban's rebellious attempt to burn Prospero's books simply anticipates
Prospero's seemingly redemptive decision to drown his book. Their intentions and methods differ, but they seem to share a belief that Prospero's
power is *materially* tied to his books.

Within the logic of the play then, this failure to divorce the book from
its contents, this confusion of inside and outside, does not seem to represent
a conceptual difficulty of Caliban's but a constitutive characteristic of Prospero's "magic." Instructing Miranda to help him divest himself of his enchanted mantle, Prospero commands:

> . . . Lend thy hand
> And pluck my magic garment from me.
> *Miranda helps him to disrobe*
> > So.
> Lie there, my art. (1.2.23–26)

By placing his magical "art" outside himself, within the very clothes he wears,
Prospero, in this moment, explicitly materializes and externalizes his power.
When they run after the glittering trifles that Prospero places before them,
Trinculo and Stephano betray their inability to understand the "true" value
of things. They fail to see them for what they are (either within the fiction of
the play or on the material stage): props in a play that is rigged to display
the clowns' ignorance for comic effect. But in valuing Prospero's clothes

"irrationally," they simply follow Prospero's lead. In Prospero's own account, *some* of his garments *are* enchanted. Prospero, then, seems to practice the very fetishism that is demystified and mocked in Caliban and the clowns. Noting that Prospero's "rough magic" is both "physical in its basis and effects" and "resides in props—the robe, staff, and book," Margreta de Grazia observes that Prospero's art displays a "basic materialism."[51] This basic materialism seems to undercut any easy distinction Shakespeare's audience might make between Prospero and Caliban, Prospero and Sycorax, enlightened European and illiterate savage.

Falling into Language

Toward the beginning and again toward the end of his writing career, Shakespeare dramatized rebellions that attacked writing and books as instruments of oppression. Viewed from a certain perspective, Shakespeare's twenty-year theatrical run—bracketed by Jack Cade and Caliban—seems to begin and end with depictions of violent threats to the book. In *2 Henry VI*—a play that like *The Tempest* dramatizes the fate of a negligent and "bookish" potentate—the revolutionary clothier Jack Cade "vows reformation"[52] by promising the abolition of private property ("All the realm shall be in common," 4.2.68; "henceforward all things shall be in common," 4.7.18–19), the reformation of sumptuary laws ("I will apparel them all in one livery," 4.2.73–74), and the burning of written documents ("burn all the records of the realm," 4.7.14). Cade and his cohort see a utopian future in which the destruction of certain kinds of texts will lead both to an Edenic egalitarianism and the restoration of their "ancient freedom" (4.8.27).

The tradition of radical dissent that Cade invokes was informed by Christian thought. From the moment the rebels enter the stage in *2 Henry VI*, their radical desire to level society is consistently framed in Christian terms. In the dramatic opening salvo of the peasants, Nick and George comically subvert the biblical notion that one must "labor in thy vocation" (4.2.16), by suggesting that the magistrates should be laboring men, "and therefore should we be magistrates" (4.2.18).[53] When his attention is called to the presence of Dick the Butcher, George is inspired to envision Old Testament retribution as butchery: "Then is sin struck down like an ox, and iniquity's throat cut like a calf" (4.2.26–27). Cade himself quotes Leviticus when he suggests that "our enemies shall fall before us, inspir'd with the

spirit of putting down kings and princes" (4.2.35–36).[54] When Cade's genealogical claims to the throne are refuted with the inconvenient fact that his
"father was a plasterer," Cade simply responds: "And Adam was a gardener"
(4.2.132, 134). Echoing the preacher John Ball's well-known adage that
"When Adam delved and Eve span / who then was a gentleman," Cade's
rhetorical turn to Genesis is a radical return to origins in which degree and
distinction are erased by a common—in both senses of the term—human
genealogy. In both Cade's retort and Ball's maxim, the commoner makes a
radical claim to equality; for Cade, however, the road to egalitarianism is
paved not only with utopian rhetoric but with the heads of clerks and lawyers, and the burnt remains of books. When Dick the Butcher pragmatically
suggests, "The first thing we do, let's kill all the lawyers" (4.2.76–77), Cade
responds with a sermon on writing and death: "Is not this a lamentable
thing, that of the skin of an innocent lamb should be made parchment? that
parchment, being scribbled o'er, should undo a man? Some say the bee stings,
but I say 'tis the bee's wax; for I did but seal once to a thing, and I was
never mine own man since" (4.2.78–83). The materiality of the text is here a
memento mori as Cade reflects on the fact that parchment is made from
animal skins.[55] That the parchment is in this instance made from "the skin
of an innocent lamb" suggests that writing, for Cade, marks a fall from
innocence. As I discussed both in the Introduction and Chapter 1, the association of writing with the law and death had a long history in Christian
thought. Early modern writers inherited a tradition extending back to the
early church fathers that taught that writing had entered the world as a direct
consequence of the Fall. For Cade this fall into writing is the undoing of a
man, a fall into hierarchy and service ("and I was never mine own man
since," 4.2.83). Throughout the play, Cade and his "rabblement" invoke a
nostalgia for an Edenic world before writing and hierarchy, labor and letters
(4.8.0.1).

While the spectators at an early modern performance of *The Tempest*
might very well have associated Caliban's desire to destroy Prospero's book
with the illiterate barbarism of non-Europeans, the example of Cade suggests
that they might also have associated it with a class-based hostility. And there
is no reason to assume that these two associations were mutually exclusive.
The radical desire of Cade and his "rabblement" to attack writing as an
instrument of oppression is expressed in the language of a Christian nostalgia
for an innocent time before letters, a nostalgia that is one of the most characteristic European responses to the New World. Above, I discussed writing as

a sign of God's grace, a sign of the spiritual and technological superiority of the literate Christian. But if figures like Purchas and Defoe read writing as a sign of God's favor, the "literall advantage" that raised the civilized and religious over the idolatrous and barbarous, others believed that the inhabitants of the New World enjoyed a pre-fallen existence without letters. The exploration and conquest of the New World famously led to depictions of the Americas as Edenic, to portrayals of New World denizens as emblems of innocence. In these versions of the New World, writing is often figured not as a mark of Christian redemption but as a mark of human corruption. In his essay "Of Cannibals," Michel de Montaigne offers one of the most famous depictions of the New World as a place of Edenic innocence. Montaigne describes an idyllic society that, in addition to having "no kinde of traffike . . . no intelligence of numbers, no name of magistrate, nor of politike superioritie; no vse of service, of riches or of povertie; no contracts, no successions," also had "no knowledge of Letters."[56] For Montaigne, it is precisely the fruit of the tree of European knowledge that will bring the New World natives out of their Edenic existence, out of their "happy estate" where they "desire no more, than what their naturall necessities direct them" and into the fallen world of European values.[57] When Shakespeare stages an Edenic vision of the New World in *The Tempest*, he famously does so by way of Montaigne's essay. In a speech that borrows freely from Florio's translation of Montaigne, Gonzalo suggests that if he had "plantation of this isle" and "were the king on't," he would "with such perfection govern" to "excel the golden age" (2.1.141–43, 165–66). Central to this nostalgic vision of a society without civilization is that "letters should not be known" (2.1.148). Whatever we make of Shakespeare's deployment of Montaigne's essay in Gonzalo's muddled utopia, the play here ostentatiously invokes the contemporary discourse of New World utopianism, a discourse that consistently expressed European ambivalence toward the technology of writing. By staging this ambivalence toward letters as part of a greater ambivalence toward "civilization," Shakespeare creates a larger frame of reference for Caliban's biblioclasm *and* Prospero's books. When Caliban articulates an animus against letters in a radical idiom ("burn but his books," 3.2.93), he evokes the *ressentiment* of Cade as well as the triumphalism of Christian notions of literacy, the cultivated nostalgia of Gonzalo's utopian vision as well as the figure of the illiterate savage.

These two antithetical contentions about literacy—that it was a sign of God's grace, and that it was a sign of a fall from that grace—gave rise, of course, to very different ways of imagining the spiritual condition of New

World societies. The competing claims that the "gift" of European letters introduced either culture or corruption to the innocent natives of the New World is especially germane to *The Tempest* given how important scenes of education are to the play's meditation on civilization and barbarism. Caliban's moral and social position on the island is a function of the Europeans' understanding of his character, and their understanding of his character seems to be of a piece with their belief in his ability or inability to learn their language and their values. According to Prospero, Caliban is "a born devil, on whose nature / Nurture can never stick; on whom my pains, / Humanely taken, all, all lost, quite lost" (4.1.188–90). This failure to have Prospero's "nurture" stick, this failure to learn from Prospero's "pains / Humanely taken" leads to the conditions that shape Caliban's existence. Like Adam ("clay"), Caliban ("earth," 1.2.314) is condemned to a life of pain and labor because of his original sin. For Caliban, the original sin was his attempt "to violate / The honour of" Prospero's daughter (1.2.347–48).[58] When this attempted violation is addressed in the play, Miranda explicitly relates it to her attempt to teach Caliban European language:

> Abhorrèd slave,
> Which any print of goodness wilt not take,
> Being capable of all ill! I pitied thee,
> Took pains to make thee speak, taught thee each hour
> One thing or other. When thou didst not, savage,
> Know thine own meaning, but wouldst gabble like
> A thing most brutish, I endowed thy purposes
> With words that made them known. But thy vile race–
> Though thou didst learn—had that in't which good natures
> Could not abide to be with; therefore wast thou
> Deservedly confined into this rock,
> Who hadst deserved more than a prison. (1.2.350–61)

For Miranda, Caliban's attempt on her honor is not only a violation of civility but an abuse of her good will toward him, a good will manifest in her desire to teach him her language. Miranda here describes an attempt to educate that is also an attempt to edify or civilize. Her judgment of Caliban as natural "slave" rests on the belief that his "abhorred" nature will no "print of goodness" take *even though* he learned her language ("Though thou didst learn"), *even though* she endowed his "purposes / With words that made them known." Miranda finds to her horror that she can imprint language but not goodness; evidently, European language cannot save Caliban from the natural depredations to which his "vile race" inclines. Caliban is in this passage the wax, paper, or metal onto which Miranda attempts and fails to imprint European values.[59] Given that the mechanical reproduction of printing was often described in the language of sexual reproduction, it is striking that Miranda uses such language to describe her pedagogic relation with Caliban.[60] From Dryden to the twentieth century, editors have attributed this speech to Prospero since its caustic tone seems indecorous coming from the seemingly innocent and virginal Miranda, but it may also be that editors were responding to the undertone of masculine presumption and aggression implicit in Miranda's desire to imprint European learning on Caliban's unyielding surface.

Miranda's failed imprinting of Caliban is, of course, interrupted by Caliban's desire to coin Calibans: "I had peopled else / This isle with Calibans" (1.2.348–49). It is important to note that Caliban's desire is explicitly political. Caliban's European education manifests itself not in a desire to be a good Christian but in a desire to establish political dominance through violence and the propagation of a people. The marriage of Claribel—the apparent reason for the fateful voyage of Alonso and his entourage—provides an important context for Caliban's political desire. Against the wishes, evidently, of his subjects and his daughter, Alonso has given Claribel to the king of Tunis, presumably to gain some political or economic advantage for Naples. Likewise, Prospero offers his daughter to the son of his enemy to help engineer his return from exile. The charm of the love story can, at times, work to blind the audience both to the political realities of the situation and to the prodigious labors Prospero undertakes to ensure this match. But when the time comes, the fact that Miranda is an object to be exchanged between men is clear. Offering his daughter to Ferdinand, Prospero figures her both as gift and as purchase: "as my gift, and thine own acquisition / Worthily purchased, take my daughter" (4.1.13–14). Prospero's ostentatious vigilance with regard to the sexual virtue of his daughter is a function both of a father's desire to preserve a daughter's innocence and an exiled ruler's desire to preserve one of the few assets he has at his disposal. With no reason to sentimentalize human relations, Caliban understands that one of the fundamental means of gaining and securing power in European society is through the effective use of women's bodies in the reproduction of the social order. Caliban, despite protestations to the contrary, learns all of his lessons well. By reading Caliban's desire as political rather than simply carnal, I do not mean to minimize the threat of sexual violence in *The Tempest*. On the contrary, I contend that the threat pervades the play. Sentimental readings of *The Tempest* attempt to contain and neutralize this threat by assigning it both to "the beast Caliban" and to a prior moment in time when the "thing most brutish" was not yet recognized as an "Abhorred slave, / Which any print of goodness wilt not take." But the threat of sexual violence is not simply a minor preoccupation of Prospero's; it shadows two of the major threads of the narrative: the love plot and the rebellion. Caliban, Stephano, and Ferdinand all offer differently articulated versions of this threat at various points in the drama. By introducing the figure of Claribel, Shakespeare expands the scope of the threat, including fathers as well as savages, churls, and charming scions in his catalogue of men with the capacity to exploit the virtue of young women.

Miranda's desire to imprint and thereby reproduce European culture in Caliban is interrupted by Caliban's desire to reproduce subjects. These desires are mirror images of each other: each expresses the desire to colonize. Caliban responds to Miranda's diatribe with that *locus classicus* of the resistance of the colonized: "You taught me language, and my profit on't / Is I know how to curse"; he might as well have said, "You taught me language, and my profit on't / Is" Adam's curse (1.2.362–63). Prospero, a man with a habit of awakening temptation in others ("I thus neglecting worldly ends . . . in my false brother / Awaked an evil nature," 1.2.89–93), has managed to reproduce both European despotism and the moral authority of Christianity on the island by finding a happy (for him) fault within the creature who was once his "own King" (1.2.342). Caliban's fall from grace is instrumental in setting up the island's moral and material economy: as Prospero says to Miranda, "We cannot miss him. He does make our fire, / Fetch in our wood, and serves in offices / That profit us" (1.2.311–13). If the curse on Adam is an etiological myth explaining the need for man to live by the sweat of his brow, then Caliban's desire to "be fruitful and multiply" ("I had peopled else / This isle with Calibans," 1.2.349–50), his desire to redistribute social relations through Miranda's fallen "labor," becomes the necessary incident explaining the establishment of slavery as the island's mode of production.

Even before Caliban's ostensible fall, however, he was already marked for labor and servitude. The truth of this marking is revealed in his first language lesson. Looking back with nostalgia to the time when Prospero first came to the isle and taught him language, Caliban says

> . . . When thou cam'st first,
> Thou strok'st me and made much of me; wouldst give me
> Water with berries in't, and teach me how
> To name the bigger light and how the less,
> That burn by day and night; and then I loved thee,
> And showed thee all the qualities o'th' isle,
> The fresh springs, brine pits, barren places and fertile. (1.2.332–38)

Of course, this utopian reverie is bracketed by Caliban's savvy genealogical claim on the island ("This island's mine by Sycorax my mother," 1.2.331) on the one hand, and his assertion of a prior claim to sovereignty ("For am I all the subjects that you have, / Which first was mine own king," 1.2.341–42) on the other. Within the passage itself, however, Caliban describes a utopia of shared resources and knowledge, a democratic communalism that separates his discourse from European social hierarchies. Ironically, however, Caliban's language lesson emerges from Christian thought and European hierarchies. The subject matter of Caliban's lesson is, of course, from Genesis:

> And God said, Let there be lightes in the firmament of the heauen, to separate the daie from the night, & let them be for signes, and for seasons, and for daies and yeres.
> And let them be for lightes in the firmament of the heauen to giue light vpon the earth. and it was so.
> God then made two great lightes: the greater light to rule the daie, & the lesse light to rule night: he *made* also the starres.
> And God set them in the firmament of the heauen, to shine vpon the earth,
> And to rule in the daie and the night, and to separate the light from the darkenes: and God sawe that it was good.[61]

By teaching Caliban "To name the bigger light and how the less, / That burn by day and night," Prospero welcomes him into the human fold on Christian terms (1.2.335–36).

In his *Lectures on Genesis*, Luther makes it clear that an understanding of both language and the firmament marks the human as human and God's special creature. For Luther, it is on "this fourth day" of creation that "our glory begins to be revealed":

> Here the immortality of the soul begins to unfold and reveal itself
> to us, inasmuch as no creature apart from man can either understand
> the motion of the heaven or measure the heavenly bodies. A pig, a
> cow, and a dog are unable to measure the water they drink; but man
> measures the heaven and all the heavenly bodies. And so here there
> gleams a spark of eternal life, in that the human being busies himself
> by nature with this knowledge of nature. This concern indicates that
> men were not created to live permanently in this lowest part of the
> universe but to take possession of heaven. . . . The human being, in
> his mind, soars high above the earth; and leaving behind those
> things that are on the earth, he concerns himself with heavenly
> things and explores them. Cows, pigs, and other beasts do not do
> this; it is man alone who does it. Therefore man is a creature created
> to inhabit the celestial regions and to live an eternal life when, after
> a while, he has left the earth. For this is the meaning of the fact that
> he can not only speak and form judgments . . . but also learns all
> the sciences thoroughly. . . . By citizenship we belong to that home-
> land which we now look at, admire, and understand, yet like strang-
> ers and exiles; but after this life we shall look at these things more
> closely and understand them perfectly.[62]

By learning to "speak and form judgments" and to comprehend the firmament, Caliban demonstrates that he, like the rest of mankind, is both citizen
and exile. Unfortunately, this passage into the human fold is also a fall. The
fourth day of Creation not only reveals human glory but also marks the
beginning of the natural, hierarchical order of the Christian cosmos. In a
marginal gloss to this passage the Geneva Bible declares that these lines speak
"Of things apperteining to natural and political ordres." The natural sovereignty of man over beast could and did become a template for the sovereignty
of one man over another. The glory of man that Luther celebrates was used
to justify the abjection of men, as the distinctively human attributes that
Luther catalogues would be used to differentiate one man from another. If it
is the glory of man to "speak and form judgments," to "understand," to
"measure," to possess "knowledge of nature" and to learn "all the sciences
thoroughly," to transcend the "things that are on the earth" and to "take
possession of heaven," then all those who fail to do so are, in some sense, less
than glorious, less than men; they are fit, it seems, only to serve. As Julia
Reinhard Lupton suggests, Prospero's theological language lesson is also a

lesson in social hierarchy and degree: "Sun and moon, Prospero and Caliban, Creator and Creature, king and subject: the image of the two lights inserts an unequal couple within the apparent innocence of the recollected lesson."[63] Prospero teaches Caliban to distinguish the greater light from the lesser and in so doing prepares him for his position in the hierarchy that, according to early modern theology, the creation story inscribed. In his idyllic recollection Caliban fails to comprehend how the utopian scene of education has already inscribed the "mooncalf" into a Christian cosmos and European social order in which he is granted a fallen humanity that condemns him to a life of subservience and labor (2.2.129).

Labor and Letters

In *Tristes Tropiques* (1955) Claude Lévi-Strauss recorded what has become one of the most well-known and controversial scenes of writing in the history of ethnography.[64] In the course of his dealings with the Nambikwara of Brazil, the anthropologist, discerning that their society did not have what he would call written language, decided to introduce pencils and sheets of paper into the culture. When the Nambikwara proceeded to make wavy lines on the paper, Lévi-Strauss interpreted this activity as their attempt to imitate the performance of writing. The chief of the Nambikwara took this mimetic venture a step further by performing his version of writing in his communication with Lévi-Strauss. When the time came for an exchange of gifts between the ethnographer's group and the Nambikwara, the chief's writing performance took center stage:

> He took from a basket a piece of paper covered with wavy lines and made a show of reading it, pretending to hesitate as he checked on it the list of objects I was to give in exchange for the presents offered me. . . . This farce went on for two hours. Was he perhaps hoping to delude himself? More probably he wanted to astonish his companions, to convince them that he was acting as an intermediary agent for the exchange of the goods, that he was in alliance with the white man and shared his secrets. (296)

This "extraordinary incident" occasions Lévi-Strauss's reflections on writing. And much of the rhetorical power of these reflections arises from the fact that Lévi-Strauss's modern parable works against generic expectations. By labeling his essay "A Writing Lesson" (*Leçon d'écriture*) and describing the introduction of the tools of literacy to those who seem not to understand this technology, he invites his readers to expect that they will witness the modern man of reason teaching the savage the wonders of letters. That literacy lifts the "primitive" out of the darkness of ignorance and superstition and into the light of freedom and progress is such a powerful cultural myth that Lévi-Strauss can expect it to shape the responses of even sophisticated readers. When the anthropologist describes the ways in which the chief seems to misunderstand the purpose of writing, the modern, Western reader expects to learn that writing is the crucial difference between the barbarous and the civilized, that the Nambikwara can only learn to be civilized, learn to learn, by learning to read. But Lévi-Strauss's "writing lesson" is not a lesson learned by the Nambikwara but by the European anthropologist; ascertaining that writing is an instrument of power, the Nambikwara chief has, in Lévi-Strauss's view, seen into the heart of things. This crucial insight stimulates Lévi-Strauss's devastating critique of the pervasive myth concerning writing and literacy:

> Writing is a strange invention. One might suppose that its emergence could not fail to bring about profound changes in the condition of human existence, and that these transformations must of necessity be of an intellectual nature. The possession of writing vastly increases man's ability to preserve knowledge. It can be thought of as an artificial memory, the development of which ought to lead to a clearer awareness of the past, and hence to a greater ability to organize both the present and the future. After eliminating all other criteria which have been put forward to distinguish between barbarism and civilization, it is tempting to retain this one at least: there are people with, or without, writing; the former are able to store up their past achievements and to move with ever-increasing rapidity towards the goal they have set themselves, whereas the latter, being incapable of remembering the past beyond the narrow margin of individual memory, seem bound to remain in a fluctuating history which will always lack both a beginning and any lasting awareness of an aim.
>
> Yet nothing we know about writing and the part it has played in man's evolution justifies this view. (298)

The lesson that the anthropologist learns is that writing is fundamentally a technology that enables the domination of peoples and the administration and control of populations. Lévi-Strauss's meditation on the role of writing in history suggests to him "that the primary function of written communication is to facilitate slavery" (299).

* * *

In *The Tempest* Shakespeare harnesses for theatrical purposes an early modern ambivalence about books, an ambivalence in which books are viewed both as instruments of enlightenment and as tools of oppression. To the extent that he intervenes in a triumphalism that celebrates the power of letters to exalt the civilized European over the barbarous non-European, he does so by placing Caliban's radical desire to burn books at the center of the play and taking that iconoclastic impulse seriously.[65] In his injunction to "possess" and "burn" Prospero's books, Caliban argues that

> . . . without them
> He's but a sot, as I am, nor hath not
> One spirit to command—they all do hate him
> As rootedly as I. Burn but his books. (3.2.90–93)

Anticipating the lesson Lévi-Strauss learns about writing, Caliban explicitly figures Prospero's books as instruments of tyrannical control. In this understanding of Prospero's magic, not only is Prospero "but a sot" without his books, but the power of Prospero's books lies in the power to command embittered and disaffected subjects. Even when reflecting on the immense power of Prospero's art, Caliban reads it as essentially the power of mastery and subjugation: "I must obey. His art is of such power, / It would control my dam's god Setebos / and make a vassal of him" (1.2.371–73). And if we look closely at Prospero's mysterious art—a power that does not seem to manifest in a meaningful way prior to his enforced exile—it is difficult to divorce it from those "natural resources" that predate his advent on the isle; it is difficult to disentangle his power on the island from the enforced labor of Ariel and the "spirits." Given Caliban's understanding of Prospero's power as, in some sense, the power of subjection, it would be tempting to argue that Prospero's book represents a mystified reification of the island's social relations, a reification in which the alienated labor of Caliban, Ariel, and the spirits appears before them as the "magical" property of this material object.[66] In this argument, the fetishization of Prospero's book arises from the peculiar character of the labor that produces it as *Prospero's book*, arises from servitude and slavery. The problem with this line of thought is that in the world of the play, Prospero's magic is very real, and the book seems to be a crucial instrument of that real power. Moreover, labor relations on the island are anything but mystified; indeed, they are often shockingly transparent. Prospero and Ariel engage in repeated negotiations about the end of Ariel's service to his master—for Ariel, a termination devoutly to be wished. And nothing could be less ambiguous than Prospero's enslaving of Caliban. As Prospero says quite plainly—and to Miranda no less, the child he seems to want to protect from knowledge of the world—"We cannot miss him. He does make our fire, / Fetch in our wood, and serves in offices / That profit us" (1.2.311–13). And to obtain this labor from Ariel and Caliban, Prospero is willing to threaten, imprison, and torture. When Ariel balks at continuing to serve Prospero, Prospero compels him with the threat of an horrific incarceration: "If thou more murmur'st, I will rend an oak / And peg thee in his knotty entrails till / Thou hast howled away twelve winters" (1.2.294–96). This is, of course, the very punishment that Sycorax had inflicted upon Ariel: "Thou best know'st / What torment I did find thee in. Thy groans / Did make wolves howl" (1.2.286–88). Morally aligning himself with the "foul witch Sycorax," Prospero threatens Ariel with "a torment / To lay upon the damned" (1.2.258, 289–90).[67] Just as Caliban's labors are more prosaic than Ariel's, so too are his prospective agonies. Insisting that Caliban continue to perform the menial tasks assigned to him ("Fetch us in fuel, and be quick," 1.2.365), Prospero menaces him with the prospect of bodily pain:

> If thou neglect'st, or dost unwillingly
> What I command, I'll rack thee with old cramps,
> Fill all thy bones with achës, make thee roar,
> That beasts shall tremble at thy din. (1.2.367–70)[68]

Through this physical torment, Prospero, according to Caliban, is able to "sty" him in "this hard rock" and keep him from the "rest o' th'island" (1.2.343–44). If Prospero contests the narrative that Caliban recounts in this scene in a general way ("Thou most lying slave," 1.2.344), he never disputes the fact that Caliban is imprisoned against his will. Given the demystified nature of labor relations on the island, and given Prospero's evident penchant for mental and physical cruelty, it seems strange that Prospero had for so long been understood as a benign figure and benevolent ruler. To understand *The Tempest*, however, it is necessary to come to terms with this curious reception history. I contend quite simply that Prospero has been read as benign because the play stages this reading of the character. That it primarily does so through Prospero's self-description, however, should give us pause. And I suggest that Prospero's vision of himself as enlightened and benign has such purchase because he presents himself as a man of letters. The conception of Prospero as a figure of benevolence is fundamentally related to his claims to learning and enlightenment, fundamentally related to his books. If the books do not work to mystify social relations, they do work to justify those relations. In *The Tempest* Shakespeare stages the fact that Prospero's mastery of books works to naturalize his mastery of others.

* * *

From the beginning of the play, Shakespeare lets his audience know that *The Tempest* will explore relations between servants and masters, authority and its discontents. According to the stage directions in the First Folio, *The Tempest* begins with a "tempestuous noise of thunder and lightning" and the entrance of a master and servant: "Enter a Ship-master and a Boatswain." From the first exchange of the drama—the master's call for the "Boatswain!" and the boatswain's response: "Here, master"—Shakespeare stages the kind of hierarchical relation that he will explore throughout the drama. (1.1.1–2). As the play opens, this social structure seems to work exactly as it should as master, boatswain, and the cohort of mariners coordinate their efforts to battle the elements. In fact, the opening exchange between master and servant seems to anticipate the characteristic exchange between Prospero and Ariel:

> *Prospero:* What, Ariel! My industrious servant, Ariel!
> *Enter Ariel*
> *Ariel:* What would my potent master? Here I am. (4.1.33–34; see also
>   1.2.187–89, 1.2.317–18, 4.1.164–65)

The simple hierarchical organization of the ship, however, is complicated when the king's party enters. Responding to the crisis at hand, the boatswain is deeply unimpressed by the powerful passengers and responds to their intrusive requests with disdain. After enjoining the king and his entourage to "keep below," the boatswain tells Antonio that their presence "mar[s] our labor" and instructs them to "keep" to their "cabins" (1.1.11, 13, 14). In response to Gonzalo's indignation at the boatswain's treatment of his betters, the boatswain commands, "Hence! What cares these roarers for the name of king? To cabin; silence! Trouble us not" (1.1.16–18). Personified, the angry waves become "roaring" or rebellious subjects who care not for the privilege and presumption of royal authority.[69] If the boatswain seems to anticipate Prospero's Ariel in his subservient and efficient relation to the shipmaster, he anticipates Prospero's Caliban in his vexed relation to the king's entourage. The poisonous repartee that the boatswain and the king's men engage in resonates throughout the play as they clash over labor ("You mar our labour," 1.1.13; "Work you, then," 1.1.42), employ the language of cursing ("A plague upon this howling!" 1.1.35–36; "A pox o' your throat, you bawling, blasphemous, incharitable dog!" 1.1.40–41; "Hang, cur, hang, you whoreson insolent noisemaker!" 1.1.42–43), and discuss the relation between character and fate ("he hath no drowning mark upon him—his complexion is perfect gallows," 1.1.28–30; "If he be not born to be hanged, our case is miserable," 1.1.32–33; "I'll warrant him for drowning," 1.1.45; "He'll be hanged yet," 1.1.57). When Sebastian curses him, the boatswain responds with the simple directive— "Work you, then" (1.1.38–42). The boatswain's injunction to work is wonderfully biting since it draws the audience's attention not merely to the uselessness of the king's entourage but to their dependence on the boatswain's labor for their very survival. When Gonzalo commands him to "remember whom thou hast aboard," the boatswain responds:

> None that I more love than myself. You are a councillor; if you can command these elements to silence, and work the peace of the present, we will not hand a rope more—use your authority. If you cannot, give thanks you have lived so long, and make yourself ready in your cabin for the mischance of the hour, if it so hap. (*To the Mariners*)—Cheerly, good hearts! (*To the courtiers*)—Out of our way, I say! (1.1.20–27)

The injunction to "use your authority" mocks Gonzalo's pretensions by highlighting the courtier's impotence in this situation. And the boatswain can refuse to recognize the authority of the royal entourage because the king and his men are literally out of their element. The discourse of authority and power that they enjoy on land becomes, at sea, an inflated rhetoric that provides them little profit, other than the ability to curse. Foregrounding the fact that the idle aristocrats are dependent upon the work of the mariners, this opening scene launches the play's exploration of the ways in which aristocratic privilege and noble idleness are subtended and sustained by the labor of others.

Of course, in the very next scene the audience learns that the roaring waves not only cared for "the name of king" but were concerned with this particular king. The noble passengers are not saved by the labor of the mariners but by the power of Prospero, the author of the storm. Nevertheless, this conception of labor as the repressed foundation of aristocratic idleness is invoked throughout the play, not only through figures like Ariel and Caliban but also through the murky and dubious drama of Prospero's backstory. Even Miranda's lone memory of her life before the island is a recollection of labor; the one thing she remembers about her pre-island existence is not her mother or the high drama of her enforced exile but that she had status, that she had servants:

> 'Tis far off,
> And rather like a dream than an assurance
> That my remembrance warrants. Had I not
> Four or five women once that tended me? (1.2.44–47)

The child raised in savage circumstances discovered to be noble is one of the most familiar conventions of romance. Because of Miranda's curious reminiscence, the audience suspects her gentility before she learns that her father was "the Duke of Milan, and / A prince of power." Miranda's birth and blood are then announced through the recollection of the servitude of others.

The story of Miranda's fall from such grace, Prospero's fall from power, is the story of service forgotten, labor taken for granted. According to his own narrative, Prospero's fall begins with his decision to delegate the "manage of my state" to his brother Antonio (1.2.70). Casting the "government" of his dukedom upon his brother, Prospero to his "state grew stranger, being transported / And rapt in secret studies" (1.2.75–77). The audience is, of course, meant to link these secret studies with the powerful magic he works on the island, but, in the first instance, Prospero refers to the object of his study as "the liberal arts" (1.2.73). "Liberal" here means "free." According to the *Oxford English Dictionary*, "liberall" was "originally, the distinctive epithet of those 'arts' or 'sciences'" that were considered "worthy of a free man," opposed to "*servile* or *mechanical.*" In "later use," "liberal" was used as both a term "pertaining to or suitable to persons of superior social station" and a term "directed to general intellectual enlargement and refinement."[70] A man of superior social station, Prospero is at liberty to pursue the "arts" or "sciences" considered "worthy of a free man."[71] Everything about Prospero's pursuit of "intellectual enlargement and refinement" seems designed to convince his audience that his engagement with the liberal arts amounts to a pursuit of transcendence. "Transported" by his "secret studies," Prospero is metaphorically carried away from the demands of his dukedom; "rapt," he transcends the workaday world of governance. Of course, the price of his freedom, the price of his rapture, is his brother's labor.

Recounting Antonio's machinations, Prospero claims that his brother had become the "ivy which . . . hid my princely trunk, / And sucked my verdure out on't" (1.2.86–87). But Shakespeare's audience might very well have noticed that the familiar figure of ivy and tree could also be used—and perhaps with more justice—to describe the parasitical relation of Prospero to his brother. Prospero describes himself as "neglecting worldly ends" as one who was "all dedicated / To closeness and the bettering of my mind" (1.2.89–90). In the narrative he relates to Miranda, he fashions this dedication *and* this neglect as the virtuous and otherworldly counterpoints to Antonio's worldly materialism. Explaining his fall from aristocratic grace, Prospero contrasts Antonio's desire for power with his own desire for learning:

> To have no screen between this part he played
> And him he played it for, he needs will be
> Absolute Milan. Me, poor man, my library
> Was dukedom large enough. (1.2.107–10)

Prospero could be bounded in a nut shell and count himself a king of infinite space if only he had his books. Ultimately, Prospero will acknowledge some culpability in the creation of Antonio's voracity ("I . . . in my false brother / Awaked an evil nature" 1.2.89–93), but his key rhetorical move is to paint himself as a guileless innocent whose pursuit of intellectual transcendence made him susceptible to the wiles of his worldly and ambitious brother. And just as Prospero draws his credulous audience in with this depiction, so too does Shakespeare. In "A Writing Lesson," Lévi-Strauss argues that the "use of writing for disinterested purposes, and as a source of intellectual and aesthetic pleasure, is a secondary result" following from its primary function as a means of organizing and subjugating labor. And as he writes, this secondary result is often deployed as "a means of strengthening, justifying or concealing" this primary function (299). One of the reasons Prospero has been championed as a benevolent figure despite the textual evidence to the contrary is that the myth of the transcendent pursuit of letters remains one of the central myths of modern, Western culture. Shakespeare, however, invites the audience to read against the grain of the story that Prospero tells Miranda. Indeed, throughout *The Tempest* Shakespeare seems intent on illustrating to his audience that Prospero's bookish pursuits—both in Milan in the past and in the present of the island—are made possible by an aristocratic idleness that depends upon the labor of others.

Both Prospero's knowledge of the "liberal arts" and his mastery of lesser creatures manifests itself most fully and clearly "as a source of intellectual and aesthetic pleasure" in the masque he stages for the betrothal of Ferdinand and Miranda. Prospero's Ovidian spectacle is an idyll of natural harmony and order. Referring to the world Prospero conjures as a "paradise," Ferdinand pronounces it "a most majestic vision, and / Harmonious charmingly" (4.1.124, 118–19). At the center of this "majestic vision," Prospero presents Ceres, the goddess of the earth, who offers the young couple a blessing:

> Earth's increase, foison plenty,
> Barns and garners never empty,
> Vines and clust'ring bunches growing,
> Plants with goodly burthen bowing;
> Spring come to you at the farthest,
> In the very end of harvest!
> Scarcity and want shall shun you;
> Ceres' blessing so is on you. (4.1.110–17)

Prospero's masque offers a vision of a fertile, bountiful nature offering up its fruits freely. In her blessing, Ceres moves directly from the end of harvest to the onset of spring, eliding the winter months in a familiar fantasy of perpetual fecundity. In Ceres' dream of natural bounty there is not only no winter but also, crucially, no mention of work, no need, it seems, for human intervention in the production of "never empty" "barns and garners." Human labor arrives in Prospero's masque belatedly and almost parenthetically when Iris invites "sunburned sickle-men, of August weary" to "Come hither from the furrow and be merry" (4.1.134–35). And it is here that the masque is famously cut short. "Rapt" once again, once again "transported" by the fruits of his secret studies, Prospero has forgotten about political realities: "I had forgot that foul conspiracy / Of the beast Caliban and his confederates / Against my life" (4.1.139–41). Into Prospero's vision of peace and harmony slouches that rough beast Caliban, his hour come round at last. And Caliban's return is a return of the repressed. Prospero's masque is a vision of bounty without labor, natural fecundity without work. It is, like Gonzalo's utopia, a fantasy in which "nature should produce / Without sweat or endeavour" (2.1.157–58). This repression of labor is wonderfully ironic, since the spirits performing the masque, performing Prospero's bidding, would seem to be the same spirits Caliban alludes to when he states that without his books Prospero "hath not / One spirit to command—they all do hate him / As rootedly as I" (3.2.90–93). And crucially, it is precisely that moment in the masque when the reapers join the dance, when human labor is alluded to, however briefly and glancingly, that Prospero remembers Caliban and his cohort. Prospero's aristocratic perspective is one that does not encompass work and thus cannot acknowledge the Calibans—or indeed, the Antonios—of the world. And on the island, this blindness, this failure to acknowledge or account for labor, once again produces rebellion.

In Prospero's story, history repeats itself in the familiar way outlined by Marx: the first time as tragedy, the second time as farce. If the tragedy of Prospero's fall is repeated in the folly of Caliban's thwarted rising, however, that repetition serves to belie distinctions between civilized and savage. And however farcical the outcome of Caliban's rebellion might be, the staging of that rebellion draws the audience's attention to the complex ways in which notions of civilization and savagery are organized around conceptions of literacy, conceptions of the proper way to read the book and the world. In the early modern period, the "literall advantage" that Purchas believed God granted European man became a defining feature establishing the difference between the civilized and Christian and the barbarous and pagan. Central to this conception of civilization is a celebration of what Prospero calls "the liberal arts," the transcendent arts pursued by a man freed from manual labor. In *The Tempest*, Prospero's narrative of his own pre-history as reclusive scholar represents an etiological myth explaining his current position of power as the natural consequence of his years spent "rapt in secret studies" (1.2.77). In this myth the noble European, in pursuit of transcendence ("neglecting worldly ends, all dedicated / To closeness and the bettering of my mind" 1.2.89–90), acquires the "literall advantage," an "advantage" that works to justify European dominion over unlettered savages.

Charms O'erthrown

Keith Thomas begins the concluding chapter of his *Religion and the Decline of Magic* with an epigraph from Prospero's address to the audience at the end of *The Tempest*:

> Now my charms are all o'erthrown
> And what strength I have's mine own,
> Which is most faint . . .[72]

Thomas employs Shakespeare's epilogue to dramatize the historical shift in the relationship between magic and religion that his history of early modern England describes. As he says, "At the end of our period we can draw a distinction between religion and magic which would not have been possible at the beginning."[73] Thomas's magisterial history tracks the movement from primitive magic to rational religion, from superstition to enlightenment.[74] His placement of Prospero's epilogue suggests an ingenious reading of the play in which *The Tempest* celebrates the redemption of Prospero as "enlightened" European man. In this reading, Prospero's abjuration of his magic and drowning of his book stages his renunciation of the superstitious materialism of a previous age. The ostentatious materiality of Prospero's magic is staged, in this understanding of the play, so that it can be abjured, so that Prospero can differentiate himself from the "barbarous" materialism of the non-European, a "barbarous" materialism that Protestantism had already discovered at the heart of the Catholic Church. Recognizing his own humanity over and against the indigenous native, Prospero accepts his role in the emergent order of a reformed imperialism, an order in which the superstitious and idolatrous things of the world are cast off like so many theatrical props.

Thomas's deployment of Prospero's epilogue follows in a long tradition of *Tempest* criticism that figures Prospero's abjuration as a turning away from magic and immanence and toward some kind of transcendence.[75] But the triumphalist reading of a transcendent Prospero emerging from the darkness of superstition is belied by the nature of Prospero's abjuration. If we are to take Prospero at his word, his abjuration of his rough magic requires both human endeavor and the harnessing of nature, requires acts of ritual destruction, requires, it seems, some kind of rough magic:

> . . . this rough magic
> I here abjure; and when I have required
> Some heavenly music—which even now I do—
> To work mine end upon their senses that
> This airy charm is for, I'll break my staff,
> Bury it certain fathoms in the earth,
> And deeper than did ever plummet sound
> I'll drown my book. (5.1.50–57)

Invoking the elements of earth and water, Prospero abjures his rough magic by vowing that these crucial props—staff and book—will be removed from human reach, withdrawn from the grasp of human hands. They are not, however, destroyed. In fact, we might expect them—buried "certain fathoms in the earth," drowned "deeper than did ever plummet sound"—to be preserved, if perhaps transformed into something "rich and strange" (1.2.402). And the invocation of prodigious depths in these lines echoes earlier moments in the play in which characters wrestled with loss and grief. The elements invoked might change, but Prospero's burial of his staff "certain fathoms in the earth" echoes Ariel's song to Ferdinand insisting upon the death of the king, his father: "Full fathom five thy father lies" (1.2.397). And Prospero's commitment to drown his book "deeper than did ever plummet sound" calls to mind Alonso's suicidal despair when faced with his culpability in his son's alleged death:

> . . . my son i' th' ooze is bedded; and
> I'll seek him deeper than e'er plummet sounded,
> And with him there lie mudded. (3.3.100–102)

If Prospero's abjuration is not a repetition of Alonso's despair, it does mirror the king's desire for some kind of essential transformation. As I discussed in Chapter 3, the ritual destruction of books was the traditional method of turning away from the diabolical letters of magical texts and toward the divine: it was a corporeal rite that gave textual conversion a dramatic form.[76] Prospero's proposed destruction of his book is an offer to convert, to transform. Like Alonso, Prospero commits to a conversion of the self, but Prospero will transform by offering up his book rather than his body. If this is not despair, the actions Prospero invokes in this scene—the commitment of staff and book to earth and sea—nevertheless suggest funeral rites, suggest a ritualized loss. His offer to commit his book to the muddy depths is an expression of a desire for a certain kind of death, an offer to surrender objects in which he has invested himself, objects that constitute him as Prospero.

The Tempest, I contend, is a play about relinquishing mastery. In the epilogue the audience bears witness as Prospero performs his lack of power, his dependence on others. In the abjuration of his magic, Prospero performs the disavowal that results in this lack of power, this lack of mastery. But the error Prospero renounces in that abjuration is not a mistaken belief in the things of this world, a mistaken belief that would tie him to Caliban and Sycorax, Catholics and savages. The ritualized actions Prospero proposes in the abjuration do not reflect the mind of a man renouncing an epistemology of immanence. Even in these acts of disavowal, Prospero accords these objects—the staff, the book—immense respect. The very material destruction of Prospero's books and props is not the final act that repudiates a fallen world of things but an acceptance of that fallen world in which he relinquishes the illusion of transcendence. At the beginning of this chapter, I suggested that in order to understand the significance of the absence of Prospero's books from the text of *The Tempest*, it would be useful to examine the central role that conceptions of literacy and materiality play in the European understanding of the "barbarous" other. As an embodiment of European letters, Prospero's books function to mark Prospero's superiority to the "primitive" Caliban. At the same time, they are potentially the marker of a "false" materialism—a materialism that must be repudiated or abjured if the European Prospero is to take his proper place in the emergent order of a "reformed" imperialism. Using anecdotes describing the awe that natives held for books and book culture, Europeans granted themselves a "literal advantage" in their own emergent understanding of the book as a text with only a contingent relation to any material form. If the audience never sees Prospero's all-important book, if *The Tempest* stages the book as a Real Absence around which all else revolves, it is so that its powers may become dislocated, transcendent. The power of the book is everywhere and nowhere. The "fetish" that Europeans decried as an object that enslaves the superstitious and unenlightened takes up its own disembodied position at the center of European dominion. Prospero's book is a fetish that charms but whose power is the more invulnerable in that we do not seem able to see it or touch it. Crucially, however,

Prospero relinquishes this absent fetish, this intangible prop; and when the book goes, so does Prospero. The cloak and the staff are the visible supplements that constitute Prospero's power, both within the fiction of the play and on the material stage of the Renaissance theater. But in the end, it is the destruction of the absent presence—Prospero's book—that will transform Prospero. In the triumphalist reading of the play, Prospero abjures his barbarous magic so that he can take his proper place in the New World of "enlightened" Europe, but on the stage the audience sees a character systematically divesting himself of the personae—the masks and prostheses—through which his person is constituted. Relinquishing the magic of things, abandoning the wonder and immanence that characterize the fictional island and the material stage, Prospero begins to undo himself.

The Tempest has long been considered a Christian play, or at least a play that invokes a Christian frame for its drama of revenge and reconciliation. Given that we have a sorcerer who abjures his magic, a wronged man who chooses noble reason over fury, virtue over vengeance, we might be forgiven if we expect a play about sin and redemption, a morality play. But if *The Tempest* is a morality play, it is a morality play that is curiously reticent about the state of the protagonist's soul. Unlike Marlowe's *Doctor Faustus*, for instance, *The Tempest* is not concerned with sin and damnation, repentance and salvation. As Stephen Orgel notes, "Faustus's magic . . . is theology, whereas Prospero's magic is art and science. . . . There is nothing whatever in *The Tempest* about magic leading to damnation; even Sycorax's putative liaison with the devil eventuates only in Caliban."[77] Firmly grounded in this world, *The Tempest* is concerned not with heaven or hell but with one man's relation to, and treatment of, other rational creatures. Rather than a play that addresses the path to eternal salvation, we seem to have a play that is interested in what we might call moral philosophy, a play that is concerned with the definition of the human, the ethics of sharing resources and dividing labor, the emotional costs of mastery and subjection, the desirability of escaping the dead and deadening hand of the past. In his abjuration, Prospero renounces not his sins but his "potent art," the power he holds over nature and his fellow creatures. He performs a disavowal of the book as that which would place him above others, beyond the human. *Doctor Faustus* is a play about a man who believes he is master of his books, only to learn that his books have mastered him. *The Tempest* is a play in which books are both sign and instrument of one man's mastery of another.

Before the abjuration of his magic, Prospero is always threatening to leave his humanity behind in a bid for some sort of transcendence. His secret studies, his arcane knowledge, separate him from and elevate him above the rest of humanity; his mastery of letters offers the illusion of freedom and autonomy, offers the illusion of some kind of divine self-authorship when, in fact, he has always been dependent on both powerfully resonant props and the labor of others. And if his books promise to make him more than a man, they also threaten to make him less than human. But this threat of losing his humanity arises not from the immanence of his rough magic, not from a fetishization of his books, but from the illusion of transcendence that his books provide. The play dramatizes a return from exile, an exile that began with Prospero's secret studies, his exile into the liberal arts. Prospero's muted redemption is not a transcendent one; it is a return to the world, a return to political realities, a return to the necessity of labor and the inevitability of death. Prospero does not, at the end of the play, think of his soul or heaven; his "every third thought" shall be of a very material "grave" (5.1.311). Prospero's story is, I contend, a story about relinquishing the illusion of transcendence that authenticates mastery, a story about relinquishing the book.

Epilogue

Bacon's Impossible Book

THE FRONTISPIECE OF the first edition of Francis Bacon's *Instauratio Magna* (1620) references the Book of Daniel: "Multi pertransibunt et augebitu scientia" (Many shall runne to and fro, and knowledge shall be increased) (Daniel 12:4; Figure 21).[1] Invoking an apocalyptic frame for Bacon's *Great Instauration*, the epigraph seems to align the Baconian project in natural philosophy with Daniel's prophecy that there will be a period of intellectual ferment before the end of time. The famous engraved image on the title page depicts a ship sailing through the pillars of Hercules, the straits of Gibraltar.[2] The pillars of Hercules were traditionally thought to mark the limits of human enterprise and discovery. According to legend, the Latin motto *ne plus ultra* was inscribed on the pillars, indicating that the straits of Gibraltar were the edge of the known world; one could not go further, there was "no more beyond" this point.[3] Dante alludes to this tradition in *The Inferno*, suggesting that these limits are marked by the Christian God and part of a Christian geography; in the twenty-sixth canto of *The Inferno*, the soul of Ulysses recounts his last journey, a journey beyond the limits of human exploration. In his desire for further adventures, Ulysses dares to go beyond the pillars of Hercules; he presumes to know and experience more than man should. His pride and presumption are rewarded with death at sea, as the will of another (*com' altrui piacque*)—the Christian God, unknown to Ulysses—denies his "longing for experience of the world" and ends his "pursuit of knowledge."[4] The frontispiece of Bacon's *Great Instauration* famously celebrates the transgressing of this ancient limit; the learning of classical antiquity had been surpassed and superseded by the discoveries of early modern exploration and the advances of natural philosophy. As Dante's revision of the story of Ulysses suggests, however, this celebration intimates a potentially

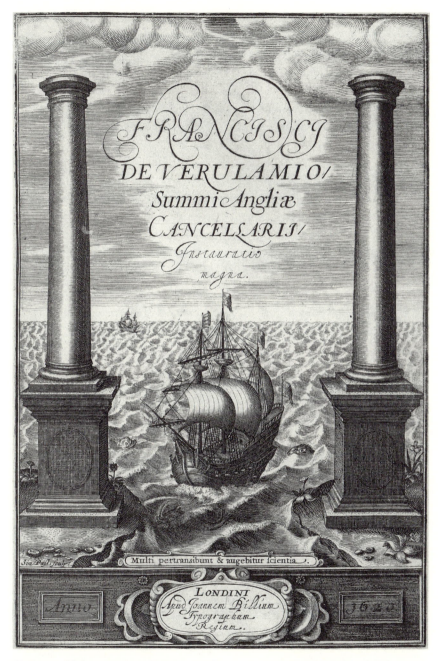

Figure 21. Title-page engraving, Francis Bacon, *Instauratio Magna* (1620). This item is reproduced by permission of The Huntington Library, San Marino, California.

dangerous pride. The Faustian dream of ever-increasing knowledge is one of the recurring cautionary tales of Christian culture; the spiritual consequences of such a dream loom over the kinds of triumphalist claims that Bacon seems to make with this frontispiece. Dante's famous continuation of Ulysses' story suggests that a Faustian desire to expand the limits of knowledge—a repetition of man's original sin—will inevitably provoke the wrath of the Christian God. Bacon's invocation of Daniel on the frontispiece of his *Great Instauration* seems designed to prevent and preclude such an understanding of the new science's ambitions, seems designed to bring natural philosophy under the auspices of religion.

Reading this passage from Daniel as a prophecy foretelling the age of discovery in which he lived, Bacon attempts to reconcile the expansion of knowledge in this age with Christian revelation. He returns to this scriptural passage at different times in his writings,[5] but his reading of it is perhaps given its fullest expression in his early work *Valerius Terminus*:

> This is a thing which I cannot tell whether I may so plainly speak as truly conceive, that as all knowledge appeareth to be a plant of God's own planting, so it may seem that the spreading and flourishing or at least the bearing and fructifying of this plant, by a providence of God, nay not only by a general providence but by a special prophecy, was appointed to this autumn of the world: for to my understanding it is not violent to the letter, and safe now after the event, so to interpret that place in the prophecy of Daniel where speaking of the latter times it is said, *Many shall pass to and fro, and science shall be increased*; as if the opening of the world by navigation and commerce and the further discovery of knowledge should meet in one time or age.[6]

The serendipity of these two epoch-shaping developments—the discoveries of natural philosophy and the "opening of the world by navigation and commerce"—meeting "in one time or age" suggests to Bacon the presence of a divine hand shaping history. Aligning the contemporary explosion of knowledge and discovery with the implacable will of the almighty, Bacon here attempts to write the endeavors of contemporary science into Christian history, apocalyptic history. Daniel's prophecy authorizes the increase of knowledge at a particular historical moment, "this autumn of the world," the evidently frenetic ("many shall runne to and fro") interim before the end times. Bacon claims this prophecy, and this interim, for natural philosophy.

In this epilogue, I offer a brief reading of Bacon's *New Atlantis* in relation to his striking appropriation of Daniel. As I suggested in the Introduction, Bacon is often considered, for better or worse, a prophet of modernity.[7] His methodological interventions helped steer early modern natural philosophy toward Enlightenment science; his conception of the proper relation to the phenomenal world anticipated modern epistemology. The image of Bacon as proleptically modern often coincides with a conviction that he was decidedly secularist in his perspective, indifferent or inimical to religion. Some scholars have suggested that Bacon's consistent positioning of his natural philosophy in relation to Christian religion is simply craft or guile. Other scholars—less insistent on claiming Bacon for modernity—have suggested that Bacon's reiterated claim that natural philosophy was consonant with Christian religion was, in fact, an expression of actual conviction.[8] Here, I want to take seriously Bacon's repeated claim that the work of natural philosophy is consistent with Christian revelation and co-extensive with a Reformation project to reject idolatry and superstition, without assuming that this claim is either defensive posturing or a confession of his true faith.[9] Like many of the natural philosophers of the sixteenth and seventeenth centuries, Bacon turned to the metaphor of the two books to describe the relation of scripture to the natural world.[10] In *The Advancement of Learning*, he writes

> For our Sauiour saith, *You erre not knowing the Scriptures, nor the power of God*: laying before vs two Bookes or volumes to studie, if we will be secured from errour: first the scriptures, reuealing the will of God; and then the creatures expressing his power; whereof the later is a key vnto the former; not onely opening our vnderstanding to conceiue the true sence of the scriptures; by the generall notions of reason and rules of speech; but chiefely opening our beleefe, in drawing vs into a due meditation of the omnipotencie of God, which is chiefely signed and ingrauen vppon his workes.[11]

Scripture is the book of God's will; the natural world is the book of God's power and works. For Bacon, this does not mean that nature is an open book, easily read. On the contrary, because of humanity's latent defects, our apprehension of the world is necessarily faulty. Bacon traces the defective and distorting "idols of the mind" he sees all around him to the fall of man, which created an epistemological gulf between man's natural faculties and God's creation.[12] For the Christian writers under discussion in *The Incarnate Text*, one bridges this gulf through faith and the divine supplement of the word of God, the book of God, even if that book only ever exists in some fallen, material form. For Bacon, one bridges this gulf by attending both to the book of God and to the book of nature. And nature's resistance to our attempts to understand it will dialectically teach us how to correct for the failings of human apprehension. Crucial to this correction is the proper separation of the two books, which for Bacon is essential to both natural philosophy and true theology. Natural philosophy concerns itself not with God's will but only with his works; to "vnwisely mingle or confound these learnings together" is to invite error.[13]

In *New Atlantis*, Bacon offers one of his most provocative and sustained articulations of the relation of natural philosophy to theology. If Bacon was a prophet of modernity, his fictional Bensalem is a vision of the promised land, a world free of the idols of the mind. In *New Atlantis*, he presents what his secretary William Rawley calls in the preface "To the Reader" both a "fable" and a "model": "This fable my Lord devised, to the end that he might exhibit therein a model or description of a college instituted for the interpreting of nature and the producing of great and marvellous works for the benefit of men."[14] Rawley's preface presents *New Atlantis* as a work that is firmly in the realm of fiction but that is also somehow historically prescriptive, theoretically reproducible in the real world. And this proselytizing intention, embedded in the notion of Bensalem as a model, dovetails with the final sentiment expressed in the narrative, when the Father of Salomon's House gives the narrator permission to make his story, and this secret society, known: "God bless thee, my son, and God bless this relation which I have made. I give thee leave to publish it for the good of other nations; for we here are in God's bosom, a land unknown" (3.166). And as the language of this endorsement suggests, other nations who read of this "land unknown" will learn of a scientific utopia that seems to be a fully Christian society. Indeed, in his only foray into fiction, Bacon produces a fable and a model of a society in which religion and science coexist happily. If Bensalem is a decidedly Christian society, however, *New Atlantis* nonetheless seems to be a valediction to a religion of the book. Christianity persists in Bensalem only insofar as it has left the book, metaphorically speaking, behind. My contention is that the relation of religion to science in *New Atlantis* is, in part, a response to the crisis of the book I have discussed throughout *The Incarnate*

Text. In *New Atlantis* Bacon imagines a utopian society that embraces Christianity even as it regards religion as a once and future concern. And this concurrent adoption and disavowal of Christian religion is made possible through a revelatory encounter with a sacred book.

* * *

When the European voyagers in *New Atlantis*, lost in the South Seas and losing hope of salvation, providentially happen upon the scientific utopia of Bensalem, they find a Christian society. Given that this is a culture set off from the rest of the world, a society of which the rest of the world seems to have no knowledge, the travelers ask how it happened that Bensalem was converted to Christianity. As the narrator recounts it, this is their most pressing question when the governor of the Strangers' House invites them to inquire about this strange land: "Above all . . . we desired to know (in respect that land was so remote, and so divided by vast and unknown seas, from the land where are Saviour walked on earth) who was the apostle of that nation, and how it was converted to the faith" (3.136–37). Their query prompts a tale within the tale, a narrative of another providential arrival and another vessel at sea, a narrative that involves the advent of a miraculous book.

About twenty years after the ascension of Christ, as the governor tells the story, a pillar of light appeared off the east coast of the island, a few miles out into the sea.[15] The column of light rose up toward heaven, and on top of the column was a brilliant "cross of light" (3.137). Struck with wonder, some of the inhabitants of Renfusa, the closest city, voyaged out to the mysterious apparition in a number of small boats. When the boats were within sixty yards of the pillar, they could get no closer. So the Bensalemites "stood all as in a theatre, beholding this light as an heavenly sign" (3.137). One of these boats happened to be carrying a man from "the society of Salomon's House"; after "attentively and devoutly" viewing and contemplating "this pillar and cross," the man lifted "his hands to heaven" and prayed:

> Lord God of heaven and earth, thou hast vouchsafed of thy grace to those of our order, to know thy works of creation, and the secrets of them; and to discern (as far as appertaineth to the generations of men) between divine miracles, works of nature, works of art, and impostures and illusions of all sorts. I do here acknowledge and testify before this people, that the thing which we now see before

our eyes is thy Finger and a true Miracle; and forasmuch as we learn
in our books that thou never workest miracles but to a divine and
excellent end, (for the laws of nature are thine own laws, and thou
exceedest them but upon great cause,) we most humbly beseech thee
to prosper this great sign, and to give us the interpretation and use
of it in mercy; which thou dost in some part secretly promise by
sending it unto us. (3.137–38)

The rapprochement between religion and science here is fascinating. The
man of science prays to God, giving thanks for the enlightenment given to
his order, knowledge of the "works of creation." This knowledge, in turn,
accords the order of Salomon's House the ability to discern the work of God
in the world. This prayer seems to suggest a Faustian dream without the
Faustian bargain: knowledge of the secrets of creation as gift of God. Moreover, the ability to discern what is and is not divine, the mandate to authenticate the true miracle and discredit the false, seems to lend the order of
Salomon's House an authority beyond the human. If the man from Salomon's House knows enough to distinguish between natural and divine, however, he claims no special insight beyond this rudimentary ability to sort or
classify. Faced with this "true Miracle," he testifies to its authenticity and
then asks for guidance, asks the deity to "prosper this great sign" to "give us
the interpretation." If this seems a humble supplication, however, the knowledge accorded the men of Salomon's House gives that supplication a pre-
sumptuous edge; their ability to engage in predictive calculation leads them
to gauge the intentions of "Lord God of heaven and earth." Since they learn
in their "books that . . . [God] never workest miracles but to a divine and
excellent end," they can presume with some confidence that God "dost in
some part secretly promise" to prosper or interpret the sign "by sending it
unto us." As I discussed in Chapter 3, this was an age in which the miraculous
was a source of great controversy. For Catholics, true religion was authenticated by the miraculous; for Protestants, the age of miracles was over, and a
belief in miracles was evidence of superstition and idolatry, a sign that one
had placed one's faith in the fallen human senses and the fallen material
world.[16] In New Atlantis none of these issues, none of these controversies,
seem to pertain. Instead, we seem to have this cordial but guarded dance
between the authority of divine revelation and the authority of human
knowledge. In this strange incident off the coast of Renfusa, it seems initially
as if natural philosophy is given the upper hand over other forms of revela-

tion, as that which authenticates the divine. But the interpretation of this event by the man of science is in turn validated by another sign, an additional miracle. Having offered this prayer, the anonymous man from Salomon's House finds that his boat, and his boat alone, can move; only he is allowed to approach the pillar. In a remarkably complementary movement, the miracle is verified by the man of science whose identity as one who can authenticate the miraculous is sanctioned by a further miracle.

As the "wise man's" boat approaches, the pillar and cross disappear, revealing a "small ark," a cedar chest with a palm branch growing out of it (3.138). Taking the ark reverently into his boat, the representative from Salomon's House opens it, revealing "a Book and a Letter," both "written in fine parchment, and wrapped in sindons of linen" (3.138). The book contains all the relevant texts of the Christian scripture. The letter is from the apostle Bartholomew, who writes that he experienced a vision wherein an angel appeared to him and told him to "commit this ark to the floods of the sea" (3.138). After the arrival of these sacred texts, the Bensalemites experience their own version of the gift of tongues at Pentecost: "There was also in both these writings, as well the Book as the Letter, wrought a great miracle, conform to that of the Apostles in the original Gift of Tongues" (3.138). In Bacon's fiction, however, the Pentecostal miracle is not a gift of speaking in tongues but a gift of reading in tongues, as all of the inhabitants, not only native Bensalemites but also "Hebrews, Persians, and Indians," find that they can read both book and letter "as if they had been written" in their "own language" (3.138–39). And through these two miraculous events—the spectacular revelation of the book and the "Pentecostal" gift of reading—Bensalem was turned once and for all to Christianity, converted to true religion: "And thus was this land saved from infidelity (as the remain of the old world was from water) by an ark, through the apostolical and miraculous evangelism of St. Bartholomew" (3.139).

Bacon's seventeenth-century readers would almost certainly have assumed that the miraculous book that effected the conversion of Bensalem to Christianity was a codex.[17] The Christian New Testament not only took the form of a codex almost exclusively, but it was also almost always represented as a codex.[18] And curiously, the miraculous book seems to be the one explicit depiction of a codex in Bacon's *New Atlantis*. There are references to "books" throughout the fiction, primarily allusions to texts from the wider world of which the Bensalemites have gained knowledge. Despite the specificity with which Bacon details the art of scientific discovery in Bensalem, however, the storage and dissemination of knowledge is left, for the most part, to the reader's imagination. Outside of a passing mention of a statue erected to the memory of the inventor of the printing press, the reader is offered little evidence to point to the ways in which text might be archived and transmitted in this technologically advanced society. Indeed, there are only three scenes in *New Atlantis* in which any kind of material text plays a prominent part. In addition to the narrative account of the miraculous book, there are two episodes featuring a very curious scroll. Upon the arrival of the sailors in Bensalem, the very first communication between the two societies is through "a little scroll of parchment" bearing a message written in Hebrew, Greek, Latin, and Spanish. The "little scroll" is described in some detail: it is "somewhat yellower than our parchment, and shining like the leaves of writing tables, but otherwise soft and flexible" (3.130). Later in the narrative, a similar scroll appears during the description of the Feast of the Family. In the ceremony, the Father of the Family is presented with "the King's Charter, containing gift of revenew, and many privileges, exemptions, and points of honour." The charter given to the Father of the Family is explicitly described as "a scroll of their shining yellow parchment" (3.149).

Scrolls were certainly not unknown in Bacon's England; they were deployed in various legal, bureaucratic, and ceremonial contexts. Here, however, Bacon calls the reader's attention to this slightly unfamiliar scroll as a way to make strange this society that is both like and unlike the world the reader knows. The fact that these shining, yellow scrolls are compared to "writing tables" when first mentioned is significant in light of recent scholarship. Peter Stallybrass, Roger Chartier, J. Franklin Mowery, and Heather Wolfe have noted the presence and evident ubiquity of the erasable writing table in early modern England.[19] This technology provided a portable, reusable, writing surface, evidently employed by a wide range of people for a variety of purposes.[20] Although these scholars track the import of such writing tables into England as early as the 1520s, the technology seems to catch on with the reading (and writing) public in the late sixteenth century. The evidence suggests that before 1581 "the average book-buyer seems to have been unfamiliar with writing-table technology."[21] This means that this writing technology entered the public sphere and the cultural imagination in the course of Bacon's life (1561–1626) and would probably have seemed a relatively recent innovation to an early seventeenth-century reader. As Stallybrass et al point out, in the passage in question Bacon seems to be comparing this "little scroll of parchment" to these erasable writing tables; the "shining" that

Bacon describes in this passage was evidently "characteristic of the mixture of glue and gesso with which the leaves" of erasable writing tables "were treated."[22] This suggests that Bacon's "little scroll" points both backward to a revered past and forward to a technologically enhanced future. Not only is the scroll understood to be a residual technology in the early modern period, but, as I discussed in Chapter 3, in certain contexts the scroll would have evoked for early modern Christians both Judaism and the law of the Old Testament. Like the designation of the central scientific institution as "Salomon's House" or the "College of the Six Days' Works," the scroll in *New Atlantis* seems designed to call to mind the significant relation of the society of Bensalem to its Judaic inheritance.[23] At the same time, this "little scroll" seems to be on the cutting edge of technologies of paper; it incorporates the contemporary, early modern technology of the erasable writing table but seems to have improved on the European model by rendering this writing surface "soft and flexible"—so "soft and flexible," in fact, that the presumably treated parchment can be rolled into scroll form.[24] The scroll seems emblematic of Bensalem itself: familiar yet strange, curiously antiquated yet technologically advanced. The scroll's evident erasability suggests that this seemingly antiquated surface is, in fact, future oriented; it can always be transformed for subsequent use. If the Bensalemite scroll seems to embrace both traditional convention and future possibility, however, the miraculous book seems consigned to a past that is no longer relevant.

When framed by references to these curious scrolls, the miraculous codex at the origin of Bensalem's Christian history seems ever more singular. The fact that the book discovered in the ark is the only codex the reader encounters in *New Atlantis* seems of a piece with the appearance of this miraculous book as a unique, nonrepeated event. And it seems that this miraculous event need not be repeated because it has succeeded perfectly, has transformed Bensalem utterly. Bacon's narrative of a second, or alternate, Pentecost is striking for a number of reasons. Not only does the man of science ground this conversion to Christianity in miraculous events, but these divine interventions are also evidently accepted by all Bensalemite Christians without question. And it is not simply that the narratives concerning these miraculous incidents are not subject to dispute but that the book so miraculously delivered is not the object of controversy. One of the more curious aspects of the miraculous book that Bacon conjures for his reader is that it contains not only "all the canonical books of the Old and New Testament" as well as "the Apocalypse itself" but also "some other books of the New Testament which were not at that time written" (3.138). Miraculously outside of time, Bacon's book includes all that is, or will be, necessary for Christian edification.[25] In Bensalem, the texts of Christianity have no history, bear no mark of human labor or struggle. As Travis DeCook observes, there is no need for the painstaking and divisive labor of canon formation or philological inquiry: "Bensalemite revelation obviates both the need for humanist philology and textual criticism, through which accurate texts and translations are achieved, and the lengthy and occasionally tumultuous councils and debates associated with canon formation. . . . Whereas Christian history entails the gradual establishment of its texts as Scripture, and, simultaneously, the ongoing and contentious canonization of various books, Bensalem is freed from these sites of potential disagreement."[26] In Bensalem, Christian scripture is miraculously always already complete. Moreover, the book's extraordinary faculty of offering itself up to every reader as if it had been written "in his own language" suggests that there is no need for translation or, it seems, interpretation (3.139).

In Chapter 1 I discussed the Pentecostal vision that Erasmus proffers in his colloquy "The Apothesis of That Incomparable Worthy, Johann Reuchlin." In the colloquy, Erasmus describes the dream of a devout Christian upon the death of Reuchlin, the august humanist who had helped revive Hebrew scholarship in Christian Europe. In this peculiar dream Reuchlin's apotheosis is accomplished when he is received into heaven by that other divine scholar, Jerome. Erasmus concludes the colloquy with a prayer for a second Pentecost: "O God thou lover of mankind, who through thy chosen servant Johann Reuchlin hast renewed to the world the gift of tongues by which thou didst once from heaven, through thy Holy Spirit, instruct the apostles for the preaching of the gospel, grant that all men everywhere may preach in every tongue the glory of thy Son Jesus."[27] This second Pentecost that Erasmus invokes here is brought about not by a charismatic speaking in tongues but by scholars like Jerome and Reuchlin, through a divinely inspired, humanist renaissance of letters. If Erasmus offers a utopian vision of the dissemination of God's word through method, through scholarship, Bacon invents a utopia in which scripture is disseminated through miraculous reading. If the narrator's limited experience of this strange society offers a true picture of Bensalem, the Pentecostal gift of reading seems to have solved, conclusively, the problem of scriptural translation and interpretation. Bacon lived in an historical moment when the translation and interpretation of scripture were matters of life and death, spiritual and physical, a moment when the reading of scripture divided nations, cultures, families. He seems to have solved this problem for his scientific utopia with the wave of a divine hand. In Bensalem we never hear of religious controversy; we never hear or see Christians debate the meaning or significance of biblical passages. In Erasmus's utopian vision, this second Pentecost will be an ongoing enterprise unfolding through time, bringing scripture to Christians through a reformation of reading practices. In Bacon's vision of utopia, reading practices are, it seems, transformed once and utterly; this second Pentecost seems to be a unique event that accomplishes its purposes completely. The two miracles of Bacon's utopia—the appearance of the book, and the Pentecost of reading—establish Christianity as the religion of the Bensalemites and, at the same time, work to fix religion as something established. Religion is practiced in Bensalem, but it does not seem to change or expand or develop; it does not seem to exist in time.

If the extraordinary event of the miraculous book seems to close off religious struggle, seems to remove Bensalemite Christianity from the vicissitudes of history, this is not to say that Bensalem itself exists outside history generally, or religious history specifically. It is important to Bacon that Bensalem is part of this world and not a vision of the next. As Marina Leslie and Christopher Kendrick have recently observed, *New Atlantis* invites an eschatological reading.[28] And this invitation to eschatology, I contend, emphatically gestures toward apocalypse as a near-future event; indeed, apocalypse seems to be an event always on the immediate horizon of Bensalem's present. One way the reader knows that Bensalem is not outside religious history altogether is that the society includes non-Christians as well as Christians. The presence of non-Christians in *New Atlantis* works both as a sign of a kind of utopian ecumenicalism, produced by the sound rationalism of a society grounded in natural philosophy, and as a sign that Bensalem is not set in a post-apocalyptic future. The key figure here, of course, is Joabin, the unconverted Jew. The central presence of Joabin in the narrative—he is one of the primary local informants—has long been a source of scholarly speculation. There are a variety of reasons for Bacon to employ the figure of Joabin as he does, but one of the fundamental purposes of Joabin's presence in the story is to evoke an eschatological frame for *New Atlantis* while firmly grounding the narrative in a pre-apocalyptic moment. As many scholars have noted, seventeenth-century natural philosophy had close ties to Christian millenarian thought.[29] Charles Whitney has shown us the ways in which Bacon consistently employs typological and apocalyptic narratives to situate his age of scientific discovery in providential Christian schemas.[30] Since the conversion of the Jews was thought to be one of the signs of the end times, the figure of the Jew was crucial to the millenarian thought of seventeenth-century England.[31]

As it happens, Joabin is the one figure in *New Atlantis* who offers an apocalyptic vision. The narrator offers an extended description of Joabin that positions him in relation to both Christianity and Bensalem:

> He was a Jew, and circumcised: for they have some few stirps of Jews yet remaining among them . . . this man of whom I speak would ever acknowledge that Christ was born of a Virgin, and that he was more than a man; and he would tell how God made him ruler of the Seraphims which guard his throne; and they call him also the *Milken Way*, and the *Eliah* of the *Messiah*; and many other high names; which though they be inferior to his divine Majesty, yet they are far from the language of other Jews. And for the country of Bensalem, this man would make no end of commending it: being desirous, by tradition among the Jews there, to have it believed that the people thereof were of the generations of Abraham, by another son, whom they call Nachoran; and that Moses by a secret cabala ordained the laws of Bensalem which they now use; and that when the Messiah should come, and sit in his throne at Hierusalem, the king of Bensalem should sit at his feet, whereas other kings should keep a great distance. But yet setting aside these Jewish dreams, the man was a wise man, and learned, and of great policy, and excellently seen in the laws and customs of that nation. (3.151)

Joabin "would make no end of commending" Bensalem not because of its effective government, or peace and stability, or, indeed, the important work and wondrous discoveries of Salomon's House, but because he believes in a special Judaic provenance for the Bensalemites: "The people thereof were of the generations of Abraham, by another son, whom they call Nachoran." In other words, everything that seems to make Bensalem a scientific utopia for the narrator is ignored in favor of dubious claims concerning ancestry and lineage. This genealogical particularism belies the avowed universalism of Christianity generally and Bensalem's Pentecostal conversion specifically, which miraculously offered a single text to all people in all languages. It also seems to belie both the universal character of the project of natural philosophy and the theoretically reproducible "model" of the College of the Six

Days' Works. And Joabin's insular perspective encompasses the future as well as the past. He envisions for Bensalem a privileged future redemption: "the king of Bensalem should sit at . . . [the Messiah's] feet, whereas other kings should keep a great distance" (3.151). This hierarchy of nations betrays a tribalism that Christianity claimed to have repudiated and a sectarianism that Bacon himself seems to have feared and rejected.[32] Both Joabin's genealogical "dream" and his eschatological vision seem atavistic in the enlightened space of Bensalem. This false eschatological vision works, however, to invoke the true apocalyptic frame of *New Atlantis*. In a remarkable study, Jeremy Cohen has traced a history of the Jew as a figure who acts as a living witness to the truth of Christian history. In this Christian conception of history, the Jew functions as a "living letter of the law," as a figure of sublation, a marker of that which must be preserved even as it is negated.[33] Joabin fulfills just this role in Bacon's *New Atlantis*. In Joabin we see a figure who is tied to a venerable past and who anticipates an apocalyptic future, but who cannot see the world around him properly, cannot understand the present moment in time. He is a champion of Bensalem, but for all the wrong reasons; "learned, and of great policy, and excellently seen in the laws and customs of that nation," he nonetheless cannot see Bensalem for what it is (3.151). The unconverted Jew refuses to acknowledge Christ's "divine Majesty" and so patiently awaits the Messiah, while the society around him proclaims, for those with eyes to see, the imminent arrival of the Second Coming. He thus misunderstands Bensalem, fails to see that it is a society occupying a pre-apocalyptic moment. At the same time, the very presence of Joabin, as an unconverted Jew, lets Bacon's readers know that we have not yet arrived at the end times. In this respect the figure of Joabin is like the miraculous book. Although they endure or persist in anticipation of a glorious future, both Jew and book have been superseded. Both living letter and miraculous book are outside of time.

The "Jewish dreams" the narrator so casually sets aside are dreams of the past and future, but the place of Bensalem exists in a curious interim; this is the time after prophecy but before apocalypse, "when many shall runne to and fro and knowledge shall be increased." I began this brief excursion to *New Atlantis* with Bacon's deployment of this apocalyptic passage from Daniel. On the frontispiece to the *Great Instauration*, however, he quotes only part of the biblical passage in question. The full passage helps us understand some of what is at stake for Bacon in this invocation of apocalypse: "But thou, O Daniel, shut vp the wordes, and seale the booke euen to the time of the ende: many shall runne to and fro, and knowledge shall bee increased."[34]

Suggesting that the words shall be shut up and the book sealed until this future apocalyptic moment when "knowledge shall be increased," Daniel's prophecy refuses to offer up any mysteries; instead, it seems content to point to a future in which such mysteries will be revealed. The Geneva Bible glosses the shutting up of words and the sealing of the book as the preservation of the mystery of the prophecy "til the time that God hathe appointed for the ful reuelation of these things."[35] It is striking that this time appointed for "ful revelation" seems to have nothing to do with words or books but with dynamic activity in the world. It is, of course, precisely the promise of worldly engagement that Bacon seizes on when suggesting that contemporary history is the fulfillment of this millennial promise. Bacon's inspired reading of Daniel produces a prophecy in which words and books, in which prophecy itself, give way to a vigorous exploration of God's mysteries in the world. As the prophecy is fulfilled, we move from book to world, from exegesis to experiment and exploration. The Geneva Bible suggests that this future time when "many shal runne to and fro" is a time to inquire into "these mysteries" that we "obteine now by the light of the Gospel."[36] In other words, according to this gloss, Daniel foretells a time when mysteries shall be revealed without the need for the light of the gospel. In Bacon's reading it would seem that Daniel's cryptic prophecy foretells the end of the time of prophecy, the end of the time of the book.

In *New Atlantis* Bacon seems to offer up a narrative of a miraculous book, miraculously read, precisely so that his scientific utopia can move beyond the book of God to the book of nature. In my reading of Bacon's fable, he conjures this mysterious book in order to embrace and obviate religion simultaneously; by fulfilling and preserving Christian revelation, this impossible book negates the impact of religious belief on Bacon's scientific utopia. The sacred book performs the same function as Joabin, the unconverted Jew: they are both living letters that are preserved so that the reader can see that the traditions that they represent have been superseded in this brave new world. Bacon's *New Atlantis* is, however, not a prophetic utterance but, crucially, the expression of a utopian desire. To the extent that Christian history, religious history, seems to begin and end with a miraculous book, the reader knows that he or she is in the realm of fantasy, of wish-fulfillment, the land of an imaginary utopia. Bacon lived in an historical moment when the book of God was the inspiration for astonishing human endeavor, when the limited resources of universities, societies, and governments were pressed into the service of textual interpretation, when a desire to understand the language of scripture consumed the careers and lives of the learned, when Christians fought and died, fought and killed, over words. He lived in a time of the crisis of language, the crisis of the book that I have attempted to address in this study. That one never hears of this religious strife or controversy in Bensalem must have marked this society as alien for Bacon's early modern readers. This conspicuous absence might have been read as sacrilegious, or amusing, or revelatory, but it would have registered as an absence. And it must have registered as a reaction to the world in which Bacon lived. The ostentatiously miraculous nature of Bacon's enchanted book has led some critics to believe that we should not take the miracle seriously; in this reading, the miraculous book is a hoax perpetrated by the fathers of Salomon's House on a credulous people.[37] I prefer to think that Bacon creates a miracle that is so ostentatious because he knows—and wants his reader to know—that this society in which religion and natural philosophy are readily compatible is not an expectation, or even a model, but the expression of a desire. In *New Atlantis*, Bacon responds to the crisis of the book by wishing it away. If Bacon was a prophet of modernity, he was a prophet who never made it to the promised land. Indeed, this is how Abraham Cowley imagined Bacon in his ode "To the Royal Society." If "Bacon, like Moses, led us forth at last" to "the blest promis'd land," he was not allowed to enter as "Life did never to one Man allow / Time to Discover Worlds, and Conquer too."[38] And from Mount Pisgah, Bacon envisions a Palestine that, in crucial ways, is utterly unlike the world he inhabited. Like the rest of us, Bacon can only realize a truly enlightened society by resorting to myth. And the myth he chooses to tell is of a time after prophecy and before apocalypse, a time when knowledge shall be increased. He describes a utopian interim in which the world is disenchanted and natural philosophy has, for a time, shut up the words and sealed the book.

NOTES

The following abbreviations appear in the notes.

CWE   *Collected Works of Erasmus*. 72 vols. Toronto: University of Toronto Press, 1974–.

CWM   *The Complete Works of Thomas More*. Edited by L. L. Martz, R. S. Sylvester, and C. H. Miller. New Haven: Yale University Press, 1963–97.

EE   *Opus Epistolarum Erasmi*. Edited by P. S. Allen. Oxford: Clarendon Press, 1906–58.

KJV   The King James or Authorized Translation of the Bible. *The Holy Bible*. London, 1611.

LB   Erasmus, *Opera Omnia*. Edited by Jean Leclerc. 10 vols. Leiden, 1703–6; reprint, Hildesheim: George Olms, 1961–62.

LW   *Luther's Works*. Edited by J. Pelikan and H. T. Lehmann. Philadelphia: Fortress, 1955–86.

OED   *Oxford English Dictionary Online*. Second Edition. Oxford: Oxford University Press, 1989–2008.

WA   *D. Martin Luthers Werke, kritische Gesamtausgabe*. Weimar: Hermann Böhlau, 1883–1999.

WA Br   *D. Martin Luthers Werke, kritische Gesamtausgabe: Briefwechsel*. Weimar: Hermann Böhlau, 1930–85.

WA DB   *D. Martin Luthers Werke, kritische Gesamtausgabe: die Deutsche Bibel*. Weimar: Hermann Böhlau, 1906–61.

WA TR   *D. Martin Luthers Werke, kritische Gesamtausgabe: Tischreden*. Weimar: Hermann Böhlau, 1912–21.

INTRODUCTION

1. There was a time when one could offer a snapshot of recent work in the history of the book in a long footnote. With the explosion of interest in the topic in recent years,

one can only gesture toward some of the work being done. Useful overviews of the field include Darnton, "What Is the History of Books?" and "First Steps Toward a History of Reading"; Price, "Reading: The State of the Discipline"; and J. Rose, "How Historians Study Reading." I have found the following studies particularly helpful: Blair, "Reading Strategies"; Chartier, *Order of Books*; Chartier and Cavallo, *History of Reading in the West*; Eisenstein, *Printing Press as an Agent of Change*; Ezell, *Social Authorship*; Febvre and Martin, *Coming of the Book*; Johns, *Nature of the Book*; Love, *Scribal Publication*; McKenzie, *Making Meaning*; McKitterick, *Print, Manuscript and the Search for Order*; Raven, Small, and Tadmor, *The Practice and Representation of Reading*; M. Rose, *Authors and Owners*; Stock, *Implications of Literacy*.

2. And, of course, such work is well under way. I see *The Incarnate Text* as contributing to an ongoing conversation; for this project some of the more important contributions to this conversation include: *Books and Readers in Early Modern England,* ed. Andersen and Sauer; *Cambridge History of the Book in Britain*, ed. Barnard and McKenzie, vol. 4: *1557–1695*; Beal, *In Praise of Scribes*; Brooks, *From Playhouse to Printing House*; Cressy, *Literacy and the Social Order*; *Uses of Script and Print,* ed. Crick and Walsham; de Grazia and Stallybrass, "Materiality of the Shakespearean Text"; Dolan, "Reading, Writing, and Other Crimes"; Elsky, *Authorizing Words*; Grafton, "Renaissance Readers and Ancient Texts"; Hackel, *Reading Material in Early Modern England*; Halasz, *Marketplace of Print*; Jardine and Grafton, " 'Studied for Action' "; Jardine and Sherman, "Pragmatic Readers"; Lamb, "Women Readers" and "Constructions of Women Readers"; Lander, *Inventing Polemic*; Lesser, *Renaissance Drama and the Politics of Publication*; Marotti, *Manuscript, Print, and the English Renaissance Lyric*; Masten, *Textual Intercourse*; Scott-Warren, *Sir John Harington and the Book as Gift*; Sharpe, *Reading Revolutions*; Sherman, *John Dee: The Politics of Reading and Writing*; Spufford, *Small Books and Pleasant Histories*; Tribble, *Margins and Marginality*; Wall, *Imprint of Gender*; Watt, *Cheap Print and Popular Piety*; Woudhuysen, *Sir Philip Sidney and the Circulation of Manuscripts*.

3. *The Incarnate Text* is particularly indebted to the following work: Cummings, *Literary Culture of the Reformation*; Fleming, *Graffiti and the Writing Arts*; Goldberg, *Writing Matter*; Kastan, *Shakespeare and the Book*; O'Connell, *Idolatrous Eye*; Stallybrass and Jones, *Renaissance Clothing and the Materials of Memory*.

4. See especially Aston, *England's Iconoclasts*; Camille, *Gothic Idol*; Diehl, *Staging Reform*; Eire, *War Against the Idols*; Freedberg, *Power of Images*; Gilman, *Iconoclasm and Poetry*; Koerner, *Reformation of the Image*; O'Connell, *Idolatrous Eye*.

5. See the important collections *Subject and Object in Renaissance Culture*, ed. de Grazia, Quilligan, and Stallybrass; *Renaissance Culture and the Everyday*, ed. Fumerton and Hunt; and *Material London, ca. 1600*, ed. Orlin. For analyses and critiques of this turn in Renaissance studies, see Bruster, "New Materialism"; and Harris, "New New Historicism" and "Shakespeare's Hair."

6. This is a monograph not on print culture but on book culture, although it will certainly engage with the historical development in the history of media that print culture represented. It sometimes seems as if scholars believe that the invention of the printing press spawned a widespread effort to gather up all extant manuscripts and send them to

the landfill. But this was not yet a culture of the disposable object, and manuscripts of this era were valuable possessions that have proven themselves to be particularly durable media objects. Moreover, the scriptoria, those factories of manuscript copying, did not go belly-up with the arrival of the printing press. As scholars such as Harold Love and Margaret Ezell have shown, new manuscripts kept being produced at a significant rate throughout the period. To imagine the culture of the codex in this particular moment, we have to imagine the manuscript and the printed book existing side by side in libraries large and small. If we see a reference to a codex in a poem or play from the sixteenth or seventeenth century, we cannot assume that we know whether the author is referring to a manuscript or printed book, or whether the author would necessarily want to make a distinction between the two.

7. Fisher, "A Sermon . . . ," 388.

8. Ibid., 393–94, 395–96.

9. The notion that we can "see" the materiality of the book with new eyes in the information age has become a commonplace in criticism addressing the relation of the history of the book to the emergence of electronic media. For a particularly compelling argument about the ways in which the "advent of electronic textuality presents us with an unparalleled opportunity to re-formulate fundamental ideas about texts," see Hayles, "Translating Media," 263.

10. To this day, when scholars describe a leaf from a parchment manuscript, they refer to the hair side and the flesh side.

11. Koerner, *Reformation of the Image*, 12. Also see Koerner's "The Icon as Iconoclash" in *Iconoclash*, ed. Latour and Weibel.

12. English translation from Chazelle, "Pictures, Books, and the Illiterate," 139. Also see Duggan, "Was Art Really the 'Book of the Illiterate'?"

13. Roberts and Skeat, *Birth of the Codex*, 1.

14. For a recent overview of the scholarship addressing this issue, see S. Hall, "In the Beginning Was the Codex." See also Roberts and Skeat, *Birth of the Codex*, especially 38–66; Gamble, *Books and Readers*, especially 42–81.

15. Cavallo, "Between *Volumen* and Codex," in *A History of Reading in the West*, ed. Cavallo and Chartier, 83–89. I am not here endorsing Cavallo's earlier claim in *Libri, Editori e Pubblico nel mondo antico* (1975) that class animus *motivated* the Christian choice of codex. For a refutation of this claim and a discussion of these issues, see Roberts and Skeat, *Birth of the Codex*, 67–74.

16. See Roberts and Skeat, *Birth of the Codex*, 24–74.

17. Peter Stallybrass observes that the codex form was "associated with women and slaves rather than with citizens." The humble form of the codex thus materializes Christianity's embrace of the "value of the valueless": "The Christian god, both as flesh and word, inhabited the waste parts of the material world: fragments of bread . . . the 'mere' notebooks of the codex." Stallybrass, "Value of Culture," 278.

18. This is the famous letter to Eustochium that contains a defense and celebration of virginity as well as Jerome's well-known dream in which he is accused of being a Ciceronian rather than a Christian for his love of pagan letters.

19. *Letters of St. Jerome*, 1:168, Epistle 22.32. For the Latin, see *Epistulae* 22.32 (*Corpus Scriptorum Ecclesiasticorum Latinorum* 54, 193).

20. Jerome, *Letters and Select Works*, 492.

21. See McGurk, "Oldest Manuscripts," 11–12.

22. See L. Kendrick, *Animating the Letter*, 36–38, and M. Williams, *Monk and the Book*, 181–84.

23. For discussions of the medieval and early modern book in relation to religious questions about language and iconicity, see Aston, *Lollards and Reformers*, 101–33; Cummings, "Iconoclasm and Bibliophobia"; Fox, "Literacy and Power"; Gamble, *Books and Readers*, 42–81; L. Kendrick, *Animating the Letter*, 36–64.

24. See especially Beckwith, *Christ's Body*; Bynum, *Holy Feast*; Gibson, *Theater of Devotion*; Harris, *Theater and Incarnation*; O'Connell, *Idolatrous Eye*; M. Rubin, *Corpus Christi*.

25. In his *Homilies on Leviticus* (ca. 238–244 C.E.), Origen explains his understanding of the relation between the embodied divinity of Christ and the letter of scripture: "The Word of God, which was clothed with the flesh of Mary, proceeded into this world. What was seen in him was one thing; what was understood was something else. For the sight of his flesh was open for all to see, but the knowledge of his divinity was given to the few, even the elect. So also when the Word of God was brought to humans through the Prophets and the Lawgiver, it was not brought without proper clothing. For just as there it was covered with the veil of the flesh, so here with the veil of the letter, so that indeed the letter is seen as flesh but the spiritual sense hiding within is perceived as divinity." *Homilies on Leviticus*, 29. Origen's "Homily" is one of many such comparisons in which the Church fathers, following certain Pauline homologies, map letter and spirit onto certain antitheses fundamental to Christianity: the flesh and spirit, the law and grace, faith and works. Here, crucially, the body of Christ is lined up with the letter of scripture: just as the Word is incarnate in Christ, so it is made flesh in scripture. Both incarnate word and textual corpus have body and soul, a material veil that clothes and obscures the spiritual reality. Origen's particular articulation of this conceit would prove hugely influential, as it was incorporated into the preface to Leviticus in the *Glossa Ordinaria*.

26. In her classic work *The Study of the Bible in the Middle Ages*, 1, n. 2.

27. For the commonplace of Christ's crucified body as manuscript in the thirteenth century, see Smalley, *Study of the Bible in the Middle Ages*, 283.

28. English translation from Gellrich, *Idea of the Book*, 17. The *Repertorium* remained a popular resource in the age of print; it was printed in 1477 (Cologne), 1489 (Nuremberg), 1517 (Lyon), 1521 (Paris), 1589 (Venice), 1609 (Antwerp).

29. See Fox, *Literacy and Power*; Gamble, *Books and Readers*, 42–81; Aston, *Lollards and Reformers*, 101–33; L. Kendrick, *Animating the Letter*, 65–146; Duffy, *Stripping of the Altars*, 209–98.

30. Curtius, "Book as Symbol," 319. My translation of the Latin.

31. Fisher, "Sermon," 394–95.

32. Walsham, "Jewels for Gentlewomen: Religious Books as Artefacts," 124. Wals-

ham's essay provides a richly informative account of sacred books as treasured objects in late medieval and early modern England.

33. Hackenbroch, *Renaissance Jewelry*, 139–40. Quoted in Walsham, "Jewels for Gentlewomen," 124.

34. For an excellent discussion of the persecution of books in sixteenth-century England, see Cummings, "Reformed Literature," especially 828–32, 839–45.

35. Daniell, *William Tyndale*, 182.

36. Fisher, "Sermon," 394.

37. Ibid., 390–91.

38. For a fascinating discussion of St. Francis and the stigmata in Fisher's sermon, see Lowell Gallagher, "The Place of the Stigmata," 101–5.

39. Fisher, "Sermon," 390.

40. See Janel Mueller's "Complications of Intertextuallity" for a discussion of the contrast between Fisher's Catholic use of the metaphor of crucified body as book and Katherine Parr's Protestant use of the same.

41. More, *A Dialogue Concerning Heresies*, CWM 1:359.

42. Ibid., 1:39–40.

43. On Luther's relationship to Müntzer, see Oyer, *Lutheran Reformers Against Anabaptists*, 6–40 and 114–39; also see Gritsch, *Reformer Without a Church*.

44. Quoted in Morgan, *Godly Learning*, 64.

45. Oberman, *Luther*, 174.

46. *LW* 1:106. For the Latin original, see *WA* 42:80–81.

47. *LW* 1:105; *WA* 42:80.

48. *LW* 1:105; *WA* 42:80.

49. See Stock, *Augustine the Reader*, 15–18; Jager, *Tempter's Voice*, 51–98. I discuss this tradition more fully in Chapter 1.

50. Ambrose, "Letters," 465.

51. Erasmus himself railed against the sentiment; see his letter to Johannes Caesarius. *CWE* 10:464 (letter 1528). *EE* v:609 (letter 1528).

52. For a succinct account of Erasmus's early influence on these and other Reformers, see Dickens and Jones, *Erasmus the Reformer*, 148–69.

53. For a discussion of Christian conceptions of the oral and aural dimensions of scripture, see Graham, *Beyond the Written Word*, 119–54.

54. "Lecture on Psalm 85," *WA* 4:9. For the English translation, see *LW* 11:160.

55. King James Version (London, 1611; hereafter KJV).

56. "Lecture on Psalm 85," *LW* 11:159, 160. *WA* 4:8, 9.

57. See Christensen, *Art and the Reformation in Germany*, 170–72.

58. I discuss Luther's conversion experience and his understanding of the "alien word" at greater length in Chapter 3.

59. Meuser, "Luther as Preacher," 136.

60. Pelikan offers a compelling analysis of these issues; see "The Theology of the Means of Grace," especially 125–31.

61. *LW* 40:99. For the German original, see *WA* 18:82–83.

62. See Hunt, "Art of Hearing," passim; Graham, *Beyond the Written Word*, 143–54; B. Smith, *Acoustic World*, 261–69.

63. In his *Guide to Godlynesse* (1629), Downame writes, "The ministery of the Word is the ordinary meanes of our new birth, and of beginning in vs Gods spirituall graces. . . . Neither are we to thinke that the Word read, either by our selues or others, is ordinarily sufficient to worke in vs grace and godlinesse . . . [for faith] commeth by hearing the Word preached." Downame, *Guide to Godlynesse*, 482; Tt1v. By the time Downame was writing, this had become one of the recurrent points of contention in debates between dissenting and more conservative Protestants.

64. Hunt, *Art of Hearing*, 10.

65. *Admonition*, B4r–B4v.

66. Ibid.

67. Hunt, *Art of Hearing*, 16, 19.

68. *Defence of the Answer to the Admonition*; Whitgift, *Works*, 3:28. Whitgift was responding to Thomas Cartwright, author of the *Second Admonition to the Parliament* and the leading voice in the nonconformist movement.

69. *Defence*; Whitgift, *Works*, 3:30–31.

70. Smyth, *Differences of the Churches* (1608), reprinted in *Works* 1:278–79.

71. Smyth, *Differences*; *Works* 1:282.

72. Ainsworth, *Defence of the Holy Scriptures* (1609), C3v.

73. Ibid., C4r.

74. Ibid., D1r. Italics in original.

75. Ibid.

76. *Defence*; Whitgift, *Works*, 3:39–40.

77. Foxe, *Actes and Monuments* (1563), 468.

78. Latimer, *Sermons*, 1:334–35.

79. Marshall, "Evangelical Conversion," 26.

80. Latimer, *Sermons*, 1:334–36.

81. Cohen, *Living Letters of the Law*, 59–60.

82. On the relation between Paul's reading of circumcision and his vision of Christian universalism, see Boyarin, *A Radical Jew*, especially 13–85, 106–35; and Lupton, *Citizen-Saints*, 37–42, 105–23. Also see Lampert, *Gender and Jewish Difference from Paul to Shakespeare*, 3–11, 21–57.

83. Galatians 3:28, KJV. See also Colossians 3:11: "Where there is neither Greeke, nor Iew, circumcision, nor vncircumcision, Barbarian, Scythian, bond, nor free: but Christ is all, and in all." KJV.

84. Romans 2:29, KJV.

85. I should stress that the fetish I invoke here is an Enlightenment concept that predates and subtends the canny appropriations of the concept by Marx and Freud. Likewise, the idol I invoke is a post-Reformation idol, called into being by the crisis of representation I address here. This is not to deny the connection between the Reformation idol

and the idol of pre-Reformation Christianity, or between the fetish as conceived in the seventeenth and eighteenth centuries and later versions of the concept. Rather, it is to insist that both the idol and the fetish are concepts with histories.

86. Weber, "Science as a Vocation," 139. Indeed, for Weber "the fate of our times is characterized by rationalization and intellectualization and, above all, by the 'disenchantment of the world.'" "Science as a Vocation," 155.

87. "Does it mean that we, today . . . have a greater knowledge of the conditions of life under which we exist than has an American Indian or a Hottentot? Hardly. Unless he is a physicist, one who rides on the streetcar has no idea how the car happened to get into motion." Weber, "Science as a Vocation," 139.

88. Ibid., 139.

89. Lee Patterson describes this familiar narrative as "the pervasive and apparently ineradicable *grand récit* that organizes Western cultural history, the gigantic master narrative by which modernity identifies itself with the Renaissance and rejects the Middle Ages as by definition premodern. According to this universal scheme, the Renaissance is the point at which the modern world begins: humanism, nationalism, the proliferation of competing value systems, the secure grasp of a historical consciousness, aesthetic production as an end in itself, the conception of the natural world as a site of scientific investigation and colonial exploitation, the secularization of politics, the idea of the state, and, perhaps above all, the emergence of the idea of individual. . . . What needs to be challenged is the crude binarism that locates modernity ('us') on one side and premodernity ('them') on the other, thus condemning the Middle Ages to the role of all-purpose alternative." "On the Margin," 92–93.

90. For a nuanced analysis of the varied historical phenomenon of "wonder" in the early modern period, see Daston and Park's excellent *Wonders and the Order of Nature, 1150–1750*. For a critique of the ways in which the historical division between enchanted and disenchanted epochs has been articulated, see Daston's "Nature of Nature in Early Modern Europe."

91. For Weber, "scientific progress is a fraction," even if "the most important fraction," of "the process of intellectualization which we have been undergoing for thousands of years." See Weber, "Science as Vocation," especially 138–39, 155.

92. Taussig, *Defacement*, 13.

CHAPTER 1. "RELICS OF THE MIND"

1. The painting is also known as *Saint Matthew and the Angel* and *Saint Matthew Composing His Gospel*.

2. *Le vite de' pittori, scultori e architetti moderni* (Rome, 1672). Reprinted and translated by Hibbard in *Caravaggio*, 365.

3. See Lavin, "Divine Inspiration"; T. Thomas, "Expressive Aspects"; Hibbard, *Caravaggio*, 144. Friedlaender expresses doubts concerning Bellori's version of events. See his *Caravaggio Studies*, 104–5.

4. In *The Golden Legend* the account of the evangelist's life begins with an etymological inquiry into the name Matthew. According to the *Legend*, the name "Matthew" is derived from "manus, that is a hand, and theos, that is God." Matthew then signifies "the hand of God," and the evangelist was named "the hand of God" for "writing . . . the gospel of God." At the end of this brief hagiography, the *Legend* insists that Matthew's Gospel had been "written with his own hand." Caxton's translation. Voragine, *Golden Legend*, 5:150, 158.

5. Jerome, *Commentary on Matthew*, 495. In his treatise *On Illustrious Men*, Jerome contends: "Matthew . . . composed a gospel of Christ at first published in Judea in Hebrew for the sake of those of the circumcision who believed," adding that "this was afterwards translated into Greek, though by what author is uncertain." Jerome insists, however, that "the Hebrew itself has been preserved until the present day in the library at Caesarea which Pamphilius the martyr so diligently gathered." *On Illustrious Men*, 10. For more on Jerome and the Hebrew Matthew, see Thornton, "Jerome and the 'Hebrew Gospel According to Matthew,'" especially 118–21.

6. As Lavin notes in a follow-up article to his classic piece on "Divine Inspiration in Caravaggio's Two St. Matthews," however, Caravaggio was not the first artist to depict Matthew writing in Hebrew: "The Antwerp painter Frans Pourbus the Elder had done something similar a quarter century before, in a panel in the Musée des Beaux-Arts, Brussels, signed and dated 1573." "A Further Note on the Ancestry of Caravaggio's First *Saint Matthew*," 113.

7. Hibbard, *Caravaggio*, 138; Langdon, *Caravaggio*, 237.

8. Muenster's text, which was dedicated to Henry VIII of England, was reprinted three times in the sixteenth century: in 1551, 1557, and 1582. See Lavin, "Divine Inspiration," 66; and *Encyclopedia Judaica*, 1st edition, s.v. "Muenster, Sebastian.".

9. Howard, "Textual Nature of an Old Hebrew Version of Matthew," 49. Schonfield, who has translated Du Tillet's text into English, suggests that the Bishop of Brieu actually found the Hebrew manuscript among books confiscated by the Inquisition. See Schonfeld, *An Old Hebrew Text of St. Matthew's Gospel*, 4.

10. Lavin hypothesizes that Caravaggio used the Muenster text and corrected it in accordance with the Vulgate. But as T. Thomas points out, it seems far more likely that Caravaggio simply had someone translate the Vulgate for him directly. See Lavin, "Divine Inspiration," 64–66, and T. Thomas, "Expressive Aspects of Caravaggio's First *Inspiration*," 639, n. 12.

11. English translation from Sutcliff, "Council of Trent," 36. For the Latin text, see *Concilium Tridentinum*, 5:91–92.

12. Furthermore, any translation of the Bible not specifically commissioned by the church was prohibited by the pope's Index of 1559. See Thompson, "Jerome and the Testimony of Erasmus," 12.

13. Calvin, *Tracts and Treatises*, 3:75. Elsewhere in the *Acts of the Council of Trent*, he writes, "But as the Hebrew or Greek original often serves to expose their ignorance in quoting Scripture . . . they ingeniously meet this difficulty also by determining that the

Vulgate translation only is to be held authentic. Farewell, then, to those who have spent much time and labour in the study of languages, that they might search for the genuine sense of Scripture at the fountainhead!" *Tracts and Treatises*, 3:68.

14. Ibid., 3:72.

15. See Rice's excellent *Saint Jerome in the Renaissance*, 187–88. Rice catalogues the range of Catholic responses to this issue.

16. Rice contends that to "embody Jerome's inspiration in a beautiful angel . . . was a recent conceit, no earlier than the end of the sixteenth century." *Saint Jerome*, 193.

17. Ibid., 189.

18. Ibid., 193.

19. This was a collaborative enterprise. Although Erasmus ultimately served as what Brady and Olin call "editor-in chief," he worked with a team of scholars. *CWE* 61:xx.

20. In a letter to Cuthbert Tunstall, Guillaume Bude wrote, "When I read what . . . [Erasmus] has published on the New Covenant . . . and what he has done for St. Jerome's works . . . then I feel how fortunate is this age of ours . . . to have that sacred body of doctrine . . . restored to us." *CWE* 4:358 (letter 583). *EE* ii:566 (letter 583).

21. In a note to Matthew 8:23 in his edition of the New Testament. See Bentley, *Humanists and Holy Writ*, 159, 202. Erasmus's contention provoked responses from Catholic theologians, including one of Erasmus's most learned and tenacious critics, Jacobus Lopis Stunica (Diego López de Zúñiga), one of the team of scholars working on the Complutensian Polyglot. For the extended polemical exchange between Erasmus and Stunica concerning the former's translation of the New Testament, see the excellent introduction to H. J. de Jonge's critical edition of Erasmus's *Apologia respondens ad ea quae Iacobvs Lopis Stunica taxaverat in prima duntaxat Novi Testamenti editione.*

22. The idea that Luther hatched the egg that Erasmus laid had become a commonplace in Erasmus's own lifetime. In a letter to Johannes Caesarius, Erasmus rails against the sentiment: "'I laid the egg and Luther hatched it!' An astounding statement . . . ! The egg I laid was a hen's egg and Luther has hatched a chick of very, very different feather." *CWE* 10:464 (letter 1528). *EE* v:609 (letter 1528).

23. Despite the fact that it was published a few months later. The *Novum Instrumentum* was published in March 1516, the edition of Jerome in September 1516.

24. In the opening lines of the *Life of Jerome*, Erasmus tackles the problem of the fictions endemic to the saint's life: "I am indeed not unaware that very many of the ancients thought it a pious and dutiful practice to make use of suitable stories, which they invented out of concern for the common weal. . . . So it was that men of good judgment in the past embellished with miraculous tales themes they wished to commend with special emphasis to the public." *CWE* 61:19.

25. *CWE* 61:22, 24.

26. Erasmus's life and work seem to revolve around the figure of Jerome. Early in life, he was educated at a Latin school that took its name from Jerome and lived with the Brothers of the Common Life, who were so associated with Jerome that they were sometimes called *Hieronymiani*. As an Augustinian canon, he studied Jerome and transcribed

all of Jerome's letters. He frequently referred to Jerome as the first among doctors of the church, famously preferring his writings to those of Augustine. His edition of Jerome's letters was a project sixteen years in the making, and when the edition finally came into being, Erasmus alleged that because of his Herculean labors it could be said that he "owned" Jerome. And as Lisa Jardine has brilliantly shown, Erasmus manipulated his persona in text and image in a largely successful attempt to *become* a modern Jerome. See Jardine, *Erasmus, Man of Letters*, especially 4–5, 55–82. Also see Rice, *Saint Jerome*, 115–36, and Olin, "Erasmus and Saint Jerome."

27. ". . . virum doctum quidem ac pium, sed tamen hominem fuisse." *EE* vii:97 (letter 1841).

28. T. Thomas provides the extended quote in Italian; see "Expressive Aspects of Caravaggio's First *Inspiration*," 639.

29. Mullett, *Catholic Reformation*, 40.

30. Although T. Thomas contends that the "guiding hand of the angel represents 'dictating' in the most physical and concrete way possible," what Caravaggio depicts in the first *Inspiration* is not, properly speaking, dictating, which would imply communication, speech. T. Thomas, "Expressive Aspects of Caravaggio's First *Inspiration*," 639.

31. For discussions of the centrality of language to Erasmus's conception of the divine, see Rummel, *Erasmus' Annotations*; Boyle, *Erasmus on Language and Method*; and Hoffmann, *Rhetoric and Theology*.

32. O'Connell, *Idolatrous Eye*, 29–30.

33. In the second edition of 1519 Erasmus changes *verbum* to *sermo* to mirror the change he makes in his translation of John 1:1. See *CWE* 3:222, n. 48. I discuss the controversial use of *sermo* in the translation of John 1:1 below.

34. *CWE* 3:222 (letter 384). For the Latin text, see *EE* ii.185 (letter 384).

35. As Brian Cummings argues, Erasmus saw his *Novum Instrumentum* as "a reordering of the mind of Europe . . . . By performing a reformation in reading practices, Erasmus proposed to reform Christian doctrine and moral life." *Grammar and Grace*, 104–5.

36. As Erasmus writes, "Quum enim Dominus diceret, 'Hic est calix Noui Testamenti', nullus erat liber Noui Testamenti proditus. Itidem Testamentum Vetus erat prius quam Moses conscriberet Pentateuchum. Porro, tabulas et codicillos in quibus pacta descripta sunt, instrumenta vocant." *EE* vii:140 (letter 1858). For a discussion of Erasmus's letter to Aldrich, see Bentley, *Humanists and Holy Writ*, 121.

37. Exceptions include Cummings and O'Connell, who both note the radical nature of similar claims in Erasmus's *Paraclesis*. See note 42 below.

38. For Erasmus's engagements with his various detractors, see Rummel, *Erasmus and His Catholic Critics*; Augustijn, *Erasmus*.

39. Translation by Olin, *Selected Writings of Erasmus*, 106. Cited as Olin hereafter. For the Latin text, see *LB* 5:144.

40. Olin, 106. *LB* 5:144.

41. O'Connell, *Idolatrous Eye*, 36. Cummings also finds this moment startling: "Although scripture has always been described as holy, to make the text the receptacle of

Christ 'fully present'—even more than in his human body or implicitly than in the sacra-ment—is a startling principle." *Grammar and Grace*, 106. Erasmus prepares the reader for this shocking conclusion earlier in the text by introducing the idea in a more qualified form: "Why have we steadfastly preferred to learn the wisdom of Christ from the writings of men than from Christ himself? And He, since He promised to be with us all days, even unto the consummation of the world, stands forth especially in this literature, in which He lives for us even at this time, breathes and speaks, I should say almost more effectively than when He dwelt among men. The Jews saw and heard less than you see and hear in the books of the Gospels." Olin, 102. *LB* 5:142.

42. I am in full agreement with O'Connell when he suggests that this passage in the *Paraclesis* "is an illustration, and a characteristic one at that, of the intensity of Erasmus's conviction that Christ was to be encountered most fully in the word, and not in any visual, material form." O'Connell, *Idolatrous Eye*, 36. Also see Eire, *War Against the Idols*, 28–53, and Boyle, *Erasmus on Language and Method*.

43. *CWE* 3:256 (letter 396). *EE* ii:212 (letter 396).

44. Erasmus fled Basel when the iconoclasts took over. See Augustijn, *Erasmus*, 158–59. For Erasmus's relationship to icons and iconoclasm, see Panofsky, "Erasmus and the Visual Arts."

45. Peter Brown, *Cult of the Saints*, 88, 86.

46. The colloquy is not iconoclastic in the narrow sense. As Erasmus says in a sup-plement to the 1526 edition of the *Colloquies*, in *Peregrinatio religionis ergo* he reproaches both "those who are mad about pilgrimages undertaken in the name of religion" and "those who with much ado have thrown all images out of the churches." *CWE* 40:1103. For *Peregrinatio religionis ergo* and the supplement, entitled *De utilitate Colloquiorum* ("The Usefulness of the Colloquies"), see *Opera Omnia*, I/3, 470–94; I/3, 741–52. For English translations, see *CWE* 40:619–74, and *CWE* 40:1095–17.

47. In *Paraclesis* Erasmus exhorts his reader to be transformed by scripture: "Let us all, therefore, with our whole heart covet this literature, let us embrace it, let us continually occupy ourselves with it, let us fondly kiss it, at length let us die in its embrace, let us be transformed in it." Characteristically, this exhortation occurs in the midst of a critique of the idolatry of things and a call for the veneration of scripture: "If anyone shows us the footprints of Christ, in what manner, as Christians, do we prostrate ourselves, how we adore them! But why do we not venerate instead the living and breathing likeness of Him in these books? If anyone displays the tunic of Christ, to what corner of the earth shall we not hasten so that we may kiss it? Yet were you to bring forth His entire wardrobe, it would not manifest Christ more clearly and truly than the Gospel writings. We embellish a wooden or stone statue with gems and gold for the love of Christ. Why not, rather, mark with gold and gems and with ornaments of greater value than these, if such there be, these writings which bring Christ to us so much more effectively than any paltry image?" Olin, 105–6. *LB* 5:144.

48. *CWE* 3:256 (letter 396). *EE* ii:212 (letter 396).

49. Of course, Erasmus's conception of books as "relics of the mind" takes its place

in a long history of metaphors relating books to bodies and bodies to books, especially the flesh of authors to their literary remains. As D. F. McKenzie writes, "The common use of the word 'Remaines' as a term for posthumous works ambiguously suggests both the items remaining to be published and, as the earthly relics of a departed soul, the close identity of a man's body and his . . . works." McKenzie, *Making Meaning*, 210. Also see Ernst Curtius's classic essay "The Book as Symbol."

50. *CWE* 3:257 (letter 396). *EE* ii:213 (letter 396).

51. As Thomas Aquinas writes, "It is evident that we are bound to hold in veneration the saints of God as being members of Christ. . . . We are equally bound, therefore, in memory of them, to accord due honour to any of their relics; and this is primarily true of their bodies, which were the temples and instruments of the Holy Spirit, dwelling and acting within them." *Summa Theologiae* (3a, q. 25.6), vol. 50: 202–3. The Council of Trent confirmed the church's position with regard to relics in the twenty-fifth session (1563): "The holy bodies of the holy martyrs and of others living with Christ, which were the living members of Christ and the temple of the Holy Ghost, to be awakened by Him to eternal life and to be glorified, are to be venerated by the faithful." *Canons and Decrees of the Council of Trent*, 215.

52. For a discussion of the ways in which Erasmus stresses the textual rather than bodily incarnation of Christ, see Eire, *War Against the Idols*, 40–41.

53. *CWE* 3:257 (letter 396). *EE* ii:213 (letter 396).

54. *CWE* 66:65. *LB* 5:27.

55. *CWE* 66:72. *LB* 5:31.

56. *CWE* 3:256 (letter 396). *EE* ii:212 (letter 396).

57. *Confessions*, 11.3.5, pp. 223–24. For the Latin text, see *Confessiones*, ed. L. Verheijen, 196–97. See also the passage in Book 13 of the *Confessions* in which Augustine, addressing his God, suggests that "divine scripture has more sublime authority since the death of the mortal authors through whom you provided it for us." *Confessions*, 13.15.16, p. 282; Verheijen, 250–51.

58. In a provocative reading of this passage, Lisa Freinkel suggests that "as Augustine understands it, the voice of truth is always already the voice of the text, a matter neither of speaking nor of presence, but a 'voice' of reading and of absence. Or rather, even more precisely, the voice of the text presents itself, but only by inscribing absence." *Reading Shakespeare's Will*, 35–37. Also see Vance, *Mervelous Signals*, 41–42.

59. *CWE* 66:72–73. *LB* 5:31–32.

60. *CWE* 73. *LB* 5:32.

61. It is characteristic of Erasmus's thought that his preference for text over authorial presence does not preclude championing the importance of preaching. On the contrary, for Erasmus preaching is essential to the dissemination of the word of scripture. For his thought on preaching, see his *Ecclesiastes*.

62. Complutum was the Latin name of Alcalá de Henares.

63. An Aramaic rendering of the Pentateuch (the Targum of Onkelos) complete with Latin translation appears at the foot of the page in the first volume. For more on the *mise en page* of the Complutensian Polyglot, see Bentley, *Humanists and Holy Writ*, 91.

64. For discussions of the production of the Complutensian Polyglot, see Bentley, *Humanists and Holy Writ*, 70–111; B. Hall, *Humanists and Protestants*, 1–51; Rummel, *Jiménez de Cisneros*, 53–65; Merton, *Cardinal Ximenes*, 131–42.

65. For a provocative discussion of this figure, see Parker, *Shakespeare from the Margins*, 116–84.

66. *Biblia Complutensis*, fol. iiiv. For an English translation, see B. Hall, "Biblical Scholarship," 51.

67. His classic statement on this is his *Ciceronianus*, in which he decries the madness of a slavish imitation of Cicero. *CWE* 28. For a discussion of Erasmus's *Ciceronianus* as an analysis of "cultural anachronism," see Greene, *Light in Troy*, 187; also see Pigman, "Imitation and the Renaissance Sense of the Past."

68. See Augustijn, *Erasmus*, 89–91; Cummings, *Grammar and Grace*, 104–5.

69. *LB* 5:32. The translation is from William Tyndale, who based his English version of the New Testament on the Greek of Erasmus's *Novum Instrumentum*. Tyndale, *New Testament,* 157. Tyndale's translation is reproduced virtually verbatim in the King James Version (London, 1611).

70. For ease of reference, these citations are keyed to the King James Version.

71. *CWE* 66:72–73. *LB* 5:31–32.

72. *Enchiridion, CWE* 66:72–73. *LB* 5:31–32.

73. *CWE* 39:251. *Opera Omnia*, I/3, 273.

74. Cave, *Cornucopian Text,* 86, n. 15.

75. *CWE* 7:169–70 (letter 1060).

76. In a 1525 letter to Celio Calcagnini, Erasmus expresses this sense of embattlement: "It seems to be my fate . . . [to] have stones thrown at me from both sides. In [Italy] . . . and in Brabant I am taken for a Lutheran, while here in Germany where I live I am considered so anti-Lutheran that there is no one whom Luther's supporters attack so savagely." *CWE* 11:112 (letter 1576). *EE* vi:77 (letter 1576). For Erasmus's attempts to negotiate a middle path between the extremists on both sides, see Augustijn, *Erasmus*, 147–60.

77. *CWE* 29:406–7. *Opera Omnia*, IV/1A, 173–74.

78. Erasmus visited England in 1499; from 1505 to 1506; 1509 to 1511; 1511 to 1514; in 1515, 1516, and 1517. He spent more time there than in any other country outside of his native Low Countries. See Dickens, *Erasmus the Reformer*, 193–96; Augustijn, *Erasmus*, 31–42.

79. Quoted passage is from the "Letter to Warham." *CWE* 3:256 (letter 396). *EE* ii:212 (letter 396).

80. According to the Edwardian *Injunctions*, Erasmus's commentary was to be "sette vp in some conuenient place, within the sayed Churche . . . whereas . . . parishioners may moste comodiously, resorte vnto the same, & read the same." Edward VI, *Inivnccions*, A4v–B1r. The Elizabethan *Injunctions* of 1559 renewed this mandate, commanding that all parishes "prouide . . . within one .xii. monethes next after the sayd visitation, the Paraphrases of Erasmus . . . in English vpon the Gospelles." Elizabeth I, *Iniunctions*, A3r.

81. This sermon is first printed in 1563 in *The seconde tome of homelyes . . . set out by*

the aucthoritie of the Quenes Maiestie: and to be read in euery paryshe churche. This collection of homilies was reprinted in 1570, 1571, 1574, 1577, 1582, 1587, 1595, 1623, 1633, and 1635.

82. "An Information," *The seconde tome of homelyes* (1563), 332 (3Rivr).

83. Ibid., 334 (3Sir).

84. Ibid., 330 (3Riiir).

85. Foxe, *Actes and Monuments* (1563), 514.

86. Erasmus, *An exhortacyon to the dylygent study of scripture*, biR–biiiiR. Erasmus addresses the subject of vernacular translation in very similar terms in a prefatory letter to his *Paraphrase of Matthew*. This letter was translated into English anonymously and printed alongside Roye's translation of *Paraclesis* in the 1534 edition of Robert Wyer. See Erasmus, *An exhortacyon to the study of the Gospell*, Eiir–Eiiv.

87. As I discuss below, Tyndale's *Obedience of a Christian Man* begins with a preface "to the Reader" that champions the translation of scripture in the vernacular. At the end of his argument, Tyndale invites the reader to turn to Erasmus: "A thousande reasons moo myght be made (as thou maist se in paraclesis Erasmi & in his preface to the paraphrasis of Mathew) vnto which they shulde be compelled to holde their peace." Tyndale, *Obedience*, C4r –C4v.

88. As Stephen Greenblatt observes, there is a "vast difference between Erasmus's 'Would that' and Tyndale's 'I will cause.' . . . What Erasmus is willing to express as a wish, Tyndale puts as his personal mission." *Renaissance Self-Fashioning*, 106.

89. As Luther writes in his *Lectures on Genesis*, "where the word is, there the church is . . . where the word is not . . . there the church is not." *LW* 2:229. *WA* 42:423–24. Or as he writes even more provocatively in the same *Lectures*, "If I were the only one in the entire world to adhere to the word, I alone would be the church." *LW* 2:102. *WA* 42:334.

90. Tyndale, *Obedience of a Christen Man*, A2r.

91. Ibid., A2r.

92. Ibid., A3r; B3r.

93. Ibid., B4r.

94. Ibid., A2r.

95. In his *Prologue unto the Epistle of Paul to the Romans*, Tyndale writes, "Where the word of god is preached purely and receaued in the herte / there ys fayth . . . . Where godes worde ys not purely preached / but mens dreames / tradicions / ymaginasion / inuencions / ceremonies and supersticion there ys no fayth." Tyndale, *A compendious introduccion, prologe or preface vn to the pistle off Paul to the Romayns*, B3v.

96. Tyndale, *Obedience*, B8r–B8v.

97. Ibid., C3r–C3v. For Tyndale the errors endemic to contemporary religion work to produce a bewildering multitude of beliefs: "euery man taketh a sondry doctoure / which doctours are as sondry and as dyuers, the one contrary vnto the other / as there are diuers facions and monstrous shappes / none lyke a nother / amonge oure sectes of religion. Euery religion / euery vniuersite & allmost euery man hath asondry dyuinite." Tyndale, *Obedience*, C2v–C3r.

98. "In so great diuersite of sprites how shall I know who lyeth and who saith

trouth? Whereby shall I trye them & iudge them? Verely by gods worde which only is true." Tyndale, *Obedience*, B8r.

99. Tyndale, *Obedience*, C3v. As Cummings notes, "This is the argument of Erasmus's *Paraclesis*. God exists in language, he is incarnated in the word." *Grammar and Grace*, 199. Also see Cummings, "The Theology of Translation," 40.

100. Tyndale, *Obedience*, C3v.

101. Luther, *The Bondage of the Will*, *LW* 33:140. *WA* 18:685.

102. See Luther, *The Bondage of the Will*, *LW* 33:138–44; *WA* 18:684–88. For Luther's distinction between an "absolute God" and "God as he is dressed and clothed in His Word and promises," see his *Commentary on Psalm 51*, *LW* 12:312. For a discussion of the distinction between the hidden and revealed God in both Luther and Calvin, see Gerrish, "'To the Unknown God.'"

103. Tyndale, *Answere vnto Sir Thomas Mores Dialoge*, 190–93.

104. On the relationship of Tyndale's thought to Luther's, see Trinterud, "Reappraisal of Tyndale's Debt"; Trueman, *Luther's Legacy*, 83–120; Clebsch, *England's Earliest Protestants*, 137–204.

105. Pelikan, *Luther the Expositor*, 50.

106. In my understanding of the polemical conflict between More and Tyndale, especially with regard to the contested ground of scripture, I am deeply indebted to the work of Brian Cummings. See especially *Grammar and Grace*, 190–206; "Reformed Literature and Literature Reformed"; and "Iconoclasm and Bibliophobia."

107. "Enforcing Statutes against Heresy; Prohibiting Unlicensed Preaching, Heretical Books." See *Tudor Royal Proclamations*, 182. In 1530 the government issued another proclamation "Prohibiting Erroneous Books and Bible Translations" that attempted to quell the flood of "heresies and erroneous opinions" that had "been late sown and spread among his subjects of this his said realm, by blasphemous and pestiferous English books" by putting forward an index of prohibited books. *Tudor Royal Proclamations*, 194.

108. Title page, *A dyaloge of syr Thomas More knyghte: one of the counsayll of our souerayne lorde the kyng and chauncelloure of hys duchy of Lancaster. Wheryn be treatyd dyuers maters / as of the veneracyon & worshyp of ymagys & relyques / prayng to sayntis / & goynge on pylgrymage. Wyth many other thyngys touchyng the pestylent secte of Luther & Tyndale / by the tone bygone in Saxony / & by the tother laboryd to be brought in to England.* (London: William Rastell, 1530). For More, as a running header informs us, "Tyndale" is "worse than Luther": "For he hath not onely sowked out the most poyson that he coulde fynde thorowe all Luthers bokes . . . but hath also in many thynges farre passed his mayster." More, *Dialogue Concerning Heresies. CWM* 6:1:424.

109. *CWM* 6:1:181. Also see 6:1:249.

110. *CWM* 6:1:181. More is presumably thinking of the *Babylonian Captivity* where Luther makes reference to the same passage in Augustine. Of course, Luther and More have very different notions of "church." See *CWM* 6:2:655.

111. Tyndale, *Answere*, 24.

112. For the ways in which John Foxe and the printer John Day contributed to the mythologizing of Tyndale, see King's "'The Light of Printing.'"

113. On the relationship of Tyndale's thought to Erasmus's thought, see Daniell, *William Tyndale*, 59–79; Mozley, *William Tyndale*, 75–109; Richardson, "Tyndale's Quarrel with Erasmus"; DeCoursey, "Erasmus and Tyndale on Bible-reading."

114. "W.T. to the Reader." *The firste boke of Moses called Genesis*, A2v.

115. It is also not true, as is often asserted, that Tyndale (or Luther for that matter) eschews figurative or allegorical reading. In the prologue to Leviticus in his translation of the *Pentateuch*, Tyndale writes, "Fynallye beware of allegoryes, for there is not a moare handsome or apte a thinge to be gile withall then an allegorye, nor a more sotle and pestilent thinge in the world to persuade a false mater then an allegorye. And contrary wyse there is not a better, vehementer or myghtyer thinge to make a man vnderstond with all then an allegory. For allegoryes make a man qwick witted and prynte wysdome in him and maketh it to abyde, where bare wordes go but in at the one eare and out at the other." *Five Books of Moses Called the Pentateuch*, 297.

116. Tyndale, *Obedience*, R6v.

117. *CWM* 6:1:115. As More says, "we be not sure by any promyse made that the scrypture shall endure to the worldes ende. . . . For where our lorde sayth that his wordes shall not passe away / nor one iote therof be lost / he spake of . . . his fayth and doctryne taught by mouth and inspyracyon. He mente not that of his holy scrypture in wrytynge there sholde neuer a iote be lost." *CWM* 6:1:115. On More's deconstruction of writing, see Cummings, "Reformed Literature and Literature Reformed," 834–38.

118. *CWM* 6:1:138.

119. *CWM* 6:1:139.

120. *CWM* 6:1:141.

121. The *Speculum Sacerdotale*, a fifteenth-century collection of sermons, outlines a common conception of Christian history: "Vnderstondeth wel we dyuyde alle the tyme of this world by thre tymes. The firste tyme is that [that] was of natural lawe fro Adam vnto Moyses. The secounde tyme is of writen lawe that was fro Moyses vnto the aduent of oure lord. The thridde tyme is tyme of grace that is fro the aduent vnto the ende of the world. The tyme that was fro Adam vnto Moyses is callid tyme of natural lawe for this skylle, that no lawe was then writen, but then was lawe to iche man as natural reson hem techid. . . . The tyme that was betwixt Moyses and Crist was callid tyme of lawe writen and to be kepte in tables of stone. . . . And the tyme fro the aduent vnto the ende of the world is called tyme of grace. For the lyffers in that tyme, whiche tyme is nowe, are born agen withoute fleschely sacrifice through baptym. . . . And so we are in the clere day." *Speculum Sacerdotale*, 7–8.

122. *CWM* 6:1:142–43.

123. For a discussion of the figure of "writing in the heart" in Christian discourse, see Jager, *Book of the Heart*, passim, and Erickson, *Language of the Heart*, 25–60.

124. *CWM* 6:1:143.

125. *CWM* 6:1:143 (emphasis mine).

126. English translation from Ebeling, *Luther*, 109. For the German text, see *WA* 50:245–46.

127. The joke concerns a "man who was charged by one of his neighbours with having given him back a borrowed kettle in a damaged condition. The defendant asserted first, that he had given it back undamaged; secondly, that the kettle had a hole in it when he borrowed it; and thirdly, that he had never borrowed a kettle from his neighbour at all." In Freud's argument, the joke illuminates the "kettle logic" common to dreams. See Freud, *The Interpretation of Dreams*, in *Complete Works,* 4:119–20.

128. Tyndale, *Answere*, 26–27.

129. Ibid., 26–27.

130. Ibid., 27.

131. As Tyndale asks, without "authentic scripture" how would "the true preacher confound the false, except he brought true miracles to confound the false?" Ibid., 26.

132. The "testament of the circumcision" comes, as Tyndale indicates, from the Acts of the Apostles 7:8.

133. Tyndale, *Answere*, 27.

134. Ibid., 29.

135. *The Whole Workes of W. Tyndall*, 255.

CHAPTER 2. REWRITING THE LETTER

1. Orgel, "Margins of Truth," 102. I am extremely grateful to Professor Orgel for sharing his transcription of the marginal notes with me. When making reference to these notes, I will cite them in relation to the book, canto, and stanza they address. Professor Orgel presented a fascinating paper on the marginalia of this reader at the "Material Texts" seminar at the University of Pennsylvania (March 31, 1997), which, in part, inspired the essay on which this chapter is based. See Kearney, "Enshrining Idolatry in *The Faerie Queene*." For Orgel's reflections on the marginalia, see "Margins of Truth."

2. Orgel, "Margins of Truth," 92.

3. Marginal note to 1.10.61. For an account of the ways in which Spenser's adapts both the saint's life and St. George to his purposes, see King, *Spenser's Poetry*, 188–99. On St. George in Spenser's poem generally, see Weatherby, "True Saint George," and Lamb, "Red Crosse Knight, St. George, and Popular Culture."

4. Marginal notes to 1.1.46; 1.10.66.

5. As Orgel notes, "Our Puritan reader . . . provides a good index to the degree to which Roman Catholicism remained an indispensable and genuinely troubling element in Protestant poetics, as in the Elizabethan religious imagination generally." "Margins of Truth," 104.

6. On the various iconoclastic stances toward the crucifix and the cross in Reformation England, see Aston, *England's Iconoclasts*, 212–13, 244–46, 302–14; Duffy, "Devotion to the Crucifix"; Cummings, "Iconoclasm and Bibliophobia," 194–97.

7. Edmund Spenser, *Faerie Queene*, 1.1.2. Subsequent citations of *The Faerie Queene* will reference book, canto, and stanza and will be cited in the text.

8. Marginal note to 1.1.2.

9. *OED*, s.v. "legend."

10. On Spenser's use of "legend" as a form of "legere," see DeNeef, *Spenser and the Motives of Metaphor*, 142; Nohrnberg, *Analogy of* The Faerie Queene, 99–100; Quilligan, *Language of Allegory*, 260.

11. For an early modern document that records these senses of the term, see Thomas Cooper's *Thesaurus linguae Romanae et Britannicae* (1578), 4B5v. Also see Lewis and Short, *Latin Dictionary*, 1048.

12. DeNeef, *Spenser and the Motives of Metaphor*, 147. I am indebted to DeNeef's excellent reading of the poem.

13. Illich, *In the Vineyard of the Text*, 58. Also see Lewis and Short, *Latin Dictionary*, 1048.

14. Marginal note to 1.2.19.

15. "Knowing how doubtfully all Allegories may be construed, and this booke of mine, which I haue entituled the Faery Queene, being a continued Allegory, or darke conceit, I haue thought good aswell for auoyding of gealous opinions and misconstructions, as also for your better light in reading thereof, (being so by you commanded,) to discouer vnto you the general intention & meaning, which in the whole course thereof I haue fashioned." Spenser, "A Letter of the Authors," *The Faerie Queene*, 15.

16. King, *English Reformation Literature*, 147.

17. For the positioning of the table in the reformed English church, see Maltby, *Prayer Book and People*, 138–39.

18. And the Catholic reaction to a perceived bibliolatry could be so vehement as to look like an attack on scripture itself. In 1569 the rebels of Durham and Yorkshire ritually burned English Bibles and prayer books while overthrowing communion tables. See Duffy, *Stripping of the Altars*, 583; Aston, *King's Bedpost*, 143.

19. *LW* 34:285. *WA* 50:658.

20. Quarles, *Shepheards Oracles*, 91.

21. My understanding of the heuristic effects of the hermeneutic wandering of both the Redcrosse Knight and the reader is indebted to the work of DeNeef, *Spenser and the Motives of Metaphor*; Miller, *Poem's Two Bodies*; Parker, *Inescapable Romance*; and Quilligan, *Language of Allegory*. My conception of Spenserian iconoclasm is made possible by the work of Gilman, *Iconoclasm and Poetry*; Gross, *Spenserian Poetics*; King, *Spenser's Poetry*; and Norbrook, *Poetry and Politics*.

22. *OED*, s.v. "tract."

23. Warner, "Dark Wood," 450.

24. Quoted in Warner, "Dark Wood," 457.

25. See especially Craig, "Secret Wit," 454–55; Parker, *Inescapable Romance*, 64–70; Quilligan, *Language of Allegory*, 33–36.

26. See the preface to the 1539 edition of his German Works, *LW* 34:285. *WA* 50:658.

27. For a discussion of Errour as a figure for the printing press, see Rhu, "Romancing the Word"; for the passages quoted, see, respectively, Spenser, *Edmund Spenser's Poetry*, 11, n. 5; and Spenser, *Faerie Queene*, 1077, n. 20.6.

28. Marginal note to 1.1.20.

29. Revelation 10:10–11: "Then I toke the litle boke out of the Angels hand, and ate it vp, and it was in my mouth as sweet as honie: but when I had eaten it, my bellie was bitter." Geneva Bible (1560). Also see Ezekiel 2:9–3:3. In a discussion of this moment in *The Faerie Queene*, Gross refers to this biblical image as the "the Bible's most radical trope of reception." See "Books in *The Faerie Queene*," 104.

30. Bale, *Image of Both Churches*, 150; sig. T6v.

31. Bale, *Apology . . . agaynste a ranke Papyst*, fol. 74; sig. K3r. Curiously, the first entry under the *Oxford English Dictionary*'s definition of "gobbet" as "A piece of a literary or musical work removed from its context" is from 1912; nevertheless, as the passage from Bale demonstrates, this understanding of the word was current in the early modern period.

32. Bacon, "Of Studies," in *Essaies* (1612), 171, M4r.

33. See Gross's insight that the Redcrosse Knight "must learn after his early defeat of a monster labeled 'Errour' that the forces of error tend to exceed any limiting names that culture or poetry might find to contain them." *Spenserian Poetics*, 58.

34. For a terrific discussion of reification in early modern thought, see Anderson, *Words That Matter*, especially 137–50. For reification as the mode of personification allegory, see Quilligan, *Language of Allegory*, 115–16.

35. As Parker notes in a brilliant reading that informs my own, the reader's desire to "make the episode wholly explicable in moral terms" is precisely the kind of erroneous reduction that Spenser allegorizes within the poem. See Parker, *Inescapable Romance*, 66.

36. M. Rose, *Spenser's Art*, 14.

37. Luther, *Table Talk*, LW 54:50. WA TR 1:146 (#352).

38. See Gross, "Books in *The Faerie Queene*," 103–4. Also see King, *Spenser's Poetry*, 47–48.

39. As Keith Thomas observes, "in Protestant mythology" Catholic authorities were frequently portrayed as "conjurers, sorcerers or enchanters." See Thomas, *Religion and the Decline*, 68–69.

40. From "dewly" rehearsing "holy things each morne and euentyde" to his constant repetition of the "Aue-Mary," Archimago's discourse is marked as that of a Catholic hypocritically or ignorantly repeating empty formulae (1.1.34–35). A Protestant reader might also be concerned by the trust he places in the beads that he bids "all day for his trespas" and the reverence with which he seems to regard the physical place of his Hermitage, with its "holy Chapell" and "sacred fountaine" (1.1.30; 1.1.34).

41. Bateman, *Christall Glasse*, M4v.

42. This is reminiscent of the title-page woodcut from Foxe's *Actes and Monuments* discussed earlier in the chapter. In this image, members of the true church experience some sort of revelation, which is figured as a glorious sun encompassing the letters of the tetragrammaton. See Figure 6.

43. Bateman, *Christall Glasse*, G4v.

44. In the interlude *Lusty Juventus*, the Vice Hypocrisy counsels the protagonist: "Let your book at your girdle be tied, / Or else in your bosom that he may be spied, /

And then it will be said both with youth and age, / Yonder fellow hath an excellent knowledge." *Lusty Juventus,* 687–90.

45. Foxe, *Actes and Monuments* (1596), 912. All references to Foxe's *Actes and Monuments* in this chapter are citations of the 1596 edition.

46. In another woodcut, depicting "the burning of Maister Wylliam Tyndall," *Actes and Monuments* dramatizes the execution of the man Foxe hailed as the architect of the English Bible while an anonymous friar looks on wearing a girdle book (Figure 15). Likewise, a friar with girdle book attends "The Burning of The Archbishop of Canterbury, D. Thomas Cranmer" (Figure 16), the man whose name would become synonymous with the English Book of Common Prayer. Finally, in two quite different woodcuts—"The maner of the popyshe Spanyards in carrying Nicolas Burton . . . to the burning" (Figure 17) and "The talke betwene M. Bradford and two Spanish fryers" (Figure 18)—*Actes and Monuments* links the girdle book to the despised Spanish friars of Mary's court.

47. Deuteronomy 6.4–9, Geneva Bible (1560).

48. Calvin, *Sermons . . . [on] Deuteronomie,* 275–76. For a discussion of this passage, see Fleming, *Graffiti and the Writing Arts,* 67.

49. On phylacteries as *tefillin,* see Tigay, "On the Term Phylacteries (Matt. 23:5)." On the term "phylactery," see the *Oxford English Dictionary.*

50. Calvin, *Sermons . . . [on] Deuteronomie,* 276.

51. For Christians the crucial New Testament text that illuminates the injunction in Deuteronomy is found in the Gospel of Matthew. In his *Paraphrase . . . vpon the Newe Testament* (1548), Erasmus explicates the relevant passage (Matt. 23) and construes the phylacteries as an emblem of a Hebraic veneration of the dead letter. See Erasmus, *The first tome . . . of the Paraphrase,* O3v.

52. Calvin, *Sermons . . . [on] Deuteronomie,* 473.

53. Tyndale, *Obedience of a Christen man,* B4v–B5r.

54. Ibid., B4v.

55. Foxe, *Actes and Monuments,* 1599.

56. For an elegant reading of this moment in relation to a Protestant semiotics of dress, see Laurie Shannon, "'His Apparel Was Done Upon Him': Rites of Personage in Foxe's Book of Martyrs."

57. See 1 Corinthians 9:24–26: "Knowe ye not, that they which runne in a race, runne all, yet one receiueth the price? so runne, that ye may obteine. . . . I therefore so runne, not as vncerteinly: so fight I, not as one that beateth the ayre." Geneva Bible (1560).

58. For another discussion of Idleness's girdle book, see King, *Spenser's Poetry,* 52–54.

59. Zechariah 11:17, Geneva Bible (1560).

60. Gross notes that "'idol shepherd' is in some ways a quite shrewd translation of the original Hebrew text, which refers not so much to . . . a 'worthless shepherd,' as a 'shepherd of worthlessness,' where 'worthlessness' translates a Hebrew noun often used as a periphrasis for the spiritual vanity of idolatry." Gross, *Spenserian Poetics,* 213, n. 4.

61. *OED,* s.v. "idol."

62. Francis Quarles uses the pun on idol and idle in reference to a book in the *Shepheards Oracle*. In the poem the radical Protestant Anarchus rejects the *Book of Common Prayer*: "Because it is an Idoll, whereunto /You bend your idle knees, as Papists doe / To their lewd Images" (91).

63. See Parker, *Inescapable Romance*.

64. On the opposition between epic and romance, see Quint, *Epic and Empire*, especially 31–41. The tension between epic purpose and romance digression was, of course, a matter of considerable literary debate in sixteenth-century Italy. Torquato Tasso famously makes this tension the thematic heart of his epic *Gerusalemme Liberata* (1581). For a terrific reading of this debate in relation to Spenser and the politics of chivalry, see Helgerson, *Forms of Nationhood*, 44–59.

65. In the "Letter to Ralegh," Spenser describes the armor that Una brings to the "clownishe young man" (who will, once outfitted, be identified by his shield as the Redcrosse Knight) as "the armour of a Christian man specified by St. Paul v. Ephes." Spenser, "A Letter of the Authors," *The Faerie Queene*, 17.

66. See Darryl Gless's perceptive remarks on the complexity of this scene. Gless, *Interpretation and Theology*, 115–22.

67. For the erotics of idolatry in *The Faerie Queene*, see Gregerson, *The Reformation of the Subject*, especially 56–62.

68. For the full prophecy, see Hosea 4:1–19. References to idolatry as whoring after false goods are sprinkled throughout the Old Testament. For a representative sample, see Exodus 34:12–17, Leviticus 20:1–7, Deuteronomy 31:14–20, Judges 2:11–22, Ezekiel 6:1–14, Judges 8:22–34.

69. On idolatry as spiritual fornication, see Gregerson, *The Reformation of the Subject*.

70. *OED,* s.v. "idle."

71. Calvin, *Institution of Christian Religion* (1587), 3.10.3; fol. 236r. Also see Psalm 115: "Their idoles are siluer and golde, euen the worke of mens hands. / Thei have a mouth and speake not: thei haue eyes and se not. / . . . / Thei that make them are like vnto them: so are all who trust in them." Geneva Bible (1560).

72. *On Christian Doctrine*, 3.10.16.

73. Ibid., 1.3–4.–3–4.

74. Ibid., 1.4.4.

75. As Bale wrote in the passage from *Image of Both Churches* quoted: "With good harte ought the scriptures to be receyued of all men, in faith deuoured, & in a pure loue digested. . . . Nothing but *idelnesse* worketh that man, which hath it not grafted within him, though he both fast & pray." *Image of Both Churches*, 150; sig. T6v. Emphasis mine.

76. *On Christian Doctrine*, 3.5.9. On Augustine's understanding of this carnal servitude, also see ibid., 3.7.11.

77. Kaske, *Spenser and Biblical Poetics*, 18–97.

78. I am grateful to Patrick Cheney for helping me understand the significance of this passage.

79. Marginal note to 1.2.18.

80. "Then those two knights, fast friendship for to bynd, / And loue establish each to other trew, / Gaue goodly gifts, the signes of gratefull mynd, / And eke as pledges firme, right hands together ioynd" (1.9.18).

81. There is, of course, an implicit and rudimentary commentary on material and spiritual value: the "boxe" embowed or encircled "with gold and gorgeous ornament" is gilt on the outside while the "booke . . . writ with golden letters" is golden on the inside; Arthur's "drops of liquor pure" are of "wondrous worth," while the Redcrosse Knight's "testament" is "of wondrous grace."

82. Although, as Roche observes in his note to the "liquor pure" in his edition of *The Faerie Queene*, Arthur seems to use this same healing substance "to cure the wounds of Amoret" in Book IV (4.8.20).

83. Quilligan, *Language of Allegory*, 36–37.

84. See Derrida's reflections on the gift of writing in *Given Time*, 99–103.

85. Augustine, "Sermon 120," *Works,* 3:4:232–33.

86. Davis, *Gift in Sixteenth-Century France*, 131.

87. On Despaire's manipulation of the arts of preaching, see Mallette, *Spenser and Reformation England*, 37–42.

88. My reading of the theology of the Despaire episode generally is influenced by Gless's *Interpretation and Theology*, 142–45.

89. As Nohrnberg demonstrates in his characteristically erudite reading of this episode. See Nohrnberg, *Analogy of* The Faerie Queene, 152–55. Also see Skulsky, "Spenser's Despair Episode"; Imbrie, "Playing Legerdemaine with the Scripture." King observes the irony of Despaire basing his argument on Paul's epistle to the Romans. King, *Spenser's Poetry*, 215–16. I am grateful to Daniel Moss for drawing my attention to the fact that Despaire quotes both Old and New Testaments; he gave a terrific paper at the Renaissance Society of America Conference in San Francisco in March 2006 entitled "Despair, Grace, and the Sufficiency of the Word: A Rereading of *The Faerie Queene* 1.9."

90. See Luther's preface to the Latin edition of his collected works (1545). *LW* 34:336–37. *WA* 54:185–86. I discuss both the narrative of Luther's conversion experience and its availability to a sixteenth-century English audience in the next chapter.

91. *LW* 34:336–37. *WA* 54:185–86.

92. See Steinmetz, "Divided by a Common Past," 256–60.

93. On the Reformation assertion of the unity and coherence of scripture, see Collinson, "Coherence of the Text." See also Coolidge, *Pauline Renaissance in England*.

94. Colossians 2:14. *KJV*. The Geneva Bible has "putting out the hand writing of ordinances that was against vs." Geneva Bible (1560).

95. For a fascinating reading of both the practice and theoretical implications of whitewashing in early modern England, see Fleming's *Graffiti and the Writing Arts*, especially 73–78.

96. See Roche's note to the "liquor pure" in his edition of *The Faerie Queene*.

97. *OED*, s.v. "requite."

98. See Mauss, *The Gift.*

99. In his *Commentary on Galatians,* Luther writes, "Mans hart doth not vnderstand nor beleeue that so great a treasure, namely, the holy Ghost, is giuen by the onely hearing of faith." *Commentarie of M. Doctor Martin Luther,* fol. 104v. I discuss this English translation of Luther's *Commentary on Galatians* as a significant text for the understanding of Luther in Elizabethan England in the next chapter.

100. *Commentarie,* fol. 5v.

101. Ibid., fol. 15r.

102. Marginal note to 1.1.30.

103. Bateman, *Christall Glasse,* G2v.

104. Cranmer, "Homily of Good Works," K3r.

105. An inscription placed upon tiles, bells, or amulets, "S. Agathe's letters" constituted a "miraculous" text traditionally said to protect homes against fire. The eight verses of St. Bernard, allegedly culled from the Psalms on the authority of the devil himself, were commonly found in editions of the Catholic Book of Hours and were thought to preserve those who recited them regularly from damnation. The "Fifteen Oes of St. Bridget" were also found in many editions of the Catholic Book of Hours; one of the most popular prayers in fifteenth- and early sixteenth-century England, it was believed to have the power to release souls from purgatory. Like "St. John's Gospel"—the first fourteen lines of the Gospel of John, which when printed out and worn around the neck by Catholics were believed to have divine powers—these texts were condemned by Protestants as abuses of the letter. They were condemned because they allegedly "worked" automatically, irrespective of God's unknowable and implacable will, and because the purported power of these texts was thought to reside in the material forms of the words themselves. See K. Thomas, *Religion,* 23, 31, 219; Duffy, *Stripping of the Altars,* 255.

106. Winston-Allen, *Stories of the Rose,* 111.

107. Ibid., 111.

108. Marginal note to 1.10.8.

109. Calvin, "Sermon upon the Epistle to Timothy," 295.

110. This understanding of the bead as prayer was current well into the sixteenth century when both meanings of the word (bead as object and bead as prayer) existed simultaneously (*OED,* s.v. "bead").

111. Spenser, *Shorter Poems,* 162.

112. Lewis, *Allegory of Love,* 322–24.

113. When Lewis suggests that "imagined buildings and institutions which have a strong resemblance to the actual buildings and institutions of the Church of Rome" will not only appear but *"ought to appear,* in any Protestant allegory," he stretches the argument beyond the breaking point. *Allegory of Love,* 323.

114. On the iconoclastic deformation rather than destruction of the image, see Koerner, *Reformation of the Image,* especially 104–36.

115. Bale, *Laboryouse Journey,* B8r–B8v.

116. Ibid., B3v, B5r–B5v.

117. Ibid., A2r–A2v. In the preface "To the Reader" he writes, "to destroye all without consyderacyon, is and wyll be vnto Englande for euer, a moste horrible infamy amonge the graue senyours of other nacyons. A great nombre of them which purchased those superstycyouse mansyons, reserued of those lybrarye bokes, some to serue theyr iakes, some to scoure theyr candelstyckes, & some to rubbe their bootes. Some they solde to the grosser and sope sellers, & some they sent ouer see to the bokebynders, not in small nombre, but at tymes whole shyppes full, to the wonderynge of the foren nacyons." *Laboryouse Journey*, B1r.

118. Ibid., B8v.

119. Ibid., A7v.

120. Ibid., A2v.

121. Simpson, *Reform and Cultural Revolution*, 17. Simpson suggests that the conflicting agendas of the antiquarian scholar and his royal patron resulted in a kind of "divided consciousness" for Leland: "Leland's *raison d'être* for constructing a British past is in part . . . the destruction of that past on the orders of Leland's own patron. Leland is himself, accordingly, an agent of destruction." *Reform and Cultural Revolution*, 17, 14. Simpson's chapter in *Reform and Cultural Revolution* is a reworking of his earlier essay, "Ageism: Leland, Bale, and the Laborious Start of English Literary History." Medieval scholars have done much in recent years to recuperate Leland and Bale as figures important to English literary history. In addition to Simpson's work, see Wallace, "Dante in Somerset," and Summit, "Monuments and Ruins."

122. Bale, *Laboryouse Journey*, B3v, B5v.

123. Simpson is particularly good on the pathos and melancholy of this text. See *Reform and Cultural Revolution*, 7–33.

124. Ibid., 16–17.

125. Cervantes, *The History of the Valorous and Wittie Knight Errant, Don-Quixote* (1612), 37–38; D3r–D3v.

CHAPTER 3. THE READING OF THE DAMNED

1. Dessen and Thomson, *Dictionary of Stage Directions*, 34–35.

2. Henslowe's *Diary* does not record the purchase of a single book. This peculiar bit of nonevidence may suggest the ease with which books could be obtained—begged or borrowed—for the stage. See Foakes, *Henslowe's Diary*.

3. Throughout the chapter, I refer to the A-Text unless otherwise noted. This argument about the presence of books as props obviously depends on how the play is staged. It would be extremely difficult to avoid books as props in the scenes to which I refer. To my mind, the only scene in doubt is scene three, where I imagine Faustus handling books—presumably the books mentioned by Valdes in the previous scene—in order to conjure Mephistopheles.

4. Dessen and Thomson, *Dictionary of Stage Directions*, 34.

5. Goldman, "Marlowe and the Histrionics of Ravishment," 23.

6. As Anthony Dawson notes, "The text's obsessive concern with books and language turns the tables on reformist reverence for the word, since it is precisely the hero's fixation on language, in particular the language of magic, that damns him." See Dawson and Yachnin, *Culture of Playgoing*, 150. I am deeply indebted to Dawson's elegant and discerning reading.

7. Dawson and Yachnin, *Culture of Playgoing*, 147.

8. I am limiting my inquiry to conversions from one version of Christianity to another.

9. From a discussion of Augustine's use of the concept of conversion in the *Confessions*. Morrison, *Conversion and Text*, viii.

10. I have borrowed the phrase "readerly conversion" from Eric Jager. See Jager's terrific *Book of the Heart*, especially 33–38.

11. Reports of the neglect of Augustine's *Confessions* in the medieval and early modern periods have been greatly exaggerated. Recent scholarship suggests that Augustine's *Confessions* was about as widely read in the Middle Ages as *De Doctrina Christiana*, if not as influential as *City of God*. See Gorman, "The Diffusion of the Manuscripts." Mary Murray has shown that early modern converts like William Alabaster model their conversion narratives on the *Confessions*, and, as I will describe below, Luther explicitly celebrates the exemplary qualities of Augustine's conversion experience in the *Confessions*. See Murray, "Literature of Conversion," 12–64.

12. I will discuss Luther's conversion experience below. For Zwingli's claim that he was converted not by Luther's teachings but by his reading of scripture, see Stephens, *Theology of Huldrych Zwingli*, 21–28; see also Bromiley, *Zwingli and Bullinger*, 16.

13. In his debate with Thomas Cartwright, John Whitgift makes exactly this point when arguing for the importance of reading scripture: "And, if you had been disposed to have called to remembrance that which you say you have so diligently read in M. Fox, you might have known that divers in the beginning came to the light of the gospel only by reading and hearing the new testament in English read." *Works* 3:39–40.

14. Foxe, *Actes and Monuments* (1563), 468.

15. Psalm 51, Geneva Bible (1560), fol. 245v.

16. Gregory, *Salvation at Stake*, 176.

17. *The lattre examinacyon of Anne Askewe*, fol. 67v. For a discussion of this passage and the use of the phoenix metaphor to describe the generation of new converts through martyrdom, see Gregory, *Salvation at Stake*, 163.

18. Murray, "Literature of Conversion," 38.

19. Morrison, *Understanding Conversion*, 185, xiii.

20. Donne, "Goodfriday, 1613. Riding Westward," lines 37–42, in *Divine Poems*, 31.

21. For discussions of the tradition of Christian meditative reading practices, see Stock, *After Augustine*, especially 8–23 and 101–14; Carruthers, *Book of Memory*, 156–88; Illich, *In the Vineyard of the Text*, passim.

22. "A frutefull exhortacion to the reading and knowledge of holy Scripture," in *Certayne Sermons*, B1v. See also the sermon "An Information for them which take offence

at certayne places of the holy scripture": "Let euery man, woman, and chylde, therefore with all theyr harte, thurste & desyre gods holy Scriptures, loue them, embrace them, haue theyr delyght and pleasure in hearyng, and readyng them, so as at length we maye be transformed, and chaunged into them." "An Information," *The seconde tome of homelyes*, 334 (3S1r).

23. This is certainly the case for Augustine and Luther. The role of scripture in Faustus's spiritual transformation is a bit more complex and will be addressed below. My understanding of the conversions of both Luther and Augustine, as well as the relation between the two conversion experiences, is indebted to Brian Cummings's brilliant work. See *Grammar and Grace*, especially 60–68.

24. Augustine, *Confessions*, 8.5.10, p. 140.

25. Ibid., 8.12.29–30, pp. 152–53.

26. On "iterability," see Derrida's "Signature Event Context."

27. Augustine's reading of the voice as a voice addressing him is authorized by the other conversion narratives that he recounts in Book Eight. Augustine famously nests his drama in the garden within other conversion narratives, establishing his spiritual transformation not as a unique event but as part of an iterative pattern, a repetition that the reader is invited to replicate. As John Freccero notes, "In the text of the *Confessions*, conversion is always a literary event, a gloss on an anterior text." "The Fig Tree and the Laurel," 36.

28. Roberts and Skeat, *Birth of the Codex*, 1. As I suggested in the Introduction to *The Incarnate Text*, the reasons for this change seem overdetermined. For a recent overview of the scholarship addressing this issue, see S. Hall, "In the Beginning Was the Codex," 1–10. See also Roberts and Skeat, *Birth of the Codex*, especially 38–66; and Gamble, *Books and Readers*, especially 42–81.

29. Jager, *Book of the Heart*, 35–36.

30. When lamenting his pre-conversion folly, Augustine describes himself as believing in practices like astrology and bibliomancy as a younger man. See *Confessions*, 4.2.2–3.5, pp. 53–55. Whatever Augustine's beliefs about the oracular use of texts, and they seem equivocal, this episode in the garden is not to be read as a sanction of bibliomancy per se; rather, it is a description of a unique if crucially generic conversion event. On bibliomancy generally and the *sortes* tradition specifically, see van der Horst, "*Sortes.*"

31. Of course, as Gamble notes with regard to Augustine's bibliomancy in this passage, "There was nothing especially Christian in this practice except the books from which omens were sought. Greeks were well acquainted with the *sortes Homericae*, and Romans with the *sortes Vergilianae*. . . . Bibliomancy was also practiced by Jews—and thus we have *sortes Biblicae*." *Books and Readers*, 239–40.

32. In an introduction to a recent collection of essays addressing technologies of cultural production, Jeffrey Masten, Peter Stallybrass, and Nancy Vickers suggest that "the codex . . . is a radical subversion of the technology of the scroll. The scroll, so central to Judaism, is a technology that depends upon a literal unwinding in which the physical proximity of one moment in the narrative to another is both materially and symbolically

significant. One cannot move easily back and forth between distant points on a scroll. But it is precisely such movement back and forth that the codex permits and encourages." *Language Machines*, 3. Stallybrass elaborates upon this premise brilliantly in "Books and Scrolls."

33. Observing the long history correlating the forefinger or pointing finger (Latin *index*) with the marking up of texts, Stallybrass contends that "the history of the hand in relation to the book is above all the history of the index (in the multiple senses of that word)." "Navigating the Book," 4. Also see William Sherman's work on the "manicule," the marginal pointing finger prevalent in manuscripts and printed books from the Middle Ages to the early modern period: "Toward a History of the Manicule."

34. In a discussion of Augustine's conversion in the *Confessions*, Geoffrey Halt Harpham contends that the referential movement of language mirrors the turning toward transcendence of conversion. See "The Fertile Word," 239.

35. As Jesse Gellrich notes, "The frustration of linguistic distraction, compared throughout the early books of the *Confessions* to the seductions of the flesh, is relentless until Augustine meets Ambrose, who teaches him how to read the Scriptures figuratively for their moral and anagogical truth. This kind of reading, an ability to see beyond the material appearance of letters to their sources of meaning, is figured for Augustine in Ambrose's 'silent reading.'" *Idea of the Book*, 117.

36. Cummings, *Grammar and Grace*, 60.

37. *LW* 34:336–37. *WA* 54:185–86.

38. Martin Luther, "Letter to Nicholaus Hausmann" (Nov. 17, 1527), *WA Br* 4:282, 6–9. English translation from Oberman, *Luther*, 226.

39. Oberman, *Luther*, 226.

40. See note 21 above.

41. See Leclercq, *Love of Learning*, passim; Stock, *Implications of Literacy*, 403–54. For a comparison of the meditative practices of Luther and Gabriel Biel, see Oberman, *Dawn of the Reformation*, 104–25.

42. *LW* 34:285. *WA* 50:658–59. *Lectio, meditatio,* and *tentatio* appear in Latin in Luther's German original.

43. *LW* 34:285. *WA* 50:659.

44. *LW* 34:286. *WA* 50:659.

45. *LW* 34:286–87. *WA* 50:660. As I mentioned briefly in Chapter 2, Luther's *Table Talk* records a conversation in which he explains that true theology is the fruit of such spiritual struggle: "I didn't learn my theology all at once. I had to ponder over it ever more deeply, and my spiritual trials [*tentationes*] were of help to me in this, for one does not learn anything without practice. This is what the spiritualists [*schwärmer*] and sects lack. They don't have the right adversary, the devil. He would teach them well." *LW* 54:50. *WA TR* 1:146 (#352).

46. The concepts of *opus alienum* and *anfechtung* have been written about extensively in Luther scholarship. I am particularly indebted to McGrath, *Theology of the Cross*, 151–58, 161–68, 169–75. See also Steinmetz, *Luther in Context*, 1–11, 23–31; and Oberman, *Luther*, passim.

47. *LW* 11:37. *WA* 3:549. This seems to be Luther's version of *compunctio*, the piercing or pricking that turns one away from sin and toward God. As Leclercq writes, "Compunction is an act of God in us. . . . God goads us as if with a spear; He 'presses' us with insistence (com-pungere), as if to pierce us." *Love of Learning*, 30.

48. Marlowe, *Doctor Faustus A-text*, 1.1.1–6. Subsequent citations from *Doctor Faustus* refer to this edition and will be cited in the text.

49. Ibid., 109.

50. As Edward Snow argues in a classic essay, "'disputing well' . . . is the 'end' (finis) of logic in the sense of final cause, abiding concern, reason for being: one is always in the midst of logic, once one has achieved its end. Yet Faustus seems instinctively to assume that having 'attained' this end means that he has arrived at the end of it, used it up, finished with it—and that as a result there is nothing to do but move on to something new." "Marlowe's *Doctor Faustus*," 78.

51. See Collinson's "Coherence of the Text" for a discussion of Protestant claims for the unity and coherence of scripture. Also see Coolidge, *Pauline Renaissance in England*.

52. *LW* 1:107–109. *WA* 42:81–82.

53. Thanks to Elizabeth Leedham-Green's catalogue of books in Cambridge inventories, we know that editions of both Augustine's and Luther's *Works* could be found at Cambridge when Marlowe was a student of divinity. See Leedham-Green, *Books in Cambridge Inventories*, 2:60–61, 2:509.

54. For a discussion of the error of reification in Reformation thought, see Chapter 2.

55. In the B-text Mephistopheles suggests that he has, in this crucial moment, directed Faustus's eye and manipulated the matter of the book: "I do confess it, Faustus, and rejoice. / 'Twas I that, when thou wert i'the way to heaven, / Dammed up thy passage. When thou took'st the book / To view the Scriptures, then I turned the leaves / And led thine eye." Marlowe, *Doctor Faustus B-text*, 5.2.97–101. By damming up the passage, he damns Faustus. By turning the leaves and averting the eye, Mephistopheles turns Faustus away from saving grace and toward a fatal justice. In the A-text we have no such demonic intervention; rather, we have what appears to be reading in the absence of divine grace.

56. Weil, *Christopher Marlowe*, 57.

57. The printer was the Huguenot Thomas Vautrollier, and the texts he printed included a collection of sermons, a commentary on certain psalms, a *Right comfortable treatise . . . containing fourteene pointes of consolation*, and *Commentarie . . . [on] Galathians*. Apart from the various translations of Luther that appeared in the prefaces to Tyndale's English versions of scripture, Luther's *Commentarie* on Galatians was one of the few extended articulations of Lutheran theology to be translated into English in the sixteenth and seventeenth centuries. Luther claimed an especial affinity with the Epistle ("The Epistle to the Galatians . . . is my epistle, to which I am betrothed. It is my Katie von Bora") and thought his exposition of it one of his most important works. *LW* 26:ix.

58. Collinson, "William Tyndale," 74.

59. Luther, *Commentarie . . . [on] Galathians*, AiiiR.

60. "And Saul arose from the grounde, and opened his eyes, *but* sawe no man. Then led they him by the hand, and broght him into Damascus, Where he was three dayes without sight, and nether ate nor dranke." Acts 9:8–9, Geneva Bible (1560), fol. 58v.

61. *Commentarie . . . [on] Galathians*, fol. 262v.

62. As he writes in his lectures on the Psalms, "It is by living—no, rather, by dying and being damned—that a theologian is made, not by understanding, reading or speculating." *WA* 5, 163.28. English translation from Gerris, "To the Unknown God," 269.

63. It is important to remember that this vision of the Bible as a single text, complete and self-sufficient, would have been alien to most Christians prior to the Reformation. For most of Christian history before Luther, single-volume Bibles and even single-volume testaments were uncommon in any language and rare for the cleric as well as the layman. David Lawton reminds us both that "Bible" is a bastardization of a term that is plural in the original Greek, and that this plural form "reflects most medieval experience." As Lawton contends, for the medieval reader who only ever reads or hears a fragment of scripture there is not only "no evident sense of privation, of the parts as somehow lacking the integrity of the whole," but there is also "little or no sense that the Bible, even if seen as single or whole, should necessarily stand alone and self-sufficient." "Englishing the Bible," 455, 457. John Milbank provocatively suggests that "the Bible as one continuous, primarily written, and initially naked, uncommented-upon text was invented by printing, humanism, and the Reformation." "Review of *Biblical Hermeneutics in Historical Perspective*," 666.

64. *LW* 34:337. *WA* 54:186.

65. For Luther's "Preface to the Epistle of James," see *LW* 35:395–97. *WA DB* 7:385–87.

66. For a nuanced and provocative discussion of the teleological thrust of interpretation in early modern hermeneutics, see Hawkes, *Idols of the Marketplace*. Hawkes observes that in early modern England, idolatry is often conceived of as "a violation of natural teleology," "a confusion of ends and means," a confusion that results in what we might call "objectification." *Idols*, 4–5.

67. For a discussion of this Augustinian hermeneutic, see Chapter 2.

68. As Miri Rubin describes it, "Using the metaphor of a legal document, the promise made by Christ's suffering body was inscribed on a parchment, the undertaking to be renewed and to offer redemption. The Charter establishes an exchange of Christ's sacrificed body which brought the hope of redemption for Man's love. It is a document inscribed on the crucified body, with the wounds as its script." *Corpus Christi*, 306.

69. Galloway, "*Doctor Faustus* and the Charter of Christ," 36–37.

70. For a comprehensive study of the Charter, see Spalding, *Middle English Charters of Christ*.

71. *Historie of the Damnable* (1592), 6–8. See Clarkson and Warren, *Law of Property*, 182; and Wilson, *Theaters of Intention*, 208.

72. Gallagher, "Faustus's Blood," 7. Also see Clarkson and Warren, *Law of Property*, 181, n. 5.

73. See Chapter 2.

74. Dessen and Thomson, *Dictionary*, 189.

75. Steiner, *Documentary Culture*.

76. See Resnick, "The Codex in Early Jewish and Christian Communities," and Stallybrass, "Books and Scrolls."

77. Wilson, *Theaters of Intention*, 207.

78. For a discussion of performative language in *Doctor Faustus*, see D. Gates, "Unpardonable Sins."

79. Wilson, *Theaters of Intention*, 209.

80. Caxton's translation. Voragine, *Golden Legend*, 3:19.

81. See Chapter 1 for the transcendence of the letter. At the death of Clare of Montefalco, it was discovered that her heart was incised with the "insignia of the Passion." See Jager, *Book of the Heart*, 94; and Bynum, *Holy Feast*, 211.

82. All quotes from Caxton's translation. Voragine, *Golden Legend*, 5:223.

83. Puccini, *St. Mary Magdalene of Pazzi*, 58–59. The work was translated into English by Thomas Smith and printed in 1687. The English translation was published with a mocking preface "To the sober and understanding Reader, of what Perswasion or Communion soever." The stated purpose of publishing this translation of the hagiography was "to give just caution against being transported beyond the bounds of true Christian piety, and good sense, by the delusions of an over-heated imagination." *St. Mary Magdalene of Pazzi*, 3.

84. See Walker, "The Cessation of Miracles." I cite here late sixteenth- and early seventeenth-century Counter-Reformation thinkers, but the charge that Reformers lacked the authenticating miracles of Catholicism had been around from the beginning. For an inventory of pre-Tridentine Catholic writings against the Reformation, see Tavard, "Catholic Reform in the Sixteenth Century."

85. See Walsham, *Providence in Early Modern England*, and Walker, "Cessation of Miracles." Edward Dering suggests that since signs and wonders are no longer necessary, the miracles that the unenlightened claim to see are the "illusions of Sathan, whose ende is superstition." The main purveyor of superstition in this age is, of course, the Catholic Church. Dering, *XXVII Lectures* (1590), 114, 116.

86. Calvin, *Institution of Christian Religion* (1587), 4.19.18, fol. 490r.

87. In his *Commentary on Galatians*, Luther makes reference to the legend of Francis's marked skin in his discussion of the stigmata that Paul claims to bear on his flesh. For Luther, the stigmata of Francis "is a pure fiction and a joke." *LW* 27:142. *WA* 40 (2):181. Curiously, Luther's discussion of Francis's stigmata is not reproduced in the sixteenth-century English translation of the *Commentary*. In Luther's reading, Paul was speaking not literally of an inscription in the flesh but metaphorically of the ways in which his body and spirit have been marked by suffering because of his devotion: "The stripes and sufferings therefore which he did beare in his body, he calleth markes: as also the anguish and terrour of spirit he calleth the fierie darts of the Deuill. . . . These be the true markes and imprynted signes, of which the Apostle speaketh in this place. The which

we also at this day by the grace of God beare in our bodies for Christes cause." Paul's "stigmata" here become emblematic of Luther's *anfechtung*. *Commentarie . . . [on] Galathians*, fols. 295r–295v.

88. Most, *Doubting Thomas*, 145.

89. Calvin, *Commentarie*, 449, 451, in *A Harmonie vpon the Three Evangelists* (1584).

90. See Walsham, *Providence in Early Modern England*; Lake and Questier, *Antichrist's Lewd Hat*.

91. *Historie of the Damnable* (1592), 7.

92. Augustine, *On Christian Doctrine*, 2.23.35–36.

93. Luther insists, however, that he "would not have wanted to shy away from him [Faustus]. I would have stretched out my hand to him in the name of the Lord, God being my protector, for I believe that many poisons were prepared to harm me." *LW* 54:241. *WA TR* 3:445 (#3601).

94. Walsham, *Providence in Early Modern England*, 229–30.

95. Here, I follow the original sequence of the A-text. Bevington and Rasmussen move a comic scene with Robin and Rafe here, inserting it between the discussion of the encyclopedic book and the discussion of the heavens. For their rationale, see their Appendix, 287–88. Obviously, I think this should be read as one continuous scene.

96. Foxe, *Actes and Monuments* (1563), 468.

97. Ibid.

98. "Many also of them which vsed curious artes, broght their bokes, and burned them before all men." Acts 19:19, Geneva Bible (1560), fol. 64v.

CHAPTER 4. BOOK, TRINKET, FETISH

1. William Shakespeare, *The Tempest*, ed. Stephen Orgel, 1.2.73. Subsequent citations from *The Tempest* refer to this edition and will be cited in the text.

2. In a fascinating essay, Barbara Mowat attempts to track down the kind of book Shakespeare's audience might have been expected to imagine, focusing on the *grimoire*, a magic manuscript used for conjuring. See "Prospero's Book." For a discussion of the place of the book in the "dialectic of seen and unseen" in *The Tempest*, see Dawson, *Culture of Playgoing*, 155–58.

3. None more inventively than Peter Greenaway's film *Prospero's Books* (Miramax, 1991). Greenaway presents a cornucopia of texts, magical and humanist, scientific and fantastic, to represent the eponymous volumes of his film. In Greenaway's vision, Prospero's books include *The Book of Water*, *A Book of Mirrors*, *A Book of Mythologies*, *A Primer of the Small Stars*, *An Atlas Belonging to Orpheus*, *A Harsh Book of Geometry*, *The Book of Colours*, *An Anatomy of Birth*, *An Alphabetical Inventory of the Dead*, *A Book of Travellers' Tales*, *The Book of the Earth*, *A Book of Architecture and Other Music*, *The Ninety-Two Conceits of the Minotaur*, *The Book of Languages*, *End Plants*, *A Book of Love*, *A Bestiary of Past, Present and Future Animals*, *The Book of Utopias*, *The Book of Universal Cosmography*, *Love of Ruins*, *The Autobiographies of Pasiphae and Semiramis*, *A Book of Motion*, *The Book*

of Games, and *Thirty-Six Plays*. Greenaway's books not only celebrate the early modern fascination with catalogues but also suggest the kind of humanist and esoteric learning that would create both a Prospero and *The Tempest*. One of the most stimulating of Greenaway's interventions in the text of *The Tempest*, this catalogue of books satisfies a need to fill in the gaps in Shakespeare's enigmatic play.

4. For an analysis of the relation of classical barbarism to early modern conceptions of Africa and Africans, see Ian Smith, "Barbarian Errors."

5. The relationship of *The Tempest* to the New World and to the European project of colonization and conquest has long been a source of dispute. For influential readings of the play that address its relationship to European imperialism, see Mannoni, *Prospero and Caliban*; Lamming, "A Monster"; Césaire, *A Tempest*; Retamar, "Caliban"; Paul Brown, "'This Thing of Darkness I Acknowledge Mine'"; Barker and Hulme, "Nymphs and Reapers Heavily Vanish"; Hulme, "Prospero and Caliban," in *Colonial Encounters*; Greenblatt, "Martial Law" in *Shakespearean Negotiations* and "Learning to Curse" in *Learning to Curse*. Scholars like David Scott Kastan, Meredith Ann Skura, and Richard Wilson have challenged postcolonial readings of *The Tempest* by suggesting that the "success in relocating *The Tempest* in Virginia has transported it too far from Virgil, and the Old World of Aeneas where its action is set." Wilson, "Voyage to Tunis," 333. Asserting the primacy of Mediterranean realpolitik and European dynastic concerns over European colonial activities and American plantation, such criticism resists "the Americanization of *The Tempest*" as "itself an act of cultural imperialism" that obscures the true literary pretexts and historical context of Shakespeare's play. Kastan, *Shakespeare After Theory*, 95. And certainly there's a salutary point here. Postwar criticism of *The Tempest* has tended to ignore the classical Virgilian and Ovidian echoes in favor of Virginia Company pamphlets and Strachey's report of the "still-vex'd Bermoothes." But this critique of American or colonialist readings obscures the fact that the Mediterranean was also an arena in which imperialist concerns were operative, a multicultural space where dominion was crucially at stake. Lest we err on the side of overcorrection, I suggest we hold fast to Jerry Brotton's measured admonition that "*The Tempest* is much more of a politically and geographically bifurcated play in the negotiation between its Mediterranean and Atlantic contexts than critics have recently been prepared to concede." "This Tunis, Sir," 24. I want to borrow Brotton's bifurcated critical lens to suggest that the play's deliberate geographic indeterminacy is both an aspect of *The Tempest*'s remarkable syncretism of sources and contexts, and the means by which the play examines the relation of Christian Europe to its various "others." For attempts to reorient the play toward the Mediterranean and Africa, see Ian Smith, "'When We Were Capital'"; Hess, "The Mediterranean and Shakespeare's Geopolitical Imagination."

6. Atkins, *Voyage to Guinea*, 84.

7. "Africa . . . is no historical part of the World; it has no movement or development to exhibit." Hegel divides Africa into three parts: European Africa (the coastal area north of the Sahara desert), Asian Africa (the Nile River valley), and Africa proper, the rest of the continent south of the Sahara. It is Africa proper that is outside of history: "historical

movements" in the continent, "that is in its northern part—belong to the Asiatic or European World." *Philosophy of History*, 99. Subsequent citations refer to this edition and are cited in the text. For the German original of this section of *Philosophy of History*, see Hegel, *Werke*, 12:120–29.

8. In Hegel's view, this objectification of the human may be the only way out of "the land of childhood." Indeed, he argues that "slavery is itself a phase of advance from the merely isolated sensual existence—a phase of education—a mode of becoming participant in a higher morality and the culture connected with it. Slavery is in and for itself *injustice*, for the essence of humanity is *Freedom*; but for this man must be matured. The gradual abolition of slavery is therefore wiser and more equitable than its sudden removal" (99). For Hegel, only the injustice of being treated as a thing, only the absolute loss of freedom will enable Africans to escape the "dark mantle of Night" and join human history.

9. Pietz, "Problem of the Fetish, I," 5. "Problem of the Fetish" consists of a series of three articles published in *Res*. See also Pietz's "Fetishism and Materialism."

10. Pietz, "Problem of the Fetish, II," 37. Subsequent citations of Pietz refer to "Problem of the Fetish, II" unless otherwise noted and are cited in the text.

11. Bosman, *New and Accurate Description, 154.*

12. I discuss the Reformation understanding of grace as radically free in Chapter 2.

13. Marees, "A description and historicall declaration of the golden Kingdome of Guinea," in Purchas, *Purchas his Pilgrimage* (1613), 941. Subsequent citations from Marees' tract refer to this edition of Purchas and are cited in the text.

14. Knapp, *An Empire Nowhere,* 145. Although my project approaches the problem of the object and value in early modern England from a different perspective, I am indebted to Knapp's provocative discussion of the "trifle."

15. Harriot, *Briefe and True Report,* 25, 45. Knapp suggests that Harriot may have been "regarded as England's resident authority on the subject of Indians misvaluing things." *An Empire Nowhere*, 304, n. 26.

16. Peckham, *True Report,* F2r–F2v.

17. Ibid., E3r.

18. Bacon, *Essayes* (1625), 108.

19. As Pietz writes, "The fetish is precisely *not* a material signifier referring beyond itself" ("Problem, I" 15).

20. Shakespeare, *The Winter's Tale,* 4.4.595–602.

21. Kaula, "Autolycus' Trumpery," 280. In addition to Shakespeare, Spenser, and Milton, Kaula finds these terms used in the following texts: Jan van der Noot's *A theatre . . . of voluptuous worldlings*, tr. T. Roest (1569); William Tedder's *The recantations as they were seuerallie pronounced by Wylliam Tedder and Anthony Tyrell* (1588); John Mayo's *The popes parliament* (1591); Francis Bunny's *A comparison betweene the auncient fayth of the Romans, and the new Romish religion* (1595); George Gifford's *Sermons vpon the whole booke of the Revelation* (1596); John Racster's *William Alabasters seven motives* (1598); John Rhodes's *An answere to a Romish rime* (1602); George Downame's *A treatise concerning*

Antichrist (1603); Samuell Harsnett's *A declaration of egregious popish impostures* (1603); Jean Chassanion's *The merchandise of popish priests* (1604).

22. *OED,* s.v. "trinket."

23. Dr. John London to Sir Richard Rich, Reading, 17 Sept. 1538, in *Three Chapters of Letters,* ed. Wright, 224.

24. Hilarie, *Resurrection of the Masse,* B8r.

25. For the "Homilie against perill of idolatrie," see *Certaine Sermons.*

26. Foxe, *Actes and Monuments* (1610), 1178.

27. H. Smith, *Six Sermons,* C2v.

28. Foxe, *Actes and Monuments* (1610), 1275–77.

29. Ibid., 1274, 1276.

30. Kibbey, *The Interpretation of Material Shapes in Puritanism,* 42.

31. K. Thomas, *Religion and the Decline of Magic,* 58.

32. Quoted in ibid., 59.

33. Most editors observe, as Stephen Orgel does, that "Trinculo" "is related to Italian *trincare,* drink deeply, and *trincone,* a drunkard." Anthony M. Esolen points out that the name is also related to the Italian word for "bauble." "The Isles Shall Wait for His Law," 237.

34. Mignolo, "Literacy and Colonization," 77–78. Also see Mignolo's "Afterword: Writing and Recorded Knowledge" and *The Darker Side of the Renaissance.* In my thinking on literacy and colonization, I have been influenced by Brotherston, "Toward a Grammatology of America"; Cheyfitz, *Poetics of Imperialism*; Clifford, "On Ethnographic Allegory"; Harbsmeier, "Writing and the Other"; Warkentin, "In Search of 'The Word of the Other'"; and Wogan, "Perceptions of European Literacy."

35. Purchas, *Hakluytus Posthumus* (1905), 1.486.

36. Greenblatt, *Marvelous Possessions,* 10.

37. As Purchas writes, "For whereas God had giuen to man two Priuiledges and principall prerogatiues, whereof other creatures are no way capable, his inward *Reason,* and abilitie to vtter the same by Speech: this benefite of God in Nature was turned into a conspiracie against God and Nature." *Purchas his Pilgrimage* (1613), 40.

38. Purchas, *Hakluytus Posthumus* (1905), 1.486–87.

39. "They know nothing of writing, either sacred or secular; indeed, they have no kind of characters that signify anything at all. When I was first in their country, in order to learn their language I wrote a number of sentences which I then read aloud to them. Thinking that this was some kind of witchcraft, they said to each other, 'Is it not a marvel that this fellow, who yesterday could not have said a single word in our language, can now be understood by us, by virtue of that paper that he is holding and which makes him speak thus?'" Léry, *History of a Voyage to the Land of Brazil,* 134–35.

40. As Léry recounts it, the "savages" of the West Indies "no longer dared to lie to the Spaniards or steal from them" because they feared the Spaniards' ability keep them under surveillance: "The Indians, knowing that the Spaniards understood each other without seeing or speaking to each other but only by sending letters from place to place,

believed either that they had the spirit of prophecy, or that the missives spoke." *History of a Voyage*, 135.

41. Ibid., 135.

42. J. Smith, *Generall Historie of Virginia*, 47–48, G4r–G4v.

43. Defoe, *Essay Upon Literature*, 5–6, A3r–A3v. Emphasis in original.

44. In his *Key into the Language of America* (1643), Roger Williams discusses the native admiration for European technology, with a special emphasis on writing: "When [the Native Americans] talke amongst themselves of the English ships, and great buildings, of the plowing of their Fields, and especially of Bookes and Letters, they will end thus: Manittowock They are Gods" (126).

45. Defoe, *Essay Upon Literature*, 21, C3r.

46. Famously, the topos of the "talking book" was co-opted by writers of slave narratives and transformed into what Henry Louis Gates has brilliantly argued is one of the founding tropes of the slave narrative. Tracing the trope of the "talking book" through the slave narratives of Gronniosaw (1770), Marrant (1785), Cugoano (1787), Equiano (1789), and Jea (1815), Gates reads this recurrent anecdote as a crucial marker on the path to full humanity. By overcoming the characteristic error of the savage who believes the book speaks and becoming a literate subject who can negotiate words and things, the slave enters into the human fold on European terms. See H. Gates, "The Trope of the Talking Book," in *Signifying Monkey*, 127–69. The fact that the "talking book" in each of these narratives is a religious artifact, either a Bible or a prayer book, illustrates that the powerful ideological force of Enlightenment "literacy" is deeply imbricated with Christian thought.

47. Harriot, *Briefe and True Report*, 27.

48. Ibid., 27.

49. In a provocative reading of the relation of colonization to European conceptions of translation, Eric Cheyfitz suggests that a crucial aspect of the history of the European colonization of the Americas is the imposition of metaphorical ways of apprehending both language and the world on indigenous populations. See *Poetics of Imperialism*, especially chapter 6.

50. Taylor, "Prospero's Books and Stephano's Bottle," 113.

51. de Grazia, "*The Tempest*," 255.

52. Shakespeare, *Second Part of Henry VI*, ed. Herschel Baker, 4.2.65. Subsequent citations from *2 Henry VI* refer to this edition and are cited in the text.

53. 1 Corinthians 7:20: "Let euerie man abide in the same vocation wherein he was called." Geneva Bible (1560).

54. Leviticus 26:8. Geneva Bible (1560).

55. For discussions of writing as a sign of sin and death, see the Introduction and Chapter 1.

56. Montaigne, "Of Cannibals," in *The Essayes,* 102. He writes that the indigenous peoples of the New World live in a state of ignorant bliss with regard to the effect of European culture upon them, since they cannot yet know "how deare the knowledge of our corruptions will one day cost their repose, securitie, and happinesse, and how their

ruine shall proceed from this commerce, which I imagine is alreadie advanced." "Of Cannibals," 106.

57. Ibid., 104.

58. Scholars have noted the ways in which Caliban's attempted crime and subsequent punishment echo the familiar racist and misogynist logic in which the virginal, white woman must be protected against the threat of the savage, non-European man. For readings that address the discourses of racism and misogyny evoked by Caliban's fall, see K. Hall, *Things of Darkness*, 141–45; and Loomba, *Gender, Race, Renaissance Drama*, 148–58. For readings that directly address the conflict between Caliban's desire for political agency and Miranda's rights to bodily integrity, see Singh, "Caliban Versus Miranda," and Slights, "Rape and the Romanticization of Shakespeare's Miranda."

59. My reading of this scene is indebted to Linton's analysis in *Romance of the New World*, 155. Also see Goldberg, "Print of Goodness," 236.

60. For the mechanical reproduction of printing as a metaphor for sexual reproduction, see de Grazia, "Imprints," and Wall, *Imprint of Gender*, especially 219–20, 279–80, 346–47.

61. Geneva Bible (1560), 1:14–18.

62. *LW* 1:45–46.

63. Lupton, "Creature Caliban," 9. As Denise Albanese notes, Prospero "uses natural categories to implicate the monster in the coercive Great Chain of Being, and by extension into the social order validated by the natural one." *New Science, New World*, 77.

64. Lévi-Strauss, "A Writing Lesson," *Tristes Tropiques*. Subsequent citations refer to this edition and are cited in the text.

65. Unlike *2 Henry VI*, *The Tempest* does not employ the rhetoric of book-burning to comic effect. The comedy of the attempted rebellion arises not from Caliban's insistence that the rebels burn Prospero's books but from the clowns' failure to do so.

66. As I argued in "Book and the Fetish." My thinking on this subject has obviously changed somewhat.

67. On Prospero's similarity to Sycorax, see de Grazia, "*The Tempest*."

68. This is a repetition of a previous threat: "For this be sure tonight thou shalt have cramps, / Side-stitches that shall pen thy breath up. Urchins / Shall, for that vast of night that they may work, / All exercise on thee. Thou shalt be pinched / As thick as honeycomb, each pinch more stinging / Than bees that made 'em" (1.2.325–30).

69. For a reading of *The Tempest* as a register of early modern republicanism generally and a radical skepticism toward the claims of monarchy as natural specifically, see Norbrook's excellent "'What Cares these Roarers for the Name of King?'"

70. *OED*, s.v. "liberal."

71. See Orgel's note on this line in his edition of *The Tempest*, 1.2.73.

72. *The Tempest*, 5.1.319–21. K. Thomas, *Religion and the Decline*, 641.

73. K. Thomas, *Religion and the Decline*, 640. While Thomas tends to adopt uncritically the Reformation understanding of such a distinction, it seems clear from his account

that by the seventeenth century, Protestants in early modern England had developed an entire system of thought that established the differences as they understood them. Indeed, as I have argued in this chapter, the language of "trinkets," "trifles," and "trumpery" was a vocabulary developed by Reformers to make just such distinctions.

74. And this is also a movement from Catholic immanence to Protestant transcendence. As Thomas writes, "Although our period ended with the triumph of religion over magic, it was religion with a difference" (640). For Thomas's contention that the medieval church helped foster the superstitious and irrational version of Christianity that he finds in popular medieval piety, see *Religion and the Decline*, 25–50.

75. For examples of this tradition, see Knight, *Crown of Life*, 252–53; and Curry, *Shakespeare's Philosophical Patterns*, 195–97. On Prospero as figure of transcendence generally, see Frye, *A Natural Perspective*, 150–59; Kermode's introduction to the Arden *Tempest*, especially xxiv–lxiii; and Still's *Timeless Theme*. For a deservedly influential critique of the sentimental reading of Prospero, see Berger's "Miraculous Harp."

76. For the scriptural precedent often cited in the early modern period, see Acts 19:19.

77. Orgel, "Tobacco and Boys," 569. For Orgel, "the worst that can be said about magic in the play is that it is in the end a retreat from reality and responsibility: that is why it must be renounced, not because it is damnable." "Tobacco and Boys," 569.

EPILOGUE

1. King James Version (1611).

2. For an extended reading of the frontispiece, see Burnett, *The Engraved Title-Page of Bacon's* Instauratio Magna.

3. *OED*, s.v. "ne plus ultra."

4. Both the Italian and the English translation are from Pinsky's parallel text edition, *The Inferno of Dante*, 221–24.

5. He reiterates this idea in *The Advancement of Learning* and *The New Organon*. See Bacon, *Works*, 3:340, 4:92. Also see *Works*, 4:311–12.

6. Bacon, *Works*, 3:220–21.

7. Most famously in Horkheimer and Adorno's devastating critique of Enlightenment rationality. See *Dialectic of Enlightenment*, especially 3–7.

8. For a recent articulation of the claim that Bacon is indifferent or hostile to Christianity, see Paterson, "On the Role of Christianity." For the claim that Bacon's natural philosophy is grounded in religious conviction, see McKnight, *Religious Foundations of Francis Bacon's Thought*. Briggs, Brooke, and Whitney offer nicely nuanced accounts of the relation of religion to natural philosophy in Bacon's thought; see Briggs, "Bacon's Science and Religion"; Brooke, *Science and Religion*, especially 52–81; and Whitney, *Francis Bacon and Modernity*. On the long history of Bacon's reception, see Rossi, "Baconianism"; and Pérez-Ramos, "Bacon's Legacy."

9. In our fascination with Bacon the man, we sometimes lose sight of Bacon as

an insightful analyst of contemporary history and his position within it. If Bacon looks proleptically modern from the perspective of the modern world, he consistently claimed that the problems with which he wrestled emerged from the age in which he lived.

10. On the use of this metaphor by a variety of natural philosophers, see Harrison, *Bible, Protestantism, and the Rise of Natural Science*, 193–204.

11. Bacon, *Two Bookes of Francis Bacon*, H4v.

12. On the "idols of the mind," see *Novum Organum* in Bacon, *Works,* 4:53–70. Also see *Works,* 4:428–34. For discussions of the relation of seventeenth-century natural philosophy to the Christian doctrine of the fall of man, see Picciotto, "Reforming the Garden"; and Harrison, "Original Sin."

13. Bacon, *Two Bookes*, B3r.

14. Bacon, *Works,* 3:127. Subsequent citations from *New Atlantis* refer to this edition and will be cited in the text.

15. David Renaker ingeniously suggests that the appearance of the miracle in the middle of the sea gets around the problem of the institutionalization of the miraculous site. At sea there can be no shrine: "No shrine, no pilgrimage; hence no temptation of a resident priesthood or monastic community to exploit the curiosity and credulity of pilgrims with sacred relics more or less authentic. . . . Simply by locating his miracle one mile offshore, Bacon has obviated millennia of superstitious practices." Renaker, "Miracle of Engineering," 188.

16. For a discussion of these controversies in relation to *New Atlantis*, see Renaker, "Miracle of Engineering."

17. In Bacon's later Latin version of *New Atlantis*, the miraculous book is referred to as *liber* (book), which does not help us distinguish between scroll and codex.

18. Moreover, the "wise man" of Solomon's House opens the ark to find "*a* Book and a Letter," rather than a collection of documents. Given that this miraculous book contains "all the canonical books of the Old and New Testament . . . and the Apocalypse . . . and some other books of the New Testament which were not at that time written," it would seem that a large manuscript codex is being described.

19. See Stallybrass, Chartier, Mowery, and Wolfe, "Hamlet's Tables."

20. Although "there is evidence for associating writing tables with merchants, tables were undoubtedly bought by a wide range of other people at a wide range of prices. . . . If the owners of writing tables varied, so did the uses to which tables were put. The blank leaves assumed the purchaser's ability to write, but surviving copies suggest that at least some owners (and/or their children) used table-books as suitable places in which to learn how to write. Tables were also used for collecting pieces of poetry, noteworthy epigrams, and new words; recording sermons, legal proceedings, or parliamentary debates; jotting down conversations, recipes, cures, and jokes; keeping financial records; recalling addresses and meetings; and collecting notes on foreign customs while traveling." Stallybrass et al., "Hamlet's Tables," 401–3.

21. Ibid., 386.

22. Ibid., 390.

23. Institutions like "Salomon's House" and the "College of the Six Days' Works" seem to predate the conversion of Bensalem to Christianity, suggesting a relation to Judaism independent of European Christianity's relation to Judaism.

24. Although Bacon offers very little evidence to suggest the ways in which texts were produced and disseminated in Bensalem, on two different occasions *New Atlantis* includes references to the invention of new kinds of paper. When the Father of Salomon's House details the technological advances of Bensalem, he says, "We have also divers mechanical arts, which you have not; and stuffs made by them; as papers . . . [etc.]." The list of desired inventions or discoveries appended to the end of *New Atlantis* includes the following entry: "Making new threads for apparel; and new stuffs; such as paper, glass, &c." Bacon, *Works*, 3:161, 168.

25. As Simon Wortham notes, the "revelation of the 'Book'" is "presented as being instantaneously and transcendentally complete." And in this transcendental completion, "the labour and temporality of writing . . . appears to have been concealed or repressed, within the fetishised spectacle of a spontaneous text, both unique and fully finished." Wortham, "Censorship and the Institution of Knowledge," 193.

26. DeCook, "Ark and Immediate Revelation," 116.

27. *CWE* 39:251.

28. See Leslie, *Renaissance Utopias and the Problem of History*, 81–118; and C. Kendrick, *Utopia, Carnival, and Commonwealth in Renaissance England*, 288–331. While my understanding of how eschatology functions in *New Atlantis* differs from both Leslie's and Kendrick's, I am indebted to their excellent essays.

29. See, for instance, the recent collection of essays edited by Force and Popkin, *The Millenarian Turn*; Jacob, "Millenarianism and Science"; Robert Merton, *Science, Technology, and Society*; and Webster, *Great Instauration*.

30. See Whitney, *Bacon and Modernity*, especially 23–54.

31. For an overview of the subject, David Katz, *Philo-Semitism*. Also see Hill, "'Till the conversion of the jews.'"

32. On Christian universalism, see Introduction, page 36–37.

33. Cohen, *Living Letters*.

34. Daniel 12:4, King James Version.

35. Marginal note to Daniel 12:4, Geneva Bible (1560).

36. Ibid.

37. Jerry Weinberger discusses this possibility in his essay, "On the Miracles in Bacon's *New Atlantis*."

38. Cowley, *Works*, 1:167–69, stanza 5.

BIBLIOGRAPHY

Ainsworth, Henry. *A Defence of the Holy Scriptures*. Amsterdam: Giles Thorp, 1609.

Albanese, Denise. *New Science, New World*. Durham: Duke University Press, 1996.

Alighieri, Dante. *The Inferno of Dante: A New Verse Translation*. Translated by Robert Pinsky. New York: Farrar, Straus and Giroux, 1994.

Ambrose. "Letters." In *Fathers of the Church*. Translated by Mary Beyenka, 26. Washington, D.C.: Catholic University of America Press, 1954.

Andersen, Jennifer, and Elizabeth Sauer, eds. *Books and Readers in Early Modern England: Material Studies*. Philadelphia: University of Pennsylvania Press, 2002.

Anderson, Judith H. *Words that Matter: Linguistic Perception in Renaissance English*. Stanford: Stanford University Press, 1996.

Aquinas, Thomas. *Summa Theologiae*. Blackfriars edition. 60 vols. London: Eyre and Spottiswoode, 1964–75.

Aston, Margaret. *England's Iconoclasts*. Oxford: Clarendon Press, 1988.

———. *The King's Bedpost: Reformation and Iconography in a Tudor Group Portrait*. Cambridge: Cambridge University Press, 1993.

———. *Lollards and Reformers: Images and Literacy in Late Medieval Religion*. London: Hambledon Press, 1984.

Atkins, John. *A Voyage to Guinea, Brazil, and the West-Indies; In His Majesty's Ships the Swallow and Weymouth*. London: Ward and Chandler, 1737.

Auerbach, Erich. "Figura." In *Scenes from the Drama of European Literature,* edited by Robert Marcellus Browning, 11–76. 1959. Gloucester, Mass.: Meridian, 1973.

Augustijn, Cornelis. *Erasmus: His Life, Works and Influence*. 1986. Translated by J. C. Grayson. Toronto: University of Toronto Press, 1991.

Augustine. *Confessiones*. Edited by L. Verheijen. Turnhout: Brepols, 1981.

———. *The Confessions*. Translated by Henry Chadwick. Oxford: Oxford University Press, 1991.

———. *On Christian Doctrine*. Translated by D. W. Robertson, Jr. New York: Liberal Arts Press, 1958.

———. *The Works of Saint Augustine*. Edited by John Rotelle. New York: New York City Press, 1992.

Bacon, Francis. *The Essaies of Sr Francis Bacon Knight*. London: John Beale, 1612.

————. *The Essayes or Counsels, Ciuill and Morall*. London: Haviland, 1625.

————. *The Two Bookes of Francis Bacon. Of the Proficience and Aduancement of Learning, Diuine and Humane*. London: Henrie Tomes, 1605.

————. *The Works of Francis Bacon*. Edited by James Spedding. 14 vols. London: Longman, 1857–74.

Bale, John. *Apology . . . agaynste a ranke Papyst*. London: Mierdman, 1550.

————. *Image of Both Churches*. London: East, 1580.

————. *The laboryouse iourney [and] serche of Iohan Leylande, for Englandes antiquitees*. London: S. Mierdman, 1549.

————. *The lattre examinacyon of Anne Askewe latelye martyred in Smythfelde*. Wesel: D. van der Straten, 1547.

Barker, Francis, and Peter Hulme. "Nymphs and Reapers Heavily Vanish: The Discursive Con-Texts of *The Tempest*." In *Alternative Shakespeares*, edited by John Drakakis, 191–205. New York: Methuen, 1985.

Barnard, John, and D. F. McKenzie, eds. *The Cambridge History of the Book in Britain*. Vol. 4: *1557–1695*. Cambridge: Cambridge University Press, 2002.

Bateman, Stephen. *A christall glasse of christian reformation, wherein the godly maye beholde the coloured abuses vsed in this our present tyme*. London: Day, 1569.

Beal, Peter. *In Praise of Scribes: Manuscripts and Their Makers in Seventeenth-Century England*. Oxford: Clarendon Press, 1998.

Beauregard, David N. "New Light on Shakespeare's Catholicism: Prospero's Epilogue in *The Tempest*." *Renascence: Essays on Value in Literature* 49, no. 3 (1997): 158–74.

Beckwith, Sarah. *Christ's Body: Identity, Culture, and Society in Late Medieval Writings*. London: Routledge, 1993.

Bentley, Jerry. *Humanists and Holy Writ: New Testament Scholarship in the Renaissance*. Princeton: Princeton University Press, 1983.

Berger, Harry. "Miraculous Harp: A Reading of Shakespeare's *Tempest*." *Shakespeare Survey* 5 (1969): 253–83.

Bible. *Biblia Complutensis*. Rome: Gregorian University Press, 1984.

————. Geneva Bible of 1560. *The Bible and Holy Scriptvres conteyned in the Olde and Newe Testament*. Geneva: Rouland Hall, 1560.

————. The Great Bible. 2nd edition. "Cranmer's Bible." *The Byble in English, that is to saye the content of al the holy scrypture . . .* London: Whytchurche, 1540.

————. The King James or Authorized Translation. *The Holy Bible*. London, 1611.

Blair, Ann. "Reading Strategies for Coping with Information Overload ca. 1550–1700." *Journal of the History of Ideas* (2003): 11–28.

Bosman, Willem. *A New and Accurate Description of the Coast of Guinea*. London: Knapton and Midwinter, 1705.

Boyarin, Daniel. *A Radical Jew: Paul and the Politics of Identity*. Berkeley: University of California Press, 1994.

Boyle, Marjorie O'Rourke. *Erasmus on Language and Method in Theology*. Toronto: University of Toronto Press, 1977.

Briggs, John. "Bacon's Science and Religion." In *Cambridge Companion to Bacon*, edited by Markku Peltonen, 172–99. Cambridge: Cambridge University Press, 1996.

Bromiley, G. W. *Zwingli and Bullinger*. Philadelphia: Westminster Press, 1953.

Brooke, John. *Science and Religion: Some Historical Perspectives*. Cambridge: Cambridge University Press, 1991.

Brooks, Douglas A. *From Playhouse to Printing House: Drama and Authorship in Early Modern England*. Cambridge: Cambridge University Press, 2000.

Brotherston, Gordon. "Towards a Grammatology of America: Lévi-Strauss, Derrida and the Native New World Text." In *Literature, Politics and Theory*, edited by Francis Barker, Peter Hulme, Margaret Iversen, and Diane Loxley, 190–209. New York: Methuen, 1986.

Brotton, Jerry. "'This Tunis, Sir, Was Carthage': Contesting Colonialism in *The Tempest*." In *Post-Colonial Shakespeares,* edited by Ania Loomba and Martin Orkin, 23–42. London: Routledge, 1998.

Brown, Paul. "'This Thing of Darkness I Acknowledge Mine': *The Tempest* and the Discourse of Colonialism." In *Political Shakespeare: New Essays in Cultural Materialism*, edited by Jonathan Dollimore and Alan Sinfield, 48–71. Manchester: Manchester University Press, 1985.

Brown, Peter. *The Cult of the Saints: Its Rise and Function in Latin Christianity*. Chicago: University of Chicago Press, 1981.

Bruster, Douglas. "The New Materialism in Renaissance Studies." In *Material Culture and Cultural Materialisms in the Middle Ages and Renaissance*, edited by Curtis Perry, 225–38. Turnhout: Brepols, 2001.

Burke, Peter. *Popular Culture in Early Modern Europe*. London: Temple Smith, 1978.

Burnett, A. D. *The Engraved Title-Page of Bacon's* Instauratio Magna. The Durham Harriot Seminar Occasional Paper 27. Durham: Thomas Harriot Seminar, 1998.

Bynum, Caroline Walker. *Holy Feast and Holy Fast: The Religious Significance of Food to Medieval Women*. Berkeley: University of California Press, 1987.

Calvin, John. *A Harmonie vpon the Three Euangelists . . . Translated by "E.P."* London: Bishop, 1584.

———. *The Institution of Christian Religion*. Translated by Thomas Norton. London: H. Middleton, 1587.

———. "Sermon upon the Epistle to Timothy." *Sermons of M. John Caluin, on the Epistles of S. Paule to Timothie and Titus*. Translated by Lawrence Tomson. London: Middleton, 1579.

———. *The sermons of M. Iohn Caluin vpon the fifth booke of Moses called Deuteronomie*. London: Henry Middleton, 1583.

———. *Tracts and Treatises in Defense of the Reformed Faith*. Translated by Henry Beveridge. Grand Rapids, Mich.: Eerdmans, 1958.

Camille, Michael. *The Gothic Idol: Ideology and Image Making in Medieval Art*. Cambridge: Cambridge University Press, 1989.

Carruthers, Mary. *The Book of Memory: A Study of Memory in Medieval Culture*. Cambridge: Cambridge University Press, 1990.

Cave, Terence. *The Cornucopian Text: Problems of Writing in the French Renaissance.* Oxford: Clarendon, 1979.

Cervantes, Miguel de. *The History of the Valorous and Wittie Knight-Errant, Don-Quixote of the Mancha.* Translated by Thomas Shelton. London: William Stansby, 1612.

Césaire, Aimé. *A Tempest.* Translated by Richard Miller. New York: Ubu Repertory Theater, 1992.

Chartier, Roger. *The Order of Books.* Stanford: Stanford University Press, 1994.

Chartier, Roger, and Guglielmo Cavallo. *A History of Reading in the West.* Amherst: University of Massachusetts Press, 1999.

Chazelle, Celia. "Pictures, Books, and the Illiterate: Pope Gregory I's Letters to Serenus of Marseilles." *Word and Image* 6 (1990): 138–53.

Cheyfitz, Eric. *The Poetics of Imperialism: Translation and Colonization from The* Tempest *to Tarzan.* New York: Oxford University Press, 1991.

Christensen, Carl C. *Art and the Reformation in Germany.* Athens: Ohio University Press, 1979.

Church of England. *The Booke of common praier . . .* London: Jugge and Cawood, 1559.

———. *Certaine Sermons appoynted by the Quenes Maiesty . . .* London: Jugge and Cawood, 1563.

———. *Certayne Sermons appoynted by the Quenes Maiestie to be declared and read.* London: Richarde Iugge and Iohn Cawood, 1559.

———. *The seconde tome of homelyes . . . set out by the aucthoritie of the Quenes Maiestie.* London: Richard Iugge and Iohn Cawood, 1563.

Clarkson, Paul S., and Clyde T. Warren. *The Law of Property in Shakespeare and the Elizabethan Drama.* New York: Gordian Press, 1968.

Clebsch, William. *England's Earliest Protestants, 1520–1535.* New Haven: Yale University Press, 1964.

Clifford, James. "On Ethnographic Allegory." In *Writing Culture: The Poetics and Politics of Ethnography*, edited by James Clifford and George Marcus, 98–121. Berkeley: University of California Press, 1986.

Cohen, Jeremy. *Living Letters of the Law: Ideas of the Jew in Medieval Christianity.* Berkeley: University of California Press, 1999.

Collinson, Patrick. "The Coherence of the Text: How It Hangeth Together: The Bible in Reformation England." In *The Bible, The Reformation and the Church*, edited by W. P. Stephens, 84–108. Sheffield: Sheffield Academic Press, 1995.

———. "William Tyndale and the Course of the English Reformation." *Reformation* 1 (1996): 72–97.

Coolidge, John S. *The Pauline Renaissance in England: Puritanism and the Bible.* Oxford: Clarendon Press, 1970.

Cooper, Thomas. *Thesaurus linguae Romanae et Britannicae.* London: Henry Denham, 1578.

Council of Trent. *Canons and Decrees of the Council of Trent.* Translated by H. J. Schroeder. Rockford, Ill.: Tan Books, 1978.

————. *Concilium Tridentinum*. Edited by Societas Goerresiana. Freiburg im Briesgau: Herder, 1964.

Cowley, Abraham. *The Complete Works in Verse and Prose*. Edited by Alexander Grosart. 2 vols. New York: AMS Press, 1967.

Craig, Martha. "The Secret Wit of Spenser's Language." In *Elizabethan Poetry: Modern Essays in Criticism*, edited by Paul Alpers, 447–72. New York: Oxford University Press, 1967.

Cranmer, Thomas. "Homily of Good Works." *Certaine Sermons appoynted by the Quenes Maiesty . . .* London: Jugge and Cawood, 1563.

Cressy, David. *Literacy and the Social Order: Reading and Writing in Tudor and Stuart England*. Cambridge: Cambridge University Press, 1980.

Crick, Julia, and Alexandra Walsham, eds. *The Uses of Script and Print, 1300–1700*. Cambridge: Cambridge University Press, 2004.

Cummings, Brian. "Iconoclasm and Bibliophobia in the English Reformations, 1521–1558." In *Images, Idolatry, and Iconoclasm in Late Medieval England: Textuality and the Visual Image*, edited by Jeremy Dimmick, James Simpson, and Nicolette Zeeman, 185–206. Oxford: Oxford University Press, 2002.

————. *The Literary Culture of the Reformation: Grammar and Grace*. Oxford: Oxford University Press, 2002.

————. "Reformed Literature and Literature Reformed." In *The Cambridge History of Medieval English Literature,* edited by David Wallace, 821–51. Cambridge: Cambridge University Press, 1999.

————. "The Theology of Translation: Tyndale's Grammar." In *Word, Church, and State: Tyndale Quincentary Essays*, edited by John Day, Eric Lund, and Anne O'Donnell, 36–59. Washington, D.C.: Catholic University of America Press, 1998.

Curry, Walter. *Shakespeare's Philosophical Patterns*. Gloucester, Mass: Peter Smith, 1968.

Curtius, Ernst. "The Book as Symbol." In *European Literature and the Latin Middle Ages*, translated by Willard R. Trask, 302–47. Princeton: Princeton University Press, 1953.

Daniell, David. *William Tyndale: A Biography*. New Haven: Yale University Press, 1994.

Darlow, T. H., and H. F. Moule, eds. *Historical Catalogue of Printed Editions of the English Bible: 1525–1961. Revised and Expanded . . . by A. S. Herbert*. London: British and Foreign Bible Society, 1968.

Darnton, Robert. "First Steps Toward a History of Reading." In *The Kiss of Lamourette: Reflections in Cultural History,* 154–87. New York: Norton, 1990.

————. "What Is the History of Books?" In *Books and Society in History*, edited by Kenneth E. Carpenter, 3–26. New York: Bowker, 1983.

Daston, Lorraine. "The Nature of Nature in Early Modern Europe." *Configurations* 6, no. 2 (1998): 149–72.

Daston, Lorraine, and Katharine Park. *Wonders and the Order of Nature, 1150–1750*. New York: Zone, 1998.

Davis, Natalie Zemon. *The Gift in Sixteenth-Century France*. Madison: University of Wisconsin Press, 2000.

Dawson, Anthony, and Paul Yachnin. *The Culture of Playgoing in Shakespeare's England: A Collaborative Debate*. Cambridge: Cambridge University Press, 2001.

DeCook, Travis. "The Ark and Immediate Revelation in Francis Bacon's *New Atlantis*." *Studies in Philology* 105, no. 1 (2008): 103–22.

DeCoursey, Matthew. "Erasmus and Tyndale on Bible-Reading." *Reformation* 1 (1996): 157–64.

Defoe, Daniel. *An Essay upon Literature: Or, an Enquiry into the Antiquity and Original of Letters*. London: Thomas Bowles, John Clark, and John Bowles, 1726.

de Grazia, Margreta. "Imprints: Shakespeare, Gutenberg, Descartes." In *Alternative Shakespeares*, vol. 2, edited by Terence Hawkes, 63–94. London: Routledge, 1996.

———. "*The Tempest*: Gratuitous Movement or Action without Kibes and Pinches." *Shakespeare Studies* 14 (1981): 249–65.

de Grazia, Margreta, Maureen Quilligan, and Peter Stallybrass, eds. *Subject and Object in Renaissance Culture*. Cambridge: Cambridge University Press, 1996.

de Grazia, Margreta, and Peter Stallybrass. "The Materiality of the Shakespearean Text." *Shakespeare Quarterly* 44 (1993): 255–84.

DeNeef, A. Leigh. *Spenser and the Motives of Metaphor*. Durham: Duke University Press, 1982.

Dering, Edward, *XXVII lectures, or readings, vpon part of the Epistle written to the Hebrues*. London: Thomas Woodcocke, 1590.

Derrida, Jacques. *Given Time: I. Counterfeit Money*. Translated by Peggy Kamuf. Chicago: University of Chicago Press, 1992.

———. *Of Grammatology*. Translated by Gayatri Chakravorty Spivak. Baltimore: Johns Hopkins University Press, 1974.

———. "Signature Event Context." In *Margins of Philosophy*, translated by Alan Bass, 309–30. Chicago: University of Chicago Press, 1982.

Dessen, Alan C., and Leslie Thomson. *A Dictionary of Stage Directions in English Drama, 1580–1642*. Cambridge: Cambridge University Press, 1999.

Dickens, A. G., and Whitney R. D. Jones. *Erasmus the Reformer*. London: Mandarin, 1995.

Diehl, Huston. *Staging Reform, Reforming the Stage: Protestantism and Popular Theater in Early Modern England*. Ithaca: Cornell University Press, 1997.

Dixon, John. *The First Commentary on* The Faerie Queene. Edited by Graham Hough. Folcroft, Pa.: Folcroft, 1969.

Dolan, Frances. "Reading, Writing, and Other Crimes." In *Feminist Readings of Early Modern Culture: Emerging Subjects,* edited by Valerie Traub, M. Lindsay Kaplan, and Dymphna Callaghan, 142–67. Cambridge: Cambridge University Press, 1996.

———. "The Subordinate('s) Plot: Petty Treason and the Forms of Domestic Rebellion." *Shakespeare Quarterly* 43, no. 3 (1992): 317–40.

Donne, John. *The Divine Poems,* 2nd ed. Edited by Helen Gardner. Oxford: Clarendon Press, 1978.

Downame, John. *A Guide to Godlynesse or a Treatise of a Christian Life*. London: Felix Kingstone, 1622.

Duffy, Eamon. "Devotion to the Crucifix and Related Images in England on the Eve of the Reformation." In *Bilder und Bildersturm im Spätmittelalter und der Frühen Neuzeit*, edited by Bob Scribner, 21–35. Wiesbaden: Harrassowitz, 1990.

———. *The Stripping of the Altars: Traditional Religion in England, 1400–1580*. New Haven: Yale University Press, 1992.

Duggan, Lawrence G. "Was Art Really the 'Book of the Illiterate'?" *Word and Image* 5 (1989): 227–51.

Edward VI. *Inivnccions geven by the moste excellent prince, Edward the sixte . . . 1547*. London: Grafton, 1547.

Eire, Carlos M. N. *War Against the Idols: The Reformation of Worship from Erasmus to Calvin*. Cambridge: Cambridge University Press, 1986.

Eisenstein, Elizabeth. *The Printing Press as an Agent of Social Change: Communications and Cultural Transformations in Early Modern Europe*. Cambridge: Cambridge University Press, 1979.

Elizabeth I. *Iniunctions geven by the Queenes Maiestie . . . Anno domini 1559*. London: Iugge and Cawood, 1559.

Elsky, Martin. *Authorizing Words: Speech, Writing, and Print in the English Renaissance*. Ithaca: Cornell University Press, 1989.

Erasmus, Desiderius. *Christian Humanism and the Reformation: Selected Writings of Erasmus*. Translated by John C. Olin. New York: Fordham University Press, 1975.

———. *Collected Works of Erasmus*. 72 vols. Toronto: University of Toronto Press, 1974– .

———. *Enchiridion Militis Christiani: An English Version*. Edited by Anne O'Donnell. Oxford: Early English Text Soc., 1981.

———. *An exhortacyon to the dylygent study of scripture: made by Erasmus of Roterodamus. And lately translated into Englysshe*. London: Robert Wyer, 1534.

———. *An exhortacyon to the study of the Gospell / Made by Erasmus of Roterodame, & lately translated in to Englysshe*. London: Robert Wyer, 1534.

———. *The first tome or volume of the Paraphrase of Erasmus vpon the newe testament*. Edited by N. Udall. London: Edwarde Whitchurch, 1548.

———. *Opera Omnia*. Edited by Jean Leclerc. 10 vols. Leiden, 1703–6; reprint, Hildesheim: George Olms, 1961–62.

———. *Opus Epistolarum Erasmi*. Edited by P. S. Allen. Oxford: Clarendon Press, 1906–58.

Erickson, Robert. *The Language of the Heart, 1600–1750*. Philadelphia: University of Pennsylvania Press, 1997.

Esolen, Anthony. "'The Isles Shall Wait for His Law': Isaiah and *The Tempest*." *Studies in Philology* 94, no. 2 (1997): 221–47.

Ezell, Margaret J. M. *Social Authorship and the Advent of Print*. Baltimore: Johns Hopkins University Press, 1999.

Febvre, Lucien, and Henri-Jean Martin. *The Coming of the Book*. London: Verso, 1976.

Fisher, John. *A sermon . . . concernynge certayne heretickes . . .* London: Berthelet, ca. 1526.

————. *The sermon . . . made agayn ye p[er]nicyous doctryn of Martin luuther. . .* London: Worde, ca. 1522.

————. "A Sermon . . . preached vpon a good Friday, by the same John Fisher, Bishop of Rochester." In *The English Works of John Fisher, Bishop of Rochester,* edited by John E. B. Mayor, 388–428. London: Early English Text Society, 1876.

Fleming, Juliet. *Graffiti and the Writing Arts of Early Modern England.* Philadelphia: University of Pennsylvania Press, 2001.

Foakes, R. A., ed. *Henslowe's Diary.* 2nd ed. Cambridge: Cambridge University Press, 2002.

Force, James, and Richard Popkin, eds. *The Millenarian Turn: Millenarian Contexts of Science, Politics, and Everyday Anglo-American Life in the Seventeenth and Eighteenth Centuries.* Dordrecht: Kluwer Academic, 2001.

Fox, Lane. "Literacy and Power in Early Christianity." In *Literacy and Power in the Ancient World.* Edited by Alan Bowman and Greg Woolf. Cambridge: Cambridge University Press, 1994.

Foxe, John, ed. *Actes and monuments of these latter and perillous dayes, touching matters of the Church . . .* London: Day, 1563.

————. *Actes and Monuments . . .* London: Short, 1596.

————. *Actes and Monuments . . .* London: Printed for the Company of Stationers, 1610.

————. *The first volume of the ecclesiasticall history contaynyng the actes and monumentes . . .* London: Daye, 1570.

————. *The whole workes of W. Tyndall, Iohn Frith, and Doct. Barnes, three worthy martyrs, and principall teachers of this Churche of England . . .* London: Daye, 1573.

Freccero, John. "The Fig Tree and the Laurel: Petrarch's Poetics." *Diacritics: A Review of Contemporary Criticism* 5, no. 1 (1975): 34–40.

Freedberg, David. *The Power of Images: Studies in the History and Theory of Response.* Chicago: University of Chicago Press, 1991.

Freinkel, Lisa. *Reading Shakespeare's Will: The Theology of Figure from Augustine to the Sonnets.* New York: Columbia University Press, 2002.

Frere, W. H., and C. E. Douglas, eds. *Puritan Manifestoes.* London: SPCK, 1909.

Freud, Sigmund. *The Interpretation of Dreams.* Vol. 4 of *The Standard Edition of the Complete Psychological Works,* translated by James Strachey. London: Hogarth Press, 1900.

Friedlaender, Walter. *Caravaggio Studies.* Princeton: Princeton University Press, 1969.

Frye, Northrop. *A Natural Perspective: The Development of Shakespearean Comedy and Romance.* New York: Columbia University Press, 1965.

Fumerton, Patricia, and Simon Hunt, eds. *Renaissance Culture and the Everyday.* Philadelphia: University of Pennsylvania Press, 1999.

Gallagher, Lowell. "Faustus's Blood and the (Messianic) Question of Ethics." *ELH* 73, no. 1 (2006): 1–29.

————. "The Place of the Stigmata in Christologiocal Poetics." In *Religion and Culture in Renaissance England,* edited by Claire McEachern and Debora Shuger, 93–115. Cambridge: Cambridge University Press, 1997.

Galloway, Andrew. "Dr. Faustus and the Charter of Christ." *Notes and Queries* 35, no. 1 (1988): 36–38.

Gamble, Harry Y. *Books and Readers in the Early Church: A History of Early Christian Texts*. New Haven: Yale University Press, 1995.

Gates, Daniel. "Unpardonable Sins: The Hazards of Performative Language in the Tragic Cases of Francesco Spiera and Doctor Faustus." *Comparative Drama* 38, no. 1 (2004): 59–81.

Gates, Henry Louis. *The Signifying Monkey: A Theory of Afro-American Literary Criticism*. New York: Oxford University Press, 1988.

Gellrich, Jesse M. *The Idea of the Book in the Middle Ages: Language Theory, Mythology, and Fiction*. Ithaca: Cornell University Press, 1985.

Gerrish, B. A. "'To the Unknown God': Luther and Calvin on the Hiddenness of God." *Journal of Religion* 53, no. 3 (1973): 263–92.

Gless, Darryl. *Interpretation and Theology in Spenser*. Cambridge: Cambridge University Press, 1994.

Gibson, Gail McMurray. *The Theater of Devotion: East Anglian Drama and Society in the Late Middle Ages*. Chicago: University of Chicago Press, 1989.

Gilman, Ernest. *Iconoclasm and Poetry in the English Reformation: "Down went Dagon."* Chicago: University of Chicago Press, 1986.

Goldberg, Jonathan. "The Print of Goodness." In *The Culture of Capital: Property, Cities, and Knowledge in Early Modern England,* edited by Henry Turner, 231–54. New York: Routledge, 2002.

———. *Writing Matter: From the Hands of the English Renaissance*. Stanford: Stanford University Press, 1990.

Goldman, Michael. "Marlowe and the Histrionics of Ravishment." In *Two Renaissance Mythmakers: Christopher Marlowe and Ben Jonson*, edited by Alvin Kernan, 22–40. Selected Papers from the English Institute. Baltimore: Johns Hopkins University Press, 1977.

Gorman, M. M. "The Diffusion of the Manuscripts of Saint Augustine's *De Doctrina Christiana* in the Early Middle Ages." *Revue Bénédictine* 95 (1985): 12–24.

Grafton, Anthony. "Renaissance Readers and Ancient Texts: Comments on Some Commentaries." *Renaissance Quarterly* 38 (1985): 615–49.

Graham, William A. *Beyond the Written Word*. Cambridge: Cambridge University Press, 1993.

Greenblatt, Stephen. *Learning to Curse: Essays in Early Modern Culture*. New York: Routledge, 1990.

———. *Marvelous Possessions: The Wonder of the New World*. Chicago: University of Chicago Press, 1991.

———. *Renaissance Self-Fashioning: From More to Shakespeare*. Chicago: University of Chicago Press, 1980.

———. *Shakespearean Negotiations: The Circulation of Social Energy in Renaissance England*. Berkeley: University of California Press, 1988.

Greene, Thomas. *The Light in Troy: Imitation and Discovery in Renaissance Poetry*. New Haven: Yale University Press, 1982.

Greg, W. W., ed. *A Companion to Arber: Being a Calendar of Documents in Edward Arber's "Transcript of the Registers of the Company of Stationers of London, 1554–1640."* Oxford: Clarendon, 1967.

Gregerson, Linda. "Protestant Erotics: Idolatry and Interpretation in Spenser's *Faerie Queene*." *ELH* 58 (1991): 1–34.

———. *The Reformation of the Subject: Spenser, Milton, and the English Protestant Epic*. Cambridge: Cambridge University Press, 1995.

Gregory, Brad S. *Salvation at Stake: Christian Martyrdom in Early Modern Europe*. Cambridge, Mass.: Harvard University Press, 1999.

Gritsch, Eric W. *Reformer Without a Church: The Life and Thought of Thomas Muntzer, 1488–1525*. Philadelphia: Fortress Press, 1967.

Gross, Kenneth. "Books in *The Faerie Queene*." In *The Spenser Encyclopedia*, edited by A. C. Hamilton, 103–4. Toronto: University of Toronto Press, 1990.

———. *Spenserian Poetics: Idolatry, Iconoclasm, and Magic*. Ithaca: Cornell University Press, 1985.

Hackel, Heidi Brayman. *Reading Material in Early Modern England: Print, Gender, and Literacy*. Cambridge: Cambridge University Press, 2005.

Hackenbroch, Yvonne. *Renaissance Jewelry*. London: Sotheby Parke Bernet, 1979.

Halasz, Alexandra. *The Marketplace of Print: Pamphlets and the Public Sphere in Early Modern England*. Cambridge: Cambridge University Press, 1997.

Hall, Basil. "Biblical Scholarship: Editions and Commentaries." In *The Cambridge History of the Bible: The West from the Reformation to the Present Day*, edited by S. L. Greenslade, 38–93. Cambridge: Cambridge University Press, 1963.

———. *Humanists and Protestants, 1500–1900*. Edinburgh: T. and T. Clark, 1990.

Hall, Kim F. *Things of Darkness: Economies of Race and Gender in Early Modern England*. Ithaca: Cornell University Press, 1995.

Hall, Stuart G. "In the Beginning was the Codex: The Early Church and Its Revolutionary Books." In *The Church and the Book*, edited by R. N. Swanson, 1–10. Woodbridge, U.K.: Boydell Press, 2004.

Harbsmeier, Michael. "Writing and the Other: Travellers' Literacy, or Towards an Archaeology of Orality." In *Literacy and Society*, edited by Karen Schousboe and Margaret Trolle Larsen, 197–228. Copenhagen: Akademisk Forlag, 1989.

Harriot, Thomas. *A Briefe and True Report of the New Found Land of Virginia*. 1590. New York: Dover Reprints, 1972.

Harpham, Geoffrey Halt. "The Fertile Word: Augustine and Hermeneutics." *Criticism* 38, no. 3 (1986): 237–54.

Harris, Jonathan Gil. "The New New Historicism's Wunderkammer of Objects." *European Journal of English Studies* 4 (2000): 111–23.

———. "Shakespeare's Hair: Staging the Object of Material Culture." *Shakespeare Quarterly* 52 (2001): 479–91.

Harris, Max. *Theater and Incarnation*. Grand Rapids, Mich.: Eerdmans, 2005.

Harrison, Peter. *The Bible, Protestantism and the Rise of Natural Science*. Cambridge: Cambridge University Press, 1998.

———. "Original Sin and the Problem of Knowledge in Early Modern Europe." *Journal of the History of Ideas* 63, no. 2 (2002): 239–59.

Hawkes, David. *Idols of the Marketplace: Idolatry and Commodity Fetishism in English Literature, 1580–1680*. New York: Palgrave, 2001.

Hayles, N. Katherine. "Translating Media: Why We Should Rethink Textuality." *Yale Journal of Criticism* 16 (2003): 263–90.

Hegel, G. F. *The Philosophy of History*. New York: Dover, 1956.

———. *Werke in 20 Bänden*. Frankfurt am Main: Suhrkamp Verlag, 1970.

Helgerson, Richard. *Forms of Nationhood: The Elizabethan Writing of England*. Chicago: University of Chicago Press, 1992.

Hess, Andrew. "The Mediterranean and Shakespeare's Geopolitical Imagination." In The Tempest*: Sources and Contexts, Criticism, Rewritings and Appropriations*, edited by Peter Hulme and William Sherman, 27–36. New York: Norton, 2004.

Hibbard, Howard. *Caravaggio*. New York: Harper, 1983.

Hilarie, Hugh. *The Resurrection of the Masse: The Masse Speaketh*. Strasburgh, 1554.

Hill, Christopher. "'Till the conversion of the jews.'" *Collected Essays*. Amherst: University of Massachusetts Press, 1965. 2: 269–300.

The historie of the damnable life, and deserued death of Doctor Iohn Faustus . . . Translated by P. F. Gent. London: Thomas Orwin, 1592.

Hoffmann, Manfred. *Rhetoric and Theology: The Hermeneutic of Erasmus*. Toronto: University of Toronto Press, 1994.

Horkheimer, Max, and Theodor Adorno. *Dialectic of Enlightenment*. Translated by John Cumming. New York: Continuum, 1994.

Howard, George. "The Textual Nature of an Old Hebrew Version of Matthew." *Journal of Biblical Literature* 105, no. 1 (1986): 49–63.

Hulme, Peter. *Colonial Encounters: Europe and the Native Caribbean, 1492–1797*. London: Routledge, 1986.

Hulme, Peter, and William Sherman, eds. *The Tempest and Its Travels*. London: Reaktion, 2000.

Hunt, Arnold. "The Art of Hearing: Preachers and Their Audiences, 1590–1640." Ph.D. diss., Cambridge University, 2000.

Illich, Ivan. *In the Vineyard of the Text*. Chicago: University of Chicago Press, 1993.

Imbrie, Ann. "'Playing Legerdemaine with the Scripture': Parodic Sermons in *The Faerie Queene*." *English Literary Renaissance* 17 (1987): 142–55.

Irvine, Michael. *The Making of Textual Culture: 'Grammatica' and Literary Theory, 350–1100*. Cambridge: Cambridge University Press, 1994.

Jacob, Margaret. "Millenarianism and Science in the Late Seventeenth Century." *Journal of the History of Ideas* 37, no. 2 (1976): 335–41.

Jager, Eric. *The Book of the Heart*. Chicago: University of Chicago Press, 2000.

————. *The Tempter's Voice: Language and the Fall in Medieval Literature*. Ithaca: Cornell University Press, 1993.

Jardine, Lisa. *Erasmus, Man of Letters: The Construction of Charisma in Print*. Princeton: Princeton University Press, 1993.

Jardine, Lisa, and Anthony Grafton. "'Studied for Action': How Gabriel Harvey Read His Livy." *Past and Present* 129, no. 4 (1990): 30–78.

Jardine, Lisa, and William Sherman. "Pragmatic Readers: Knowledge Transactions and Scholarly Services in Late Elizabethan England." In *Religion, Culture and Society in Early Modern Britain: Essays in Honour of Patrick Collinson*, edited by Anthony Fletcher and Peter Roberts, 102–24. Cambridge: Cambridge University Press, 1994.

Jerome. *Epistulae*. Edited by I. Hilberg. *Corpus Scriptorum Ecclesiasticorum Latinorum*. Vol. 54. Leipzig: G. Freytag, 1910.

————. *The Letters of St. Jerome*. Vol. 1. Translated by Charles Mierow. *Ancient Christian Writers*. No. 33. Edited by Johannes Quasten and Walter Burghardt. London: Longmans, Green and Co., 1963.

————. *On Illustrious Men*. Translated by Thomas P. Halton. Washington, D.C.: Catholic University of America Press, 1999.

————. *Letters and Select Works*. Translated by W. H. Fremantle. *A Select Library of Nicene and Post-Nicene Fathers of the Christian Church*. 2nd ser. Vol. 6. Grand Rapids, Michigan: Wm. B. Eerdmans, 1892.

Johns, Adrian. *The Nature of the Book: Print and Knowledge in the Making*. Chicago: University of Chicago Press, 1998.

Jones, Ann Rosalind, and Peter Stallybrass. *Renaissance Clothing and the Materials of Memory*. Cambridge: Cambridge University Press, 2000.

Jonson, Ben. *Timber: or Discoveries*. Edited by G. B. Harrison. Edinburgh: Edinburgh University Press, 1966.

Kaske, Carol. *Spenser and Biblical Poetics*. Ithaca: Cornell University Press, 1999.

Kastan, David Scott. *Shakespeare After Theory*. Newark: University of Delaware Press, 1999.

————. *Shakespeare and the Book*. Cambridge: Cambridge University Press, 2001.

Katz, David S. *Philo-Semitism and the Readmission of the Jews to England, 1603–1655*. New York: Oxford University Press, 1982.

Kaula, David. "Autolycus' Trumpery." *Studies in English Literature, 1500–1900*. 16 (1976): 287–303.

Kearney, James. "The Book and the Fetish: The Materiality of Prospero's Text." *Journal of Medieval and Early Modern Studies* 32, no. 3 (2002): 433–68.

————. "Enshrining Idolatry in *The Faerie Queene*." *English Literary Renaissance* 32, no. 1 (2002): 3–30.

Kendrick, Christopher. *Utopia, Carnival, and Commonwealth in Renaissance England*. Toronto: University of Toronto Press, 2004.

Kendrick, Laura. *Animating the Letter: The Figurative Embodiment of Writing from Late Antiquity to the Renaissance*. Columbus: Ohio State University Press, 1999.

Kermode, Frank. Introduction to *The Tempest,* by William Shakespeare, xi–lxxxviii. Edited by Frank Kermode. London: Methuen, 1954.

Kibbey, Ann. *The Interpretation of Material Shapes in Puritanism: A Study of Rhetoric, Prejudice, and Violence.* Cambridge: Cambridge University Press, 1986.

King, John N. *English Reformation Literature: The Tudor Origins of the Protestant Tradition.* Princeton: Princeton University Press, 1982.

———. "'The Light of Printing': William Tyndale, John Foxe, John Day, and Early Modern Print Culture." *Renaissance Quarterly* 56, no. 1 (2001): 52–85.

———. *Spenser's Poetry and the Reformation Tradition.* Princeton: Princeton University Press, 1990.

———. "Was Spenser a Puritan?" *Spenser Studies* 6 (1985): 1–31.

Knapp, Jeffrey. *An Empire Nowhere: England, America, and Literature from* Utopia *to* The Tempest. Berkeley: University of California Press, 1992.

Knight, G. Wilson. *The Crown of Life: Essays in Interpretation of Shakespeare's Final Plays.* Oxford: Oxford University Press, 1947.

Koerner, Joseph Leo. *The Reformation of the Image.* Chicago: University of Chicago Press, 2004.

Lake, Peter, and Michael Questier. *The Antichrist's Lewd Hat: Protestants, Papists and Players in Post-Reformation England.* New Haven: Yale University Press, 2002.

Lamb, Mary Ellen. "Constructions of Women Readers." In *Teaching Tudor and Stuart Women Writers*, edited by Susanne Woods and Margaret P. Hannay, 23–34. New York: Modern Language Association, 2000.

———. "The Red Crosse Knight, St. George, and the Appropriation of Popular Culture." *Spenser Studies* 18 (2003): 185–208.

———. "Women Readers in Mary Wroth's *Urania*." In *Reading Mary Wroth: Representing Alternatives in Early Modern England*, edited by Naomi J. Miller and Gary Waller, 210–27. Knoxville: University of Tennessee Press, 1991.

Lamming, George. "A Monster, a Child, a Slave." In *The Pleasures of Exile,* 95–117. 1960. Ann Arbor: University of Michigan Press, 1992.

Lampe, G. W. H., ed. *The Cambridge History of the Bible.* Vols. 1–3. Cambridge: Cambridge University Press, 1969.

Lampert, Lisa. *Gender and Jewish Difference from Paul to Shakespeare.* Philadelphia: University of Pennsylvania Press, 2004.

Lander, Jesse. *Inventing Polemic: Religion, Print, and Literary Culture in Early Modern England.* Cambridge: Cambridge University Press, 2006.

Langdon, Helen. *Caravaggio: A Life.* New York: Farrar, Straus and Giroux, 1998.

Latimer, Hugh. *Sermons by Hugh Latimer.* Edited by G. E. Corrie. Cambridge: Cambridge University Press, 1844.

Latour, Bruno, and Peter Weibel, eds. *Iconoclash: Beyond the Image Wars in Science, Religion and Art.* Cambridge, Mass.: MIT Press, 2002.

Lavin, Irving. "Divine Inspiration in Caravaggio's Two *St. Matthews*." *Art Bulletin* 56 (1974): 59–81.

————. "A Further Note on the Ancestry of Caravaggio's First *Saint Matthew.*" *Art Bulletin* 62, no. 1 (1980): 113–14.

Lawton, David. "Englishing the Bible, 1066–1549." In *The Cambridge History of Medieval English Literature*, edited by David Wallace, 454–82. Cambridge: Cambridge University Press, 1999.

Leclercq, Jean. *The Love of Learning and the Desire for God.* Translated by Catharine Misrahi. New York: Fordham University Press, 1961.

Leedham-Green, E. S. *Books in Cambridge Inventories: Book-lists from Vice-Chancellor's Court Probate Inventories in the Tudor and Stuart Periods.* 2 vols. Cambridge: Cambridge University Press, 1986.

Léry, Jean de. *History of a Voyage to the Land of Brazil, Otherwise Called America.* Translated by Janet Whatley. Berkeley: University of California Press, 1990.

Leslie, Marina. *Renaissance Utopias and the Problem of History.* Ithaca: Cornell University Press, 1998.

Lesser, Zachary. *Renaissance Drama and the Politics of Publication: Readings in the English Book Trade.* Cambridge: Cambridge University Press, 2004.

Lévi-Strauss, Claude. "A Writing Lesson." In *Tristes Tropiques,* translated by John and Doreen Weightman, 294–304. New York: Atheneum, 1974.

Lewis, C. S. *Allegory of Love: A Study in Medieval Tradition.* Oxford: Oxford University Press, 1938.

Lewis, Charlton T., and Charles Short. *Latin Dictionary.* New York: American Book Company, 1907.

Linton, Joan Pong. *The Romance of the New World: Gender and the Literary Formations of English Colonialism.* Cambridge: Cambridge University Press, 1998.

Loomba, Ania. *Gender, Race, Renaissance Drama.* Manchester: Manchester University Press, 1989.

Love, Harold. *Scribal Publication in Seventeenth-Century England.* Oxford: Clarendon Press, 1993.

Luborsky, Ruth, and Elizabeth Ingram. *A Guide to English Illustrated Books, 1536–1603.* Tempe, Ariz.: Medieval and Renaissance Texts and Studies, 1998.

Lupton, Julia Reinhard. *Citizen-Saints: Shakespeare and Political Theology.* Chicago: University of Chicago Press, 2005.

————. "Creature Caliban." *Shakespeare Quarterly* 51 (2000): 1–23.

Lusty Juventus. 1550. *Four Tudor Interludes.* Edited by J. A. B. Somerset. London: Athlone, 1974.

Luther, Martin. *A Commentarie of M. Doctor Martin Luther vpon the Epistle of S. Paule to the Galathians.* London: Thomas Vautroullier, 1588.

————. *D. Martin Luthers Werke, kritische Gesamtausgabe.* Weimar: Hermann Böhlau, 1883–1999.

————. *D. Martin Luthers Werke, kritische Gesamtausgabe: Briefwechsel.* Weimar: Hermann Böhlau, 1930–85.

————. *D. Martin Luthers Werke, kritische Gesamtausgabe: die Deutsche Bibel.* Weimar: Hermann Böhlau, 1906–61.

———. *D. Martin Luthers Werke, kritische Gesamtausgabe: Tischreden.* Weimar: Hermann Böhlau, 1912–21.

———. *Luther's Works.* Edited by J. Pelikan and H. T. Lehmann. Philadelphia: Fortress, 1955–86.

Mallette, Richard. *Spenser and the Discourses of Reformation England.* Lincoln: University of Nebraska Press, 1997.

Maltby, Judith. *Prayer Book and People in Elizabethan and Early Stuart England.* Cambridge: Cambridge University Press, 1998.

Mannoni, Octave. *Prospero and Caliban: The Psychology of Colonization.* Translated by Pamela Powesland. New York: Praeger, 1956.

Marlowe, Christopher. *Doctor Faustus A- and B-texts (1604, 1616).* Edited by David Bevington and Eric Rasmussen. Manchester: Manchester University Press, 1993.

Marotti, Arthur. *Manuscript, Print, and the English Renaissance Lyric.* Ithaca: Cornell University Press, 1995.

Marshall, Peter. "Evangelical Conversion in the Reign of Henry VIII." In *The Beginnings of English Protestantism*, edited by Peter Marshall and Alec Ryrie, 14–37. Cambridge: Cambridge University Press, 2002.

Masten, Jeffrey. *Textual Intercourse: Collaboration, Authorship, and Sexualities in Renaissance Drama.* Cambridge: Cambridge University Press, 1997.

Masten, Jeffrey, Peter Stallybrass, and Nancy Vickers. "Introduction: Language Machines." In *Language Machines: Technologies of Literary and Cultural Production*, edited by Jeffrey Masten, Peter Stallybrass, and Nancy Vickers, 1–16. New York: Routledge, 1997.

Maus, Katharine Eisaman. *Inwardness and Theater in the English Renaissance.* Chicago: University of Chicago Press, 1995.

Mauss, Marcel. *The Gift: The Form and Reason for Exchange in Archaic Societies.* Translated by W. D. Halls. London: Routledge, 1990.

McConica, James Kelsey. *English Humanists and Reformation Politics Under Henry VIII and Edward VI.* Oxford: Clarendon, 1965.

McGrath, Alister E. *Luther's Theology of the Cross: Martin Luther's Theological Breakthrough.* Oxford: Basil Blackwell, 1985.

McGurk, Patrick. "The Oldest Manuscripts of the Latin Bible." In *The Early Medieval Bible: Its Production, Decoration and Use*, edited by Richard Gameson, 1–23. Cambridge: Cambridge University Press, 1994.

McKenzie, D. F. *Making Meaning: "Printers of the Mind" and Other Essays.* Edited by Peter D. McDonald and Michael F. Suarez. Amherst: University of Massachusetts Press, 2002.

McKerrow, R. B. *An Introduction to Bibliography for Literary Students.* 1927. Oxford: Clarendon, 1967.

McKitterick, David. *Print, Manuscript and the Search for Order, 1450–1830.* New York: Cambridge University Press, 2003.

McKnight, Stephen. *The Religious Foundations of Francis Bacon's Thought.* Columbia: University of Missouri Press, 2006.

Merton, Reginald. *Cardinal Ximenes and the Making of Spain*. London: Kegan Paul, Trench, Trubner and Co., 1934.

Merton, Robert. *Science, Technology and Society in Seventeenth-Century England*. New York: Howard Fertig, 1970.

Meuser, Fred W. "Luther as Preacher of the Word of God." In *The Cambridge Companion to Martin Luther*, edited by Donald K. McKim, 136–48. Cambridge: Cambridge University Press, 1993.

Mignolo, Walter. "Afterword: Writing and Recorded Knowledge in Colonial and Postcolonial Situations." In *Writing Without Words: Alternative Literacies in Mesoamerica and the Andes*, edited by Elizabeth Boone and Walter Mignolo, 293–310. Durham: Duke University Press, 1994.

———. *The Darker Side of the Renaissance: Literacy, Territoriality, and Colonization*. Ann Arbor: University of Michigan Press, 2003.

———. "Literacy and Colonization: The New World Experience." In *1492–1992: Re/ Discovering Colonial Writing*, edited by René Jara and Nicholas Spadaccini, 51–96. Minneapolis: Prisma Institute, 1989.

Milbank, John. Review of *Biblical Hermeneutics in Historical Perspective*, edited by M. S. Burrows and P. Rorem. *Journal of Theological Studies* 46, no. 2 (1995): 666–70.

Miller, David Lee. *The Poem's Two Bodies: The Poetics of the 1590 Faerie Queene*. Princeton: Princeton University Press, 1988.

Montaigne, Michel de. *The Essayes*. Translated by John Florio. London: Sims, 1603.

More, Thomas. *The Complete Works of Thomas More*. Edited by L. L. Martz, R. S. Sylvester, and C. H. Miller. New Haven: Yale University Press, 1963–97.

———. *A dyaloge of syr Thomas More knyghte*. London: William Rastell, 1530.

Morgan, John. *Godly Learning: Puritan Attitudes towards Reason, Learning, and Education*. Cambridge: Cambridge University Press, 1986.

Morrison, Karl F. *Conversion and Text: The Cases of Augustine of Hippo, Herman-Judah, and Constantine Tsatsos*. Charlottesville: University Press of Virginia, 1992.

———. *Understanding Conversion*. Charlottesville: University Press of Virginia, 1990.

Moss, Daniel. "Despair, Grace, and the Sufficiency of the Word: A Rereading of *The Faerie Queene* 1.9." Essay presented at the Renaissance Society of America Conference, San Francisco, Calif., March, 2006.

Most, Glenn W. *Doubting Thomas*. Cambridge, Mass.: Harvard University Press, 2005.

Mowat, Barbara. "'Knowing I Loved My Books': Reading *The Tempest* Intertextually." In *The Tempest: Sources and Contexts, Criticism, Rewritings and Appropriations*, edited by Peter Hulme and William Sherman, 27–36. New York: Norton, 2004.

———. "Prospero, Agrippa, and Hocus Pocus." *English Literary Renaissance* 11 (1981): 281–303.

———. "Prospero's Book." *Shakespeare Quarterly* 52, no. 1 (2001): 1–33.

Mozley, J. F. *William Tyndale*. New York: Macmillan, 1937.

Mueller, Janel. "Complications of Intertextuallity: John Fisher, Katherine Parr and 'The Book of the Crucifix.'" In *Texts and Cultural Change in Early Modern England*, edited by Cedric Brown and Arthur Marotti, 15–36. New York: St. Martin's Press, 1997.

Muenster, Sebastian. *Evangelium secundum Matthaeum in lingua hebraica cum versione latina atque succinctis annotationibus Sebastiani Munsteri.* Basel, 1537.

Mullett, Michael A. *The Catholic Reformation.* London: Routledge, 1999.

Murray, J. A. H. *The Oxford English Dictionary: Being a Corrected Re-Issue with an Introduction, Supplement, and Bibliography of A New English Dictionary on Historical Principles.* Oxford: Clarendon Press, 1933.

Murray, Mary Pollard. "The Literature of Conversion in Early Modern England." Ph.D. diss., Yale University, 2004.

Nohrnberg, James. *The Analogy of* The Faerie Queene. Princeton: Princeton University Press, 1976.

Norbrook, David. *Poetry and Politics in the English Renaissance.* London: Routledge, 1984.

———. " 'What Cares These Roarers for the Name of King?': Language and Utopia in *The Tempest.*" In *The Politics of Tragicomedy: Shakespeare and After,* edited by Gordon McMullan and Jonathan Hope, 21–54. London: Routledge, 1992.

Oberman, Heiko A. *The Dawn of the Reformation: Essays in Late Medieval and Early Reformation Thought.* Edinburgh: T. and T. Clark, 1986.

———. *Luther: Man Between God and the Devil.* 1982. Translated by Eileen Walliser-Schwarzbart. New York: Doubleday, 1992.

O'Connell, Michael. *The Idolatrous Eye: Iconoclasm and Theater in Early-Modern England.* Oxford: Oxford University Press, 2000.

O'Donnell, Anne M. "Scripture Versus Church in Tyndale's *Answer unto Sir Thomas More's Dialogue.*" *Moreana* 28, no. 106–7 (1991): 119–30.

Olin, J.C. "Erasmus and Saint Jerome: The Close Bond and Its Significance." *Erasmus of Rotterdam Society Yearbook* 7 (1987): 33–53.

Orgel, Stephen. "Margins of Truth." In *The Renaissance Text: Theory, Editing, Textuality,* edited by Andrew Murphy, 91–107. Manchester: Manchester University Press, 2000.

———. "Tobacco and Boys: How Queer Was Marlowe?" *GLQ: A Journal of Lesbian and Gay Studies* 6, no. 4 (2000): 555–76.

Origen. *Homilies on Leviticus 1–16,* translated by Gary Wayne Barkley. Washington, D.C.: Catholic University of America Press, 1990.

Orlin, Lena Cowen, ed. *Material London, ca. 1600.* Philadelphia: University of Pennsylvania Press, 2000.

Oyer, John S. *Lutheran Reformers Against Anabaptists.* The Hague: Nijhoff, 1964.

Panofsky, Erwin. "Erasmus and the Visual Arts." *Journal of the Warburg and Courtauld Institutes* 32 (1969): 200–227.

Parker, Patricia. *Inescapable Romance: Studies in the Poetics of a Mode.* Princeton: Princeton University Press, 1979.

———. *Shakespeare from the Margins: Language, Culture, Context.* Chicago: University of Chicago Press, 1996.

Paterson, Timothy. "On the Role of Christianity in the Political Philosophy of Francis Bacon." *Polity* 19, no. 3 (1987): 419–42.

Patterson, Lee. "On the Margin: Postmodernism, Ironic History, and Medieval Studies." *Speculum* 65 (1990): 87–108.

Pearson, A. F. Scott. *Thomas Cartwright and Elizabethan Puritanism.* Cambridge: Cambridge University Press, 1925.

Peckham, George. *A True Reporte, of the Late discoveries . . . of the Newfound Landes.* 1583. In *The Voyages and Colonizing Enterprises of Sir Humphrey Gilbert*, edited by D. B. Quinn. Hakluyt Society, 2nd ser. Vol. 84. London, 1940. 2: 435–82.

Pelikan, Jaroslav. *Luther the Expositor: Introduction to the Reformer's Exegetical Writings.* Companion Volume to *Luther's Works*, edited by J. Pelikan and H. T. Lehmann. Philadelphia: Fortress, 1955–86.

———. *Reformation of Church and Dogma (1300–1700).* Vol. 4 of *The Christian Tradition: A History of the Development of Doctrine.* Chicago: University of Chicago Press, 1983.

———. "The Theology of the Means of Grace." In *Accents in Luther's Theology*, edited by Heino Kadai, 124–47. St. Louis: Concordia, 1967.

Pérez-Ramos, Antonio. "Bacon's Legacy." In *Cambridge Companion to Bacon*, edited by Markku Peltonen, 311–34. Cambridge: Cambridge University Press, 1996.

Phillips, John. *The Reformation of Images: Destruction of Art in England, 1535–1660.* Berkeley: University of California Press, 1973.

Picciotto, Joanna. "Reforming the Garden: The Experimentalist Eden and Paradise Lost." *English Literary History* 72, no. 1 (2005): 23–78.

Pietz, William. "Fetishism and Materialism: The Limits of Theory in Marx." In *Fetishism as Cultural Discourse*, edited by Emily Apter and William Pietz, 119–51. Ithaca: Cornell University Press, 1993.

———. "The Problem of the Fetish, I." *Res* 9 (1985): 5–17.

———. "The Problem of the Fetish, II." *Res* 13 (1987): 23–45.

———. "The Problem of the Fetish, IIIa." *Res* 16 (1988): 105–23.

Pigman, G. W. "Imitation and the Renaissance Sense of the Past: The Reception of Erasmus' *Ciceronianus*." *Journal of Medieval and Renaissance Studies* 9, no. 2 (1979): 155–77.

Price, Leah. "Reading: The State of the Discipline." *Book History* 7 (2004): 303–20.

Puccini, Vincenzio. *The Life of St. Mary Magdalene of Pazzi, a Carmelite Nunn.* Translated by Thomas Smith. London: R. Taylor, 1687.

Purchas, Samuel. *Hakluytus Posthumous, or Purchas His Pilgrimes.* 20 vols. Glasgow: MacLehose, 1905.

———. *Purchas his Pilgrimage.* London: Stansby, 1613.

Quarles, Francis. *The Shepheards Oracles.* London: M.F., 1646.

Quilligan, Maureen. *The Language of Allegory: Defining the Genre.* Ithaca: Cornell University Press, 1979.

Quint, David. *Epic and Empire.* Princeton: Princeton University Press, 1993.

Raven, James, Helen Small, and Naomi Tadmor, eds. *The Practice and Representation of Reading in England.* Cambridge: Cambridge University Press, 1996.

Renaker, David. "A Miracle of Engineering: The Conversion of Bensalem in Francis Bacon's 'New Atlantis.'" *Studies in Philology* 87, no. 2 (1990): 181–93.

Resnick, Irven M. "The Codex in Early Jewish and Christian Communities." *Journal of Religious History* 17, no. 1 (1992): 1–17.

Retamar, Roberto Fernández. "Caliban: Notes Toward a Discussion of Culture in Our America." In *Caliban and Other Essays*, translated by Edward Baker, 3–45. Minneapolis: University of Minnesota Press, 1989.

Rex, Richard. "The English Campaign Against Luther in the 1520s." *Transactions of the Royal Historical Society.* 5th ser. 39 (1989): 85–106.

Rhu, Lawrence. "Romancing the Word: Pre-Texts and Contexts for the Errour Episode." *Spenser Studies* 11 (1994): 101–10.

Rice, Eugene. *Saint Jerome in the Renaissance.* Baltimore: Johns Hopkins University Press, 1985.

Richardson, Anne. "Tyndale's Quarrel with Erasmus: A Chapter in the History of the English Reformation." *Fides et Historia* 25, no. 3 (1993): 46–65.

Roberts, Colin H., and T. C. Skeat. *The Birth of the Codex.* Oxford: Oxford University Press, 1983.

Rose, Jonathan. "How Historians Study Reading." In *Literature in the Marketplace*, edited by John O. Jordan and Robert Patten, 195–212. Cambridge University Press, 1995.

Rose, Mark. *Authors and Owners: The Invention of Copyright.* Cambridge, Mass.: Harvard University Press, 1993.

———. *Spenser's Art: A Companion to Book One of* The Faerie Queene. Cambridge, Mass.: Harvard University Press, 1975.

Rossi, Paolo. "Baconianism." In *Dictionary of the History of Ideas,* ed. Philip P. Wiener, 1: 172–79. New York: Scribner's, 1973.

Rubin, Miri. *Corpus Christi: The Eucharist in Late Medieval Culture.* Cambridge: Cambridge University Press, 1991.

Rummel, Erika. *Erasmus and His Catholic Critics.* 2 vols. Nieuwkoop: De Graaf, 1989.

———. *Erasmus'* Annotations on the New Testament: *From Philologist to Theologian.* Toronto: University of Toronto Press, 1986.

———. *Jiménez de Cisneros: On the Threshold of Spain's Golden Age.* Tempe: Arizona Center for Medieval and Renaissance Studies, 1999.

Schonfield, Hugh J., ed. and trans. *An Old Hebrew Text of St. Matthew's Gospel.* Edinburgh: T. and T. Clark, 1927.

Scott-Warren, Jason. *Sir John Harington and the Book as Gift.* Oxford: Oxford University Press, 2001.

Shailor, Barbara A. *The Medieval Book.* Toronto: University of Toronto Press, 1991.

Shakespeare, William. *The Second Part of Henry VI.* Edited by Herschel Baker. In *The Riverside Shakespeare*, edited by G. Blakemore Evans and J. J. M. Tobin, 630–70. Boston: Houghton, 1974.

———. *The Tempest.* Edited by Stephen Orgel. Oxford: Clarendon, 1987.

———. *The Winter's Tale.* Edited by Hallett Smith. In *The Riverside Shakespeare*, edited by G. Blakemore Evans and J. J. M. Tobin, 1569–1605. Boston: Houghton, 1974.

Shannon, Laurie. "'His Apparel Was Done Upon Him': Rites of Personage in Foxe's Book of Martyrs." *Shakespeare Studies* (2000): 193–98.

Sharpe, Kevin. *Reading Revolutions: The Politics of Reading in Early Modern England*. New Haven: Yale University Press, 2000.

Sheppard, Gerald. *The Geneva Bible: The Annotated New Testament 1602 Edition*. Facsimile ed. New York: Pilgrim, 1989.

Sherman, William. *John Dee: The Politics of Reading and Writing in the English Renaissance*. Amherst: University of Massachusetts Press, 1995.

———. "Toward a History of the Manicule." In *Owners, Annotators and the Signs of Reading*, edited by Robin Myers, Michael Harris, and Giles Mandelbrote, 19–48. New Castle, Del.: Oak Knoll Press; London: British Library, 2005.

Shuger, Debora. *The Renaissance Bible: Scholarship, Sacrifice, and Subjectivity*. Berkeley: University of California Press, 1994.

Sidney, Philip. *An Apology for Poetry or The Defence of Poesy*. Edited by G. Shepherd. 1965. Manchester: Manchester University Press, 1989.

Simpson, James. "Ageism: Leland, Bale, and the Laborious Start of English Literary History, 1350–1550." *New Medieval Literatures* 1 (1997): 213–35.

———. *Reform and Cultural Revolution. The Oxford English Literary History*. Vol. 2: *1350–1547*. Oxford: Oxford University Press, 2002.

Sinfield, Alan. *Literature in Protestant England, 1560–1660*. London: Croom Helm, 1983.

Singh, Jyotsna. "Caliban Versus Miranda: Race and Gender Conflicts in Postcolonial Rewritings of *The Tempest*." In *Feminist Readings of Early Modern Culture: Emerging Subjects*, edited by Valerie Traub, M. Lindsay Kaplan, and Dympna Callaghan, 191–209. Cambridge: Cambridge University Press, 1996.

Skulsky, Harold. "Spenser's Despair Episode and the Theology of Doubt." *Modern Philology* 78 (1981): 227–42.

Skura, Meredith Anne. "Discourse and the Individual: The Case of Colonialism in *The Tempest*." *Shakespeare Quarterly* 40 (1989): 42–69.

Slights, Jessica. "Rape and the Romanticization of Shakespeare's Miranda." *Studies in English Literature, 1500–1900*, 41, no. 2 (2001): 357–79.

Smalley, Beryl. *The Study of the Bible in the Middle Ages*. 2nd ed. 1952. Reprint, Notre Dame, Ind.: University of Notre Dame Press, 1964.

Smith, Bruce R. *The Acoustic World of Early Modern England: Attending to the O-Factor*. Chicago: University of Chicago Press, 1999.

Smith, Henry. "The Sweete Song of Old Father Simeon, in Two Sermons." In *Sixe Sermons Preached by Maister Henry Smith*. London, 1593.

Smith, Ian. "Barbarian Errors: Performing Race in Early Modern England," *Shakespeare Quarterly* 49 (1998): 168–86.

———. "'When we were capital'; or, Lessons in Language: Finding Caliban's Roots." *Shakespeare Studies* (2000): 252–56.

Smith, John. *The Generall Historie of Virginia, New-England, and the Summer Isles*. London: Printed by I[ohn] D[awson] and I[ohn] H[aviland] for Michael Sparkes, 1624.

Smyth, John. *The Differences of the Churches of the Seperation*. 1608. Reprinted in *Works of John Smyth*, edited by W. T. Whitley. Cambridge: Cambridge University Press, 1915.

Snow, Edward A. "Marlowe's Doctor Faustus and the Ends of Desire." In *Two Renaissance Mythmakers: Christopher Marlowe and Ben Jonson*, edited by Alvin Kernan, 70–110. Selected Papers from the English Institute. Baltimore: Johns Hopkins University Press, 1977.

Spalding, Mary Caroline, ed. *The Middle English Charters of Christ*. Bryn Mawr, Pa.: Bryn Mawr College, 1914.

Speculum Sacerdotale, edited from British Museum MS. Additional 36791. Edited by Edward H. Weatherly. Early English Text Society, Original Series, No. 200 London: Oxford University Press, 1936.

Spenser, Edmund. *Edmund Spenser's Poetry: A Norton Critical Edition*, 3rd ed. Edited by Hugh Maclean and Anne Lake Prescott. New York: Norton, 1993.

———. *The Faerie Queene*. Edited by Thomas P. Roche, Jr. London: Penguin, 1978.

———. *The Works of Edmund Spenser: A Variorum Edition*. 10 vols. Edited by E. Greenlaw, Charles Grosvenor, Frederick Morgan Pedelford, and Ray Heffner. Baltimore: Johns Hopkins, 1943.

———. *The Yale Edition of the Shorter Poems*. Edited by W. Oram, Einar Bjorvand, and Ronald Bond. New Haven: Yale University Press, 1989.

Spufford, Margaret. *Small Books and Pleasant Histories*. London: Methuen, 1981.

Stallybrass, Peter. "Books and Scrolls: Navigating the Bible." In *Books and Readers in Early Modern England: Material Studies*, edited by Jennifer Andersen and Elizabeth Sauer, 42–79. Philadelphia: University of Pennsylvania Press, 2002.

———. "Navigating the Book." Unpublished paper, University of Pennsylvania, 1998.

———. "The Value of Culture and the Disavowal of Things." In *The Culture of Capital: Property, Cities, and Knowledge in Early Modern England*, edited by Henry S. Turner, 275–92. New York: Routledge, 2002.

Stallybrass, Peter, Roger Chartier, J. Franklin Mowery, and Heather Wolfe. "Hamlet's Tables and Technologies of Writing in Renaissance England." *Shakespeare Quarterly* 55, no. 4 (2004): 379–419.

Steiner, Emily. *Documentary Culture and the Making of Medieval English Literature*. Cambridge: Cambridge University Press, 2003.

Steinmetz, David. "Divided by a Common Past: The Reshaping of the Christian Exegetical Tradition in the Sixteenth Century." *Journal of Medieval and Early Modern Studies* 27, no. 2 (1997): 245–64.

———. *Luther in Context*. Bloomington: Indiana University Press, 1986.

Stephens, W. P. *The Theology of Huldrych Zwingli*. Oxford: Oxford University Press, 1986.

Still, Colin. *The Timeless Theme*. London: Ivor Nicholson and Watson, 1936.

Stock, Brian. *After Augustine: The Meditative Reader and the Text*. Philadelphia: University of Pennsylvania Press, 2001.

———. *Augustine the Reader: Meditation, Self-Knowledge, and the Ethics of Interpretation*. Cambridge, Mass.: Belknap, 1996.

———. *The Implications of Literacy: Written Language and Models of Interpretation in the Eleventh and Twelfth Centuries*. Princeton: Princeton University Press, 1983.

Summit, Jennifer. "Monuments and Ruins: Spenser and the Problem of the English Library." *English Literary History* 70, no. 1 (2003): 1–34.

Sutcliff, E. F. "The Council of Trent on the *Authentia* of the Vulgate." *Journal of Theological Studies* 49 (1948): 35–42.

Taussig, Michael. *Defacement: Public Secrecy and the Labor of the Negative.* Stanford: Stanford University Press, 1999.

Tavard, George. "The Catholic Reform in the Sixteenth Century." *Church History* 26, no. 3 (1957): 275–88.

Taylor, Mark. "Prospero's Books and Stephano's Bottle: Colonial Experience in *The Tempest.*" *Clio* 22, no. 2 (1993): 101–13.

Thomas, Keith. *Religion and the Decline of Magic.* New York: Scribner, 1971.

Thomas, Troy. "Expressive Aspects of Caravaggio's First *Inspiration of Saint Matthew.*" *Art Bulletin* 67, no. 4 (1985): 636–52.

Thompson, Craig R. "Jerome and the Testimony of Erasmus in Disputes over the Vernacular Bible." *Proceedings of the PMR Conference* 6 (1981): 1–36.

Thornton, Timothy C. G. "Jerome and the 'Hebrew Gospel According to Matthew.'" *Studia Patristica* 28 (1993): 118–22.

Tigay, Jeffrey. "On the Term Phylacteries (Matt. 23:5)." *Harvard Theological Review* 72, nos. 1–2 (1979): 45–53.

Tribble, Evelyn. *Margins and Marginality: The Printed Page in Early Modern England.* Charlottesville: University Press of Virginia, 1993.

Trinterud, Leonard J. *Elizabethan Puritanism.* New York: Oxford University Press, 1971.

———. "A Reappraisal of William Tyndale's Debt to Martin Luther." *Church History* 31, no. 1 (1962): 24–45.

Trueman, Carl R. *Luther's Legacy: Salvation and English Reformers, 1525–1556.* Oxford: Clarendon Press, 1994.

Tudor Royal Proclamations. Vol. 1. Edited by Paul L. Hughes and James F. Larkin. New Haven: Yale University Press, 1964–69.

Tuveson, Ernest. *Millennium and Utopia: A Study in the Background of the Idea of Progress.* New York: Harper and Row, 1964.

Tyndale, William. *An Answer to Sir Thomas More's Dialogue.* Edited by Henry Walter. Cambridge: Cambridge University Press, 1850.

———. *A compendious introduccion, prologe or preface vn to the pistle off Paul to the Romayns.* Worms: P. Schoeffer, 1526.

———. *The firste boke of Moses called Genesis newly correctyd and amendyd by W.T.* Antwerp: M de Keyser, 1534.

———. *The Five Books of Moses Called the Pentateuch. Being a Verbatim Reprint of the Edition of M.CCCCC.XXX.* Edited by J. I. Mombert. Carbondale: Southern Illinois University Press, 1967.

———. *The obedience of a Christen man and how Christen rulers ought to governe.* Antwerp: M. de Keyser, 1528.

———. *Tyndale's New Testament, Translated from the Greek by William Tyndale in 1534.* Edited by David Daniell. New Haven: Yale University Press, 1989.

————. *The Whole Workes of W. Tyndall, Iohn Frith, and Doct. Barnes, three worthy Martyrs, and principall teachers of this Churche of England.* Edited by John Foxe. London: John Daye, 1573.

Vance, Eugene. *Mervelous Signals: Poetics and Sign Theory in the Middle Ages.* Lincoln: University of Nebraska Press, 1986.

van der Horst, Pieter W. "*Sortes*: Sacred Books as Instant Oracles in Late Antiquity." In *The Use of Sacred Books in the Ancient World,* edited by L. V. Rutgers, P. W. van der Horst, H. W. Havelaar, L. Teugels, 143–73. Leuven: Peeters, 1998.

Voragine, Jacobus de. *The Golden Legend or Lives of the Saints as Englished by William Caxton.* Edited by F. S. Ellis. 7 vols. London: J. M. Dent, 1900.

Walker, D. P. "The Cessation of Miracles." In *Hermeticism and the Renaissance: Intellectual History and the Occult in Early Modern Europe,* edited by Ingrid Merkel and Allen G. Debus, 111–23. Washington, D.C.: Folger Books, 1988.

Wall, Wendy. *The Imprint of Gender: Authorship and Publication in the English Renaissance.* Ithaca: Cornell University Press, 1993.

Wallace, David. "Dante in Somerset: Ghosts, Historiography, Periodization." *New Medieval Literatures* 3 (1999): 9–38.

Walsham, Alexandra. "Jewels for Gentlewomen: Religious Books as Artefacts in Late Medieval and Early Modern England." In *The Church and the Book,* edited by R. N. Swanson, 123–42. Rochester, N.Y.: Boydell and Brewer, 2004.

————. *Providence in Early Modern England.* Oxford: Oxford University Press, 2001.

Warkentin, Germaine. "In Search of 'The Word of the Other': Aboriginal Sign Systems and the History of the Book in Canada." *Book History* 2, no. 1 (1999): 1–27.

Warner, Lawrence. "The Dark Wood and the Dark Word in Dante's *Commedia*." *Comparative Literature Studies* 32 (1995): 449–78.

Watt, Tessa. *Cheap Print and Popular Piety, 1550–1640.* Cambridge Studies in Early Modern British History. New York: Cambridge University Press, 1991.

Weatherby, H. L. "The True Saint George." *English Literary Renaissance* 17, no. 2 (1987): 119–41.

Weber, Max. "Science as a Vocation." In *From Max Weber: Essays in Sociology,* translated and edited by H. H. Gerth and C. Wright Mills, 129–56. New York: Oxford University Press, 1946.

Webster, Charles. *The Great Instauration: Science, Medicine and Reform, 1626–1660.* New York: Holmes and Meier, 1975.

Weil, Judith. *Christopher Marlowe: Merlin's Prophet.* Cambridge: Cambridge University Press, 1977.

Weinberger, Jerry. "On the Miracles in Bacon's *New Atlantis*." In *Francis Bacon's New Atlantis: New Interdisciplinary Essays,* edited by Bronwen Price, 106–28. Manchester: Manchester University Press, 2002.

Whitgift, John. *The Works of John Whitgift.* Edited by John Ayre. 3 vols. Cambridge: Cambridge University Press, 1851–53.

Whitney, Charles. *Francis Bacon and Modernity.* New Haven: Yale University Press, 1986.

Williams, Megan Hale. *Monk and the Book*. Chicago: University of Chicago Press, 2006.

Williams, Roger. *A Key into the Language of America*. Edited by Howard Chapin. Bedford, Mass.: Applewood Books, 1936.

Wilson, Luke. *Theaters of Intention: Drama and the Law in Early Modern England*. Stanford: Stanford University Press, 2000.

Wilson, Richard. "Voyage to Tunis: New History and the Old World of *The Tempest*." *ELH* 64, no. 2 (1997): 333–57.

Winston-Allen, Anne. *Stories of the Rose: The Making of the Rosary in the Middle Ages*. University Park: Pennsylvania State University Press, 1997.

Wogan, Peter. "Perceptions of European Literacy in Early Contact Situations." *Ethnohistory* 41, no. 3 (1994): 407–29.

Wortham, Simon. "Censorship and the Institution of Knowledge in Bacon's *New Atlantis*." In *Francis Bacon's* New Atlantis*: New Interdisciplinary Essays*, edited by Bronwen Price, 180–98. Manchester: Manchester University Press, 2002.

Woudhuysen, H. R. *Sir Philip Sidney and the Circulation of Manuscripts, 1558–1640*. Oxford: Clarendon Press, 1996.

Wright, Thomas. *Three Chapters of Letters Relating to the Suppression of Monasteries; Edited from the Originals in the British Museum by Thomas Wright*. London: Nichols, 1843.

INDEX

ACKNOWLEDGMENTS

This book, like all books, is the work of many hands. I have been extraordinarily fortunate in the help I have received along the way.

My greatest intellectual debt is to Peter Stallybrass, whose brilliance and generosity continue to inspire me. I was extraordinarily fortunate to have Margreta de Grazia and Rebecca Bushnell as mentors early in the book's conception; they encouraged and challenged me at crucial stages, shaping both the project and my approach to scholarship. This project began at the University of Pennsylvania, where I was surrounded by a remarkable group of people; for their support, scholarly and otherwise, I want to thank Hester Blum, Jon Eburne, Jim English, Jean Feerick, Carolyn Jacobson, Rayna Kalas, Vicki Mahaffey, John Pollack, Maureen Quilligan, Phyllis Rackin, Erik Simpson, and the members of the Medieval and Renaissance Seminar.

The argument of the book has been shaped by my colleagues at Yale University and the University of California, Santa Barbara, many of whom have read parts of the manuscript. I want particularly to acknowledge the following colleagues and friends from my time in New Haven: Nigel Alderman, Jessica Brantley, Thomas Fulton, Larry Manley, Annabel Patterson, David Quint, Nicole Rice, Joe Roach, John Rogers, and Elliott Visconsi. The scholarly community in the English Department at Santa Barbara has proven to be astonishingly generous, and I am especially grateful to Giles Bergel, Jan Caldwell, Bob Erickson, Paddy Fumerton, Bishnu Ghosh, Ken Hiltner, Alan Liu, Michael O'Connell, Carol Braun Pasternack, Rita Raley, Mark Rose, Russell Samolsky, Bill Warner, and the late and much-missed Richard Helgerson.

Brian Cummings offered expert advice and generous encouragement in the late stages of the project; his work and his humane approach to the profession have been an inspiration. Juliet Fleming and Katie Craik were there at the beginning, and I extend warm thanks to them and to the 1994–95 Renaissance M.Phil. group at Cambridge.

I would also like to thank Jerry Singerman, my editor at the University of Pennsylvania Press, for his guidance and patience. The readers for the press, Ritchie Kendall and Michael O'Connell, offered excellent advice that helped clarify and enhance the argument. This project benefited tremendously from a year's leave, courtesy of the Morse Fellowship from Yale University. I am grateful to Annie Abrams for her indefatigable research assistance. Parts of Chapters 3 and 5 appeared in *English Literary Renaissance* and the *Journal of Medieval and Early Modern Studies,* and I thank the editors of these journals for their permission to reprint them here. I am grateful to have permission to reproduce images from the collections of the Rare Book and Manuscript Library at the University of Pennsylvania, the Beinecke Rare Book and Manuscript Library at Yale University, the Huntington Library, and Art Resource. I would also like to thank audiences at the British Studies Colloquium at Yale University, the Early Modern Seminar at Columbia University, the Group for Early Modern Cultural Studies Conference, the History of Material Texts Seminar at the University of Pennsylvania, the Inhabiting the Body, Inhabiting the World Conference at the University of North Carolina, the Medieval and Renaissance Seminar at the University of Pennsylvania, the Renaissance Society of America Conference, and the Shakespeare Association of America Conference. My students at the University of Pennsylvania, Yale University, and the University of California, Santa Barbara offered stimulating discussion that helped hone many of the book's ideas. I would especially like to thank the remarkable group of graduate students affiliated with the Early Modern Center at Santa Barbara.

My family has been supportive of me in everything I have done. I dedicate this book to my parents, Kate and Jerry Kearney, who showed me how to work hard and taught me to love books. I thank Marylynn, Dan, Gavin, and Zachary Stecher; Bernadette and Kathleen Kearney; and Tom, Jan, and Olivia Zinn for being the weird and wonderful people they are. Leo arrived as this book was being written; he is one of the wisest and funniest people I know, and I could not be more grateful for his presence in my life.

This book could not have been written without Emily Zinn, who knows that there are no words.